# In Their Own Interests

## Race, Class, and Power in Twentieth-Century Norfolk, Virginia

### Earl Lewis

**UNIVERSITY OF CALIFORNIA PRESS**
Berkeley   Los Angeles   Oxford

University of California Press
Berkeley and Los Angeles, California

University of California Press, Ltd.
Oxford, England

c *C*

**Library of Congress Cataloging-in-Publication Data**

Lewis, Earl.
 In their own interests : race, class, and power in twentieth-
century Norfolk, Virginia / Earl Lewis.
  p.  cm.
 ISBN 0–520–06644–8 (cloth)
  1. Afro-Americans—Virginia—Norfolk—Social conditions.  2. Afro-
Americans—Virginia—Norfolk—Economic conditions.  3. Working
class—Virginia—Norfolk—History—20th century.  4. Norfolk (Va.)—
Social conditions.  5. Norfolk (Va.)—Economic conditions.
I. Title.
F234.N8L48  1990
305.8′960730755521—dc20                                    90–42819
                                                                CIP

boo3602895

Printed in the United States of America
9 8 7 6 5 4 3 2 1

The paper used in this publication meets the minimum requirements of
American National Standard for Information Sciences—Permanence of Paper
for Printed Library Materials, ANSI Z39.48–1984. ⊗

# In Their Own Interests

*For Susan J. and Clifton J.,*
*who inspired the telling of this story*

# CONTENTS

# LIST OF ILLUSTRATIONS

## FIGURES

1. Sketch of black men shucking oysters

2. Black woman sorting peanuts, ca. 1910

3. View of Church Street

4. Black dockworkers unloading cotton, 1908

5. A river baptism

6. The 1926 graduating class of Booker T. Washington High School

7. Norfolk's segregated public library for Afro-Americans

8. Black and white men gather to hear the World Series broadcast, 1931

9. The Philharmonic Glee Club, 1927

10. Relief recipients awaiting distribution of benefits, 1933

11. Chapel Street day-nursery school

12. Residents of a segregated wing of the Norfolk Poor Farm

13. Black longshoremen on strike, 1934

14. Black women workers on relief receiving instructions from a WPA supervisor

15. Dedication of the Smith Street USO

*Figures follow page 88*

## MAPS

# LIST OF TABLES AND GRAPHS

## TABLES

## GRAPH

# ACKNOWLEDGMENTS

In a community where much was shared and "home" meant a great deal, Susan and Clifton J. loaned me their stories. On their front porch in the mid-1960s, I learned about migration, visiting, conjuring, Daddy Grace, sweet potato pies, Virginia hams, work, racism, dignity, and determination. I learned how a partially educated, working-class black couple struggled to send their three children to college because it was "in their interests." I watched their expressions as the intoxicating smells from a nearby cigar plant filled their house, as a poorly designed sewage system rendered their street impassable and unhealthy after an August thunderstorm, and as a steady parade of neighbors passed their stoop. Both are dead now, but I am forever in their debt. Appropriately, this book is dedicated to them.

Over the course of the past eight years, several institutions, grants, and individuals have helped transform a reservoir of impressions into a book. I would like to take a moment to thank as many as possible and to apologize to any I may forget. This book would not have been possible without the fine counsel and assistance I received as a graduate student at the University of Minnesota. Several fellowships, a computer grant, and the invaluable help of the Interlibrary Loan Department greatly facilitated the completion of the first phase, my dissertation. More important was the help I received from Russell Menard, Clarke Chambers, John Modell, Allan Spear, Lansiné Kaba, and Allen Isaacman.

I left Minneapolis in early 1985 for the warmer surroundings of Berkeley, California. Without question, my former students and colleagues there made this a much better book. A few programs and individuals deserve special note. A career development grant, a computer grant, and assorted research monies provided much-needed finances and release time. Students in my Afro-American urban history courses, perhaps unknowingly, contributed handsomely to the reframing of the conceptual framework. I will never forget their blank stares as I lectured about work and home—because of them, this book is more comprehensible. David Organ, who later co-wrote an article with me, deserves special recognition, as do Ethnic Studies graduate students Helen Lara-Cea, Lupe Gallegos, Gabrielle Foreman, Gin Pang, Ed Park, Tim Fong, Caridad Souza, and June Murray-Gill.

When I arrived at Berkeley as a new, young assistant professor, several people, who became good friends, aided my transition. Heading the list were my colleagues in the Afro-American Studies Department. In an atmosphere that was supportive and friendly, they encouraged and nurtured my development. Bob Brentano and Reginald Jones became mentors, whether or not they intended to, and they taught me much about the culture of the institution. The decision to leave them was the most difficult I have yet made.

Other colleagues interrupted their schedules and accepted the demanding job of reading parts or all of the manuscript. Included in this group were members of the American history reading group, as well as William Banks, Bob Blauner, Lawrence Levine, Carol Stack, Jim Gregory, and several anonymous readers. I may not have satisfied all of their concerns, but I am forever indebted. A special thanks is owed to my good friend Jon Gjerde, who read and criticized several versions of the book with great dispatch, and to Larry Levine, who shepherded me through the world of academic publishing.

Several other agencies and individuals were equally helpful. The staffs of both the Manuscript Division at the Library of Congress and the Labor and Economic Division at the National Archives provided invaluable assistance. Likewise, I was well served by the Sargeant Memorial Room at the Norfolk Public Library, the Alderman Library at the University of Virginia, the Perkins Library at Duke University, the Virginia State Library in Richmond, and the libraries at Old Dominion University, the University of Minnesota, and the University of California at both the Berkeley and Los Angeles campuses.

Although the writing of a book is a consuming enterprise, the wise counsel and good cheer of a few friends have made the undertaking bearable. I am grateful to Coretha Rushing and Howard Smith, who housed me on several trips to Washington, D.C. My aching knees thank Charles Henry, who reminded us that nothing is more important than a good game of three-on-three. And to Joe Trotter, a friend since graduate school, my warmest thanks. Few have shown such genuinely unselfish support and encouragement—even when we disagree.

This book would not have been produced without the able and professional support of many people. Over the past eight years, Mary Chisolm and Elmirie Robinson deciphered my handwriting and typed numerous drafts with humor and commitment. Although Elmirie never admitted it, I am sure she is glad I finally learned to type. My research assistant at the University of Michigan, Mary Alice Parker, has been a godsend. A number of people at the University of California Press have also provided professional support and help. Sheila Levine and Mark Jacobs have been all that editors should be. The work of copyeditor Mary Renaud has made this a better book.

Finally, to my family much more than thanks is owed. My wife, Jayne London, has alternated between being my harshest critic and my strongest supporter. Our daughter, Suzanne, however, has been the master of indifference. Like all four-year-olds, she believes that swimming, playing, and running are immensely more important than being squirreled away with notes and computer. Unlike many well-paid engineers, my brother Rudolph twice volunteered for work as a research assistant. So did my parents. As lifelong residents of Norfolk, they took particular interest in seeing this project concluded. Although I am responsible for any errors, the book is as much theirs as mine. I trust they will recognize *In Their Own Interests* as their story.

# INTRODUCTION

In 1857 Frederick Douglass told the nation: "Power concedes nothing without a demand. It never did and it never will." Half a century later, Francis J. Grimké exhorted from his Washington pulpit:

> If we are ever to be free from invidious distinction in this country based upon race, color, previous condition, we have got to be alive, wide-awake to our own interest. . . . We are not going to secure our rights in this country without a struggle. We have got to contend, and contend earnestly, for what belongs to us. Victory isn't coming in any other way. . . . We have got . . . to keep up the agitation until right triumphs and wrong is put down.

As the nation mobilized for World War II, A. Philip Randolph declared that "if Negroes [are to] secure their goals . . . they must win them and to win them they must fight, sacrifice, suffer, go to jail and, if need be, die for them. These rights will not be given. They must be taken."[1] These three leaders lived at different times and adopted different political orientations, but they shared a common understanding. The America in which they lived conceded nothing without a demand. If Afro-Americans expected a share of the nation's bounty, then Afro-Americans would have to act in their own interests.

Just before the mantle of Negro leadership passed from Frederick Douglass to Booker T. Washington, Thomas Hill left North Carolina and headed for Norfolk, Virginia. At first glance, his actions seem far removed from the powerful words of Douglass, Grimké, and Randolph. But Thomas Hill, like many Afro-Americans, proved how much, and in what ways, blacks were prepared to act in their own interests. Arriving in Norfolk in 1892, Hill resided there for the next forty-seven years. By

*1*

1939, when he was sixty-nine, Hill had much to tell Edith Skinner, an interviewer for the Virginia Writers' Project.

Hill's early years in Norfolk were difficult financially; he survived by working as a day laborer. Then, in 1904, he went to work at the Norfolk Navy Yard (in Portsmouth) as a woodcutter's helper, a job he retained for more than twenty-five years. He retired at age sixty-two with a pension. Steady employment had enabled him to marry in 1904; his wife bore two children before her death in 1908. By the time he remarried four years later, his youngest child had also died. Working-class by all measures, Hill nonetheless managed to purchase a seven-room, two-story, brown-shingled house for his daughter and new wife. Lit by electricity and warmed by a heatrola, the house with its fine amenities became a testament to his hard work, although it set him apart from most others of similar background.[2]

In relating his life's story, Hill adumbrated the history of black Norfolk. Pushed by deteriorating economic and social conditions and pulled by the lure of the city, many Afro-Americans emigrated from farms and small towns in Virginia and North Carolina during the late nineteenth and early twentieth centuries. In Norfolk, they struggled to find jobs that promised a better future. The Norfolk of those years was neither an industrial wasteland nor an industrial oasis. Because the city was blessed with a naturally deep harbor and strategically located within the Atlantic coast transportation system, its commercial fortunes improved and its economic base grew as its port expanded. For most blacks, this economic expansion translated into additional jobs in the transportation and service fields. Like Hill, a few managed to obtain industrial employment. Fewer still became teachers, preachers, lawyers, and entrepreneurs— the Afro-American elite. Only the coming of World War II altered the general contours; then, more than ever before, black residents landed industrial jobs.

As a middle-sized southern city, Norfolk is an ideal setting in which to study how Afro-Americans balanced the competing inclinations of conscious inaction and purposeful agitation. Norfolk remained wedded to the traditions, customs, and mores of the region, but, as an Upper South port city, it also experienced the profound changes of World War I, the Depression, and World War II; the radicalizing influence of the Communist party and the CIO; and the general shifts in tastes, ideas, and philosophies that occurred throughout the nation. Norfolk was also a military town and thus an important southern industrial site. It was a terminus in the North-South transportation complex and played an important role in the ferrying of southern blacks north and south and between the countryside and the city. It had a reasonably well developed civic and business infrastructure, including what was at the time the nation's largest black-owned and -operated bank. The *Norfolk Journal and Guide*, headed by editor P. B. Young, was the South's leading black newspaper—a paper that, notwithstanding its openly middle-class bias, provides us with a unique entree into the world blacks created. And, finally, Norfolk contained a broad spectrum of Afro-Americans—active Garvey followers, Daddy Grace supporters, Communist enthusiasts, conservative race leaders, and teachers who successfully challenged the legality of a race-based wage structure. Though their viewpoints were often strikingly different, they frequently agreed on matters of race. Their disagreements underscored the complexity of the race-class dynamic and the importance of studying southern Afro-American urbanites.

Equally important, during the years between the Civil War and the civil rights movement, as Norfolk Afro-Americans struggled to improve their material conditions, they also fought for equal treatment, sometimes quietly and sometimes visibly. They never abided racism, "polite" or otherwise, well;[3] instead, they boycotted, rioted, petitioned, cajoled, demonstrated, and sought legal redress. During moments of introspection, some even vocalized the irony they found in accepting a policy of separate-but-equal that led to an unwanted reality of inequality.

It would be incorrect to conclude, however, that blacks in Norfolk merely reacted to white racism. Long before emancipation, Afro-Americans had ceased simply reacting to whites. The Norfolk that Thomas Hill knew had its own sights, sounds, and tastes, its own urban flavor, accounted for in large part by Hill and his neighbors. They filled the porches and windowsills, attended the churches, lodges, and parades, set the rhythm, and regulated the pace. As much as possible, they transformed the city to meet their needs. Always cognizant of racism, they were never all-consumed by its presence; throughout, they remained actors in a fluid social drama.

This book is about Thomas Hill and other Norfolk blacks—members of the working class and the elite, marginally educated and learned, folksy and refined, lesser knowns and power brokers—who came to live in the city between 1862 and 1945. It seeks to recreate the texture of Afro-American urban life. Thus it is concerned with the lives of the migrants after they moved to the city—the jobs they obtained, the assistance they secured, the houses they lived in, the families they built, the battles they waged, the victories they realized, the defeats they suffered, the institutions they developed, and the culture they shared.

It is also a book about a southern place, during the period of Jim Crow's codification, during the lean, troublesome 1930s, and during the conversely bountiful but equally troublesome 1940s. It is concerned with the internal, external, and structural factors that affected the city and its Afro-American residents.[4] Unavoidably, it considers the little-explored nexus between race, space, and class—that is, race relations, spatial formation, and elements of what Joe William Trotter, Jr., labels proletarianization. Norfolk's southern character dictates, however, that we cannot blindly adopt previous approaches, especially because most earlier analyses have concerned case studies of northern urban centers.

If few urbanists have studied southern city dwellers, even fewer have studied the larger issue of Afro-Americans at work and at home (which in black parlance signifies both the household and the community). Most studies have instead detailed black-white contact or ghetto formation. Although these are important considerations, Afro-American history is much more complicated than the history of race relations or ghettoization. Such studies have made significant historiographical contributions, but they render little assistance to those interested in the intersection of industrialization, urbanization, and Afro-American history.[5]

Profoundly interested in this intersection, Trotter argues that historians should focus on the making of an urban-industrial Afro-American proletariat and should abandon their seemingly unreflective attachment to the approaches that concentrate on race relations or ghetto formation. Offering the phenomenon of proletarianization as an alternative approach, Trotter defines it as the movement of blacks "into the industrial labor force as wage earners whose lives were shaped by racism as well as by the competitive interplay between labor and capital under capitalism."[6]

Although proletarianization offers a fresh perspective and avoids the theme of tragic sameness that pervades much of the existing literature, it is not without its limits. First, any study of the Afro-American urban experience must consider the culture that blacks constantly recreated, a culture that bound blacks to one another, even while it distinguished the working class from the elite. Second, any such study must include, where possible, a serious consideration of the Afro-American family and its role. Finally, the current application of the proletarianization approach fails to examine fully how the "complex convergence of class and race consciousness" informed changing patterns of interracial labor solidarity and fragmentation.[7]

If the Norfolk story proves typical, previous scholars may thus have erred in choosing only the most rapidly industrializing northern urban settings for study. Through the 1960s, Afro-Americans in such cities were a clear-cut minority, dominating few occupations and controlling few labor associations. Emphasis on industrial jobs also contradicts the general employment history of blacks. In Norfolk, where blacks composed at least a third of the population, dominated several occupational categories, and had important independent, all-black, nonindustrial unions, the story of labor solidarity and fragmentation is not one story but three—the first beginning in 1910 and ending in 1930; the second dating from the Depression until the start of World War II, and the last spanning the war years, 1941–1945. Furthermore, each story highlights the complex interplay between conditions at work and at home.

To explore those complexities adequately, we need a new conceptual framework. This perspective must build on the strengths of earlier approaches while avoiding their weaknesses. An analysis of the ways in which blacks acted in their own interests, the strategies they devised to empower themselves, accomplishes this. More specifically, we should examine the interaction between shifts in social relations and changes at work and at home. Several scholars have observed that the melding of urban and industrial development had by 1900 produced individuals who identified themselves as workers at work and ethnics at home. This was true for all groups *except* Afro-Americans, who remained "racial ethnics" at work and at home.[8] This peculiar half-status in the urban setting shaped their search for empowerment.

Through this perspective, we discover a story distinctly American in form and Afro-American in substance. In its American form, it is a story about the relationship between power and culture in the industrial phase of American history.[9] In substance, it is a story about how Afro-Americans acted in their own interests and how their peculiar place in the political economy shaped those actions. This story also considers the culture that Afro-Americans both transferred and transformed, often in such a way as to sidestep the contentious debate over relative degrees of autonomy.[10] For Norfolk's black residents, the issue was more than autonomy—their success in carving out some social and psychic space exemplified their determination to achieve power in whatever way possible (see Chapter 4).

Essentially, this book argues that as shifts in social relations intersected with conditions at work and at home, blacks modified their strategies. As we discover in Chapter 1, the basic strategic outline appeared soon after emancipation, inspired by the search for both well-being and equality, that is, material gain as well as equal treatment and privileges before the law. Fully aware of their tenuous position in the local setting, Norfolk's Afro-American residents attempted to fulfill these goals by combining advancement in the workplace with improvements in the home sphere.

In a setting where *home* meant both the household and the community, the term *home sphere* enables us to understand more clearly how blacks framed their own world. The word *sphere* can be defined as the environment in which one lives. That environment exists on several different levels—the household, the neighborhood, the black community, the city, the state, and so forth. Few blacks lived a completely balkanized existence, and their environment was informed by the interaction between the different levels, which in turn was shaped by shifts in values, ideologies, and norms over time. But at the level of local mobilization, our concern is the intersection between the household and the community, or the home sphere, where Norfolk blacks struggled to align their needs, expectations, desires, and cultural traditions to improve their place in the city.

By 1900 the formation of a racially stratified labor market, coupled with changes in social and political structures, called the initial strategic equation into question. At work, blacks found themselves relegated to the worst jobs, increasingly at odds with their white counterparts, and unable to take advantage of their numerical superiority in certain trades. At home, they lost the franchise, were forced to endure the spread of Jim Crow restrictions, and lost out to working-class whites in the battle for city services. As a result, Afro-Americans modified their strategy. Workplace advancement remained an important concern, but it became less of a priority than progress in the home sphere. Most believed that the greatest losses had occurred in that area and that more individuals would benefit from an approach that produced better roads, more city services, and a larger say in the political process. Once framed, it was this perspective that Afro-American residents took into the first decades of the twentieth century.

Except for a brief moment during World War I, blacks in Norfolk followed this strategy into the early days of the Depression (see Chapters 2–4). This is not to imply that the strategy was not challenged at various points, for it was. At times, for example, the needs and actions of working-class blacks diverged from the stated interests of the larger community. Black workers frequently purchased goods from white ethnic merchants who offered lower prices rather than from their black friends or neighbors. One's allegiance to home was as often determined by one's class and racial positions as it was by race alone. Thus the interests of a particular household might contradict professed community interests. And in this complex and contradictory world, neither the black community nor the white community was a monolith. Internal differences highlight the intricate nature of race and class concerns. But the enveloping political economy did compress the range of choices open to those seeking power. As a result, in the final analysis, blacks agreed more than they disagreed over which strategy to pursue.

A pivotal modification came during the Depression years, as discussed in Chapters 5 and 6. A sharp decline in collective material well-being and the introduction of a new protest rhetoric led some to equate true development in the home sphere with sustained advancement in the workplace. The convergence this formulation suggests never completely materialized. For example, as part of this shift, black workers were advised to form alliances with white workers. A few managed to do so, but most wondered whether they had surrendered too much in the process, for such coalitions existed only at work. Beyond the workplace, the same groups remained locked in an ongoing battle for city services. Many believed that alliances that failed to contribute to development in the home sphere produced more harm than good. Nonetheless, the seed for change was planted.

The most dramatic realignment in perspective came during World War II. For the first time in more than half a century, large segments of the community agreed that an equation for full empowerment must link employment advances with progress in the home sphere. This time, however, as Chapter 7 describes, black workers received wider encouragement to form prudent alliances with whites. In turn, white laborers made a more serious effort to move the language of competition beyond black versus white to haves versus have-nots. This shift paralleled a larger discussion among blacks about the true meaning of democracy. The acceptance of a strategy based on advances at work and at home heralded the birth of a new chapter in the history of Afro-Americans in the industrial age.

During the heady days of the civil rights movement, blacks across the region began to alter their strategy once again, with mixed results. In the name of progress in the home sphere, they valiantly invaded the citadels of racism and white supremacy, eventually crippling Jim Crow through the combined weight of moral force and social pressure. Through their efforts, they gained access to political office, removed the most egregious symbols of segregation, produced a new black middle class, and in the process acquired a new sense of self. But they could not check a decline in the nation's industrial fortunes, and thus, in spite of the numerous improvements, power remained elusive. For a time, lulled by their own success, even blacks in Norfolk forgot that improvements in the home sphere without advancement in the workplace produces hollow gains. Sadly, a generation after the 1963 March on Washington, it is now conventional wisdom—and the conclusion of this book—that in black America everything has changed and nothing has changed.

Hence this is not only a book about Afro-Americans in Norfolk and the social world they created or about a southern city and its black residents. It is also a book suggesting the history of a region and its people, a book about the complex interplay between race and class and how that interplay changed over time. Through that perspective, it explains how shifts in social relations intersected with altered conditions at work and at home to frame Afro-Americans' interpretation of their own interests.

# ONE

# Framing a Perspective, 1862–1910

It was an act of political and economic empowerment: the decision to liberate her nameless slave-child. After a night of merriment that advertised her admittance into Cincinnati's community of free blacks, Sethe's ugly past collided with her hopeful future. The slavekeeper and his attendants approached, intent on reenslaving her and her children. Quickly, she grabbed the closest one, her first daughter and third child, and slit her throat. Before she could emancipate the other three, friends intervened, preventing her from doing what a war would later partially accomplish. In this simple, horrific manner, Sethe, the central character in Toni Morrison's *Beloved*, exercised one of the few political options open to a runaway determined to escape slavery. It was also an economic act: destroying the property of another, negating the property's economic worth. Afterward, the slavekeeper abandoned his quest, overawed by the weight of Sethe's resolve and her comprehension of her power.[1]

Afro-Americans who filed into Norfolk during and after the Civil War were equally committed to freedom and equally determined to act in their own interests. They realized early on, however, that the full attainment of freedom—economic, social, and political—depended on the final negotiations between their bitter past and their hope-filled present. Therefore, Norfolk blacks, who first labored to construct a shared definition of freedom, campaigned openly to preserve freedom's guarantees. The broad outline of their perspective appeared almost immediately, and their articulation of this viewpoint became increasingly focused as the twentieth century replaced the nineteenth. From the beginning, they sought both advancement in the workplace and improvements in the home sphere—unhampered access to well-paid jobs, along with better roads, new schools, improved living conditions, and the right to vote as equals. To these ends, they joined labor unions, built strong, enduring institutions, and engaged in electoral and protest politics. But as most of the benefits gained during the immediate postwar years were lost, a subtle shift in priorities emerged. By the end of the Gilded Age, Norfolk blacks had come to champion development in the home sphere over workplace advancement, a strategy that would change only modestly between 1910 and 1930. If we are to understand why black Norfolkians responded as they did to issues at work and at home during the first half of the twentieth century, an overview of what unfolded between the Civil War and Jim Crow's coming of age is critical.

## FORMULATING THE EQUATION

Looking out to the sea and inward to the plantation belt, Norfolk had become an important southern city by 1862. With a deep harbor and a strategic location at the confluence of the Chesapeake Bay and the Atlantic Ocean, the city's fortunes as a commercial center were on the rise. Plans to connect Norfolk with the interior of Virginia by railroad and with North Carolina by canal promised an even brighter future, one in which Norfolk might shed its image as a sleepy seaport town and compete with the more dominant Baltimore to the north. This future hinged, however, on the continued survival of slavery, an integrated economic, social, and political system predicated on unequal relations. Although individual residents opposed the institution, the city as a whole was quintessentially southern, and slaves and freedpeople, because of law and custom, lived a circumscribed existence.[2]

The arrival of Union troops in 1862 and the establishment of contraband camps resulted in a dramatic influx of former slaves and a permanent change in a way of life. Almost immediately, Norfolk became a haven for runaways and others seeking sanctuary. Years later, Charles Grandy told an interviewer from the Works Progress Administration (WPA), "Durin' slavery de white folks didn' treat de niggers right, an' de niggers start gettin' tired of it."[3] Grandy's experience proved somewhat typical. Like him, many blacks desired to escape the institution that defined and treated them as property, and they saw in the North-South conflict the opportunity to correct those injustices by fleeing the plantations and farms. Although the responses of Afro-Americans to the Civil War were complex and varied, many responded as Grandy did: when he learned that a camp had been established near Norfolk, he risked all and fled from a plantation near Hampton.[4]

Emancipation intensified the rate of migration, causing Norfolk's black population to grow dramatically between 1860 and 1870. As Grandy observed, "Nobody owned de niggers; so dey all come to Norfolk,

TABLE 1    Norfolk's Population, 1860–1910

| | Black | | Native White[a] | | Foreign-Born White | | Total Number |
|---|---|---|---|---|---|---|---|
| | Number | Per-centage | Number | Per-centage | Number | Per-centage | |
| 1860 | 4,330 | 29.6 | 10,290 | 70.4 | — | — | 14,620 |
| 1870 | 8,765 | 45.6 | 10,462 | 54.4 | — | — | 19,227 |
| 1880 | 10,068 | 45.8 | 11,898 | 54.2 | — | — | 21,966 |
| 1890 | 16,244 | 46.6 | 17,509 | 50.2 | 1,108 | 3.2 | 34,861 |
| 1900 | 20,230 | 43.5 | 24,711 | 53.1 | 1,606 | 3.4 | 46,547 |
| 1910 | 25,039 | 37.1 | 38,789 | 57.6 | 3,564 | 5.3 | 67,392 |

SOURCES: U.S. Bureau of the Census, *Ninth Census of the United States* (Washington, D.C.: Government Printing Office, 1872), vol. 1, *Population, 1870,* p. 281; U.S. Bureau of the Census, *Tenth Census of the United States* (Washington, D.C.: Government Printing Office, 1883), vol. 19, pt. 2, *Report of the Social Statistics of Cities,* pp. 65–70; U.S. Bureau of the Census, *Eleventh Census of the United States* (Washington, D.C.: Government Printing Office, 1890), vol. 1, *Population, 1890,* p. 126; U.S. Bureau of the Census, *Twelfth Census of the United States* (Washington, D.C.: Government Printing Office, 1901), vol. 2, *Population, 1900,* p. 139; U.S. Bureau of the Census, *Thirteenth Census of the United States* (Washington, D.C.: Government Printing Office, 1911), vol. 1, *Population, 1910,* p. 287.

[a]Figures for the years 1860–1880 represent the total white population, both native and foreign-born.

look lak to me."[5] In 1860 Afro-Americans accounted for 29.6 percent of the city's population; a decade later this figure had risen to 45.6 percent. Blacks remained nearly this same proportion of the population through 1910, although the actual numbers of both blacks and whites more than doubled between 1870 and 1910 (see Table 1).

The men and women who came to live in the city after 1865 hailed from a number of states, though the largest numbers came from Virginia, North Carolina, and Maryland. Samuel Walden, a thirty-year-old steamer fireman, and Sarah, his twenty-four-year-old wife, were both native Virginians. Marrinda Jane Singleton, born in 1840, came to Norfolk from rural North Carolina sometime after the war; as she recalled years later, "I was married soon after de war and came to Norfolk wid my husband, Robert Singleton, and lived wid him for 40 years." Born in 1846 in St. Mary County, Maryland, Cornelius Garner first came to Norfolk in 1864 as part of a military detail, only to remain after the war's end.[6]

Both blacks and whites who migrated to the city joined in the complicated attempt to define freedom. Their differences in viewpoint contributed to fractures in social relations and ultimately shaped black perspectives on larger economic and social matters. Essentially, emancipation not only had freed blacks but also had dissolved old lines of authority. Before the Civil War, laws had prohibited black residents from learning to read and write, narrowed their occupational choices, and established where they could venture, when, and for how long. Blacks who violated either law or custom flirted with corporal punishment, banishment, or, worst yet, reenslavement. Minor, irregular transgressions had been tolerated in the past, but emancipation and Reconstruction now amounted to a permanent breach. At least, that was what many whites feared and many blacks hoped.[7]

Although the responses of Afro-Americans to freedom were wide-ranging, Norfolk blacks, chastened by a series of race riots pitting them against Union troops and whites who believed them inferior, framed a shared public perspective.[8] In 1865 several leading black residents composed the *Equal Suffrage Address*, which bore the subtitle *Also an Account of the Agitation Among the Colored People of Virginia for Equal Rights.* The authors included, among others, Dr. Thomas Bayne, a former runaway who had become a dentist and an ardent Republican; Joseph T. Wilson, author of two books on blacks in the military and publisher and editor of several post-emancipation journals; and the Reverend Jno. Brown, the first black pastor at St. John African Methodist Episcopal (AME), one of the city's oldest black churches.

In both style and content, the *Equal Suffrage Address* was a true political sermon, a classic Afro-American jeremiad. It highlighted America's democratic promise and celebrated the role of Afro-Americans in the preservation of national independence. Independence and liberty were important symbols and cherished rights, and blacks therefore defined freedom to mean the full enjoyment of equal economic, social, and political rights, the full guarantee of independence and liberty. As in all jeremiads, there was a concern over declension, over a retreat from noble principles. Hence any action by whites that threatened the integrity of Afro-Americans' freedom caused alarm and prompted blacks to ask: "The honor of your country should be dear to you . . . but is that honor advanced . . . when America alone, of all Christian nations, sustains an unjust distinction against four millions and a half of her most loyal people, on the senseless ground of a difference in color?"[9]

The authors recommended extending the franchise to blacks to counter such charges of antidemocratic behavior, but they understood that, alone, the vote was no panacea. They tendered a three-pronged strategy, encouraging blacks to form political organizations, as well as both labor and land associations. Members of the Colored Union Monitor Club, who joined in writing the *Address*, advised:

> Let Labor Associations be at once formed among the colored people throughout the length and breadth of the United States, having for their object the protection of the colored laborer, by regulating fairly the price of labor, by affording facilities for obtaining employment by a system of registration, and last, though by no means least, by undertaking, on behalf

of the colored laborer, to enforce legally the fulfillment of all contracts made with him.

They concluded: "Then be up and active, and everywhere let associations be formed having for their object the agitation, discussion and enforcement of your claims of equality before the law, and equal rights of suffrage." Otherwise, the authors argued, blacks risked becoming the economic pawns of their former owners, who, it was believed, were "forming Labor Associations for the purpose of fixing and maintaining . . . the prices to be paid labor."[10]

The plan proposed by the Equal Suffrage Committee, created by Norfolk blacks at a public meeting on 5 June 1865, highlighted the tension between the American ideal and the American reality. Ideally, citizens in a democracy should disregard differences in color. But because most people were conscious of color, equity in society was predicated on racial considerations. Consequently, leaders such as Bayne, Wilson, and Brown advised blacks to form associations among themselves, not with equally situated whites. For the authors of the *Equal Suffrage Address,* race, under certain conditions and in certain social calculations, informed perspectives in a way class could not. Many Afro-Americans accepted the essential logic of this reasoning, even when their actions diverged from its implications. Hence the history of blacks at work and at home became the degree to which racial and class concerns changed as shifts in the political economy altered formulations for empowerment.

## MODIFYING THE EQUATION

By encouraging blacks to form labor associations, the framers of the *Equal Suffrage Address* rightly made the attainment of sustained political and social freedom dependent on economic advancement and basic improvements in employment. Throughout the South, this strategy became increasingly significant after the war. In rural areas, former planters, themselves victimized by the lack of currency and usurious loans, connived to keep blacks dependent through the sharecropping system. In urban areas, competition with white workers, a constant feature of southern life, threatened the few examples of labor solidarity that had existed. Even before the Civil War, white mechanics at the Norfolk Navy Yard had campaigned to eliminate black workers from the yard. And after the war, the 1865 joint strike of black and white workers along the New Orleans docks faded into memory as interracial competition for control of waterfronts throughout the South intensified. Furthermore, state and local governments, using everything from the infamous "Black Codes" and their vagrancy provisions to the convict lease system, prevented blacks from competing freely and successfully. As a result, black workers in Norfolk began to organize and agitate, efforts that reflected their commitment to act in their own interests.[11]

Blacks' concern for economic opportunity and progress coincided with a slow industrial awakening in the region that promised additional jobs. Tobacco plants, iron and steel foundries, and paper and textile mills filled in the formerly underdeveloped antebellum landscape. As they did, manufacturing investment in cities such as Richmond, Birmingham, and Durham, North Carolina, increased substantially.[12]

Norfolk's postwar aspirations hung on becoming a major port city and commercial hub. In part, the dream was realized. By the time of Ulysses Grant's election in 1869, railways linked the city to important cotton centers in the interior. Fourteen years later, the Norfolk and Western Railway began the almost daily transfer of the rich bituminous coal buried in the mountains of western Virginia and West Virginia to Norfolk's newly constructed Lamberts Point pier. Over the next twenty years, the city became the world's leading coal port. By 1910 it had also grown into the country's fourth largest cotton port, the leading peanut production center, and the South Atlantic's preeminent site for exporting lumber. A trade in perishables rounded out the economy. Bound by an exceptional truck farming industry, the flourishing coastwide trade in foodstuffs netted millions annually.[13]

In manufacturing, Norfolk proved to be somewhat of a laggard in comparison to Richmond and Birmingham. Nevertheless, the city was anything but an industrial wasteland. Fifteen years after the Civil War, a walk down the main thoroughfares of Norfolk rendered this tally: nine bakeries; eight blacksmith shops; seven cigar, cigarette, and tobacco companies; four flour and grist mills; and three shipbuilding plants. Considerable growth occurred over the next two decades. Between 1880 and 1900, capital investment increased 1,027 percent, while the labor force nearly quintupled.[14] State officials in 1899 listed

> fourteen manufactories of lumber, three of farming implements, six cotton knitting mills, ten fertilizers, seven peanut cleaning, three rice factories, two flour mills, one brewery, two creosoting plants, cotton compresses, foundries, machine shops, and manufacturers of wagons, coaches, cigars, candy, celluloid goods, boxes, pickles, furniture, shirts, silverplated ware, silk, peanut oil and meal, etc.[15]

The growth in the city's commercial and industrial fortunes provided jobs but not necessarily the economic independence or material advancement Afro-Americans had hoped for, particularly after 1890. Slaves and free blacks had held a wide variety of jobs before the Civil War. In the years after the war, many black men worked as laborers, as Willis Williams, Adam Bush, Lewis Keeling, and James Bush did. Others were fishermen, oyster shuckers, or dockworkers. Like Francis Nichols, a fifty-year-old blacksmith, or George Townsend, a shoemaker, a select few managed to find employment as skilled artisans. In most cases, the jobs black males obtained paid little and denied them the economic independence and rewards they sought.[16]

Black women also held jobs, but, as household patterns suggest, this too failed to counter the problem of underemployment. Eliza Taylor, for example, was a washerwoman who was forty-five years old in 1870 and headed a household of five children. She owned no real estate or personal property. As was the case for many black female-headed households in urban America, survival depended on income brought in by several of the children. Like most of their contemporaries, both of Eliza Taylor's daughters—Caroline, eighteen, and Prudence, fourteen—worked as domestics. John, twenty-one, worked as a farm laborer in a nearby rural area. George, eleven, and Anthony, seven, remained at home; but even they may have brought in wages of some kind.[17]

Only a small number were able to use occupation and associated status to catapult themselves into the world of the black middle class. Born in 1844, James E. Fuller belonged to this elite group. Fuller owned five pieces of property in the city by 1877, accumulating them during a period in which the value of property held by blacks never exceeded 2 percent of the city's total. In numerous ways Fuller was exceptional. While many others became laborers, he worked as a gauger, clerk, and shopkeeper for the U.S. Customs House, important political patronage jobs that may have been the spoils of contacts made while serving on the Common Council (a body similar to a board of aldermen).[18]

Others entered the status-dependent black middle class in more traditional ways. Like Richard Langley, some worked as the city's draymen, an occupation blacks had long dominated and one whose steady income had enabled several individuals to accumulate notable real estate holdings.[19] Some secured employment at the post office, while others entered the ministry, the legal profession, medicine, or private business. Among those who went into business was Moses Williams, who owned a variety store at 292 Church Street. He had as a business neighbor the mortuary at 185 Church, owned by James Edwards. And over on Market Street, blacks owned and operated the Paige Hotel. These business people and professionals formed the backbone of Norfolk's emergent black middle class.[20]

Through 1910, the general pattern of employment changed only negligibly. A large number of black men continued to work as laborers, and most women worked as domestics or personal servants. The manuscript censuses (house-to-house surveys of all Americans) for the period reveal that blacks lacked the range of occupational options open to whites. In fact, new competition and conflict with white workers removed Afro-

Americans from certain skilled trades, such as plumbing, altogether. Yet the growth of the city's black population and the attendant demand for services expanded opportunities for an evolving business class among blacks, which would in time play a central role in articulating the community's post-1910 agenda.[21]

Black workers meanwhile struggled to devise a coherent strategy for realizing basic progress in the workplace. Individual workers, of course, could go their own way, but in the wake of capitalist development and larger capital concerns such a course was pure folly. Although the *Equal Suffrage Address* had advised blacks to form independent labor associations, whites dominated organized labor, and in reality blacks needed their support to overcome the problem of underemployment. Otherwise, white employers could easily use white strikebreakers to undermine the efforts of blacks.

The depth of this problem was reflected in the efforts of Isaac Myers, a black resident of Baltimore, who was first sent to Norfolk in 1869 by the National Labor Union (NLU). In that year, he successfully organized the large contingent of black workers on the Norfolk docks. A year later, however, he returned with a different emphasis. As a representative of the Colored NLU, he again urged blacks to join unions, but now he insisted that the time had passed "for the establishment of organizations based on color." He reasoned: "Labor organization is the safeguard of the colored man. But for real success separate organization is not the real answer. The white and colored mechanics must come together and work together." Nevertheless, Myers had to acknowledge that a racially stratified labor market characterized by one group's dominance or near-dominance in certain jobs made it feasible for blacks and whites to continue in separate unions for the time being.[22] This confession mirrored the reality of local labor conditions. Both blacks and whites favored separation, because through it they expected to achieve greater racial economic security.

Twenty years later, positions were even more entrenched. Locally, the Knights of Labor, the new national labor body, failed to scale the wall of racial segregation in the labor market. It failed in part because blacks, fearful of surrendering what little power they possessed, rejected the myth of interracial labor solidarity. Some argue that at this critical juncture Afro-Americans lived history in reverse: for all others, the confluence of urbanization and industrialization broke down ethnic boundaries in the workplace. In Norfolk, it was not so much that blacks lived history in reverse; rather, they lived a sort of "shadowed" existence. In broad outline, their world resembled the world of their white counterparts. But in substance there were both qualitative and quantitative differences. The shadow reflected the body but lacked the body's power of independent action. And black workers wanted more than a shadow's existence. Consequently, black longshoremen and female domestics, who dominated their respective occupations, organized segregated union locals. Opposed to joining District Assembly (DA) 123 in Norfolk (a council of various union locals), they affiliated with the all-black DA 92 in Richmond.[23] Nearly two decades after Myers's entreaty, black workers' reading of contemporary conditions suggested that a workable formula for advancement was not to be found in integrated district assemblies, where blacks ceded power to whites.

In rejecting interracial labor solidarity, blacks never rejected unionization itself or what it promised. They were willing to employ any tactic that would improve their condition. Blacks saw unions as vehicles through which they could agitate for better pay and working conditions and for overall workplace advancement. They preferred all-black locals, because the social climate dictated such a structure and because, through them, they retained some element of control and power.

Norfolk Afro-Americans illustrated their commitment to organized labor on several occasions. On the eve of the new century, several hundred black longshoremen walked off the docks rather than work with nonunion men, even though these nonunion workers were probably black. Union members believed that nonunion workers threatened the National League of Longshoremen, an all-black union, and its goals of improved working conditions and control of the docks. Similarly, in an attempt to assert their power and realize improved conditions, fifteen hundred mostly black, unionized oyster shuckers went on strike, alleging illegal tactics by the oyster shucking firms. In both instances, blacks willingly used unions to advance their interests, especially when they retained control of the locals.[24]

By the turn of the century, the geographic and social boundaries separating blacks and whites had grown sharper, and the likelihood of labor solidarity had become more remote. Increasingly affected by the enveloping social paradigm predicated on the alleged superiority of whites, members of Norfolk's white working class became some of the most ardent believers in and strident transmitters of the doctrine of white supremacy. Both the white union leadership and the rank and file proposed measures designed either to eliminate blacks from certain trades or, at the very least, to exclude them from the more powerful white-dominated unions.

For example, in a letter sent to the *Plumber's Journal* in March 1903, C. H. Perry, a member of Norfolk's Plumbers' and Steamfitters' Union, advised the national body to promote the "Virginia plan" for eliminating black plumbers: "I believe the enclosed Virginia State plumbing law will entirely eliminate [the Negro] and the imposter from following our craft and I would suggest to the different locals that if they would devote a little time and money they would be able to secure as good if not better law in their own state."[25] The bill to which he referred required that all would-be plumbers successfully pass a test administered by an examining board. Under the terms of the law, the board, made up of union members, determined if a candidate possessed the necessary knowledge and skills to become a plumber. Policing power was bequeathed to each Virginia municipality. The practice opened the doors for the creation of a racially stratified trade.

In light of the mounting racial hostility, the structure of the industrial order, and their place in it, some blacks continued to reason that separate unions headed by blacks were in their long-term best interests. Indeed, Norfolk blacks, as longshoremen would tell interviewers in the 1920s, preferred separate, racially exclusive unions, because this structure ensured the presence of blacks in the conference rooms during contract negotiations.[26] If one listened closely, the authors of the *Equal Suffrage Address* could still be heard in 1910, declaring that it was important for Afro-Americans to form labor associations—their own associations.

Changing conditions, however, dictated something other than a blind allegiance to earlier strategies for empowerment and advancement. In the wake of diminishing social and political rights, Afro-American residents of Norfolk astutely began to assign more importance to the home sphere than to the workplace. Ironically, this shift came at a time when blacks might have used their numerical dominance of certain trades to wrest concessions from whites. But they did not do so for the same reasons some chose DA 92 over the alternative: black workers, like white workers, understood how deeply fragmented labor remained. Equally significant, neither group was able to transcend or transform substantially the vocabulary of race—the pseudoscientific racial hierarchies derived from Social Darwinism, the race-specific laws, and the racial stereotypes in popular culture. Events coalesced so quickly that by 1904 solidarity of any kind was even more unlikely. As this happened, a modified perspective arose among blacks. This perspective considered advances in the workplace to be of continued importance but saw their value as limited to those in the targeted trades, whereas progress in the home sphere—improved social services and fuller political and social rights—was seen as benefiting the entire community. This understanding directed those who struggled to check the advances of Jim Crow.

## THE SEARCH FOR EMPOWERMENT
## IN THE AGE OF JIM CROW

In postwar Norfolk, as in prewar Norfolk, race and economic status were, to varying degrees, the primary determinants of residence, although Afro-Americans lived in all of the city's wards in 1870, constituting a majority only in the Second Ward. A decade after the war, most of the city's influential and prominent white citizens lived west of Granby Street and the central business district in a section called Smith's Point. Middle-class whites resided in the central part of town bounded by Brewers, Banks, and Cumberland streets, extending across Church Street out toward Briggs' Point. The city's small but important Jewish community tended to concentrate at the eastern end of Main Street. Poor whites and a few blacks lived in the alley tenements just south of Main Street. Most blacks lived in the northeast quadrant of the city, primarily along Church Street, north of Charlotte-Bute Street. This section extended beyond Princess Anne Road, stopping just south of Cedar Grove Cemetery.[27]

Ward breakdowns, though illuminating, nevertheless obscure important information about the potential for interracial social intercourse. Throughout the South, working-class blacks and working-class whites had long lived near one another; Norfolk was no exception.[28] This was true after the Civil War as well. Along one thoroughfare in Norfolk's First Ward in 1870, blacks and whites lived next door and across the street from one another. Mary Ryan, for example, a native of Ireland and a grocer, lived next to a boardinghouse that had ten black residents. Her immediate neighbors were Annie Nelson, a thirty-two-year-old white seamstress; two young males, one clearly Annie's son and the other an unspecified relative; and Mary Dudley, a mattress maker. A couple of doors away lived Georgina Robinson, Caroline Watts, and a woman named Sarah, whose last name is unknown; these three women were black domestics. Next to them lived another white family. This key-board pattern of alternating rows of black households and white house-holds was repeated many times.[29] Here, the common denominator seemed to be class. Well-to-do whites distanced themselves from working folks of any color.

This pattern changed over the ensuing decades, causing distinct black and white neighborhoods to emerge, although there were no geograph-ically expanding ghettos. The process was neither fast nor complete. In 1900 twenty-three blacks in five households, thirty-eight whites in nine households, and two Asians in one household lived between 459 and 479 Church Street. Many clearly defined clusters of black residences had be-gun to emerge, however. The Fourth Ward, for instance, which included Church Street, was overwhelmingly black, whereas the First Ward was disproportionately white (see Table 2).[30]

The establishment of racially distinct neighborhoods proved to be an important complement to increased racial fragmentation in the work-place, and it figured centrally in black strategies. For some time, city ser-vices had gone first to the wealthy west of Granby Street and last to the

TABLE 2 Norfolk's Population by Ward and
Race, 1870 and 1890

| | | 1870 | |
| Ward | Black | Native White | Foreign-Born White |
| --- | --- | --- | --- |
| One | 1,108 | 2,373 | 171 |
| Two | 3,224 | 1,160 | 98 |
| Three | 1,820 | 2,228 | 202 |
| Four | 2,614 | 3,239 | 268 |

| | | 1890 | |
| Ward | Black | Native White | Foreign-Born White |
| --- | --- | --- | --- |
| One | 2,272 | 5,152 | 455 |
| Two | 1,526 | 2,580 | 265 |
| Three | 3,122 | 4,020 | 211 |
| Four | 8,617 | 1,232 | 81 |
| Five | 157 | 3,290 | 51 |
| Six | 550 | 1,267 | 64 |

SOURCES: U.S. Bureau of the Census, *Ninth Census of the United States* (Washington, D.C.: Government Printing Office, 1872), vol. 1, *Population, 1870*, p. 281; U.S. Bureau of the Census, *Eleventh Census of the United States* (Washington, D.C.: Government Printing Office, 1890), vol. 1, *Population, 1890*, p. 483.

working-class neighborhoods east of Granby. With working-class whites moving increasingly into the Brambleton district, interracial competition for these services accelerated. In the minds of many blacks, race rather than class now became the common denominator. Of course, class did not disappear as a salient feature in Afro-American life. Middle-class blacks who believed that it had were truly confounded by working-class black neighbors who ignored their entreaties and shopped at white-owned businesses that offered lower prices.

But neither did blacks belong to the world of the white working class described by Katznelson; they were neither workers at work nor ethnics at home. Instead, in the social milieu in which they lived, they were "racial ethnics" at work and blacks (or some less flattering term) at home. In both settings, they lived beyond the boundary of acceptance. But this status did not hurt them as much outside work, because community politics were most often ethnically or racially based. Thus, locked in a battle with the white working class for city services, yet somewhat

dependent on those same whites for lasting workplace advances, it became clear they were on more solid ground promoting development in
the home sphere.[31]

The decision to adopt this strategy for group empowerment stemmed
in part from a decline in political clout and an increase in obtrusive Jim
Crow laws. After slavery, blacks had used the franchise to play a prominent role in local political affairs. Possessing a slight majority in 1867,
black voters supported several issues advanced by white Radical Republicans and initiated some of their own, such as integrated free public education. Thomas Bayne, co-author of the *Equal Suffrage Address* and a fi-
ery orator and unabashed champion of Afro-American rights, led the
charge. At the 1867 state constitutional convention, he told delegates
that he and other blacks were determined to ensure a black presence in
local, state, and federal politics.[32]

Whites were frightened by such proclamations and the general prospect of black political ascendancy. The stridently anti-Radical *Norfolk
Journal* declared before the 1870 mayoral election that, if blacks won, the
"subordination of property, intelligence, and industry to pauperism, ignorance, and sloth" would be ensured. Further, a victory by blacks would
mean "the debasement of Christian civilization and of Anglo-Saxon enterprise beneath the heels of Fetish Superstition and African unthrift.
It means negro magistrates on your benches, negro policemen on your
streets, negro legislators in your councils . . . negro commissioners in
your schools." Peter Dilworth, nominated by the "black-and-tan" Republicans, lost the election to John B. Whitehead, the Conservatives' candidate. Blacks controlled four of the nine city council positions, however;
others served on the Common Council, and black men of property such
as Norfolk County resident Richard "Dick" G. L. Paige (reportedly the
offspring of a prominent white woman and a slave father) represented
area interests in the state legislature.[33]

The political ascent of local Afro-Americans crested in the mid-1880s,
paralleling the statewide pattern. From the beginning, black Virginians,
Norfolkians included, wedded themselves to the party of Lincoln. But
this union proved untenable; it remained viable only so long as few
whites could vote. Once this changed, the relationship between black
Republicans and white Republicans, which was already somewhat
strained, deteriorated. Left without a strong political ally, blacks found
it nearly impossible to thwart the changes in the political order. This
situation played into the hands of the Democratic party.[34]

Aware of changes at the state level, Afro-American residents living in
Norfolk's mostly black Fourth Ward worried about losing an even wider
spectrum of political gains. A local group formed, calling itself the
Union Republican League. It set as its priorities ousting ward chairman

Charles Beslow, whom many saw as unattentive to blacks' needs, and identifying "men of pluck and intelligence [to] be the vanguard of the race." Citywide, however, voters rejected the Republican party, and the summer of 1896 marked the arrival of Democratic hegemony.[35]

At the state constitutional convention in 1901–1902, matters totally degenerated. A. P. Thom of Norfolk summarized popular sentiment when he labeled the gathering a meeting to disfranchise blacks.[36] Carter Glass, delegate from Lynchburg and future U.S. senator from Virginia, put it more forcefully when he proclaimed:

> Discrimination! Why, that is exactly what we propose; that exactly is why this convention was elected—to discriminate to the very extremity of permissible action under the limitations of the Federal Constitution with the view to the elimination of every Negro who can be gotten rid of, legally, without materially impairing the strength of the white electorate.[37]

After the convention agreed on a combination of the "understanding clause" (potential voters had to prove to the attending registrar that they were able to interpret the constitution) and the poll tax (a capitation tax paid for three consecutive years), Glass boasted, "This plan will eliminate the darky as a political factor in this state in less than five years."[38] His quip proved prophetic. Within two years of the plan's passage, the number of black voters in Norfolk declined from 1,826 to 504; by 1910 only 44 paid the poll tax, a prerequisite to voting.[39]

The complete pacification of black political activity required additional action at the local level. Beginning in the 1890s and continuing through 1920, several efforts at municipal reform aided this cause. Reformers had as their first target the saloons and saloonkeepers. The newly formed Prohibition party of 1896, composed of anti-"Ring" Democrats and lower-class and lower-middle-class moral reformers from the predominantly white suburbs of Brambleton and Atlantic City, sought to undercut the saloonkeepers' influence at city hall. The moralists sanctimoniously campaigned to rid the city of the pernicious influence of alcohol and associated evils such as prostitution. To do so, they hoped to dilute the control the tavern owners and their allies—a group called the "Ring"—exercised over city politics. The Ring drew much of its strength from the First, Second, and Fourth wards, all areas with fairly large black populations. In fact, Fourth Ward boss Napoleon Bonaparte "Bonnery" Joynes, who was black, supported the Ring's desire for an open town.[40]

Although the Prohibition party met with only modest success, it did serve as the launching point for the next wave of political reform. Middle-class white progressives worked steadily between 1904 and 1908 to eliminate the ward system, to cut the number of city council members, and to force the city to adopt a city-manager governmental structure. These reforms hurt Afro-Americans in profound ways. In a period of black disfranchisement, aspiring black politicians now campaigned for fewer seats in a citywide election that robbed them and their backers of the power of the black vote. The progressives, and their successors in the Citizen's party who led the reform movement through 1920, succeeded in the long run in changing both the style and the complexion of the individuals involved in local politics. Although not all reformers set out to remove blacks from political life, that became the end result.[41]

As their political influence declined and as the city enacted more racially restrictive laws and policies, more Afro-Americans saw improvements in the home sphere as the most critical means of realizing group advancement. For instance, Norfolk's territorial growth in the last quarter of the nineteenth century emphasized the need for an urban transportation system. Something had to be done to link the suburban communities of Brambleton, Ghent, Huntersville, and Atlantic City to downtown businesses. In 1880 the area's transportation system consisted of a twelve-car, thirty-two-horse, twenty-one-man operation. Between 1880 and 1887, the city switched to electric trolley cars. By 1895 streetcar lines connected many suburbs to the city. These lines traversed most major thoroughfares, particularly in the city's wealthiest neighborhoods. But, as geographer William Ainsley notes, "no streetcar lines went along streets in the predominantly Negro neighborhoods."[42]

Between 1890 and 1910, various aspects of Jim Crow society slowly enveloped daily life. Norfolk eventually found itself in lockstep with the regional ethos, as the city divided along lines of black and white. Ten years after the U.S. Supreme Court's *Plessy* decision validated separate-but-equal public accommodations, the city began to codify the separation, passing an ordinance that regulated seating assignments on Norfolk streetcars. In the process, the ordinance transformed the streetcar from a symbol of technological progress into an emblem of social retrogression.

Afro-Americans quietly accepted some of the Jim Crow restrictions but vehemently protested others. Their reaction to the streetcar ordinance was swift and direct: residents called for a total boycott of the segregated conveyances. They even created their own Metropolitan Transfer Company as an alternative to riding the city streetcars. The company, which probably lacked sufficient operating capital, eventually failed to garner a sizable ridership, and, in the end, the boycott collapsed.[43]

Whereas the boycott itself failed, the principle on which it was based survived into the middle years of the twentieth century. Faced with changes in social and political relations they had little power to halt, Afro-Americans, at least in the short term, accepted aspects of the Jim Crow system and its promise of separate-but-equal. They understood, however, that a loss of power never meant absolute powelessness. They protested loudly and forcefully whenever they perceived a threat to the *Plessy* decision's promise of equal opportunities. Furthermore, in momentarily surrendering a claim to certain rights, they never surrendered their quest for equality. Thus the legal reference point for most blacks was not the *Plessy* doctrine; rather, it remained the "statutes of liberty," the Thirteenth, Fourteenth, and Fifteenth amendments.

At the same time, blacks used Jim Crow's formative years to develop their institutional infrastructure further. In time, these institutions would play a critical role in helping blacks advance in both the home sphere and the workplace. A spectrum of churches, schools, social organizations, and small businesses appeared in response to the spiritual, educational, social, and material needs of Afro-Americans. The birth of these institutions testified to the ability of blacks to live beyond the stare of the white world, even though they were not independent of the evolving political economy. Some scholars frame the discussion of these developing institutions in terms of degrees of autonomy. But blacks sought more than autonomy: they sought a means of empowerment, and all-black institutions provided this. In these institutions, blacks gained critical leadership experience, channeled their opposition to setbacks in civic conditions, and gained momentary respite from the unpredictable world of American racism.[44]

At the hub of every black community sat the church. As a place of worship, a concert hall, and a general meeting place, it represented black independence. By 1870 several black churches were listed in Norfolk's city directory—Bute Street Baptist, Catherine Street Baptist, St. James Methodist Episcopal, and the largest and oldest, St. John AME.[45] As the community diversified, the number of churches grew; and the denominations, as well as the role of the churches and their ministers in community affairs, also became more diverse.

If the church remained the symbol of black autonomy, education remained a key to black advancement. To blacks generally, including those in Norfolk, knowledge was power, and education was the means of acquiring knowledge. Schooling therefore took on a special meaning and importance. From the beginning, the city objected to funding education for blacks. This refusal prompted the American Missionary Association to send teachers to the area in 1863; the association established and maintained a separate school system for blacks through 1871. In that year, at the constant urging of blacks, the city established an administratively unified, though segregated, public school system. From its inception, it was separate and unequal.[46]

The struggle for quality education for blacks continued, however. Although the two races made up nearly equal proportions of the population, the city had provided six schools for whites and only one for blacks by 1886. As a consequence, Afro-American educators faced a much higher student-teacher ratio: seventy-four children per black teacher, compared to forty-two children per white teacher. The burdens of white teachers were eased further by a dozen private schools. The only private school to admit blacks was Norfolk Mission College, affiliated with the Presbyterian church.[47] More high school than college, this institution trained blacks in the basics from 1883 to 1916.[48] In fact, its opening made it the city's first secondary school for Afro-Americans. Continued agitation by black residents brought a new public school building, the S. C. Armstrong School, in 1886. Other improvements followed the an-nexation of Barboursville, Huntersville, and Lamberts Points in 1911.[49]

Other institutions, though further removed from the world of whites, were no less influenced by larger social forces. Following the war, but es-pecially after 1880, a plethora of secret and benevolent societies ap-peared. The Good Samaritans, the Masons, the Odd Fellows, the Knights of Gideon, and the Knights of Pythias, among others, provided fellow-ship and economic protection.[50] Alexander Coprew, for example, a driver for Santos and Company Coal, belonged to the King David Lodge, the 1412 Grand United Order of Odd Fellows, the Rose of Sharon House-hold of Ruth 100, the Saint Joseph Lodge 4, the Seven Wise Men, and the Bute Street Baptist Church.[51] Such a wide assortment of affiliations provided social contacts that aided urban adjustment. Membership in benevolent organizations with burial plans also benefited an individual's family when a death occurred—an important consideration, for few in-surance companies sold policies to blacks.[52]

The YMCA, the YWCA, and a number of social welfare agencies also helped blacks attend to their many needs. The national YMCA move-ment actually started among blacks in Norfolk. According to contempo-raries, the Y's work began there "ten to fifteen years before it was regu-larly organized and recognized by the parent body." Officially, the Y movement originated with the arrival of William A. Hunton in 1888. Hunton then spent three years in Norfolk before leaving for New York to head the colored division of the national body. During its life, the Norfolk YMCA provided an employment service, a sanctuary, and moral guidance to black men.[53]

The Y movement also spread among the female population. During the initial years (1892–1906), women officially belonged to the Ladies' Auxiliary of the YMCA. This changed in October 1906, when the women filed an application to become charter members of the YWCA. Their request was finally honored in 1908, when the Ladies' Auxiliary became the Phyllis Wheatley Branch of the YWCA. The women's organi-zation stressed the importance of caring for both the "moral and physical development of girls and young women of the race." Most important, it arranged sleeping quarters for an average of twenty young women who were working in the area as domestic servants, and it functioned as a clearinghouse and employment agency for those looking for help or work.[54]

The urgency blacks felt about forming their own organizations must be viewed in the context of the values and expectations of the Gilded Age. Novelists and social thinkers canonized the "self-made man" and promulgated theories of endless mobility. Examples abounded of men who escaped humble backgrounds to amass immense personal wealth and secure celebrity status, men with names such as Carnegie, Morgan, and Hill. Afro-Americans could not help absorbing elements of this prevailing value system, dreaming the thousand what-ifs even when confronted by the brutal reality of an extremely racist society. Moreover, leaders such as Booker T. Washington encouraged these dreams. Washington was a firm believer in the progressive march of time, waiting for a day when merit would negate caste. His prescription for accelerating the pace of change advised blacks to work hard, become self-sufficient, and emulate the captains of industry. On these points, few of his Afro-American contemporaries challenged his basic formula for empowerment. They too celebrated the virtues of hard work, initiative, and capital accumulation; they too believed internal development critical to social empowerment. Black institutions, in this scheme, became the apparatus for channeling the individual and collective efforts of the race.[55]

Among black residents of Norfolk, P. B. Young, editor of the influential *Norfolk Journal and Guide,* came to represent the new group of somewhat similarly opinioned middle-class leaders. Born in Littleton, North Carolina, in 1884 to solidly middle-class parents, Young moved to Norfolk in 1907 after attending Reedy Creek Academy and St. Augustine College. In Norfolk he worked for several years as plant foreman for the *Lodge Journal and Guide,* a paper distributed by the Knights of Gideon.

Young was no neophyte in the publishing world when he arrived in Norfolk, however. As a youth, he had spent several years helping his father produce the *True Reformer,* a Littleton newspaper dedicated to temperance and the self-help philosophy of Washington. Although the senior Young did not endorse Washington's complete program for racial advancement, those elements of the program that he did endorse impressed his son. The son also remained somewhat cautious, but he did not fail to appreciate Washington's importance. When the twenty-year-old began publication of a magazine, *The Argus,* sometime around 1904, he turned to the "wizard of Tuskegee" for counsel. Like other editors in the region, Young agreed with Washington that economic nationalism promised considerable material gain for blacks. He and

Washington communicated often during the first decade of the twentieth century about projects to buttress the economic base of the Afro-
American community.

Coming to Norfolk in 1907 slowed Young's plans. As plant foreman,
he no longer controlled a newspaper's editorial content. Fortunately, he
was able to purchase the lodge's printing equipment when its lending institution defaulted, and in 1910 Young launched his newest and last
newspaper venture. Dropping the word *Lodge* and substituting *Norfolk* in
the paper's name, Young founded the *Norfolk Journal and Guide*. Under
his leadership, it became the most respected black newspaper in the
South, and, over the next four decades, Young became one of the region's leading race men. He continually advised blacks to build from
within, to promote advancement in the home sphere.[56]

On Independence Day 1910, the benefits of such a strategy became
crystal clear to most black residents. On that day, Jack Johnson, who was
black, and Jim Jeffries, who was white, battled for the title of heavyweight boxing champion of the world. The bout, pitting the first black
heavyweight champion and the first "Great White Hope," became a met-
aphor for an age.

For years, the boxing ring, precisely measured and expertly cordoned,
had represented society's boundaries, with whites on the inside and blacks
on the outside. If blacks wanted to box, they would do so with other
blacks, in separate rings. This situation remained unchanged until the
day when an arrogantly confident white fighter, Tommy Burns, showed
the temerity to let Jack Johnson into an Australian boxing ring as an
equal. Burns violated the intraracial covenant on which segregation rested
and then, in the minds of whites, compounded his error by losing to
Johnson. Now Johnson was heavyweight champ, and the social calculus
that had kept other blacks outside the ring was questioned. Two years
later, boxer Jim Jeffries had the job of reestablishing white dominion
and reminding blacks of their inferiority. Throughout white America,
the outcome seemed predetermined: Jeffries would annihilate Johnson.
But the outcome was different, and Johnson whipped Jeffries. In doing
so, he taunted Jeffries, and, by extension, he taunted white America.[57]

White residents of Norfolk, like whites across the nation, reacted vio-
lently to news of Johnson's triumph. In Norfolk, "when news came
through of Jack Johnson beating Jeffries," one Afro-American bemoaned, "the white folk began pulling the Negroes off the streetcars . . .
and beating them just to vent their rage, they were so sore."[58] The riot
had been sparked when some whites heard two unnamed black men,
who were walking down Plume Street, shout in exhiliration, "Oh, you
Johnson!" This simple pronouncement began what one visitor to the city
described as a pogrom, likening it to what he had seen in his native

Russia.[59] In the eyes of the leading white daily, the riot stemmed from the "insolence of jubilant negroes." The key word, of course, is *insolence*. According to the guardians of the white power structure, Johnson had threatened the existing social order and its clear division of power. Black identification with Johnson posed a similar—or, if it spread, perhaps an even greater—threat. Thus, reasoned the paper, whites had no alternative but to insist forcefully that blacks recall their place in the political economy.[60]

In its broadest context, therefore, the Independence Day riot represented an attempt to exorcise the community of the profane assertion that whites were not superior, an assertion that Johnson's victory symbolized. At the national level, such an exorcism meant eliminating Jack Johnson, the country's proverbial "bad nigger." Federal officials realized this end when Johnson went to jail for violating the Mann Act.[61] At the local level, it meant coercing blacks back inside the geographic and social boundaries of their circumscribed existence.

Ironically, the riot had a function that the predominantly working-class white participants and their middle-class supporters surely failed to anticipate. It served to transform the individualistic Gilded Age language of Booker T. Washington into a mutualistic Afro-American language for empowerment. If doubts lingered about the correctness of promoting development in the home sphere, the riot erased them. To say this is not to ignore the remaining divisions in the black community. But the riot dramatically illustrated the need for communal action. Individually, blacks were vulnerable; Henry Alston was attacked on "Cove Street near Chesapeake Lane, outnumbered eight to one." But in concert they demonstrated real power. Afro-Americans understood that the riot stopped only after they returned to their community and erected a human wall of defense. Without assistance, they—blacks themselves—halted the riotous onslaught.[62]

Set against the backdrop of entrance into the urban-industrial order, such incidents helped Norfolk blacks shape a strategic perspective. From the start, they wanted the full range of rights and privileges guaranteed all citizens of the republic. Equally important, they were prepared to fight to gain those rights. At first, they believed it was in their interests to achieve advancement both in the workplace and in the home sphere, somewhat equally. Structural changes in the orgranization of the urban setting, characterized by the unique bifurcation between work and home faced by blacks, forced modifications. A segregated job market hampered prospects for interracial labor solidarity. Chances for real improvements in employment hinged on interracial cooperation, which could prevent employers from using white strikebreakers to undercut the efforts of black workers. But the likelihood of such cooperation declined as the Jim Crow system spread.

Furthermore, as Jim Crow matured, black and white workers moved into separate neighborhoods and found themselves in increasing competition for scarce city resources. The combination of interracial fragmentation in the workplace, interracial civic competition, and racism led to the framing of a modified perspective. By the end of the nineteenth century, Afro-Americans were assigning greater emphasis to promoting development in the home sphere. Here, blacks thought they could best marshal their resources for the benefit of the majority. Through 1930 this strategic emphasis intensified, despite temporary shifts and internal class differences.

Two

# Migration, Jobs, and Race-Conscious Urban Workers, 1910–1930

In the earliest years of the twentieth century, Norfolk Afro-Americans remained committed to pursuing improvements in the home sphere. During the years of World War I, however, they briefly adjusted their calculations, influenced by the rapid in-migration that not only affected Norfolk but also shaped the evolving northern ghettos and produced the emergent northern urban-industrial proletariat.[1] Spurred by the need for labor, encouraged by the language of democracy that was so much a part of the country's war effort, and believing that the time for workplace advancement had come, black residents shifted emphasis in their tireless fight for material improvements. They promoted progress in employment in the belief that well-situated workers enhanced the development of the home sphere and benefited the entire community. This shift, which lasted only for a brief moment, was linked to the past; for example, those who joined labor associations joined all-black organizations. After 1920, following a recession and the complete codification of segregation, new priorities emerged, and development in the home sphere regained favor. As the interwoven stories of migration, jobs, and the making of race-conscious urban workers reveal, the strategies Afro-Americans pursued were complex and fluid, clearly the result of increasing integration into a political economy in the throes of significant change.

## MIGRATION, OPPORTUNITY, AND EMPLOYMENT

George W. Bennett recalled that he was nearing adulthood when his father abandoned a comfortable position as a sawyer for an Edenton, North Carolina, lumber company to take a job in Norfolk. It was war-

TABLE 3     Black Population of Norfolk, 1910–1930

|  | 1910 | 1920 | 1930 |
|---|---|---|---|
| Males | 11,887 | 21,794 | 20,790 |
| Females | 13,152 | 21,598 | 23,153 |
| Total | 25,039 | 43,392 | 43,943 |
| Percentage of total population | 37.1 | 37.5 (73.3)[a] | 33.9 (1.27)[b] |

SOURCES: U.S. Bureau of the Census, *Thirteenth Census of the United States* (Washington, D.C.: Government Printing Office, 1911), vol. 1, *Population, 1910*, p. 287; U.S. Bureau of the Census, *Fourteenth Census of the United States* (Washington, D.C.: Government Printing Office, 1921), vol. 3, *Population, 1920, p. 1069; U.S. Bureau of the Census, Fifteenth Census of the United States* (Washington, D.C.: Government Printing Office, 1932), vol. 3, pt. 2, *Population, 1930*, p. 1166.

[a]Number in parentheses is percentage increase from 1910 to 1920.
[b]Number in parentheses is percentage increase from 1920 to 1930.

time, and the once sleepy seaport needed laborers, for it was about to be transformed into the foremost naval base of the Atlantic coast. Bennett, Sr., in migrating to Norfolk, became part of a national phenomenon. During the period from 1900 to 1920, about 1.5 million blacks left the rural South. More than half of these migrants settled in southern cities, indicating that the rural-to-urban and South-to-North migration streams were not identical.[2]

As federal officials noted and as in-migration rates vividly illustrate, movement to Norfolk followed this call for labor.[3] The city's black population increased by an average annual rate of 7.3 percent during the war decade, the greatest war-associated population increase of any large southern city. Over the next ten-year period, however, when many northern cities experienced a second surge, more blacks left Norfolk than became permanent residents (see Table 3).[4] Thus the period between 1910 and 1930 was characterized by an initial phase of intense in-migration, followed by a phase of equally substantial out-migration.[5]

Those who migrated to Norfolk followed existing migration streams along the eastern seaboard rather than through the Mississippi Valley corridor.[6] In fact, most Afro-American migrants came from the surrounding region, other parts of Virginia, or North Carolina, a proximity that allowed them to maintain contact with kith and kin. Between 1910 and 1930, Norfolk County, an immense rural hinterland abutting the city's eastern edge and sprawling south toward North Carolina, lost population. In part, the decline followed the city of Norfolk's annexation of portions of the county in 1911 and 1923 (see Map 1); it also resulted from the movement of residents to the city, especially during World War I.[7]

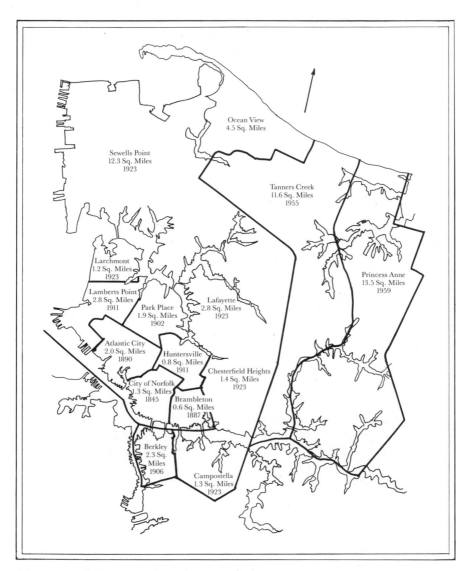

Map 1. Norfolk's Changing City Boundaries
SOURCES: Norfolk Planning Commission; *Virginian-Pilot* (Norfolk).

Family members often facilitated the move from Norfolk County into the city by providing the new migrants with living quarters and financial assistance during the initial adjustment period. Such movement vividly illustrates the process of chain migration, defined "as that movement in which prospective migrants learn of opportunities, are provided with

transportation, and have initial accommodation and employment arranged by means of primary social relationships with previous migrants." Lloyd D., for example, recalled his family having to make room
for a female cousin, Susan J., who took up semi-temporary residence in
their household during the late 1910s. This cousin, Lloyd remembered,
had come in search of work from rural St. Brides, an area of black concentration in Norfolk County.[8]

Migrants who did not come from nearby Norfolk County were likely
to have come from other Virginia locations or from North Carolina.
Throughout the period, two thirds of all blacks who settled in Norfolk
claimed Virginia as their state of birth.[9] Occasionally, movement to
Norfolk was part of a process of stepwise migration, as migrants moved
from small town to larger city. Maria Ruffin described such a process to
Virginia Writers' Project interviewer Edith Skinner; Ruffin settled in
Norfolk after moving from several small Virginia towns to Petersburg
and then to Norfolk.[10] Although the recorded data are not as precise
for non-Virginian newcomers, it seems that, at the state level, most of
them were from North Carolina. Many undoubtedly resembled George
Bennett's father, who, already integrated into a wage economy, was predisposed to migrate to improve his life choices.[11]

The majority of those who poured into the city between 1910 and
1930 may have hoped for unimpeded occupational advancement, but
they got much less. They discovered an employment opportunity structure that made blacks' participation in the labor force highly sensitive to
fluctuations in the economy, female labor exceedingly important, and
intraracial class tension increasingly obvious. The structure of the labor
force also exposed the material gap between black and white workers.
This gap, paired with the absence of interracial labor solidarity, tended
to validate the claims of those who argued at various times for an emphasis on development in the home sphere because it was more attainable. To examine the composition of the labor force and the associated
occupationally defined class structure of the black community, we must
rely largely on published census data.[12] Unfortunately, systematic data
for 1910 are not available, and we are thus forced to restrict our discussion primarily to 1920 and 1930.

The rate of participation in the labor force dramatizes the extent to
which work was available and also highlights the underemployment of
black men. Spread across the occupational spectrum—although over-
represented as laborers, unskilled more often than semi-skilled or
skilled—nearly nine of every ten working-age black men found employment in 1920. Their rates of both concentration in unskilled laboring
jobs and participation in the labor force were higher than those of native
whites. Foreign-born whites had a higher participation rate than blacks,

but the difference is attributable to a dissimilar age structure: 94 percent of foreign-born males were more than twenty years old, compared to only 81 percent of black males. As a result, many black households depended on the earnings of teenage sons, who were preponderantly errand boys and bootblacks.[13]

More important, although many black men found employment, few secured lasting, better-paying industrial jobs. In part, this reflected the varied makeup of Norfolk's economy and the central importance of its waterways and port. Because of the region's dual, or segmented, labor market, in which certain jobs became the exclusive province of blacks and others the domain of whites, most Afro-American men worked in occupations traditionally held by blacks. Most of these jobs were low-paying, which placed added pressure on wives and children to work for wages. For generations, Norfolk's ample waterways had provided employment for black men such as Charlie Johnson, a fisherman; others worked as seamen or in the many secondary trades such as oyster shucking.[14] In further keeping with past practices, in 1920 the greatest number of black men worked in transportation jobs. Of the 31.7 percent who constituted this occupational grouping, more than half joined J. C. Skinner on the docks as longshoremen or stevedores.[15] The remainder worked in a mixture of middle-class and laboring jobs—draymen or chauffeurs, on the one hand; sailors, deckhands, or general laborers, on the other (see Table 4).

Norfolk experienced a boom in its manufacturing sector during the war years. New companies, such as American Chain and Standard Oil, appeared. They brought increased employment opportunities but not always openings for skilled workers. The 1920 census showed that 30 percent of all black males had found jobs in manufacturing and mechanical industries; nearly half of these workers (44 percent) were identified as laborers. (The percentage of laborers may have been even greater, for many occupational headings failed to specify the nature of the job.) Others worked in occupations not generally considered industrial, such as baking and carpentry. Edward Weller, who moved to Norfolk in 1922, held several odd jobs before he found employment as a baker's helper, a job he held as late as 1939.[16]

World War I and the accompanying search for skilled labor produced new pressure to liberalize hiring and promotion practices at local military installations, the area's primary employers of skilled labor. Blacks added to this pressure by demanding improved opportunities, and to some extent their hopes were realized. A census taken among the residents of Truxton—a showcase all-black community built for black Norfolk Navy Yard employees by the U.S. Housing Corporation (USHC)—indicates that one quarter of the men worked at the yard as skilled

TABLE 4    Male Occupations by Race, Norfolk, 1920

| Occupation | Native White | Foreign-Born White | Black |
|---|---|---|---|
| Agriculture, forestry, animal husbandry | 118   (0.5) | 11   (0.3) | 173   (1.0) |
| Extraction of minerals | 24   (0.1) | 1   (0.0) | 14   (0.1) |
| Manufacturing and mechanical | 8,302 (36.6) | 1,338 (32.2) | 5,101 (30.5) |
| Transportation | 3,182 (14.0) | 805 (19.4) | 5,308 (31.7) |
| Trade | 4,575 (20.1) | 1,129 (27.2) | 1,668 (10.0) |
| Public service | 1,153   (5.1) | 84   (2.0) | 1,531   (9.2) |
| Professional services | 1,427   (6.3) | 157   (3.8) | 241   (1.4) |
| Domestic and personal service | 655   (2.9) | 490 (11.8) | 2,446 (14.6) |
| Clerical | 3,279 (14.4) | 141   (3.4) | 238   (1.4) |
| Total | 22,715 | 4,156 | 16,720 |

SOURCE: U.S. Bureau of the Census, *Fourteenth Census of the United States* (Washington, D.C.: Government Printing Office, 1923), vol. 4, *Occupations, 1920*, pp. 1183–84.

NOTE: Figures in parentheses are percentages of the particular ethnic or racial group. As a result of rounding, not all columns total exactly 100.0 percent.

workers or helpers. Examples include E. B. Williams, driller; Henry Jones, pipefitter's helper; and P. J. Sharp, shipfitter's helper.[17]

In general, however, black men gained little ground, as wage differentials for black and white navy yard workers reminded everyone. Such differences continued to be an obstacle to interracial labor solidarity by highlighting the advantages whites maintained. Personnel records indicate that 83 percent of the yard's black employees earned between $21 and $25 per week. Although these wages were better than the pay received by most laborers in the area, they were inferior to the wages paid to whites. Whereas 19 percent of whites earned between $21 and $25 per week, more than 60 percent earned in excess of $34 per week. Fewer than 10 blacks out of 2,086 earned that much. Black men, it seemed, remained disproportionately underemployed, even after entering the ranks of the industrial work force.[18]

More telling is what happened to the privileged few who saw an opportunity, seized it, and overcame the barriers of race. In 1918 Charles N. Hunter, already sixty-seven years old and a prominent North Carolina educator and political activist, left his job as a school principal in Method, North Carolina, for a more lucrative job at the Norfolk Navy Yard as a laborer. He quickly deduced that this position was below his level of skills, however. Long years of political activism had brought him into contact with a number of prominent southern whites, including Secretary of the Navy Josephus Daniels. He used this contact and his own considerable skills to become one of only two black foremen at the installation. He held this rating through 1921, when cutbacks in personnel and the resignation of Daniels hastened his downfall. In a letter to W. H. Hays, head of the Republican National Executive Committee, Hunter explained his turn of fortune and begged for help:

> Since the Armistice and especially since the election of last November, there has been going on a gradual, but sure process of elimination by which all Negroes, who have attained higher ratings are being disposed of. The motive is quite apparent. These men are without any means of representation or protection save through you. They deserve better treatment and should get it. . . . as soon as Secretary Daniels term of office expired I was recommended for demotion to a common laborer. . . . Other engagements are opened to me. But I do protest against this as a policy of my party.[19]

The Republican party failed to protect its loyal worker. After appeals to Hays, Assistant Secretary of the Navy Franklin D. Roosevelt, and many others, Hunter accepted a discharge at the permanent rating of laborer. Hunter's rise and fall marked both the high and the low points in the search for well-paid industrial jobs. The Afro-Americans who did secure industrial employment clearly faced many pitfalls at this stage, given their place in the political economy.

Hunter belonged to a less-than-exclusive fraternity. Economic recessions at both the start and the conclusion of the next decade put many black men out of work, although they did little to alter the occupational class structure of the community. Hunter returned to Raleigh, North Carolina, to a series of one-year teaching appointments. Others left for cities further north. By 1930 the proportion of employed black males had dropped from nine in ten to eight in ten, reflecting a net loss of nearly three thousand jobs. Whites, conversely, gained forty-five hundred jobs, thereby erasing the earlier racial differentials. The only groups of black males to fare well were agricultural workers and professionals (see Table 5). Aside from individuals such as medical doctors Coppage and Trigg, attorney Edwards, and several schoolteachers, most black professionals in Norfolk were members of the clergy. Some, like Rev. Richard Bowling of First Baptist Church, were established and well respected; others, dubbed "jack legs," were preachers without formal training or a permanent church.[20]

High rates of labor force participation by black men, even during the recession-plagued 1920s, cloak the sobering realization that black households were overwhelmingly dependent on the productive capabilities of black women. Black women were twice as likely as native-born white women to be part of the labor force, and nearly three times as likely as foreign-born white women.[21] These comparisons clearly bespeak the

TABLE 5    Male Occupations by Race, Norfolk, 1930

| Occupation | Native White | Foreign-Born White | Black |
|------------|-------------|--------------------|-------|
| Agriculture | 169   (0.6) | 13   (0.6) | 308   (2.2) |
| Forestry and fishing | 62   (0.2) | — | 50   (0.4) |
| Extraction of minerals | 10   (0.0) | — | 14   (0.1) |
| Manufacturing and mechanical | 7,995 (29.1) | 575 (23.6) | 4,482 (32.8) |
| Transportation and communication | 2,923 (10.6) | 251 (11.2) | 3,969 (29.1) |
| Trade | 5,665 (20.6) | 833 (37.1) | 1,664 (12.2) |
| Public service | 5,292 (19.3) | 136   (6.1) | 503   (3.0) |
| Professional services | 1,642   (6.0) | 130   (5.8) | 410   (3.0) |
| Domestic and personal service | 628   (2.3) | 221   (9.8) | 2,163 (15.8) |
| Clerical | 3,096 (11.3) | 86   (3.8) | 98   (0.7) |
| Total | 27,482 | 2,245 | 13,661 |

SOURCE: U.S. Bureau of the Census, *Fifteenth Census of the United States* (Washington, D.C.: Government Printing Office, 1933), vol. 4, *Occupations, 1930,* pp. 1673–74.

NOTE: Figures in parentheses are percentages of the particular ethnic or racial group. As a result of rounding, not all columns total exactly 100.0 percent.

structural characteristics of employment. Female labor was essential because black males and females were underemployed relative to whites. Few women, moreover, could expect to bridge the employment gap. Throughout most of the period between 1910 and 1930, more than four in five black women worked as domestics or personal servants in nonskilled, labor-intensive, poorly paid jobs (see Table 6).

Employment in one of the city's manufacturing and mechanical industries provided the only real alternative to the drudgery of domestic service. Ironically, the mix of firms enabled black women to dominate this sector, and they claimed more than half of these jobs. This did little to ease underemployment, however, because most worked for low wages in industries that paid by the piece. The largest group (253 out of 1,013) worked as dressmakers in a nonfactory setting. In 1920 the vast majority of black women who worked in factory settings were employed as tobacco stemmers at the American Cigar Company. Others worked for one of the smaller clothing manufacturers such as the Mar-Hof Company or the Chesapeake Knitting Mills. The former produced "cotton, linen [and] woolen middy blouses and skirts," and the latter manufactured "union-suits, drawers and shirts."[22]

Industrial employment may have meant relatively better wages for these women, but it did not free them from the dual burden of race and

TABLE 6    Female Occupations by Race, Norfolk, 1920

| Occupation | Native White | Foreign-Born White | Black |
|---|---|---|---|
| Agriculture, forestry, animal husbandry | 3  (0.0) | — | 26  (0.3) |
| Extraction of minerals | — | — | 1  (0.0) |
| Manufacturing and mechanical | 740 (13.2) | 42 (11.7) | 1,013 (11.7) |
| Transportation | 166  (3.0) | 3  (0.8) | 29  (0.3) |
| Trade | 885 (15.8) | 128 (35.6) | 123  (1.4) |
| Public service | 18  (0.3) | — | 22  (0.2) |
| Professional services | 788 (12.1) | 43 (12.0) | 296  (3.4) |
| Domestic and personal service | 680 (12.1) | 74 (20.6) | 7,094 (81.9) |
| Clerical | 2,320 (41.4) | 69 (19.2) | 61  (0.7) |
| Total | 5,600 | 359 | 8,665 |

SOURCE: U.S. Bureau of the Census, *Fourteenth Census of the United States* (Washington, D.C.: Government Printing Office, 1923), vol. 4, *Occupations, 1920*, pp. 1184–85.

NOTE: Figures in parentheses are percentages of the particular ethnic or racial group. As a result of rounding, not all columns total exactly 100.0 percent.

gender. In December 1919, the Mar-Hof Company had a work force of fifty-three men and women—five white men, two black men, thirty-five white women, and eleven black women. The white men were fabric cutters and were responsible for the upkeep of the machinery, while the black men performed custodial duties. White women ran the power machines, inspected the finished products, and worked in supervisory positions. Black women had the hot and arduous job of standing over the pressing machines day after day. It is not clear from the description provided by the company whether or not these women were actually semi-skilled or unskilled laborers.[23] What is certain is that few black women, including the 104 black seamers at Chesapeake Knitting Mills, had an opportunity to become skilled laborers or managers.[24]

Although the percentage of black women who found professional jobs was greater than that of their male counterparts, females on the whole had a smaller range of employment options. Occupational mobility, and thus class mobility, primarily hinged on landing one of the coveted teaching jobs. Of the 296 female black professionals in 1920, 71.6 percent were teachers. But mobility could be erased as quickly as it was achieved. Ruth V. was a teacher who married in the 1920s; her marriage ended her teaching career. Her financial contribution was important to her family, however, and so, with few alternatives, she became a beautician.[25] Bertha L. Douglass, a graduate of Norfolk Mission College, became an

TABLE 7    Female Occupations by Race, Norfolk, 1930

| Occupation | Native White | Foreign-Born White | Black |
|---|---|---|---|
| Agriculture | 1 (0.0) | 1 (0.4) | 191 (2.0) |
| Manufacturing and mechanical | 859 (12.4) | 38 (13.2) | 1,276 (13.4) |
| Transportation and communication | 201 (2.9) | 3 (1.1) | 11 (0.1) |
| Trade | 1,241 (18.0) | 103 (36.1) | 110 (1.2) |
| Public service | 9 (0.1) | — | 6 (0.1) |
| Professional services | 1,373 (19.9) | 38 (13.3) | 428 (4.5) |
| Domestic and personal service | 818 (11.8) | 57 (20.0) | 7,482 (78.3) |
| Clerical | 2,405 (34.8) | 45 (15.8) | 55 (0.6) |
| Total | 6,907 | 285 | 9,559 |

SOURCE: U.S. Bureau of the Census, *Fifteenth Census of the United States* (Washington, D.C.: Government Printing Office, 1933), vol. 4, *Occupations, 1930,* pp. 1673–74.

NOTE: Figures in parentheses are percentages of the particular ethnic or racial group. As a result of rounding, not all columns total exactly 100.0 percent.

exception to the experience of downward mobility. After taking correspondence classes and studying under attorney J. Eugene Diggs, she passed the state bar exam in December 1926 and became the city's first black female lawyer.[26] Almost all the other black women who held professional jobs were nurses, musicians, or music teachers.

Ironically, employment losses during the 1920s by black males came as black women realized gains in sex-segregated occupations. A historical lock on domestic service jobs, coupled with improved opportunities for whites, tendered black women a dubious advantage: an additional one thousand jobs as domestics during the 1920s. They made other gains as well. Between 1920 and 1930, more than two hundred new jobs were acquired in the manufacturing and mechanical trades, reversed only as the Depression worsened (see Table 6, compared to Table 7). But, although it was significant that some women acquired industrial jobs, the fact that eight in ten Afro-American women continued to work as domestics meant that blacks remained underemployed, a condition some tried to remedy by joining unions and seeking improved wages.

## THE STRUCTURING OF THE BLACK MIDDLE CLASS

Against the backdrop of an underemployed working class emerged a modest entrepreneurial middle class. This group found its fortunes inescapably tied to those of the working class. Consequently, its members frequently counseled that community development hinged on racial cooperation and challenged the laboring class's commitment to the community and ultimately to the race. But black laborers had a measure of independence, which manifested itself in displays of both race consciousness and class consciousness. At times, this dual consciousness led to disagreement between these two classes.

The Afro-American business community in Norfolk remained steadfastly race-oriented, which fanned intraracial disagreements. Many members of this community came under the direct or indirect influence of Booker T. Washington. Washington's influence can be traced in the formation of a local Negro Business League and in the frequency with which his message of self-help and economic self-sufficiency appeared in public discourse. Truxton resident D. H. Haywood, for example, advised in Washingtonian language that although politics and education were important, the race's survival depended on attaining economic self-sufficiency. Self-sufficiency, he warned, required new industries to provide an intergenerational exchange of capital and skills. It was not enough to say, "Let them come up as I did," he admonished, concluding that this may have been acceptable advice for earlier generations because "they did the best they knew, but we must go further than that and take up where they left off."[27]

William A. Hewlett was more emphatic. He maintained: "We cannot hope to survive unless we begin to provide for the employment of our people; this we should not expect other races to do for us in this age of our American advancement. We must manufacture, we must become commercial."[28] Neither man belonged to the visible black leadership in the area. Nonetheless both Haywood and Hewlett effectively articulated the most often-repeated views of the period. Certain blacks heeded their counsel and struggled to build an enduring business community.

The life of a business person was indeed one of struggle and frustration, despite an apparent lock on black trade. Blacks in Norfolk shared the same problem faced by blacks in other cities: inadequate start-up capital to turn dreams into sound business ventures. As a result, the business community came to be dominated by small, volatile enterprises: corner groceries, nickel-and-dime retail operations, beauty parlors. Buena Kelly's experience was typical. She quit her job at a Norfolk beauty salon in 1916 in order to open her own shop. From the outset, however, she was plagued by insufficient funding. She compensated by converting her O'Keefe Street residence into her salon.[29]

Although undercapitalization militated against the likelihood of success, some overcame the obstacles. To circumvent money problems, a few merged their resources: F. S. Ryan, L. J. Layton, and W. R. Leary, who jointly opened a grocery store after World War I; R. T. Brown, Charles H. Robinson, and J. D. Archer, who opened a steam laundry; and several other individuals who consolidated their capital to open the Union Progressive Shoe Company. Cooperative ventures had been tried by blacks in other cities and towns since the end of the Civil War, and World War I renewed the tendency. Layton spoke for a broader constituency when he suggested that joint ventures enabled black grocers to increase their buying power and thereby offer the best products to the black consumer for the lowest price.[30]

But only a few found others to share the financial risk. Average business owners lived close to the edge. Their stories dramatized both the dependence of the petty merchant on black workers and the reasons why some shortsightedly championed development in the home sphere more than advancement in the workplace. Rarely did black entrepreneurs make a public connection between their economic welfare and improved wages for black workers. As they teetered on the edge, most members of the business community endorsed any actions that maximized profits and minimized risk. These conservative practices marked their general approach to labor activism as well. More than once, their strained relationship with the rank and file spelled economic doom.

The story of a merchant named Mr. Porter illustrates these points. He moved to Norfolk in 1918 from Hertsford, North Carolina, and opened a grocery store on the corner of Chapel and Goff streets. Because his business thrived during the war years, he allowed his working-class customers to buy on credit, a practice he continued after the war ended. All went well until the recession hit in 1921 and people all over the city lost their jobs. Porter faced a dilemma. To weather the recession, he needed to maintain his clientele, who needed credit now more than ever; but to replenish his depleted inventory and remain in business, he needed to settle delinquent accounts. He could not find a successful strategy, and his store closed in 1924. Porter showed both a surprising resiliency and a striking typicality, however. Two years later, embittered but determined, he announced his intention to reopen.[31] Nonetheless, because of undercapitalization and a marginally capitalized clientele, his business, and others like it, remained on the edge. How many individuals slipped in and out of the business class we may never know; if the business turnover rate along Church Street (the heart of the black business district; see Map 2) is an accurate barometer, the number was large.

Small merchants faced the added problem of white competitors. Segregation separated blacks from whites in many areas, but it always seemed to be to the advantage of whites. For example, there were no restrictions keeping nonblack merchants out of the black business district. Ostensibly, local officials adopted the most insidious aspect of Booker T. Washington's "Altanta Compromise" speech, in which he said

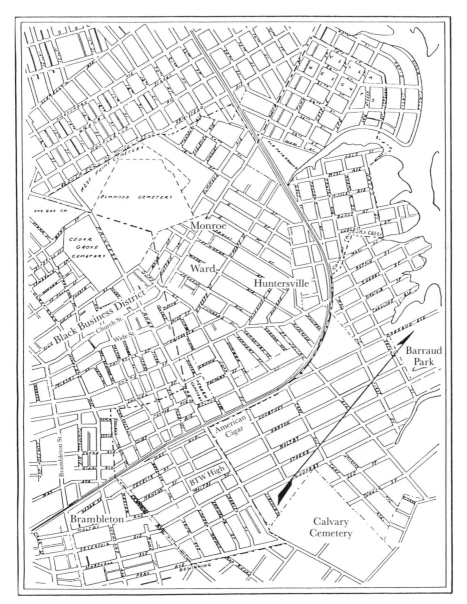

Map 2. The Heart of Norfolk's Black Community, 1910–1930

that blacks and whites should be as separate as the five fingers in things social and political and like a closed hand in things economic.[32]

A perusal of the city directories reveals that Jews, Italians, Greeks, and Asians entered into business on Church Street long before the city wrote its first segregation ordinance. By 1910 the south end of Church

Street near the Elizabeth River housed the residences and shops of Jewish merchants. Between Main Street and Plume Street, Marx Shapiro owned a clothing store; a block further north, Diamondstein and Schneider worked as tailors. A block away was Bernard Lilienfeld's pawn shop. Further up the street, one encountered L. L. Cohen's millinery store, M. A. Cohen's tailor shop, Mendal Reuben's grocery store, Max Brenner's bakery, Jacob Crockin's furniture store, and Samuel Schneider's dry goods store. Other merchants included A. Z. Levine, a saloonkeeper; W. Richenstein, a jeweler; David Freidman, a clothier; Aaron Bernstein, a baker; and Abraham Swartz, a cobbler. To a black community profoundly aware of its place in the political economy, these merchants came to embody the barriers thwarting the dream of economic self-sufficiency, and their presence frequently served as the agency for race-conscious mobilization.[33]

The Italian merchants who operated along Church Street throughout the 1910s and 1920s remained few in number, and thus, as a specific ethnic group, they did not threaten the dream in the same manner as the Jewish merchants did. Often, however, in the eyes of blacks, ethnicity blurred, and the color scheme reverted to black and white, with little intragroup differentiation. Italians, in this context, also became a group to oppose.

In a black and white world, Asian merchants confounded the picture. At least through 1930, blacks viewed them in a different fashion than they viewed other nonblacks. In part, this resulted from the relatively small size of the Asian population; nonblack minorities made up less than 1 percent of the population and thus did not represent the same entrepreneurial threat. In addition, the racial ethos shaped residential patterns, association, and ultimately identity. Whereas in the West segregation worked to create an autonomous and distinct Asian community, Asians in the South, after the *Gong Lum* decision, increasingly became part of surrounding black communities.[34] Because the Jim Crow world emphasized a black and white color scheme, Asians functionally became coloreds and hence "blacks." Racial and ethnic cultural identities were not completely blurred, of course; several Chinese in Norfolk, for example, opened restaurants that specialized in Asian cuisine. Rather, segregation southern style forced the formation of rudimentary transethnic color consciousness.

The funeral of George Wong brought into the open the consequences of marginality in a southern setting. Wong owned a business in the black community. Either because of the small size of the Chinese community or because of his identification with blacks, he joined a black association, the Elks. His attachment to that organization was so great that, when he was stricken with appendicitis, he delayed treatment to attend the funeral of a lodge brother, and he subsequently died of complications. Black residents gazed in wonderment at the Elks' processional bearing Wong's body. His funeral and his association with the Elks highlighted the contradictions of a dichromatic world.[35]

Although some Asians were accepted, the presence of nonblack merchants along Church Street generally caused much rancor. A society consistently structured along racial lines should have guaranteed black exclusivity; that it did not underscored the one-sided nature of the restrictions and brought protests from Afro-Americans. In fairness, ethnic merchants, despite their greater access to capital, were pawns in the larger political economy. With their own choices delimited by life in a southern city, they frequently set up shop wherever possible.

Striving to enter the middle-class world, black merchants who tied their success to that of the community, blamed not only white competitors but also working-class blacks for business failures. Recalling the events that had culminated in his bankruptcy in 1924, grocer Porter unwittingly pointed to the symbiosis between the black classes. The same patrons he carried on credit, he complained, deserted him to patronize white merchants when he demanded payment. Their actions, he concluded, sealed his fate and caused his bankruptcy.

The belief that when one black succeeded all blacks shared in the success and that when one black individual failed all black people failed informed Porter's attack. Porter envisioned a community fortified with a heavy dose of race consciousness. To him, economic empowerment hinged on group support; without such support, advancement of any kind was hopeless. Hence race defined one's ultimate identity; or, as others would ponder, "How can working folks continue to give their hard-earned money to white merchants who then take the money and build their own communities?"[36]

Wedged between the petty merchants and the successfully capitalized businesses rested a declining handful of highly specialized black artisans, who catered to a racially mixed clientele and were, by and large, very successful. Individuals like Charles S. Carter, an officer of the Business League and owner of the oldest clothing and tailoring shop in the city, found themselves in a fairly comfortable financial position by the mid-1920s. Joining Carter was H. F. Fonville, who owned the Southern Furniture Repair and Novelty Company. At his Bank Street location, Fonville reconditioned and built furniture. They, as well as Mr. Omohundro, who owned the city's leading mirror factory, managed to stay afloat during the volatile 1920s without publicly criticizing potential black patrons.[37] They knew that blacks constituted only a percentage of their clientele. These individuals may have been race-conscious in other ways, but this consciousness was not based on a dependence on black customers.

Within Norfolk's black business community one also found a handful of larger business units. Like the proprietor of the corner grocery, they too relied heavily on black customers. Because they did, they adopted a public posture and used a public rhetoric that keyed community development to cooperation between the middle class and the working class.

One of the oldest of these companies was C. C. Dogan's Home Building and Loan Association (HBLA). Dogan came to Norfolk in 1892 from Spartanburg, South Carolina, to become secretary of the YMCA. From that vantage point, he surveyed the community's needs and concluded that a lending agency to loan money to aspiring business owners and homeowners was essential to black progress. Several residents agreed, and in 1905 they backed his plan, which created HBLA, with Dogan as its financial secretary. By 1920 the company held assets totaling $82,782.73, stock profits of $9,135.73, and receipts equaling $61,847.05. It paid out $11,400 to individuals whose stocks reached maturity.[38]

By the mid-1920s, Norfolk had not one but two notable financial institutions. Four years after Dogan persuaded his group to underwrite the creation of HBLA, E. C. Brown, with ten thousand dollars drawn largely from his own savings, founded Brown Savings and Banking Company. The new bank opened in a converted grocery store. Brown undertook such a speculative venture because he earnestly believed blacks needed a full-fledged bank. A survey of local conditions had both saddened and inspired him: it found only about five hundred savings accounts bearing the names of black residents; a severely underdeveloped business community; a poor housing situation exacerbated by the lack of secure, black-owned lending institutions; and individuals entrapped by the usurious methods of loan sharks. Against this backdrop he chose to act.[39]

Within the first three years of its founding, the bank made significant strides. W. M. Rich, a graduate of Hampton Institute, was hired to assist Brown. Together, they charted the bank's future development. Then, in 1912, the bank benefited from a reorganization: within a year, the number of depositors nearly doubled, growing from eight hundred to fifteen hundred; and the deposits nearly tripled, rising from nine thousand dollars to twenty-three thousand. In 1919 Brown Savings and Banking Company became Metropolitan Bank and Trust Company, with stock capitalized at two hundred thousand dollars. The newly formed bank claimed one thousand depositors and deposits totaling between a quarter-million and a half-million dollars. Meanwhile, the bank came under new leadership. W. M. Rich, who had first joined the bank as Brown's assistant and a cashier, quickly moved his way through the organizational structure to assume the presidency. In 1922 the bank merged with the Tidewater Bank and Trust Company, another all-black establishment that had been created in 1918 by several of the city's leading businessmen. With the merger of the two banks, Norfolk claimed the largest black-owned financial institution in the country.[40]

The merger both buttressed the fiscal foundation of Metropolitan and contributed to the growing involvement of a small coterie of men in the community's financial dealings. M. R. Jackson, with experience in the insurance field, became vice-president of Metropolitan and HBLA. Dr. G. Hamilton Francis, who had been vice-president of the Tidewater Bank and Trust Company, continued in the same capacity with Metropolitan. Similarly, C. C. Dogan, manager of HBLA (which merged with Seaside Building and Loan Association in May 1922), joined the newly combined board of directors. P. B. Young, editor of the *Norfolk Journal and Guide* and the most persistent purveyor of the racial solidarity message, also assumed a position with the new bank as a member of the board of directors.[41]

Although the merger resulted in a company with fifteen thousand depositors and approximately $1.5 million in deposits, the growth camouflaged several basic problems that underscored the link between the banker and the corner grocer. Despite the bank's phenomenal growth, the rest of Norfolk's business community remained largely underdeveloped, which invited financial catastrophe. As Rich noted in 1927, "The growth of business has not been comparable to that of increased home-ownership, churches, and fraternal organizations." Growth in these other sectors, important though it was, did not produce the revenue needed to underwrite development. Because there were few businesses, the bank was forced to rely heavily on the earnings of its depositors to balance accounts. Such a practice could, as Rich realized, lead to long-term disaster, for the bank spent considerable administrative resources to monitor and service many very small accounts (most less than fifty dollars). These accounts actually cost the bank more money than they brought in, but to jettison them would have jeopardized the bank's somewhat tenuous relationship with people who needed encouragement to save money and utilize financial institutions. Rich was painfully aware of the impossible balance and diplomatically complained, "It [is] rather difficult to eliminate these accounts without materially discouraging the very thing undertaken by way of educating and encouraging the masses to save." To compound the situation, the bank paid out 4 percent interest on savings accounts, mostly to small savers, which "cut down . . . net earnings materially," given that 70 percent of all deposits involved savings accounts. Rich encouraged business development as a remedy; a diagnosis of the problem proved much easier than finding the appropriate means of implementing the remedy, however.[42]

Black residents nevertheless knew that a successful business could be built locally. All they had to do was take note of the *Norfolk Journal and*

*Guide* and its companion, the Guide Publishing Company. When P. B. Young assumed the helm of the insolvent lodge paper, its future had seemed dismal. But under the tutelage of Young and his brother W. H., the paper grew to be the most important black weekly in the South. Historian Henry Lewis Suggs, the leading authority on the newspaper's history, estimates that between 1910 and 1935 the number of subscriptions grew from five hundred to twenty-nine thousand. By 1928 it had entered markets in Connecticut, Chicago, Kansas City, and Omaha, seeking in the process to shed the cloak of regionalism and emerge as a national voice. Although its equipment could not fully rival that owned by the *Baltimore Afro-American* or the *Pittsburgh Courier,* the *Journal and Guide* employed twenty-five people, more than any other black-owned business in the city.[43]

Men and women like W. M. Rich, Mr. Porter, Buena Kelly, and P. B. Young also assumed leadership roles in the community, which gave them a platform to tout their race-conscious economic program. The black working class selectively responded to their invocations, at times disregarding middle-class pleas. At other times, the working class wedded its race and class interests in a manner that defies simple explication but is related to what sociologist Charles S. Johnson aptly labels "the ideology of the color line."[44] To understand when and why black workers heeded the advice of the middle class, we must understand what made urban workers race-conscious.

## AN IMPORTANT HISTORICAL MOMENT

The eldest in a family of eighteen children, Clifton J. joined the thousands of blacks who migrated from the farms to the nation's cities and towns during the 1910s in search of work. His reasons for leaving rural Norfolk County were similar to those of most other migrants: essentially, he yearned to escape agricultural labor and the life it accorded. He reached Norfolk as employment opportunities diminished, the result of a postwar recession. Through a combination of determination and luck, he nonetheless secured a series of jobs as a laborer and membership in the city's broad working class.

We know very little of Clifton's attitudes about work. Unlike others, he never joined a union, even during World War II, when he obtained permanent industrial employment. Undeniably, Clifton was race-conscious, but he was seemingly indifferent even to race-conscious labor associations.[45] Clifton's experiences both at work and at home (the household and the community) must have shaped his perspective—how this happened remains an unanswered question.

Fortunately, where Clifton's story goes mute, the larger story of black labor through 1930 finds voice. That story complements and challenges what others have written about the Afro-American urban working population by emphasizing the complex social calculus that made up worker consciousness.[46] During World War I, for example, Norfolk blacks used the racial structure of the dual labor market to promote race-exclusive unionization. At this stage, both industrial and nonindustrial workers responded to the summons. Moreover, through 1920, black workers received tentative support from middle-class spokespersons who linked advancements in the workplace to improvements in the home sphere.

At the war's end, however, various groups of workers followed different paths. Those who could continued to advance unionization; others devised different strategies to secure workers' control. Still others ignored collective action entirely. The changes had to do both with different opportunities and circumstances and with black Norfolk's growing class stratification. Increasingly, after 1920, middle-class leaders appropriated management's language, advising black workers to be more productive, efficient, and reliable. Workers, divided by jobs and approaches, failed to muster a strong counterargument. Furthermore, the general trend during these years was to treat the workplace as an important but subordinate sphere of concern. This trend was strengthened by the fact that racism proved such a great leveler. Blacks realized that outside work their white counterparts continued to enjoy a status unrelated to their class position. This status undermined labor solidarity both at work and at home and influenced what it meant to be race-conscious urban workers in a maturing industrial economy.

Despite the limited successes and the later changes, the period of the late 1910s through 1930 proved to be very significant for the black working class of Norfolk. One of the hidden ironies of segregation was the power it unwittingly bequeathed to blacks. Forced to accept Jim Crow's proscriptions, Afro-Americans transformed the racial segmentation of the labor market into a vehicle for the organization of black workers. This was the case especially during the war years. The organizing campaign began among black longshoremen in 1917. After winning concessions from shipping lines in the areas, including recognition of their union, they tried to guarantee similar gains for other black workers in local industries. Although the longshoremen's success was not to prove transferable, this episode dramatized a growing commitment to progress in the workplace and the ongoing importance of race-conscious unionization.

Changes in the material makeup of the city's economic base, which offered the possibility of raising black workers' low wages, partially explains why the push toward race-exclusive unions shadowed the city's transformation into a vital war center. In 1913 more than three million dollars' worth of marine foodstuffs left ports in the lower Chesapeake Bay for national consumption; these same ports employed a disproportionate number of black men. A year later, Norfolk boasted invested capital of thirty million dollars in 362 manufacturing plants. The federal government, another major employer, annually spent fourteen million dollars to maintain several military installations. Additional revenues came from maritime trade; in 1917 alone, 8.5 million tons of cargo entered and another 9 million tons left Norfolk's ports.[47]

Growth in all sectors spurted during the war years, producing a noticeable industrial expansion. E. I. Dupont leased a new building for the storage of cotton liners, while the British-American Tobacco Company opened four large plants to manufacture cigarettes. Texas Oil increased its holding capacity; the Hampton Roads Shipbuilding and Drydock Company and the Norfolk Shipbuilding and Drydock Company enlarged their facilities; and the government pumped in large sums of money in its quest to buy new land for its expanding military operations.[48]

As the city's economic base increased, so did black expectations. Afro-Americans wanted new jobs and new opportunities, ones that could eliminate underemployment. Most understood that race had been an impediment to advancement, and they wanted such barriers removed. When approached by a representative of Norman R. Hamilton, the collector of customs, about using their pulpits to announce openings at the Norfolk Navy Yard, members of the Colored Interdenominational Ministers Union responded:

> We have . . . requested your representative to bear to you our earnest wish that you use the great influence of your position to have the honorable Secretary of the Navy and others to do their utmost to break down every barrier . . . so that the opportunity not only for labor but for promotion and the loftiest patriotic effort may be opened to [black workers] according to their several abilities.[49]

Here, middle-class black leaders and black workers were of one mind: advancement depended on securing permanent, better-paying jobs.

Relatively few blacks got the better-paying jobs: the American Chain Company hired several individuals, and the Norfolk Navy Yard added openings for five hundred, mostly laborers.[50] Yet blacks managed to advance the cause of improved wages, despite underrepresentation in traditionally unionized trades. The combination of a labor shortage, blacks' numerical domination of certain trades, and the growth and development of the nationwide labor movement accounted for increased union activism. As Arthur Kyle Davis notes in a history of the city during World War I, "there were no less than eight strikes in Norfolk during the war and even more threats."[51] Afro-Americans planned and orchestrated several of these strikes, all of which followed the emergence of race-conscious black unions.

Longshoremen were at the hub of black labor organization during the first three decades of the twentieth century. Several thousand strong, these workers formed two unions, the Coal Trimmers Union Local 15277 and the Transportation Workers Association (TWA). The former, which obtained a charter from the American Federation of Labor (AFL) in 1914, represented several hundred coal trimmers who worked on the railway piers. (Coal trimmers worked in gangs of forty, manually spreading crane-loaded coal throughout the bottom of a ship.) Soon after receiving its charter, the union demanded better pay and improved working conditions; in particular, the workers wanted time for meals. The companies responded by firing the head of the union, George Milner. The workers called for his immediate reinstatement; the companies refused. The coal trimmers responded by striking, promising to remain out until Milner was rehired. Once they were convinced of the workers' resolve, the companies capitulated and reinstated Milner. The union also obtained a pay raise for the workers and a written contract.[52] Its success marked the beginning of a major new chapter in local labor annals.

The TWA, in contrast, began as a quasi-fraternal organization sometime between 1910 and 1913. Its initial function was the disbursal of burial benefits to members. By 1916 it had made the transition into a full-fledged labor association, although critics screamed that this change violated its state charter. Perhaps the shift was spurred by the arrival of the Industrial Workers of the World, the radical IWW, which courted blacks in other South Atlantic cities and maintained a Norfolk office. Or the change may have been inspired by other examples of successful labor organization locally and nationally.[53] Whatever the impetus, the TWA and its strong membership, which varied between five thousand and eleven thousand, demonstrated a newfound determination to change conditions along the Hampton Road docks.

In many ways, the TWA's history is unique. As the most recent entries into the industrial work force in the North, blacks often felt pressured to choose between white unions and white employers. Some joined the unions; the majority refused. Those who refused questioned the benefits of union membership, mindful of the exclusionary provisions in many union charters. Interracial clashes outside work, where black and white workers often had competing and conflicting community needs, further undermined potential workplace solidarity. As a result, many blacks allied with management, for employers offered them the opportunity to escape the world of sharecropping and domestic service.[54]

Through the early 1920s, black workers in Norfolk avoided lasting alliances with either white laborites or white employers, although circumstances occasionally dictated interracial dealings. According to federal agents investigating purported pro-German activities in the black community, members of the Coal Trimmers Union, for example, obtained help in tightening their organizational structure from W. C. Drewans, a sympathetic white unionist and navy yard boilermaker.[55]

Black workers also marched with white workers in what some called the first joint Labor Day parade in southern history. A black reporter viewed this as a momentous occurrence and enthusiastically observed that "white unions and industries . . . are beginning to recognize the Negro as an important factor in the industrial world."[56] Important though it was, few black participants saw the parade as more than a symbolic gesture designed to draw attention to labor's universal needs. Certainly the black carpenters, coal trimmers, working women, and longshoremen who participated would have questioned any other interpretation, especially given that social proscriptions allowed whites to march at the front and required blacks to secure the rear of the parade. Black laborers in general remained wary of the intentions of white workers—but not so wary as to side with white employers.

Black workers remained cool to white employers because, throughout the South, white businesses sanctioned a dual wage structure that suppressed the wages of Afro-Americans and guaranteed their underemployment. Of course, the dual labor market suppressed white wages, too, but underemployment handicapped blacks—especially black men—more than it did whites, causing proportionally more black women and children to work for wages.[57] Furthermore, the expressed attitudes and behavior of employers betrayed a deeply held opposition to any organization, tactic, or idea that threatened to alter the worker-employer power tilt by improving wages. In Norfolk, Barton Myers, scion of one of the oldest merchant families and president of the Chamber of Commerce, spoke for most:

> We frequently are not discriminating enough in our reference to negroes, referring to them all as the same undesirable character. We are fortunate in having such a population instead of some of the radical foreigners who have been attracted to large manufacturing centers. No doubt some agitators are seeking to mislead negroes and organize them . . . but . . . we [must] . . . secure the cooperation of the better class to aid in restraining those who might otherwise be led astray.[58]

Even if the "better class" had wished to dictate to black workers, it lacked the power to dissuade them from organizing, as TWA members quickly demonstrated. As nearly 90 percent of all stevedores and longshoremen, blacks took advantage of their numerical strength. First, they made racial exclusivity a positive attribute, emphasizing the rewards of an all-black union with black representatives to engage in labor negotiations.[59] Second, they made it clear that there was a natural link between race and unionism, arguing that the union would protect the interests of black men and women. Finally, they refused to believe that unskilled and casual workers could not be organized, and hence they brought all dockworkers under the umbrella of the association— dockhands, teamsters, and gang laborers.

When TWA representatives approached the Furness-Witty Company, the W. B. Treadwell Company, and the United States Shipping Company in September 1917 about better working conditions, improved pay, and more reasonable hours, they began with the universal backing of their charges and thus from a position of power. Their position was also strengthened by timing: their demands were raised as Norfolk was becoming an important military center. The federal government deemed it imperative that the port remain open. Wanting to push, but not wanting to push too hard, TWA leaders J. C. Skinner and Arkansas Gray agreed to delay all strike activity for thirty days while government negotiators hammered out an agreement. On 11 October, almost exactly thirty days after the union had filed an intent to strike, the parties reached an accord. Under the provisions of the new contract, the longshoremen received a 31 percent pay increase and a guarantee of improved working conditions. In turn, the shipping concerns averted a strike, and the government avoided the closure of the ports.[60]

Had TWA organizers succeeded only in organizing the longshoremen, this episode would have been noteworthy. But in fact they accomplished much more. The threatened strike highlighted a growing awareness among Afro-Americans of the potential of collective bargaining, demonstrating that when they were in a position of power they could wrest concessions from white employers. It established the groundwork for the continued growth of the longshoremen as an important labor group in the city, and it underscored the intricate balance of race and class consciousness among blacks. In addition, real improvements in working and living conditions resulted. TWA officials sought and secured improved salaries and a guaranteed daily minimum wage, important to low-wage black workers and the community in which they lived.

The new contract required the shipping lines to pay crew leaders forty-five cents per hour and laborers forty cents per hour, wages that placed them among the area's highest-paid black workers. The workday commenced at seven in the morning and concluded at six in the evening, with a one-hour lunch break between noon and one in the afternoon. Anyone who worked either through a lunch period or on the night shift was paid time and a half, as were those who worked beyond 6 P.M. on a weekday or 4 P.M. on Saturday. All longshoremen received an additional two and a half cents per hour for handling cotton, because of the hazards of prolonged contact with cotton dust.[61]

From the workers' perspective, one of the more significant planks in the new contract involved the guaranteed daily minimum wage, which brought regularity to their pay and helped to improve living standards. It had been common practice for men to leave Longshoremen's Hall at Princess Anne Road and Wide Street believing that work awaited them at the docks—only to arrive and find that there was no work and that they had invested their time without hope of remuneration. In the new contract, the companies agreed to pay workers for the time spent in transit to the docks and for the time spent waiting there in anticipation of work. If a worker decided that the assignment looked too hazardous and refused to work, then and only then did the worker forfeit the right to a paycheck.[62]

The union also agreed, however, to certain concessions that lessened its ability to police its own members and threatened the solidarity based on race. Management constantly worried about productivity and attributed its decline to worker insobriety. The union accordingly promised to prohibit alcoholic beverages on the docks. Those caught drinking, as well as those who reported to work under the influence, would face immediate dismissal. The union also agreed that "the parties of the second part will not try to uphold incompetency, shirking of work, pilfering or poaching of cargo; any man found guilty of these offenses shall be dealt with as parties of the first part may see fit, or as the circumstances may require." Consequently, whenever the company discovered someone stealing or loafing, the contract obliged the TWA to "immediately discharge from membership" the accused individual.[63] These concessions placed labor and management in a partnership. More important, this partnership seemingly undermined the union's manifest concern, safeguarding the interests of black longshoremen.

Racial matters nevertheless remained at the forefront of plans devised and decisions reached by the TWA. These plans also underscored the nature of the battle being waged. Aware of the meager gains achieved when only one segment of the labor force organized, TWA organizers surveyed the local labor scene and discovered that blacks dominated other occupations as well. They spent the autumn's remaining weeks trying to gain TWA recognition among female cigar stemmers, male and female oyster shuckers, and female domestics—such efforts were in their collective interests. What followed highlighted the complex intersection between race and class among black workers during the 1910s.

TWA organizers approached the female cigar stemmers first, a group with a work profile somewhat comparable to the longshoremen's and one that had been previously targeted for organization. Norfolk had one primary stemmery in 1917, the American Cigar Company, with a labor force of slightly more than three hundred workers, almost exclusively female and black. Two or three generations of some families worked in the plant; other workers had just arrived from the farm. In a craft-oriented industry, these workers held the undervalued job of separating the stem from the tobacco leaf and washing and then stacking the leaves in large piles for shipping.[64] Like the longshoremen, however, they were indispensable to plant operations. This indispensability, coupled with low wages, had caused the short-lived Women's Trade Union League to send Mildred Rankin, a black social worker, and "several colored organizers" to Norfolk to organize the stemmers. Coming about a year before the TWA's overtures and plagued from the outset by insufficient funding, the league's efforts failed; but a seed was planted, one cultivated by the TWA.[65]

World War I brought an increase in the cost of living, which caused the women to seriously question the wages they received for the hours worked.[66] Despite rising early in the morning and working past 5 P.M., many of the women earned less than five dollars a week, the industry's prevailing wage. As an editorial in the *Norfolk Journal and Guide* revealed, most of them earned less than subsistence-level incomes. Because many stemmers lived on their own, or at least contributed a substantial portion of household finances, they came to feel that some adjustment was warranted.[67] Aware of the women's dissatisfaction with work conditions and their belief that management's promise to negotiate was disingenuous, TWA officials proposed that the women form a union local. The women quickly accepted the invitation, becoming Sisterhood No. 1. Following consultation with TWA organizer Arkansas Gray, the women asked the company to increase their pay to $1.25 per day, to shorten the work week to fifty-five hours, and to recognize the union as their legitimate bargaining agent. Initially, the company refused all demands. From its perspective, seventy cents a day exceeded a fair wage for unskilled labor. The company's failure to negotiate proved to be an unwise tactic, however. The women, quite determined, went out on strike, halting operations at the plant for several weeks.[68]

At the end of the third week, official spokesman and plant manager J. T. Long demonstrated a newly discovered willingness to bargain. He agreed to discuss a pay increase and shorter hours, but he remained opposed to the union. He informed a reporter for the city's white daily, the *Virginian-Pilot and Norfolk Landmark,* that he would rather close the plant and send the work to the company's other locations than allow an outside agent like the union to have a say in the company's labor policy.[69]

When Long and the women sat down to bargain, radical differences in their salary proposals threatened the negotiations. The women wanted a 100 percent increase in wages. Female stemmers throughout the industry had always been paid by the piece. A fast stemmer could earn eleven to twelve dollars per week, but the typical pay averaged six to seven dollars a week, and many earned less than five dollars. From the women's point of view, the outer limit of the range seemed so unattainable that something had to be done for the productive, but average, worker who lacked the dexterity and skill to attain a higher wage. Long, however, contended that a 15 percent increase was more than adequate. In time, both parties reached a tentative salary agreement, but the company remained opposed to the union. As an alternative, it proposed the formation of a company union. After considerable deliberation, the women rejected the entire offer.[70]

The strike lasted for another two months, with the workers and the company deadlocked over the issue of union recognition. Throughout, the male leadership of the TWA publicly reiterated its opposition to strikes. Arkansas Gray told local newspaper reporters that although his organization had presented the women's demands to the company, neither he nor his union had authorized the strike. Gray may have been technically correct that the TWA had not officially authorized the strike, but the union did establish a strike relief fund that enabled the women to endure as long as they did.[71]

Finally, the women's determination and patience gave out, and they returned to work. Two years later, in December 1919, a survey of the plant by the U.S. Women's Bureau reported that little had changed. Black women still constituted the entire female labor force, working conditions remained onerous, and, based on the comments of the surveyor, management's policies capricious. Higher pay seemed the only tangible benefit of the failed experiment with unionization in the fall of 1917. The attempt illustrated the conditions under which race, class, and gender prompted black workers to organize.[72] The failure illustrated the opposition to unionization in Norfolk, particularly to the unionization of black women. It also underscored the unique position of the longshoremen.

Meanwhile, TWA organizers expanded their efforts to organize all black workers. They again targeted blacks in a trade they numerically dominated, oyster shucking. As always, they hoped that workplace advances would translate into financially secure workers who would invest in the community and help develop the home sphere. Conditions, however, were never so simple, and neither was the response of black Norfolkians. Few could ignore the implications of such a strategy. Hopes for sustained progress in the workplace rested on the faulty foundation of interracial labor cooperation. Most knew that in reality black and white workers remained apart, at work and at home. The *Norfolk Journal and Guide* hoped this could be changed, and it called on all white unions to open their doors to blacks and on all blacks to join labor's cause.[73] This plea proved futile, for whites made little effort to change. Nevertheless, the Afro-Americans of Norfolk were not prepared to abandon the cause of labor entirely or the prospect of improved conditions. But their economic viewpoint turned on the politics of race: for now, although perspectives modified in time, blacks organized blacks. They did so because the community's welfare remained critical to their long-range goals. In the end, a shift in priorities and the troubled nature of the workplace would make the call for greater development in the home sphere an acceptable alternative.

City officials viewed the expanding labor activism, race-based or not, with trepidation and wanted it stopped. After oyster shuckers at all ten plants in the city went out on strike—the result of a labor-management impasse over the companies' refusal to raise wages by a nickel per eight pints shucked—the police received orders to disperse all picketers who congregated on street corners.[74] In addition to the problems caused by hostile police activity, this strike was also weakened from the beginning by irreparable internal divisions, in contrast to the labor actions of the longshoremen and the stemmers, which had been characterized by near-unanimity. Divided by age, tenure, family peculiarities, disposition, and the seasonal nature of the occupation itself, some shuckers refused to support the union's goals. The companies, allied with city officials, used this division as a weapon. Not only were the police instructed to disperse crowds, but, in the wake of threatened reprisals, they also received instructions to escort all would-be strikebreakers to their jobs.[75]

Given the clear dissension among the workers, the owners made a major thrust to kill the strike once and for all. Some argued that strikes of this nature not only violated local custom but also bordered on sedition. The secretary of war had issued a plea for increased productivity by the nation's fishing and oyster industries. The local oyster companies reasoned that a strike in the Chesapeake Bay area, one of the most bountiful estuaries in the nation, would endanger the nation's security. They called on the government to bar the TWA from interfering with oyster operations. In case this proved impossible, they also sought a judicial restraining order that would limit TWA activity to the docks.[76]

Before the federal government could respond, the strike ended. While awaiting the government's decision, the companies went on the offensive. They transferred workers from the fishing divisions to the oyster shucking divisions to meet the daily labor needs. This action punctured the strikers' spirits, because it showed that the companies could contravene the strike's impact on day-to-day operations. Company officials also enlisted the assistance of the police and persuaded them to arrest all "industrial slackers," which further dampened the workers' enthusiasm for the strike. Within a few days of the police roundup, the pro-business *Virginian-Pilot and Norfolk Landmark* reported that by "standing pat" the companies had forced TWA-affiliated shuckers to return to work. And, indeed, within a few weeks, most of the shuckers had returned, without attaining any of their initial goals.[77]

Almost like brush fires, however, labor actions spread; as soon as tension on one front was dowsed, tension on another front ignited. Still committed to organizing all black workers, the TWA shifted its focus. Organizers had previously restricted their efforts to the manufacturing and transportation sectors. By doing so, they had effectively excluded the majority of working women, namely, domestic servants. This was an important oversight. In 1920, 87.1 percent of all female domestics in large South Atlantic cities (those with populations greater than one hundred thousand) were black. In Norfolk, 81.9 percent of all employed black women worked as domestics or personal servants. Working hours were typically long and irregular because the needs of the employer's household varied from day to day, and wages fluctuated, depending on the job. At the upper end of the wage range were cooks, and at the lower end were day workers, who strung together a living by going from house to house. In between were women like Essie Weller, a former schoolteacher who took in laundry after her marriage ended her teaching career.[78]

To the race-conscious organizers from the TWA, these women deserved a better life. Moreover, the women themselves were not oblivious to the benefits of organization. A year earlier, the Working Women's Union, mostly domestics, had formed to "unite laboring women and bring about a closer relationship between them."[79] What this group actually did is not known, but, clearly, black women had independently fashioned a worldview linking gender, race, and class. Therefore, as campaigns at the cigar factory and oyster shucking companies continued, TWA organizers approached this largest bloc of black working women. During the first week in October 1917, the women answered by threatening to strike for a guaranteed dollar per day and predetermined work hours.[80]

The larger white community found the thought of black domestics on strike unconscionable, as it found the thought of blacks in unions generally. Only a couple of weeks before the women's pronouncement, white residents had bemoaned the disappearance of the "antebellum auntie" who lived in their homes and manifested a happy, hardworking, and diligent demeanor. Her modern version, they lamented, was a complete antithesis. Earlier that spring, one white resident had actually reported his cook's actions to federal agents, because she "had recently been indulging in frequent and lengthy dissertations on the great injustice done the negroes by the whites."[81] The cooks, maids, waitresses, laundresses, and others who proposed to take part in the strike simply validated the antipathy whites felt toward the modern domestic and made them long for her predecessor.

Whites did more than simply pine for a return to the past, however. Housewives and others linked this activism to the other ongoing strikes. They interpreted the women's demands as evidence of growing insolence. Middle-class black spokespersons countered that the demands were legitimate and reflected real changes in the marketplace. Black women, they argued, were determined to gain some control over their work lives. The police muted all explanations by stopping the incipient strike before it started. Following the arrest of the oyster shuckers, Norfolk police chief C. G. Kizer easily redirected his forces to arrest all "loafers" and "slackers" among the entire black laboring class, including the domestics.[82]

The ramifications of the police intrusion did not escape the black community, for events at work could not be completely divorced from events at home. Commenting on the actions of the police, the *Norfolk Journal and Guide* wrote that, instead of responding to the domestics' demands for better wages in a forthright manner, city officials had resorted to force and intimidation. The entire episode left the *Journal and Guide* to ask why officials, when whites struck—as they had in recent weeks— expressed a willingness to negotiate, whereas when blacks struck, the same officials responded with intimidation.[83]

Differences between black and white workers—especially during the war, when federal authorities investigated both all-black unions and private citizens who were alleged to harbor pro-German sentiments[84]— provided clues for answering the *Journal and Guide*'s query. In a two-dimensional social system, the battle between labor and management produced clear battle lines. But the specter of Jim Crow and the ubiquitous concern with race altered the constituencies throughout the country, particularly in the South. There, race became the central mediating variable and what might have been two-dimensional became four-dimensional: black-white, labor-management. When all was said and done, black workers remained black.

With aid from the TWA, blacks in the four instances discussed above remolded this social geometry to wed race and unionism. It is important to note that many were not factory workers. Too often, we ignore the union activities of nonindustrial laborers. As the TWA proved, most employees, factory and nonfactory workers alike, were poised to improve their station. When convinced of the centrality of their role, most would listen to a plea to improve wages, working conditions, and benefits. Race, however, remained an important reference point, for blacks and whites worked in different and unequal segments of the labor market.

It seems premature to argue that this worker consciousness manifested itself in a traditionally class-conscious manner. The TWA focused on organizing black workers because they remained racial ethnics at work and at home. These efforts reflected a sharp and focused racial critique of the economic system. In the process of organizing black women and men, the TWA also both challenged and reinforced certain gender conventions. For example, the longshoremen and the cigar stemmers worked in sex-segregated work environments, in which the jobs themselves and the work culture reproduced and reaffirmed the belief that certain jobs were for men and certain jobs were for women. Nevertheless, members of the TWA were able to part with such conventions long enough to attempt to organize all black workers—male longshoremen, female cigar stemmers and domestics, and male and female oyster shuckers. This is an excellent example of how the search for empowerment could and did transform relations.

In addition, the near-exclusivity of blacks in the four trades targeted—longshore work, cigar stemming, oyster shucking, and domestic service—worked against the development of a nonracial class perspective. In the world in which these workers lived, nearly everyone was black, except for a supervisor or employer. Even white workers who may have shared a similar class position enjoyed a superior social position because of their race. Thus, although it appears that some black workers manifested a semblance of worker consciousness, that consciousness was so imbedded in the perspective of race that neither blacks nor whites saw themselves as equal partners in the same labor movement.

## AFTER THE HISTORICAL MOMENT

The war's conclusion signaled the end of this important historical moment. With it came a fine-tuning of the equation for empowerment. Most notably, the longshoremen opted against organizing all black workers. They did not abandon their racial perspective entirely, but they did broaden their perspective on unionization. For their part, nonunion workers, in particular the female stemmers, gained a modicum of control over the work setting by other means. Residents also increased their agitation on behalf of improvements in the home sphere, which effectively diminished the community's role in achieving broad advances in the workplace. As a result, better working conditions became the responsibility of individual workers. The turnabout had a dulling effect on organized labor activity and indicated that Afro-Americans were rethinking what was in their interests. The turnabout also illustrated a resiliency, a willingness to try several different strategies for group and community advancement.

The transition began when the War Shipping Board, which set policy for the ports, bequeathed organizational hegemony in Hampton Roads to the International Longshoremen's Association (ILA) in late 1917. By 1921 the ILA had subsumed the old Coal Trimmers Union as well as much of the TWA. Affiliation with a national union was important because it gave black longshoremen greater clout. It also eliminated management's ploy of bringing in white longshoremen from New York as strikebreakers, a device that had been successfully used in the 1880s and in 1914.[85] Moreover, the workers realized that a strike in Hampton Roads now stood a better chance of being recognized by all Atlantic coast ports in which the ILA had similar control. But in acquiring such a national focus, the longshoremen lost the local focus that had made them attractive to so many other workers in 1917. Perhaps more important, affiliation with the ILA meant that power lay in New York with ILA president Joe Ryan, not solely with the workers on the piers of Norfolk. The appointment of George Milner, former head of the Coal Trimmers Union, as thirteenth vice-president of the ILA made the change palatable, but it did not negate the consequences.[86]

Unquestionably, affiliating with an interracial body committed to bread-and-butter unionism, as compared to creating and being a member of an all-black union, marked a significant shift in behavior, if not attitudes. The shift, of course, was not complete. The structure of the local labor market ensured that blacks would continue to dominate work on the docks numerically, which enabled them to retain positions of authority in the local longshore council and to protect the interest of black workers. What that meant to the larger community and its mission changed, however. As members of the ILA, longshoremen moved beyond the perspective that had fueled their organizing efforts a few years earlier. They were now black longshoremen in a larger labor body, not black longshoremen in a body of other black workers. In addition, affiliation with the national union meant a transfer in allegiance. Primarily, the community of reference changed. No longer was this community simply black workers or black Norfolk; rather, it was now all ILA members. At times, solidarity with union brothers in other ports had little to do with conditions in Norfolk. The world at work became visibly more detached from the world at home as a consequence.

Without question, the economic crises that followed the war convinced the longshoremen of the importance of continued labor affiliation, even with a union foisted on them by the federal government. The postwar recession erased most visions of sustained prosperity. In March

1920 the *Associated Negro Press* had reported, "Norfolk has not slackened pace because of the close of the war, and labor which commanded high wages then, continues to earn good pay with jobs awaiting everyone who comes prepared to work." But these words rang hollow by the next year, as the bleak reality of layoffs, business closures, and general cutbacks set in.[87]

The economic downturn forced dockworkers to accept a 20 percent pay reduction in 1921. Some lost jobs permanently; others recovered lost jobs in October 1923, following an intense three-week strike marred by the shooting of several black strikebreakers. Only intervention by federal mediators helped defuse the situation. Federal negotiators eventually convinced the longshoremen to accept seventy-five cents an hour for straight time rather than the eighty cents demanded. In turn, the mediators also convinced the shipping companies to agree to recognize the ILA as the official bargaining agent. By the end of 1923, an uneasy coexistence characterized the relationship between the longshoremen and the shipping companies, although its intrinsic adversarial structure by no means dissolved. Well into the late 1920s, the two sides traded charges and countercharges of intimidating workers.[88]

However beneficial it was to the longshoremen, bread-and-butter unionism escaped most other black workers. AFL locals remained committed to the exclusionary rule, and the state body remained indifferent, if not hostile, to the needs of unorganized blacks. As a result, many black workers either retreated to time-tested protest methods or formed independent, job-specific labor bodies. In each instance, their decision stemmed more from existing limitations than from an expressed hostility toward or lack of interest in unionization. Postal carriers, for instance, formed a branch of the National Association of Letter Carriers in 1923 to work for an "increase in salaries, more liberal retirement and compensation, and promotion within the service."[89]

For black women employed at American Cigar, little had changed since the aborted strike of 1917. They worked the same hours in 1919–1920 as they had worked previously. Moreover, conditions were as abysmal in Norfolk as in other locations. The workers sat on seemingly endless rows of backless wooden benches on the second and third floors of the plant. The air remained heavy with the sickly sweet smell of tobacco. Just outside the third-floor shop room was a dimly lit, poorly ventilated bathroom. Since the 1919 drought, water rationing had been encouraged, and using the bathroom thus meant a penetrating assault on the senses.[90]

Physical discomforts aside, a position at the cigar plant continued to be one of the best-paying jobs for black women. Given the economic reality, the fresh memory of the 1917 failure, and the understanding that domestic service was their primary alternative, many women preferred this job, even with its drawbacks. But getting hired was no easy task. As one federal investigator noted, the company had no firm hiring policy. Under existing guidelines, each departmental supervisor hired and fired, with only minimal interference from the shop manager. Labor policy, as a consequence, was so capricious that an investigator for the U.S. Women's Bureau recommended that "a definite employment policy should be adopted and records kept of hiring, firings, transfers, promotions, demotions, wages, labor, turnovers, etc."[91]

Although the cigar workers offered no hint of considering another attempt to unionize, they did not relinquish all say in workplace conditions. Instead, they and their peers in other industries gained a degree of control over their work settings in a less obvious manner. The owner of the Bosman and Lohman Company, which processed peanuts and manufactured peanut candy bars, depended heavily on black labor (92 of the company's 105 workers were black). He complained bitterly about the irregular work habits of blacks and even questioned their suitability as industrial laborers, failing to see the connection between irregular hours and the nature of the labor. Most men and women were pieceworkers. Piecework, like the old slave-mode task system, enabled workers to set their own rhythm. Thus, within certain limits, the Bosman and Lohman employees sought to control when they reported to work and how long they stayed, actions that placed them at odds with the captains of industry and the rhythm of industrial time.[92]

Because of preconceived notions of who possessed power in the work setting, owners often misconstrued other signs of workers' control. Black women at American Cigar, for example, often sang while they worked. But we must question those who interpreted their music as clear evidence that they were contented Christians, "because they so much enjoy singing religious songs." Even a reporter for the *Norfolk Journal and Guide* mistook the sound of gospel music as evidence of the women's contentment.[93] To the student of history, an alternative explanation quickly comes to mind. For generations, blacks had resorted to song to transcend stifling work regimens. Although these women may have been Christians, in all likelihood singing helped them to regulate the pace of work, escape the temporal and spatial constraints of the workplace, and gain a bit of control over the work environment.[94]

At other times, blacks did not organize because they were shut out of jobs. As Norfolk became more industrialized, employers invoked exclusionary provisions, to the detriment of black workers. The Ford Motor Company, which opened a local plant in 1921, immediately barred blacks in the name of promoting amicable race relations. The American Chain Company, however, adopted the opposite strategy, hiring blacks at all job levels, even employing an Afro-American, Dr. G. Jarvis Bowen, as "director of the department of hygiene and welfare." Because of its enlightened hiring policy, pressure mounted for the company to bow to racial and social etiquette by firing or at least segregating black employees. Rather than capitulate, the company left town.[95] In both instances, blacks lost.

Of course, some white businesses had employed Afro-Americans for some time without any problems and had little reason to fear black labor activism or white opposition to hiring blacks. Often, these black workers were employed at a branch store safely sheltered in the black community, such as D. P. Penders's grocery, or in the service department at one of the large department stores. These companies maintained employee loyalty by combining a decent wage and periodic displays of company paternalism.[96] Miller, Rhoads and Swartz, for example, a major department store, sponsored a daylong excursion for its black employees on 21 July 1923; the family and friends of Linwood Billups, Ammon Mann, Louvinia Whidbee, Louis Colden, Bertha Jackson, and Ursula James, among others, spent a day at Little Bay Beach in Hampton. Following the success of Miller, Rhoads and Swartz, other companies adopted similar tactics.[97] It was, after all, a reasonable price to pay to raise employee morale and maintain company loyalty.

Another factor must also be considered in explaining the shifts that occurred during the postwar years: the rural dimension of Norfolk's economy. From the beginning, Norfolk's identity as an urban place, like that of many southern cities, extended beyond the city's boundaries. Many Afro-Americans turned to truck farming on the urban fringe to supplement household budgets, thereby fusing the country and the city. The seasonal and casual nature of these jobs limited formal labor activism. And the nature of the jobs, in all probability, made truck farming a workplace strategy for those who wanted to determine when they worked and for how long.

Norfolk abutted one of the country's primary truck farming regions. Although the typical Norfolk County farm averaged only 78.4 acres, as compared to the national average of 148.2 acres, by the 1920s truck farms in the area produced more than forty crops, ranging from kale, melons, and peas to sweet potatoes, tomatoes, and strawberries. Unlike the truck farming regions in southern New Jersey, which employed predominantly foreign-born workers, and Anne Arundel County in Maryland, with its racially mixed labor force, "[in] the Norfolk area labor [was] reconnoitered chiefly from the colored race."[98]

Occasionally, Susan J., who married Clifton J. in 1926, answered the seasonal call of truck farmers and their agents for strawberry hands or other produce pickers. By all accounts, Clifton secured steady, adequate employment during most of their forty-nine years of marriage. But times did arise when Susan asserted her independence, defied Clifton's wishes, and worked to supplement the household income. Most often she worked as a domestic, but on occasion she made the journey to one of the truck farms and picked strawberries, kale, or other produce. Ordinarily, she could earn about $1.50 per day, or fifteen cents per hour; on some days, the wages might be less.[99]

The pay compared favorably to domestic work, and the jobs afforded enough latitude to make labor activism a nonissue. More important, workers were typically paid by the day, meaning that they could quit if and when they wanted without fear of penalty. Many seemed to find this agreeable. Aside from the summer of 1917, when blacks exchanged the fields for factories in Norfolk and other defense sites, there was an abundant supply of labor. Also, because the jobs were temporary, thus requiring little emotional investment or long-term commitment, the idea of unionization probably never crossed the workers' minds.

Furthermore, for some, work on the truck farms was an economic imperative; they dared not do anything to jeopardize their earnings. A survey by the U.S. Children's Bureau in 1923 found that most of the black women working on the farms were supplementing a family's budget, as Susan was. Farm work was the primary source of income for only 15 percent of those surveyed. This was less true of households with an employed male head than in households in which the male was absent or unemployed. In the 20 percent of the households where the mother was the chief breadwinner, and particularly if the mother was chiefly a domestic servant, the farm income supported a family on the economic brink.[100]

Black workers responded as they did after 1919 also because they agreed with the anointed spokespersons for the race that community development was essential, perhaps more essential than the broad organization of black workers. Perhaps, too, black workers, after careful calculation, decided that advances in the community were more attainable than those in the workplace. But it was never a question of incompatibility. Advancement in the workplace and development in the home sphere were compatible; the question turned on priorities and strategies. Given the conditions of economic retrenchment, interracial labor fragmentation, and the maturation of Jim Crow, certain battles became more important than others. Blacks in Norfolk never abandoned the quest for progress on the job; they simply redirected the bulk of their resources.

This redirection was aided by the fact that most workers were race-conscious, that worker organization had been based on race, and that middle-class leaders delivered race-based appeals for community improvement. On more than one occasion, the Reverend Richard Bowling, pastor of First Baptist, P. B. Young, and others asked residents to put community needs above other concerns. In early 1923, for instance, Young published an editorial in the *Norfolk Journal and Guide* in which he requested more community spirit, spirit that hinged on racial cooperation. The message, plainly stated, was that blacks must look out for their own. In making this appeal, Young recited the oft-heard plea made by such notables as Booker T. Washington, W. E. B. Du Bois, Calvin Chase, and Marcus Garvey. Young wrote: "There are business enterprises that need encouragement; churches that need assistance; a Y.M.C.A. and Y.W.C.A. that need refinancing and revitalizing; a community Health and Thrift Center that needs support; a Traveler's Aid and United Charities Organizations that are entitled to a much more liberal existence." A week later, the prominent black physician Frank Trigg endorsed Young's idea.[101]

The same Afro-American spokespersons who advised black workers to patronize their own remained somewhat ambivalent about the efficacy of membership in organized labor. They understood the importance of well-situated workers for both the household and the community; the appeal of ministers on behalf of potential navy yard workers, for example, reflected this comprehension. Yet an uncertainty clouded their overall appraisal of the benefits of extended labor activism. P. B. Young wrote in 1917 that the war gave "the working man a chance long sought by some to reach an adjustment in matters of wage, working time and working conditions." That same year, the *Journal and Guide* demanded: "Open All Labor Unions to Colored." Over the span of several years, the newspaper reported the meetings and organizational efforts of men and women from a range of occupations. As late as 1928, Young openly supported the organizational efforts of local pullman porters.[102] But often the middle-class spokespersons offered black workers other counsel, too. Be more attentive to timeliness, demeanor, and productivity, they instructed. As natural allies of business, members of the middle-class leadership applauded the infrequency of strikes, which marred labor relations elsewhere. And through a public relations campaign directed by the Colored Chamber of Commerce, they fabricated the image of a pliant, diligent, and employable black labor force.[103] They may have favored labor activism under certain conditions, but, more generally, they feared the image it portrayed.

Above all, bettering the place of Afro-Americans in the political economy required shrewd and flexible strategists. Workplace advancement, and the resultant labor activism, remained a priority as long as it produced positive results. Once this progress slowed, Norfolk blacks, understanding the pernicious effects of racism and discrimination, adjusted their priorities to emphasize development in the home sphere. More than that, this was a strategy many believed they could pursue independent of entangling coalitions with whites. The lessons of time showed that power was elusive and that to harness and direct its potential they must act in their own interests.

Afro-Americans flocked to Norfolk during the war decade in hopes of improving their material condition. Many—men, women, and children—found jobs. High employment rates, though positive in one sense, also revealed the degree to which blacks, who entered a labor market structured by race, were underemployed. But as longshoremen proved, the market's structure and the attendant black underemployment could be used to mobilize black laborers. In the long run, the racial divisions that divided workers at work and at home dulled labor activism and the benefits it potentially offered blacks. Black workers did not totally abandon attempts to win control in the workplace; but in varying degrees they endorsed the community's interest in progress in the home sphere, although their class position at times gave the endorsement a different shading.

# THREE

# Race Relations, Institutions, and Development in the Home Sphere, 1910–1930

Years after it happened, Ella Baker, grand lady of the civil rights movement, recalled a fortuitous childhood encounter with a white youth who was determined to convince her of the rightness of white supremacy:

> I have had about forty or fifty years of struggle, ever since a little boy on the streets of Norfolk called me a "nigger." I struck him back. And then I had to learn . . . I had to learn that hitting him back with my fist, one individual, was not enough. It takes dedication. It takes a willingness to stand by and do what has to be done, when it has to be done.[1]

This incident galvanized her resolve to fight discrimination, as similar incidents fortified the resolve of other Norfolk Afro-Americans. Her youthful response was bold and pointed; adults had to be more circumspect, more circuitous. But blacks in Norfolk refused to abide racism, whether direct or indirect. Like Ella Baker, they attacked the forces that worked to subordinate them, to define and treat them as inferiors. In the process, they built institutions, engineered protest campaigns, and engaged in politics. Throughout, events reminded them of the saliency of white racism; they, meanwhile, reminded one another of the need to influence their own futures and the importance of development in the home sphere, particularly in the community.

## THE POWER OF RACE

Examples of white racism proliferated between 1910 and 1930. Some were nearly invisible and hard to pinpoint; others were highly visible and hard to ignore. From his bench, acting Police Court Justice J. O. Pitts said, "A nigger will get a pint of liquor and sell it for a couple of dollars; thus he'll lay around on the money and won't work."[2] All blacks took offense at such a claim—which was contradicted by their high rate of participation in the labor force—and demanded an apology. Other acts were terrifying. Flaunting white robes and platitudes of hate, the Ku Klux Klan surrounded the home of W. B. Trent one late summer night, threatening him with physical harm. Fortunately, his son scared the nightriders off with rifle fire. Following this incident and the kidnapping of Father Warren, principal of St. Joseph's Catholic High School for black youths, whites such as Louis Jaffe, editor of the *Virginian-Pilot*, joined blacks in supporting passage of an anti-mask ordinance in the city.[3]

Other cues, though no less racist, proved more inscrutable, and the responses were therefore not as clear. This enabled the *Virginian-Pilot* to continue using the terms *pickaninnies, darky*, and *dusky* as synonyms for Afro-Americans.[4] A casual glance by a white mechanic or routine questioning by a white police officer proved even harder to decipher—was it a discriminatory act or not? Likewise, the language chosen often softened the racism expressed and thus confused the course of action. A Norfolk clubwoman who was asked to explicate her racial views stated, "They should be free, but they are more capable of domestic arts than the fine arts. All human beings are fashioned to certain places, and theirs is utilitarian rather than artistic. It's due to their savage background and slavery. I may be wrong. After centuries of civilization they may compare."[5] Her words, coated with a paternalistic veneer, perfectly summed up the belief system of southern whites: that circumstance and biology had colluded to make blacks inferior to whites.[6]

Had these displays been simply the personal memories of individual Afro-Americans, the commitment to advancement in the home sphere might have remained unfocused. But because each incident became part of the collective racial memory of all blacks, the goal remained clear: Norfolk Afro-Americans sought to share power in the evolving political economy. They understood, however, that full participation hinged on their ability to promote their own interests. For the time being, this meant developing the home sphere. This strategy became imperative because the codification of the Jim Crow system, which threatened the once-important voice of blacks in local affairs, coincided with significant changes in the demographic makeup and geographic boundaries of Norfolk's black community.

Blacks, always a sizable proportion of city residents, congregated in distinct neighborhoods, though the geographic distribution never approached that of a northern-style ghetto. Instead, Norfolk resembled Richmond, Atlanta, and other southern cities where blacks, despite being clustered in a few pockets, tended to scatter across the urban landscape.[7] The 1910 dispersal of Norfolk Afro-Americans, who were

TABLE 8   Black Population of Norfolk by Ward, 1910

| Ward | Number | Percentage of Ward Population |
|---|---|---|
| One (Old Town) | 1,577 | 21.1 |
| Two (Old Town) | 4,316 | 49.8 |
| Three (Old Town) | 2,298 | 34.7 |
| Four (Old Town) | 12,770 | 92.6 |
| Five (Brambleton) | 43 | 0.6 |
| Six (Atlantic City) | 835 | 7.6 |
| Seven (Park Place) | 53 | 1.3 |
| Eight (Berkley) | 3,147 | 40.9 |
| Total | 25,039 | 37.1 |

SOURCE: U.S. Bureau of the Census, *Negro Population in the United States, 1790–1915* (Washington, D.C.: Government Printing Office, 1918), p. 107.

then more than a third of the city's population, confirms this general pattern. More than half of all black residents lived in the Fourth Ward, which was 92.6 percent black (see Table 8). But no ward lacked a black presence: Afro-Americans accounted for more than two fifths of the population in wards Two and Eight, between one fifth and one third of wards One and Three, and slightly fewer than one tenth of the residents of Ward Six. In only two wards, Five and Seven, was the black presence negligible. Of these, only Ward Five—Brambleton, with its white working-class population—erected social barriers to black residency.

Little altered this basic pattern through 1920, although the city pared down its wards from ten to five in 1912.[8] The newly created Monroe Ward encompassed the old Fourth Ward and a good part of Huntersville (with its mostly black population), which was annexed in 1911. Yet blacks constituted only half of Monroe Ward's total. They composed more than half the population in Adams and Jefferson wards and no less than one tenth of the population in any ward (see Table 9).

Thus by 1930 Norfolk lacked a spatial ghetto, although clearly defined residential pockets contributed to the formation of what Hirsch has called an institutional ghetto.[9] Many blacks lived in the uptown section (Monroe Ward) in the heart of Old Norfolk. This section contained Church Street, the center of the black business district, and several lodges, churches, and schools. Other blacks lived in Berkley, annexed in 1906, and in Lamberts Point on the city's western edge, annexed in 1911. Additional clusters emerged in the Titustown section of Sewells Point and in the Campostella area, wedged between Brambleton and Berkley (see Map 1).

TABLE 9     Black Population of
Norfolk by Ward, 1920

| Ward | Number | Percentage of Ward Population |
|------|--------|------------------------------|
| Adams | 11,232 | 67.1 |
| Jefferson | 9,165 | 50.8 |
| Madison | 3,160 | 10.1 |
| Monroe | 16,052 | 53.5 |
| Washington | 3,783 | 19.1 |
| Total | 43,392 | 37.5 |

SOURCE: U.S. Bureau of the Census, *Fourteenth Census of the United States* (Washington, D.C.: Government Printing Office, 1921), vol. 3, *Population, 1920*, p. 1078.

Although a spatial ghetto failed to form, it was not because politicians ignored the city's residential contours. In fact, a series of segregation ordinances laid the foundation for a possible geographic ghetto. In 1914 Virginia officials instructed local municipalities to follow Baltimore's lead and devise a plan that would result in residential segregation. As C. Vann Woodward notes, this directive broadening the scope of segregation was implemented by three different methods across the state. Portsmouth and Roanoke developed a policy similar to the one in Baltimore, which prohibited blacks and whites from living in the same district. Richmond adopted a plan that based residence on the proportional makeup of each block: where whites composed the block's majority, blacks had to sell their houses and move; wherever blacks constituted the majority, whites had to move.[10]

Norfolk adopted a more complicated plan that incorporated both the race of the majority on a given block and who owned the particular property. The ordinance, written in March 1914, made it "unlawful for any white person to use as a residence or place of abode any house, building, or structure, or any part thereof, located in any colored block." Similar restrictions applied to blacks when whites composed the block's majority. The law excluded two groups: servants who lived in their employer's home and those who resided in the specified areas before the law went into effect. A block was defined as "that portion of any street or alley, upon only one side of the same, between two adjacent intersecting or crossing streets." A "white block" referred to a block "in which, at the time of the passage of this ordinance, white persons shall be residing," one where blacks did not reside unless they were live-in servants. A "colored block" was "construed to mean a block . . . in which at the time of the passage of the ordinance, colored persons will be residing, and in which . . . no white person shall be residing," except as live-in servants. These restrictions did not apply to owning property; thus, although whites or blacks would have to move, they could still maintain control over their property. The penalty for violating the ordinance was a fine of not less than five dollars but not more than fifty dollars.[11]

Afro-Americans turned to a bevy of institutions to protest what they felt was rank discrimination. As the Reverend Richard Bowling of First Baptist complained from his pulpit one Sunday morning, if the community failed to mobilize to protect its interests, it legitimized the actions of the majority. He declared that "the movement to the suburbs is halted by a segregation ordinance that hems the black brother in and keeps his death and sick rates high; his living conditions crowded and a disgrace to any modern city" and that unless this was overcome Norfolk would become a full-fledged Jim Crow town.[12] Individuals like Bowling accepted racial distinctiveness, but they refused to accept racism. Because they had their own vision of society and their place in it, they challenged segregation ordinances, discriminatory distribution of city services, the lack of recreational facilities, and other examples of white racism.

## INSTITUTIONS AND COMMUNITY EMPOWERMENT

A wide range of institutions assisted local residents in their efforts to thwart white racism and promote advancement in the home sphere. The church formed the bedrock of this institutional infrastructure. According to newspaper advertisements, city directory entries, and other sources, almost every denomination was represented in Norfolk by 1910—African Methodist Episcopal (AME) churches, Colored Methodist Episcopal (CME) churches, Presbyterian churches, Episcopal churches, Baptist churches, various Holiness churches, and a Catholic church—and all had active memberships.[13]

The structure of this religious community was revealed by a series of federal censuses completed between 1906 and 1936. The picture is clearest for Methodists and Baptists. Black Methodists maintained seventeen churches in Norfolk, and in 1916 they claimed more than 4,200 members. Women parishioners outnumbered men 2,709 to 1,562, indicating that they no doubt played an important role in the internal affairs of the churches.[14] No Methodist church commanded as much stature or acquired as many members as St. John AME. During the period between 1913 and 1938, it was directed by six pastors, and its membership swelled to 1,447. Continued growth enabled it to pay off its mortgage and to direct the birth of St. Mark's and John M. Brown AME churches.[15]

In 1916 fifteen tremendously popular black Baptist churches accounted for an additional 7,696 churchgoers. A few of the churches traced their roots back to slavery. No one church dominated the Baptist community in the way that St. John dominated the AME churches, although several were equally large and important. Bank Street Baptist and First Baptist led most others in membership and community prominence. A visitor described the latter as a "charmingly built church . . . contrived in graceful horseshoe style, with graduated, sloping gallery, richly-stained windows, and a vast array of red-cushioned seats." Another visitor wrote:

> One cannot write in a brief space of the many things to be seen in Norfolk, but you cannot leave without saying a word about its church edifices. . . . The First Calvary Baptist Church, the Second Calvary Baptist Church are large new structures while Bank Street Baptist Church . . . is a worthy place for a king to worship with its modern arrangements and art windows in which have been painted colored subjects.

The Reverend Richard A. Bowling, First Baptist's pastor for about forty years, became one of the community's leading religious and civic leaders.[16]

The sudden influx of migrants after 1916 had a telling effect on the religious infrastructure. Overall, the population increased by 73 percent, but recorded church attendance lagged. Among Baptists, membership grew by one quarter during the decade 1910–1920. This growth warranted the addition of seven new churches, but the average membership dropped from 513 to 458. The Methodists experienced a similar increase in membership, although no new edifices were constructed. Like First Baptist, most congregations consisted of a working-class and elite admixture. On this point, a white visitor observed: "In the full congregation were all types of Negroes. The men were undistinguished, but the women were striking. . . . Two Cleopatras sat in front of me. . . . They were evidently of the elite of Norfolk. On the other hand, there were numbers of baggy and voluminous ladies." Many of the Afro-Americans who moved to the city chose to go to different established denominations, whereas others flocked to the many storefront churches that followed the black migration to the city.[17]

Movement into these new denominations fueled considerable interfaith competition and in subtle ways undermined the struggle for group empowerment. Bank Street Baptist Church's congregation, also a mixture of the working class and the elite, forced its highly respected minister, Charles Satchell Morris, to surrender his pastorate for flirting with Pentecostalism. A majority considered Morris's new interest in conflict with the church's stated mission. The controversy even caused the Conference of Baptist Ministers to expel him. In tendering his resignation to the church, the unrepentant Morris announced his intention to "devote his whole time to preaching a full gospel of both justification and sanctification." This incident highlighted interreligious struggles, as well as the appeal of Pentecostalism to some urbanites, particularly those who were new additions to the urban working class.[18]

In other ways, however, the church brought people of divergent views together. After all, the church was a religious place and a social place, a place to worship and a place of entertainment; it was spiritual sanctuary and meeting hall; it was, as C. Eric Lincoln notes, a place where the sacred and the secular wedded. Norfolk blacks who braved a blinding snowstorm on a cold night in 1927 to listen to opera singer Marian Anderson perform at First Baptist Church understood this. So did those who attended lectures by W. E. B. Du Bois and other prominent guests.[19]

Afro-Americans also owed allegiance to organizations other than the church. Several benevolent societies and social clubs, which helped to ease the move from the country to the city, provided working-class blacks with leadership opportunities and offered crucial financial assistance to members. Many blacks belonged to the Knights of Gideon, the Knights of Pythias, the Elks, the Sons of Norfolk, the Ladies Aid No. 1, the White Lily Social and Benevolent Association, the Fraternal Order of the Beavers, the Daughters of the Forest, or the Grand United Order of Tents. Other organizations such as the Oriole Social Club, the Eutopia Social Club, the Vincent Lodge No. 139, and the Harvest Lodge functioned more as social clubs than benevolent associations. Whether a club or a lodge, such an organization offered recent migrants a point of entry into the community, as Du Bois noted in 1899 and others have since confirmed. At lodges, one made friends and became entangled in the larger social web. The lodge, like the church, drew many into a family beyond the threshold of the household and helped redefine the meaning of home.[20]

Certainly group membership could prove divisive, especially if this identification supplanted others. But several factors minimized the likelihood of such a problem. First, few individuals belonged to only one organization. When an elevator crashed in 1922, killing Albert Lassiter, the *Norfolk Journal and Guide* reported that "all [five] of the orders or clubs of which he was a member turned out" for the funeral.[21] Second, many associations had a very specific focus, such as providing burial insurance. Third, membership in a spate of institutions enhanced one's ties to the community and, conceivably, one's willingness to work on behalf of broader community interests.

From the churches, benevolent associations, and lodges came the membership for a complex array of organizations focused on social protest and betterment that ranged from the National Association for the Advancement of Colored People (NAACP) to Marcus Garvey's Universal Negro Improvement Association (UNIA). During its inaugural decade, the NAACP, an interracial body with a white leadership, pursued the protest politics favored by Du Bois's fabled "talented tenth." Over the next two decades, it moved blacks into key leadership positions within the organization, intensified efforts to organize blacks in most major cities, and began its gradual assault on the legality of Jim Crow. By 1930 the NAACP had established itself as the preeminent civil rights organization.[22]

The UNIA, founded and led by Jamaican-born Garvey, started from the outset as a grassroots organization. At its peak, Garvey claimed a worldwide following surpassing two million. Whereas the NAACP proclaimed in language and actions a belief in the inherent goodness of America and its ability to be redeemed for black Americans, Garvey held little hope that America would alter its course. He preached a revitalization message that called on black Americans to make at least a mental, if not a physical, return to Africa—a glorious, resplendent Africa of a nobler time. In Norfolk, the social and ideological makeup of these two organizations illustrates the black community's class diversity, its different approaches to its problems, and the degree to which there was nevertheless a shared vision.[23]

Unmistakably bourgeois, the local NAACP counted no whites in its leadership but did boast several leading members of the black middle class. The charter membership list of the Norfolk branch read like a who's who of local black society: doctors A. B. Green, Jr., G. Jarvis Bowens, J. A. Byers, R. J. Mathews, and J. R. Brown; business figures C. C. Dogan, M. R. Jackson, F. E. Puryear, J. T. Tanner, C. H. Oliver, F. M. Johnson, Robert A. Cross, and P. B. Young; Professor Harvey Robinson; attorney Walter L. Davis; Mrs. L. E. Titus; Mrs. F. S. Barber (or Barbour), a teacher; and Mrs. E. L. Young, a clerk. The elected officers included P. B. Young, editor of the *Norfolk Journal and Guide,* president; M. R. Jackson, a local insurance executive, vice-president; Mrs. L. E. Titus, secretary; and Mrs. F. S. Barber, treasurer. The local branch, like the parent body, advocated a brand of what Kelly Miller calls radical conservatism—challenging the most egregious aspects of segregation but within preexisting and sanctioned structures. In most cases, this meant that the organization tried to dismantle Jim Crow's legal foundation.[24]

The domination of the black elite among the leadership positions does not mean that the NAACP lacked a following among the broader classes of Afro-Americans. On the contrary, average citizens frequently depended on the branch for help and were counted among its members. Ella Tucker, for instance, sought the NAACP's aid in reclaiming land that had been left to her by her late father but was now controlled by a white neighbor. Through 1930, however, none of these individuals played a dominant role in branch leadership. Moreover, the local branch, like the parent body, remained committed to legal remedies, which contrasted sharply with the UNIA.[25]

Members of the UNIA favored other approaches, reflecting that organization's class composition and reading of contemporary conditions. Available records indicate that, in general, UNIA Liberty Halls in the Norfolk area—such as Norfolk No. 1, Norfolk No. 22, Berkley, Campostella, Oakward, and Suffolk—drew both members and leaders primarily from the laboring classes (60 percent of the members were unskilled laborers). In this regard, the UNIA's leadership and membership differed from those of the NAACP, at least at the outset. Those who belonged to the Norfolk branches also differed from the lower middle class, or middling group, Judith Stein posits formed the backbone of the UNIA in Detroit, Cincinnati, Gary, and other enclaves (see Table 10).[26]

Clearly, most members joined because they liked the nature of Marcus Garvey's message. When he boomed, "Up, You Mighty Race," it struck a responsive chord, penetrating the inner psyche and stimulating the collective unconscious of African peoples worldwide. The words walked them through the hazy world of oppression and degradation to remind them of what they had been, what they were, and what they could be. Garvey's message created a windfall for UNIA recruiter Allen Hobbs when he arrived in Norfolk in 1919. Even those who shied away from formally joining the organization crammed into the Queen Street Liberty Hall to hear E. L. Gaines, Minister of African Legions, speak on behalf of Garvey and the UNIA. And an overflow crowd packed the centrally located Attucks Theater in July 1922, when Garvey intoned that prayer without work produced little. Everywhere his message was heard, Garvey's dreams became the dreams of many, his message of revitalization their personal anthem. They rejoiced over Garvey's plans to produce black dolls, to organize a black nursing corps, and to establish an Afro-centered brand of Christianity; over a proposal to build the Black Star Shipping Line to ferry African peoples throughout the diaspora; and over a call to develop an economic and social infrastructure that would thrust black people onto the world's stage as equals.[27]

Followers in Norfolk clung to those dreams and the companion message of revitalization, despite words of reproach from middle-class spokespersons who were fearful of Garvey's style and methods. These critics disliked the colorful UNIA parades, Garvey's military garb, and his successful appeals to the masses for financial support. Many feared that Garvey's business ventures would fail and leave the average black American unable to trust other leaders who proposed programs. But supporters of Garvey ignored the plaintive vow of the Baptist Pastors' Union to use all its members' skills and abilities to "convince our people that this Movement is doomed to failure." Many castigated the ministers

TABLE 10
## Occupations of UNIA Members in the Norfolk Area, 1920s

| Occupation | Number |
|---|---|
| Laborers | 33 |
| Domestics | 11 |
| Carpenters | 5 |
| Helpers | 5 |
| Farmers | 4 |
| Barbers | 4 |
| Porters | 3 |
| Laundresses | 2 |
| Shoe repairers | 2 |
| Teachers | 2 |
| Drivers | 2 |
| Lathe operators | 2 |
| Longshoremen | 2 |
| Mill hands | 2 |
| Reverend | 1 |
| Cleaner and presser | 1 |
| Cook | 1 |
| Grocer | 1 |
| Ironworker | 1 |
| Foreman | 1 |
| Chauffeur | 1 |
| Sawyer | 1 |
| Butcher | 1 |
| Caulker | 1 |
| Cement worker | 1 |
| Total | 90 |

SOURCES AND NOTE: UNIA members noted in the *Negro World* as belonging to one of the Norfolk area branches were cross-referenced with the *City Directory of Norfolk*. Only those who could be positively identified are included above. Individuals with common names that minimized the likelihood of a positive identity were eliminated.

and agreed with W. H. Johnson, a Norfolk delegate to the UNIA convention, that "the people in Norfolk are going ahead, . . . there is no doubt about it."[28] Others dismissed charges that Garvey was a buffoon and a master showman whose methods threatened the long-term welfare of black America. Instead, they concurred with P. B. Young, himself a vocal and frequent critic of Garvey, that "if he can succeed and benefit himself and the race we shall be glad of it." Black residents of Norfolk such as C. M. Brown, who wrote a long letter of support published in the UNIA's journal, the *Negro World,* provided Garvey, architect of the largest mass movement in Afro-American history, with his local base.[29]

After Garvey's arrest for mail fraud, many sent letters of protest. Hundreds—reflecting their social backgrounds and meager resources—contributed small amounts, never exceeding a dollar, to the defense fund established to pay Garvey's mounting legal expenses. Jos. E. Easton explained why in a letter: "Through his teachings Negroes of the world today are living a hope, one of an unshaken faith and confidence. . . . It is not because they have never heard fine lectures or flowery speeches, not because they had not followed other men with zeal, faith, love and hope for better things."[30] Those who followed Garvey considered him in the vanguard of the movement to advance the cause of the race. Garvey, of course, did not create race-conscious urbanites; as Lawrence Levine comments, blacks were always race-conscious.[31] Rather, Garveyism provided the political channel and global perspective through which blacks could address their needs.

Nonetheless, interracial class disagreement between the middle-class preachers and the working-class Garveyites never thwarted the overriding commitment to betterment in the home sphere, for both the preachers and the Garveyites harbored similar goals. Garveyism in many ways represented the coming of age of an older plan for Afro-American success, which had originated during the Gilded Age with national black leaders such as Booker T. Washington, T. Thomas Fortune, and Calvin Chase. These leaders believed in individual accomplishment as the key to greater mobility, believed that the sum total of individual achievement by many would eventually lead to progress for the race. Garvey simply changed the emphasis from the singular *I* to the plural *we.* Garveyism therefore represented a subtle shift in the language of black protest.[32]

But as the actions of blacks in Norfolk reveal, protest was not restricted to any single class or group. No matter how strained intraracial relations became, the coalescing of both more and less visible cues to the depth of white racism reminded the various parties of their commonality. Although they did not always share the same means, they understood their common place in history and shared the same goal: empowerment. The varying perspectives and approaches underscored the amount of experimentation that went into fine-tuning their calculations. Through 1930 each new adjustment gave greater weight to the desire for progress in the home sphere.

## WHY HOME SPHERE DEVELOPMENT?

A series of issues and events tested the commitment to developing the home sphere, refined what this came to mean, and shaped the form of protest campaigns. For instance, although Norfolk's residential segregation ordinance eventually proved unworkable, the city supported its legality for several years, undeterred by the U.S. Supreme Court's ruling in *Buchanan v. Warley* (1917) that residential segregation ordinances violated the constitution. As late as 1925, I. Walke Truxton, who had succeeded Colonel W. B. Causey and Charles E. Ashburner as city manager, maintained that the Norfolk ordinance was different and thus constitutional. This belief culminated in the rewriting of the ordinance in 1925.[33]

The city's commitment to the ordinance stemmed from pressure exerted by working-class whites, who lived in separate neighborhoods with their own needs. From the start, racist responses merged with fears of economic loss. This group watched with ever-increasing apprehension during the late 1910s and early 1920s as the black community spread east and south toward Brambleton. The problem seemed to be settled when these whites badgered both black and white realtors, the mayor, and city manager Ashburner into holding Coprew Avenue (known in local parlance as the "dead line") as a buffer zone. But World War I and the attendant population increase produced new demands for housing. The tension grew after a very spirited debate—which was dominated by Brambleton residents who projected falling property values and increasing crime rates—ended in the construction of the new Booker T. Washington High School for blacks near the "dead line."[34]

Working-class whites grudgingly accepted the new arrangement on the condition that blacks honor the prohibition against residing on Coprew Avenue. In 1923 one black family violated the ban. A group of between eighty and one hundred armed whites, including Hugh L. Butler, a member of the city council, converged on the home and ordered the family to move immediately. Impressed by the size of the mob and the group's intimidating posture, the family acquiesced. Norfolk blacks watched curiously as this episode unfolded, because although the whites called the family black, the family considered itself white. Nonetheless, the message was clear.[35]

Two years later, another group of whites voiced disapproval when blacks moved too close to the buffer zone. After black families purchased two homes on Coprew Avenue, whites informed both families that they had twenty-four hours to vacate. To accentuate the seriousness of their demand, this same crowd of whites marched to the home of O. W. C. Brown, the black realtor who had sold the homes. Brown had not been a party to the original agreement, but the whites found this explanation wanting. Luckily for Brown, he was not at home when they arrived. In his absence, they ordered his wife to tell him to refrain from selling property in that area to other blacks.[36]

Blacks who moved into contested neighborhoods thus received a welcome similar to that which awaited Afro-Americans in Cleveland in the 1920s and in Chicago between 1920 and 1960: armed, marauding vigilantes. But in Norfolk, white reaction benefited from the added security of Jim Crow; working-class whites who suffered from status anxiety had the comfort of knowing that a bevy of laws legalized separation. The distinction highlighted their advantages vis-à-vis their black counterparts.[37] And, in an overstated way, it reminded blacks that the character of racial politics had not changed. Black progress depended on group action.

With the white working class and the city committed to the ordinance as their reference point, the local branch of the NAACP mounted a legal challenge, at the behest of Robert Bagnall, director of branches for the national body. Bagnall advised P. B. Young, who he erroneously thought was still president of the Norfolk branch, that a communitywide meeting should be held to discuss the ordinance's negative effect on living conditions for blacks. Following the meeting, the new branch president, attorney David H. Edwards, filed suit against Nathan Falls, a Jewish merchant who operated a shop in the black community. According to the deposition, Falls's family came to reside above his place of business after passage of the 1925 ordinance. This clearly violated the ordinance, which prohibited whites from moving into a predominantly black block. Edwards therefore charged that Falls, who may have been a willing defendant, had violated the city ordinance.[38]

Police Court Justice Spindle decided the case. Citing what he viewed as clear-cut parallels between the overturned Louisville ordinance in the *Buchanan v. Warley* case and the Norfolk ordinance, Spindle ruled the latter unconstitutional. City officials countered that the Norfolk law differed in one important respect: the Louisville ordinance prohibited blacks from owning property in white neighborhoods as well as from living in those neighborhoods, whereas the Norfolk law did not include the former restriction. Because of this difference, city officials argued, Norfolk's ordinance resembled a New Orleans law that had recently been declared constitutional by the Louisiana Supreme Court. Spindle remained unconvinced, but NAACP officials thought it wise to address this issue in a higher court, where a precedent would affect similar laws in other jurisdictions. Whether or not the NAACP followed through is not clear. It is clear, however, that de facto patterns of residential segregation replaced de jure measures and that both were effective.[39]

Although this incident was both ironic and tragic, it represented what development in the home sphere could accomplish. It was ironic that blacks would be the ones to charge a white person with moving into their block when the law's real intent was to keep blacks out of white areas. It was tragic that blacks had to resort to such tactics to strike down a law that inhibited their ability to live as they wished. Yet the legal maneuver was part of a grander design to make the system work for them. By charging Falls with violation of the ordinance, the principals hoped to expose the idiocy of the provision and nullify it. They were clearly acting in their own interests.

Afro-Americans agitated not only because of what they were denied but also because of what they expected. Primarily, they expected the basic rights and privileges guaranteed to all under the law—of course, within socially negotiated parameters. When Israel Banks shot eleven-year-old Leroy Strother in 1926, the incident inflamed the black community. Banks was Jewish and operated a business with a sizable black clientele. Many black entrepreneurs already chafed under what they considered a racial double standard: whites (often Jewish merchants) could do business in black neighborhoods, but blacks could not establish themselves in white areas. Despite the somewhat marginal status of Jews in the New South, many blacks believed that Jews identified with and acted like other white southerners. Business locations and residential patterns led to a fairly high level of interracial contact; although a government survey in 1939 reported that many of the city's "better class Jews" had moved into more fashionable neighborhoods such as West Ghent, conversations with black residents reveal that blacks and Jews remained neighbors through 1945.[40] This contact did not bring increased understanding, however; rather, it magnified the discord. After Strother's death, David Edwards, head of the local NAACP, wrote to James Weldon Johnson, the national secretary:

> Evidence has been adduced which shows that Leroy had been employed by Banks to put away a load of wood; having completed his job the child asked for his pay, Banks offered him $0.05 and Leroy retorted that "this is not what you promised," and it was then that Banks reached under the counter for his gun and fired a bullet in Leroy's head. . . .
>
> This is not the first time that colored men and boys have been shot down in this City without just cause and to my knowledge this is the third child under thirteen years of age that has been killed by jews within the last ten months.

When the jury returned a verdict of involuntary manslaughter and the judge fined Banks only six hundred dollars, blacks received a bitter reminder that their position in the political economy was unique and their need to agitate imperative.[41]

The city's indifference to the many civic needs of Afro-Americans, rather than a judicial double standard, often compelled the course of action. Inadequate city services, which plagued both wealthy and working-class black neighborhoods, headed the list of grievances. A black physician critical of the city's disbursal of civic improvement monies confided to a white visitor:

> We pay equal taxes, but because colored people live in these streets the city won't repair the roads. They are all rich people living in these houses, all Negroes. Several of them own cars. . . . Now look on the other hand at this street. It's a white street, all smoothly repaired. What a beautiful surface; see the difference!

What, asked an editorial in the *Norfolk Journal and Guide*, were blacks to do when through no fault of the residents the fire department found the streets in the black community impassable after a heavy rain? Why, the editorial continued, must blacks bear the burden of paying higher insurance rates simply because the city refused to widen the streets, improve the drainage system, or pave the roads?[42] Huntersville residents asked the same questions. Despite their comfortable homes, residents in the wealthier sections awoke from each rainstorm to the exasperating sight of water-covered, impassable roads.[43] The city's indifference to such problems lessened the social distance between the classes in the black community and gave the middle class a greater incentive to work for improvements.

Whereas middle-class blacks found living conditions a discomfort, working-class blacks found them deadly. Through at least 1930, 80 percent of all Afro-Americans were renters, many living in dwellings in desperate need of repair. At a 1915 conference in Baltimore, Norfolk was singled out for its deplorable housing for blacks, a situation that was greatly exacerbated two years later with the sudden influx of war workers. Afro-Americans living in those tenements did not need conferees at the National Conference of Charities to tell them about the poor state of residential housing. They knew all too well that the "double six domino" tenements—small, stuffy, and unsanitary dwellings that had the visual appearance of a number six domino—contributed significantly to the high death rate among blacks. A report distributed by Powathan S. Schneck, the city health commissioner, verified their suspicions. According to his figures, the death rate for Norfolk whites in 1920 approached 8.5 per 1,000, but the death rate for blacks stood at 20 per 1,000. A disproportionate number of the dead were children, who lacked the immunities to disease granted by age. Schneck found that whereas one in every twenty white babies died before the age of one in 1920, one in every six black babies died. Some speculated that the rate for blacks was even higher, because not all black midwives reported deaths to the city. It was clear that poor housing conditions and stagnant city water in low-lying areas aggravated the problem.[44] Many blacks, despite their proclivities toward class partisanship, came to see that problems such as inadequate city services affected the entire community.

Consequently, several community and neighborhood groups emerged to battle the city for improvements. In the process, efforts to secure advances in the home sphere were pushed to the top of the agenda. It is not clear whether the various groups coordinated their efforts, but their public responses suggest a shared goal. Residents of Lindenwood, one of the more exclusive residential areas, organized the Lindenwood Improvement League. A few miles away, others formed the Monroe Ward Citizens' League, made up of residents from Huntersville, Barboursville, Douglass Park, Washington Heights, and Lindenwood. In 1923 the Norfolk Civic and Welfare League was formed "to serve as a medium of public expression on important civic matters as particularly related to the welfare of colored people of Norfolk." Headed by the Reverend C. M. Long, pastor of Bank Street Baptist, the new league succeeded the Norfolk Civic League, which had encouraged widespread community involvement by all organizations, believing that "only through a large, united organization" was there "hope for relief from the conditions that oppress us."[45]

Members of these groups targeted important issues and used available channels to seek redress. But progress was slow and the struggle often frustrating. The Monroe Ward Civic League, for example, agitated for a long time before Ashburner, the city manager, finally outlined a two-million-dollar project to pave Avenue A, Anne Street, and Rugby Street. But even after the announcement, it was hard not to be cynical. Similar promises had been made to George Haynes, head of the U.S. Labor Department's Division of Negro Economics, after complaints by the local Negro Workers Advisory Committee, which had been established by the federal government to inform the Labor Department about local labor and civic problems during World War I. Ashburner had been the country's first city manager, serving in Staunton, Virginia, in 1908; he came to Norfolk after additional stints in Richmond and Springfield, Ohio. When he arrived in 1918, he inherited a city constructed to accommodate 70,000 but forced to house nearly 130,000 and plagued with an inadequate water supply system, an antiquated sewage system, and poor roads. The city's Afro-American population lived in areas where all of these problems were especially acute. Hence, they, even more than others, were attracted to Ashburner's two-million-dollar proposal. But a year later, residents of the same streets noted with indignation the city's failure to implement the improvements. Finally sensing that blacks would not capitulate, the city again agreed to rectify problems in a quick and equitable manner.[46]

The frequency of such delays was extremely frustrating. Each instance dramatized the virtues and perils of protest politics and the limits of a strategy predicated on progress in the home sphere. On another occasion, the city decided to transform the tranquil Lindenwood section, with its flowery gardens and manicured lawns, into a site for urban waste disposal. The city converted a low-lying, marshy expanse that ran between Lindenwood and Cottage Heights into a dumping ground laden with trash and animal carcasses. In time, the land became a breeding ground for cockroaches, according to complaints from nearby residents. Residents repeatedly begged the city to correct the situation, but the city responded only after the *Journal and Guide* reported an unfavorable story chronicling the failed efforts of the citizens. Without questioning whether they had erred in placing a city dump so close to residences, officials dispatched city crews to spread lime on the dumpsite, in hopes of destroying the roaches—clearly, they opted to treat the symptoms rather than the causes.[47]

It was not that the city was totally deaf to the pleas of Afro-Americans. In one 1929 communiqué, city manager Truxton acknowledged the city's neglect: "The sanitary living conditions of our colored citizens should be materially improved. I refer particularly to the need for sewers in the colored residential area. . . . Many of the owners of these modest homes can ill afford to bear the pro rata portion of the cost . . . and the matter resolves itself into a problem and responsibility of our entire community."[48]

Despite the neglect, the problems, and the delays, protest politics based on development in the home sphere worked as a strategy in the context of an industrializing America. With it, blacks chipped away at the armor of segregation. They also seized power, even where it supposedly did not exist, because they discovered that the system would bend. In turn, the concessions gained became measured victories whose meaning did not go unnoticed. During moments of introspection, black residents concluded, "We have not gotten all that we wanted, nor all that we deserved, but it is worth while occasionally to take inventory of what has been done as a basis of comparison, and in the interest of correct thinking and acting."[49]

The harsh realities of urban racial paternalism tempered the frequency of such moments, however. Afro-Americans in Norfolk, like those in other cities, found that their inability to directly influence municipal elections bound them to the good graces of whites.[50] This vulnerability proved troublesome, particularly when blacks asked for money for major, capital-intensive projects.

One would not expect Norfolk to have had a problem providing recreational facilities, for it is surrounded by beachfront on almost all sides. But, as of 1923, the city had neither a park nor a beach for its black citzenry. The fight for a beach consumed the community during the early Depression years. During the 1920s, the debate raged over whether the city planned to adhere to the spirit of the *Plessy* decision and provide a separate-but-equal park for blacks. The debate understandably reinforced the saliency of racism and the commitment of blacks to struggling for improvements in the home sphere.

Before 1923, blacks had used a segregated portion of Lafayette Park (also known as the City Park); but unkempt grounds, a solitary drinking fountain, and only four park benches dissuaded many Afro-Americans from using the facility. The entire physical surroundings served as a "silent but sinister reminder that Negroes were not welcome anywhere in the park." This perception grew when the city finally ended the charade and removed the benches and the water tank.[51]

Some middle-class whites found the discrepancies unconscionable. In 1921 Robert W. Coates, a member of the Kiwanis Club, noted several black children wistfully watching white children scurry from swing to slide. Moved by the episode, he urged his civic-minded club to help right a wrong. The group pledged support and approached city officials about building a park for black children. Officials told the Kiwanis Club the same thing they had told a delegation of blacks several months earlier: they would look into the matter.[52]

Many blacks actually approved of the city's stall, at least initially. They feared that the creation of a separate facility smacked of Jim Crow— and, as many realized, Jim Crow meant inequality. They did not object to a fair share of their tax dollars being used for a park, but they did object to the money being used to support Jim Crow facilities.[53]

This principled opposition had decreased by 1923. During the intervening two years, conditions had worsened. Although the city had reserved a third of its playground space for black children, the issue was not solely one of quantity. A real difference existed in the quality of recreational facilities. White children had access to both citywide and neighborhood facilities. In contrast, because the city failed to provide a public park for blacks and because social custom prohibited blacks from utilizing playgrounds in white neighborhoods, black children largely went without, able to use only the limited facilities available at a handful of scattered school sites.

Moreover, such facilities were a poor substitute for a spacious commons. Across the nation, urban reformers celebrated the virtues of urban parks. These progressive reformers believed that urban residents needed a slice of the old pastoral way of life. Parks provided the best of the country—open land and wildlife, in particular—in a controlled environment in the city. Blacks, too, wanted this experience, but playgrounds next to old school buildings failed to recapture the flavor of rural America. Thus, although the playgrounds at John H. Smallwood, John H. Smythe, John T. West, and Abraham Lincoln schools proved important to blacks, they were not substitutes for parks.[54]

Nor did continued agitation by the black community or support from a few white allies such as city council member E. Seft Robertson, who criticized the city for neglecting its civic responsibility, produced the desired result. Each time the council proposed a site for a park for blacks, city manager Truxton vetoed the selection. At the same time, the city acquired further land for white usage, thereby heightening the disparities. By mid-May of 1926, the city owned or controlled twenty-one parks for whites and none for blacks. In early 1926 alone, it purchased a forty-seven-acre tract at Willoughby and a twenty-three-acre tract near Larchmont. The inequities became so blatant that the *Journal and Guide* editorialized: "Norfolk remains behind every southern city in the matter of justice to its colored population."[55]

Less than two weeks after the newspaper issued its opinion, the council approved the purchase of the seventeen-acre Barraud Farm. Aware of the scope of the conflict, few blacks jumped at the news of this decision; all too often the council had promised blacks something, only to renege later. Afro-Americans recalled hearing the council's hollow claim that it would complete the sewer lines along A Avenue between Hunter and Freemont and finish paving Johnson Avenue. Their caution seemed even more warranted when word slipped out that it had taken five years (1921–1926) to purchase the Barraud Farm, because the city wanted to find parkland that was "convenient" to whites (meaning a location that would not require blacks to pass through white neighborhoods). Although the Barraud Farm, situated east of Huntersville and just north of Lindenwood, fulfilled the prerequisites established by whites, a full two years later black residents still awaited the council's authorization to clear the land.[56]

Capitulation came in 1928, after a prominent white citizen, Mrs. Frank Anthony Walke, made an urgent plea on behalf of those who felt that a park for the city's colored children was of paramount importance.[57] It is not altogether clear whether the council's and city manager's final nod was a cynical attempt to placate Mrs. Walke and others or whether it reflected a growing awareness that it was morally reprehensible to deny blacks so basic a right as a park. Whatever the reason, the park episode exposed the tension between race and power. As citizens, blacks had certain rights and therefore certain power. As blacks, they had fewer rights and therefore less power than whites. But by agitating forcefully and continually, they asserted their claim to their rights and demonstrated the nature of their power. Thus despite its limitations, the pursuit of home sphere development paid dividends.

Afro-Americans realized, however, that if they wanted the pace of this development altered, they had to combine protest and electoral politics. As it stood, local politicians could ignore them, for they elected no one. By changing this, they would stand a better chance of getting what they desired. To do so, blacks had to be encouraged to pay the poll tax, an obstacle that denied many a role in political affairs, because one had to pay the tax to qualify to vote. According to poll tax lists kept by the city, only 44 blacks paid in 1910, 93 in 1911, and 148 in 1912, an election year. The numbers of those able to pay $1.50 per year for three years increased substantially when Norfolk annexed portions of Norfolk County in 1923 (see Table 11). As economic conditions for blacks worsened, the 1924 peak could not be sustained, and the number of registrants dropped by half in three years' time. By 1931 only 57 more individuals paid the poll tax than the number who had paid in 1921.[58]

Frequencies provide a general sense of the pattern of payment, but what is more crucial is the number of individuals who paid as a percentage of all potential voters in the population. Blacks constituted one third of the eligible voters, but at no time did more than 7 percent of those eligible pay the tax. Furthermore, 1916 resembled 1931: in both years, 3 percent paid. The poll tax proved to be an effective means of disfranchising the majority of black voters.

Increasingly, however, some black residents managed to overcome this obstacle. A sample from the list of payees in 1915 reveals a clear pattern (bearing in mind the constitutional limitations placed on voter participation).[59] Of the twenty-five randomly selected individuals, three were laborers, eight were managers or independent entrepreneurs, two or three appear to have been skilled operatives, and the remainder belonged to a loosely defined group of semi-skilled operatives and middle-class personal servants (e.g., porters, carriers, bartenders, oystermen, and drivers). Clearly, whether or not one voted was both a function of race and class, for laborers constituted nearly 80 percent of the overall population.

The fusion of class background with agitation to secure the franchise is unmistakable. In 1923 young professionals in the Berkely section organized the Citizens' Club with the express purpose of pushing for voting rights. Addressing the group at its inaugural meeting, Dr. F. F. Bradley implored, "Our young men and women must be taught the obligations that they owe this nation, and the obligations this nation

TABLE 11    Tabulation of All Black Poll
Tax Registrants in Norfolk for
Selected Years Between 1910 and 1931

|  | Number of Black Registrants | Black Registrants as a Percentage of Potential Black Voters |
|---|---|---|
| 1910 | 44 | .54 |
| 1911 | 93 | 1.14 |
| 1912 | 148 | 1.82 |
| 1913 | 175 | 2.15 |
| 1914 | 187 | 2.30 |
| 1915 | 205 | 2.52 |
| 1916 | 248 | 3.05 |
| 1917 | 274 | 3.37 |
| 1918 | 344 | 4.23 |
| 1919 | 283 | 3.48 |
| 1920 | 300 | 1.97 |
| 1921 | 822[a] | 2.78 |
| 1924 | 2,082[b] | 7.05 |
| 1927 | 1,194 | 4.04 |
| 1931 | 879 | 3.05 |

SOURCE: The number of registrants is derived from a hand count
of those individuals noted in the Capitation Tax Rolls, the Norfolk Public Library. Potential black voters are the number of
men (and, later, women) twenty-one years of age and older (U.S.
Bureau of the Census, *Thirteenth Census of the United States* [Wash-
ington, D.C.: Government Printing Office, 1911], vol. 1, *Population, 1910*, p. 287; U.S. Bureau of the Census, *Fourteenth Census
of the United States* [Washington, D.C.: Government Printing Office, 1921], vol. 2, *Population, 1920*, pp. 356–57; U.S. Bureau of
the Census, *Fifteenth Census of the United States* [Washington,
D.C.: Government Printing Office, 1932], vol. 3, pt. 2, *Population, 1930*, p. 1156).

[a]In 1921, 208 black women paid the poll tax, reflecting the passage of the Nineteenth Amendment.
[b]A large portion of Norfolk County was annexed in 1923.

owes them." Bradley's statement went to the core of the language used
to encourage blacks to fight for their rights.[60] The vote became the lit-
mus test for citizenship.

Two years later, the Commercial Thrift Club issued another call for
blacks to pay the poll tax and qualify as voters.[61] Many apparently heeded
the plea. Although the absolute number of those paying the poll tax declined between 1924 and 1927, those who did pay came from more diversified class backgrounds. Whereas very few laborers registered in 1915,
analysis of a 1927 sample discloses a growing democratization of the reg-

istration rolls. Forty-four percent in the 1927 sample were laborers, while
an additional 38 percent were part of a broadly defined middle-class
group of business owners, chauffeurs, farmers, merchants, and waiters.
Further, 40 percent of the taxpayers were homeowners; of this 40 percent, more than half were laborers. Clearly, this fight, which was ori-
ented toward development in the home sphere, bridged the class divide.[62]

Moreover, the impediments to voting—the poll tax, hostile white reg-
istrars, and an underemployed black electorate—and the inexperience
of blacks with electoral politics undercut even the little intraracial class
conflict that might have found public expression. When blacks disagreed, the argument came from the modest leadership elite. In one
case, the difference of opinion foreshadowed a major cleavage that
would emerge in the late 1930s. In 1921 John Mitchell, editor of the
*Richmond Planet,* along with attorney J. T. Newsome of Newport News,
tendered an all-black slate for the 1921 state Republican ticket. Although the historical link between blacks and the party of Lincoln was
well established, Mitchell, Newsome, and others were angry because the
state party machinery willfully neglected black Republicans and their
needs and interests. P. B. Young shared their outrage but deemed it political suicide for blacks to go it alone. The final vote tallies indicated that
most blacks agreed with Young. Nonetheless, a more militant political element was emerging, which came to challenge the ideas of moderate
conservatives.[63]

Challenges to the leadership elite and challenges to various approaches adopted by the community characterized the years from 1910
to 1930, but none of these challenges significantly altered the black community's overall decision to pursue progress in the home sphere more
vigorously than improvements in the workplace. Afro-Americans were
not ignorant of the value of advances in employment. Individually and
collectively. black workers fought for higher wages, better working conditions, anu union representation. And in many instances the black middle class endorsed these efforts. But within the context of the industrial
age, with a racially divided labor market and with companies willing to
use black or white workers as strikebreakers when it satisfied management's needs, long-term progress on the job required interracial labor
solidarity. Members of Norfolk's black proletariat understood, however,
that race was the great divide and that the necessary interracial solidarity was unlikely to materialize.

Influenced by the fragmentation of the working class and the crystal-
lization of the Jim Crow system, blacks turned inward. Making use of
both old and new institutions, they combined protest and electoral politics to obtain certain civic improvements from city officials. In every in-

stance, they remained fixed on the tension between what was desired and what was possible. Although they would not abandon this understanding over subsequent years, they would change the means by which they sought to realize their goals and, in the process, rethink the relationship between the work and home spheres. Each shift underscored the complexity of acting in their own interests.

Fig. 1. Black men working at one of the several oyster shucking plants, presumably during the late nineteenth century. Courtesy of the Norfolk Public Library.

Fig. 2. Black woman sorting peanuts at a local peanut plant, ca. 1910. This was one of the few factory jobs open to black women. Courtesy of the Norfolk Public Library.

Fig. 3. A view of Church Street, the major artery of the black business district. Courtesy of the Norfolk Public Library.

Fig. 4. Black dockworkers at a cotton warehouse in 1908. Black men held a wide range of jobs involving manual labor, particularly along the city's many wharves. Courtesy of the Norfolk Public Library.

Fig. 5. The area's many waterways made river baptisms popular. This photograph shows black men and women taking part in this important religious rite. Courtesy of the Norfolk Public Library.

Fig. 6. The 1926 graduating class of Booker T. Washington High School, the city's only public high school for Afro-Americans. The school played an important role in the educational and social activities of the community. Courtesy of the Norfolk Public Library.

Fig. 7. Norfolk opened a modestly endowed public library for Afro-Americans in 1921, the first public library for blacks in the state. Named for Edward Blyden, the West Indian–born architect of the pan-African movement, the library was housed in Booker T. Washington High School for several years. Although this photo was probably staged, it depicts not only the library's cramped conditions and poor heating but also its importance to black residents. Courtesy of the Norfolk Public Library.

Fig. 8. Black and white men gather to hear the public radio broadcast of the World Series on an autumn day in 1931. The exclusion of women distinguishes this otherwise democratic use of public space. Courtesy of the Borges Collection, Norfolk Public Library.

Fig. 9. Class differences often played themselves out in cultural expressions. The majority of Norfolk blacks preferred Mamie Smith, but a sizable minority favored groups such as the Philharmonic Glee Club, featured in this 1927 photograph. Courtesy of the Norfolk Public Library.

Fig. 10. Relief recipients awaiting distribution of benefits, 18 December 1933. As the Depression worsened, more and more people turned to the federal government for assistance. Courtesy of the Borges Collection, Norfolk Public Library.

Fig. 11. The poor material condition of this Chapel Street day-nursery school during the 1930s cannot be disguised by children's happy faces. Children were often the invisible victims of the Depression. Courtesy of the Borges Collection, Norfolk Public Library.

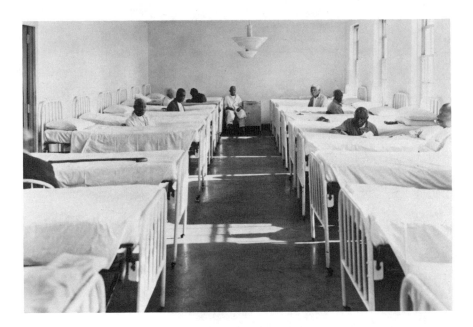

Fig. 12. In the shadow of poverty, many elderly Afro-Americans lived their last days as residents of a segregated wing of the Norfolk Poor Farm. This photo from the 1930s captures the shattered dreams and hopes of the industrial age. Courtesy of the Norfolk Public Library.

Fig. 13. Black longshoremen on strike, 3 May 1934. Judging from the date, this is probably a photograph of MWIU workers. Courtesy of the Borges Collection, Norfolk Public Library.

Fig. 14. Black women workers on relief receiving instructions from a WPA supervisor, at the Municipal Gardens near the city airport. Many displaced black females turned to federal programs for employment. Courtesy of the Norfolk Public Library.

Fig. 15. The dedication of the Smith Street USO. Courtesy of the Norfolk Public
Library.

# FOUR

# Culture and the Family:
# Defining Their World,
# 1910–1930

During a moment of introspection, the protagonist in Ralph Ellison's *Invisible Man* ponders the changes the city has occasioned in him. At this point, he is like those individuals described by early urbanologists: isolated, atomized, and alienated. Then he has a chance encounter with an older fellow who is plying his trade as a yam seller. The protagonist stops and purchases one and then another of the butter-drenched, piping hot Carolina yams. In a matter of moments, his whole being is altered. For the first time, he recognizes the rural part of himself he has tried so desperately to ignore. Eating the yams functions as a cultural lifeline linking the old and the new, the rural and the urban. It also symbolizes a much deeper truth: individuals who moved to the city brought their cultural traditions and perspectives with them.[1]

Scores of blacks in Norfolk underwent a somewhat similar process. They too brought elements of their culture with them, particularly their folk traditions. They also encountered a city with its own rhythm, its own sights, sounds, and tastes, which recast old traditions. The family at times functioned as a conduit through which change was realized, channeling old images and new displays, as visiting and travel habits vividly suggest. Thus, although blacks could never forget their unique place in the local setting, they allotted time to enjoy life's precious moments, even as they struggled over issues at work and at home.

The nature of the struggle directs our attention to the relationship between power and culture in the industrial phase of American history. Soon after the end of the Civil War, Norfolk's black residents dedicated themselves to sharing in the fruits of democracy, and they crafted a strategy based on the desire to win improvements both in the workplace and in the home sphere. Poor interracial relations and shifts in the political economy eventually forced a reconsideration. The new strategy did not ignore improvements in the workplace, but it did shift emphasis to development of the home sphere. Although this approach did not always pay immediate dividends, it nevertheless proved informative. Afro-Americans discovered that even though they could not always secure the range of improvements desired, they could begin to frame their own reality. In their efforts, they modified the political language so that segregation became congregation; in so doing, they used structural limitations to achieve a certain degree of autonomy and, by extension, power. This is not to imply that blacks somehow stepped outside their social milieu. It does imply, however, that the battle for empowerment operated on several fronts and that, like Ellison's protagonist, Norfolk Afro-Americans used cultural references to define themselves and their world.

## THE SIGNIFICANCE OF CONGREGATION

For years, most denied that Afro-Americans even had a culture. Many believed that blacks—forcibly removed from Africa and denied any chance of reaffirming ancestral ties—had lost their cultural bearings and had simply mimicked white culture upon arrival in the Americas. In this view, blacks were a sort of tabula rasa, eventually becoming quintessentially American.[2]

These early commentators were wrong. Black culture had not been erased; instead, blacks adjusted and adapted as they went along. Lawrence Levine observes that "black Americans forged and nurtured a culture: they formed and maintained kinship networks, made love, raised and socialized children, built a religion, and created a rich expressive culture in which they articulated their feelings and hopes and dreams."[3] Culture therefore was not a sterile process, but rather all-engaging, encompassing life in its totality. For the world in which the black residents of Norfolk lived, this meant many things.

The weekly list of events in the *Norfolk Journal and Guide* provides entry into the public displays of that world. It also shows how segregation led to congregation and a measured autonomy. Those interested in spiritual matters needed only to consult the newspaper's religious directory to find a preview of the week's forthcoming ecclesiastical activities (the paper came out on Saturdays). Sports enthusiasts could find stories of local and regional importance, such as the much-anticipated annual showdown between the football teams of Booker T. Washington and St. Joseph's high schools.

Interspersed throughout the sports section were entertainment features, with prominent coverage devoted to movies showing at the local theaters. On occasion, a story announcing the upcoming arrival of a star performer like Roland Hayes or Mamie Smith drew attention. Ads described the black-owned and -operated Bailey's Amusement Park, its open-air pavilion, 250-seat capacity, and modern soda fountain. More mundane day-to-day concerns were addressed by ads from grocery stores and furniture stores, feature articles on local social organizations, obituaries, want ads, and divorce announcements. These sections, as well as editorials and letters to the editor, provided an insider's view into the community's culture. It is impossible to recapture the whole of that culture, but examining even a portion offers an important glimpse into that often neglected part of black city life.

For visitors venturing up any street in the black neighborhoods, the sounds, sights, and smells of Afro-American life and culture were everywhere. On the stoops, in the alleys, and along the lanes, children played, adults talked, and folks gathered. If visitors listened closely, they might have overheard residents discussing the annual Emancipation Day celebration, an upcoming baseball contest featuring the Norfolk Giants, Marcus Garvey's latest visit, or life on the docks.[4] On payday, they might have heard the worldly wise soliloquies of men who sat on front stoops and back porches and mused about the world's problems.[5] No doubt they could have smelled the pleasant sweetness of a freshly baked sweet potato pie or the salty smell of seasoned collard greens.[6]

The layout of the streets and the design of the structures they contained contributed to this symphony of sounds, sights, and smells. Fewer than fifteen feet separated many buildings, but more typically structures shared a common wall.[7] Especially during the hot and humid summer months, windows were thrown open all around. Residents used these opportunities to engage their neighbors, to view the sights on the streets below, or to listen to the sounds of the city. Each household thereby eclipsed its structural function as a self-contained place of residence; rather, in a sort of synchronization, the household flowed into the community.

This interweaving of self and community enabled residents to transform the language of segregation. The presence of segregation attested to blacks' limited power; by the same token, it endowed all whites, regardless of class, with tremendous power. Because of this, few whites noticed that segregation also vested blacks with the power to redefine aspects of their own existence. On public conveyances, in downtown shops, at voting booths, and in innumerable other ways, segregation cast blacks as second-class citizens. But at other times and in critical ways, blacks lived within reach yet beyond the world of white control. At home, they chose the people with whom they would interact, and in most cases they interacted with their own.

Here the operative word is *congregation*. Afro-Americans who lived in communities as diverse as Chicago, Norfolk, and Buxton, Iowa, congregated—sometimes along class lines, but always together. In the southern context, congregation was important because it symbolized an act of free will, whereas segregation represented the imposition of another's will. Slyly and modestly, blacks in Norfolk substituted the one for the other in daily dealings, adroitly inverting the language of oppression.[8] They discovered, however, that congregation in a Jim Crow environment produced more space than power. They used this space to gather their cultural bearings, to mold the urban setting.

Aspects of Afro-American material culture reveal the contour. As the story of Ellison's invisible man suggests, a penchant for certain foods accompanied the migration to the city. Although this diet had long been shaped by the vagaries of slavery, each city nevertheless left its imprint on tastes. In Norfolk, a wide selection of seafood joined standards like pork, greens, and yams.[9] In fact, the smell of seafood along Church Street was so strong that one visitor later recalled this as the city's signature.[10]

Residents wanted to be sure they could continue to eat the foods they liked. A wide range of eateries catered to blacks' tastes. In 1910 sixteen of the twenty-four eating establishments along Church Street belonged to blacks. (Whites owned all of the saloons, however.) For an unknown reason, the number of restaurants listed in the city directory had dropped by three quarters by 1918. Of the six remaining, blacks owned three. Many restaurateurs offered a menu similar to that offered by Jones and Pinner, proprietors of the Blue Front Delicatessen at 517 E. Brambleton Avenue. In an attempt to solicit patrons, their ads promised much: "When hunger calls, glance down our menu, which was change [sic] daily and order your favorite dishes. Fried chicken, salads and sandwiches of all kinds. Fish and sea food Dinners our specialties."[11] This advertisement appealed to the community's impulse to eat familiar foods.

Because windows were wide open and individuals were clustered outside, procuring food was not limited to restaurant purchases. Sometimes, merchants simply loaded their wares onto a cart and took to the streets. Their voices could be heard above the rumble of city life, announcing the day's inventory of fresh seafood, produce, and other items. For those who liked their food already prepared, there was also the black cartman, who catered to the working crowd. He proved to be a lunchtime success among the female stemmers at American Cigar.[12] Yet whether the offering was from the local fishmonger or the culinary trader, in all likelihood the smells and the sights did not challenge the known. Chicken, pork, collard greens, and cornbread remained dietary mainstays.

But the city—unlike the country, where the diet was tied to the soil and had a long tradition—did afford broader eating opportunities. Anyone who dared challenge the city's penchant to segregate could travel to the upper end of Church Street, toward the Elizabeth River, for new adventures. How many took the challenge is not known; by 1923, however, white ethnics had replaced many of the black proprietors on the lower end of Church Street itself, making the cultural journey longer than the physical journey by miles. The black-run New York Restaurant at 720 Church Street was only four blocks up the street from Amdursky's Kosher Restaurant at 346 Church. There, or at the Italian Spaghetti House at 130 Church, the opportunity to eat new foods awaited the adventurous (or at least the adventurous who would tolerate using backdoor entrances). Asians had by 1923 also come to live and cook in the heart of the black community. Nestled between Bill's Cafe and the New York Cafe, two black establishments, was the Japanese Lunch Box. Here, as was true further up the street, the city helped introduce blacks to a world beyond the boundaries of their upbringing. In part, the city transformed rural folk into city folk, even if their racial perspectives were not always transformed; and in turn those rural folk altered the contours of the city by bringing their chickens, gardens, and desire for familiar foods.[13]

The exchange between the country and the city also helped shape Afro-American culture. Religion served to keep the interchanges between the rural and the urban, the old and new alive. Moreover, religious gatherings promoted congregation. Clifton J., for instance, maintained cultural contact by returning each September to his boyhood church in Norfolk County for revival meetings.[14] Amid the singing and the shouting, the praising of the Lord and the testifying, the preaching and the converting, there was also fellowship. Revivals, whether in the city or in the country, brought together friends and relatives who shared a wide sampling of food, conversation, and laughter. Revivals were, as Joseph Earnest observed in 1911, primarily religious expressions, but such a narrow categorization unnecessarily straitjackets black culture. For decades, such gatherings served as fantastic celebrations.[15]

Religion, particularly in the urban setting, had many manifestations in the black community. On the one hand, affiliation with some church was very important; on the other, people realized that God worked in various ways. A coterie of palmists, healers, and clairvoyants promised to "reunite the seperated [sic], cause speedy and happy marriages," help patrons overcome "enemies, rivals, lovers' quarrels, evil habits, stumbling blocks and bad luck of all kinds." John Jones assured all that with the aid of "soul power" and "his herb medicines" he could provide sought-after relief "as if by magic."[16] Jones made such a claim because he knew his audience had long ago fashioned a worldview that included belief in conjuring and mysticism, beliefs that made the passage across the Atlantic, survived two hundred years of bondage, endured the transition to freedom, and seemingly survived the migration to the city.

Faith healing never replaced a devout belief in Christianity, however. Instead, it supplemented and piggybacked on a belief in God's omniscience and omnipotence. All along, the institutionalized church remained the focal point of social and cultural activity, because it aided the search for autonomy in an otherwise circumscribed world.

At the center of the religious universe was the minister, who cared for the social and spiritual needs of the community. On any given Sunday, at any church, congregations heard their pastors blend secular and spiritual elements into a varied, meaningful message. Some ministers chastised teachers who frequented nightclubs for endangering the morals of impressionable youths. Others prophesied the near-complete unraveling of the moral fabric. Still other ministers conscripted churchgoers into the war against sin: bring sinful friends to church, they implored.[17]

A sermon on thrift delivered by the Reverend C. M. Long of the Bank Street Baptist Church captures the connection between secular and spiritual matters, long a central feature of Afro-American religious expression. This sermon also illustrates how residents used culture in the battle for power. Rev. Long praised the virtues of thrift. He labeled Jesus Christ "the world's most perfect and inspiring example of Thrift." Then Long sermonized that the black community desperately needed to start saving its money. He channeled his appeal through the church and its collective character. Members were told that they could make the congregative aspects of segregation work for them. Thus a sermon using allegorical references to Jesus had as its premise the economic solidification of the black community.[18]

It is not hard to imagine that Long's sermon provoked his congregates to respond individually and collectively with "Amen," "That's right," and "Praise the Lord." Exchanges such as these captured the essence of what has been called the aesthetic of the Afro-American religious form and were critical to the performed Afro-American sermon. Ministers like Long understood the rules. They were obligated to help the churchgoers bridge the expanse between the spiritual and the secular. The most successful ministers therefore transformed the intellectual and abstract into something personal and tangible.[19]

Religious imagery extended well beyond the confines of spiritual edifices, however. Organizers of secular protest movements often wedded religion and the cry for social justice. No one was more successful in this effort than Marcus Garvey and his followers. On Sundays, typically after the city's churches recessed, members of various chapters of the Universal Negro Improvement Association convened. As was the case in other locales, the structure of UNIA services bore a striking resemblance to services at established churches like St. John AME, Bank Street Baptist, and even Grace Episcopal.

The Men's Day celebration on Sunday, 19 October 1924, typified the pattern. The service began with the UNIA's ode "From Greenland's Icy

Mountain," after which J. C. Johnson, president of the Norfolk division, prayed and commented. The choir then sang a selection, Mrs. L. J. Johnson read the Lord's Prayer, and members at-large explained why they were Garveyites. Carrie Goodwin sang a solo, "His Eyes Are on the Sparrow," and Joseph Drew spoke on the subject "Practice What You Preach." Drew's address was followed by a duet sung by J. E. Ballard and Carrie Goodwin. Finally, the principal speaker, Rev. V. B. Clark, spoke on the theme "Let the Kingdom Come, Let Thy Will Be Done." Because the UNIA service was so similar to that of any church in town, local UNIA members could confidently assert that they not only drew from the community's culture but also were a vital part of it. It is not surprising that some of the city's most prominent black ministers shared the group's platform at one time or another. Although the Garvey rhetoric struck many as inflammatory and worth repudiating, the style, if not the substance, was quite palatable—a fact that in no small way contributed to Garvey's amazing success.[20]

Manifestations of culture, even in the black community, varied along class and gender lines. Class differences were obvious in public displays, exemplified by the concerts one attended, the movies one chose, and the church to which one belonged. Gender differences could also be seen in public settings. In some cases, the contrasts emanated from a sense of fraternity or sorority derived from workplace conditions. In other cases, an event or a setting defined the participants and thereby closed the activity to the other gender.

Housing for blacks in Norfolk was deplorable. On the exceptionally hot, humid days of summer, the inner rooms of many houses became unbearable. Searching for relief, many residents fled to stoops, porches, and windowsills, where they found neighbors and friends similarly positioned. In these public spaces, the individual became one with the community, although some feared that "to the uninitiated the crowd [was] a group of idlers, wasting time in meaningless banter." Such a description robs these scenes of their real importance and ignores the centrality of congregation in a segregated setting. Such gatherings wrote the history of a people as they struggled to be included in a rapidly changing and industrializing economy. In these public spaces, men and women both mixed and segregated themselves.[21]

Away from the house, participation rights changed. Men and boys assembled in tightly connected knots under shade trees to play checkers and dominos. The first thing a casual observer might have noticed was the exclusivity of the gathering: the tree marked one's entrance into a male, but not always working-class, dominion. Why this was so is not clear, but even today gnarled men and inquisitive youths gather to play the old games by the old rules.[22]

At times, interracial public displays challenged the politics of racial congregation, though seldom for long and never completely. When they did, we get a nuanced sense of the complex social matrix that made up life in the urban South. Scholars have written that baseball, for example, was a caricature: it represented the embodiment of democratic principles and practices. Throughout black America, Afro-Americans attended games without regard for class. In the race-segregated world of early twentieth-century American sports, however, blacks and whites often attended the same game but did not sit together. Nevertheless, when Norfolk's white radio station broadcast a World Series game from its Plume Street office, numerous citizens—black and white, poor and rich, worker and employer, sailor and civilian—joined the crowd to be a part of the event, standing together as a group. This picture of democracy, transcending the usual race and class cleavages, would have been complete except that the gathering was almost exclusively a male affair. Among the hundreds of men pictured, only two women are to be found, neither of them black (see Figure 8 in the section of illustrations).[23]

## THE CULTURAL MATRIX OF RACE AND POWER

Popular culture, especially movies and concerts, also figured in the shaping of the urban environment. When America began to industrialize in the mid–nineteenth century, live theater dominated popular culture. Patrons got a steady diet of Shakespearean plays, minstrel shows, and musicals. Advances in technology in the twentieth century gave birth to a new medium: silent movies, which spread across the country in the 1910s and 1920s. In their wake, old theater stages changed to accommodate the new moviehouses. Simultaneously, working-class populations imprinted their tastes on the medium.

The movie industry competed with vaudeville for the ostensibly fickle loyalties of urban residents. In some places, as movies gained in popularity they siphoned patrons from vaudeville houses. But vaudeville, a nineteenth-century cultural entry, offered the varied entertainment that appealed to the multiracial and multiethnic urban working class—songs, comedy acts, skits, and minidramas—and before long, patrons returned, which threw the management of moviehouses into a quandary. Norfolk's Palace Theater, operated by the Levy Brothers and built exclusively for blacks, switched from being a movie theater to a vaudeville house in 1917 because of what the management described as a shift in taste.[24]

Unbeknownst to the Palace management, however, such shifts were transitory. Owners of all the theaters in the black sections, including the Palace, the Manhattan, the Colonial, and the Attucks, discovered that in order to be successful and draw black patrons, they had to offer a full

range of events and entertainment: public speakers like Garvey, vaudeville acts, concerts, and movies—but especially movies. Through 1930,
a good cross-section of the standard fare available nationwide played in
Norfolk, from *The Red Circle* to D. W. Griffith's *Broken Blossoms* to the
Keystone comedies. Blacks, particularly children, longed to see the latest celluloid offering, be it an Oscar Micheaux race film like *The Brute*
or a western. When the industry introduced talkies in 1929, Afro-
Americans, enticed by full-page advertisements for *College Love, Broad-
way,* and *Thunder,* paid their twenty cents and continued their love relationship with the new medium.[25]

Movies proved to be an important diversion in the urban setting. Sitting back and losing oneself in a western or an adventure tale afforded
a temporary retreat from events outside the theater. A few minutes
spent laughing at the latest episode of the Keystone Cops or other comic
shorts provided the time to carve out a psychic buffer against the en-
croaching social world predicated on black inferiority.

Movies, however, were an imperfect diversion. The movie screen was
a vehicle for transmitting values and mores, and the early silent movies
reinforced rather than challenged society's stereotypes. Norfolk theaters, which were housed squarely in the center of the geographic black
community, assisted in this transmittal.[26] Black residents may have de-
lighted in the cowboys' victories over the Indians, or even in D. W. Griffith's portrayal of the conniving, villainous Oriental in *Broken Blossoms,*
but there was something very disquieting about these storylines. Without exception, all the heroes and heroines were white, and the villains
were nonwhite, or at least non-Anglo. Although they lived in a preponderantly segregated world, blacks, whites (both native-born and foreign-
born), Hispanics, Native Americans, Asians, and others learned about
race, power, and America from the same cultural lesson plan, transmitted via the silver screen.

Storylines may have sought equilibrium—hero versus antihero—but
blacks found no such equilibrium; even in the movies, they became pris-
oners of race. This was especially true with the appearance of *Birth of a
Nation* (1915), which seemed to cleanse some of the psychic wounds in-
flicted on whites by Reconstruction. This film taught a central and acceptable lesson: Reconstruction had been a terrible chapter in the nation's history, a period when reason, honor, and civility lost out to Negro
domination and debauchery, ending only when southern whites united
to restore "majority rule." After the movie's debut, the mechanism existed to reintroduce the "true Negro" to the American people. Unlike
the much-ballyhooed New Negro advertised by black writers and aca-
demics in the 1920s, the "true Negro" fashioned by white moviemakers
resembled the old Negro born of slavery and long a cultural stereo-

type—happy, superstitious, and, most important, childlike. The cultural ancestors of this stereotype, as personified by Stepin Fetchit, were the title characters in the old darky stories. In action and in deed, this Negro looked a lot like the blackfaced figure whites had created in the early nineteenth century. Like the minstrel character, the new "true Negro" remained a caricature of the multidimensional persons who lined Church Street in Norfolk and the many other such streets in black America. Because a caricature seemed safer than a multidimensional person, white America conspired to define blacks in a way that robbed them of a place on the cultural seesaw between the heroes and anti-heroes who loomed large on the screen.[27]

Blacks, of course, did not sit back and allow whites to take all the initiative. Individuals such as Oscar Micheaux sought to give blacks their own heroes and heroines, separate from those offered by white America. Yet in some ways Micheaux, the most famous of the "race movie" directors and producers, failed to make a complete break and himself fell victim to the symbiotic relationship between whites and blacks. Consequently, the characters with white ancestry in Micheaux's *The Brute* ended up as tragic figures for the same reason whites depicted mulattoes as tragic—their mixed blood.[28]

Because power remained in some respects a question of perception, Afro-Americans battled on to shape their world. Many blacks, exercising one form of working-class power, responded to white movies by boycotting the theaters. As J.E. Kelly, manager of the Attucks Theater, noted, by the mid-twenties Norfolk blacks no longer liked the "mediocre pictures" with "Negroes in traditional monkey shine [sic] roles." Instead, they sought a more realistic re-creation of their world in the films they watched. Kelly contended that they still wanted entertainment; but he also noted that although in the past "if a film produced a laugh, that was enough," now the laugh had to be supplemented by "something that gives them a thought."[29]

Kelly's assessment of Afro-Americans' taste illustrates the complexity involved in trying to pinpoint when individuals of one subculture affect the dominant culture in which they live. The phenomenon of minstrel shows is another example of this complexity. For the most part, the northern-created, urban aesthetes outgrew that form of entertainment in the twentieth century; but it still flourished in rural settings, particularly in the South. On occasion, a local men's club or secret society in Norfolk or elsewhere might stage a minstrel show during membership week. For those in attendance, minstrelsy remained the surest introduction to the genre of the absurd. It enabled white men to don black faces and to be, for several hours, what it was impossible to be, what they allegedly never wanted to be, and what they never were: black. In this contrived world, whites released themselves and shed their inhibitions. In the end, minstrelsy said more about white America than about black America. The characters portrayed were not blacks; they were the darker side of whites.[30]

Such an assessment appears fairly straightforward until one realizes that blacks, too, donned blackface and became "white blacks." The Antigua-born Bert Williams survived in New York theater because he agreed to darken his tan color for pay. Although the success of the form eventually helped to move it beyond the most extreme caricatures, the highly acclaimed Williams never had the luxury of performing as himself; he always had to wear blackface. Miles away, and a year before William's death in 1922, the Laughland Club at Norfolk's black Booker T. Washington High School presented what was billed as a "High Class Minstrel Show."[31] For a quarter, the club provided viewers with what was in effect a journey into the depths of both psychological oppression and liberation—oppression, because the motivation for the performance went unexplained, suggesting that blacks might have internalized their subordinate status; liberation, because perhaps they wore the masks to escape, to consciously play a role they knew lacked any basis in reality. And perhaps, by laughing at the characters, they sought to accentuate the absurdity of contemporary social relations. Whatever the reasons, the minstrel show remained a curiosity in the cultural family of events and behavior that shaped black Norfolk.

The sights Afro-Americans viewed on the silver screen or the high school stage represented only a small percentage of the attractions that formed the cultural fabric. While music aficionados among the black middle class attended concerts by Marian Anderson and Roland Hayes, those in search of a more modern tempo listened to Mamie Smith and the other purveyors of the newly created blues sound.[32] For many years, blues and Mamie Smith were synonymous. Crowds packed the Attucks Theater to hear Smith and the Jazz Hounds perform the tunes popularized on the Okeh Records label. Aware of how important her performance was to local blacks, Smith commented before one of her Norfolk engagements, "I realize that thousands of people who come to hear me at my concerts expect much, and I do not intend that they shall be disappointed. They have heard my phonograph records and they want me to sing my songs the same as I do in my own studio in New York."[33] Her insight reflected the core element of Afro-American culture, its expressive and interactive quality. Listeners swayed to the sounds of recordings or live performances, clapped their hands, tapped their feet, and totally immersed themselves in the spirit of the moment. In the process, many probably sought to emulate Smith, others undoubtedly identified with her, and many enjoyed the success she achieved.

Through the blues, Smith and her counterparts became more than troubadours. They furnished a running digest of blacks' integration into the rapidly changing industrial economy. In some ways, the songsters became contemporary equivalents of West African griots, preserving and recalling for the audience the triumphs and travails of a people. Some, like Eddie "Son" House, who sang "Dry Spell Blues," described the conditions in the South that had prompted migration:

> The dry spell blues are falling drove me from door to door
> The dry spell blues are falling drove me from door to door
> The dry spell blues have put everybody on the killing floor
> Now the people down South soon won't have no home
> Lord it's people down South soon won't have no home
> 'Cause this dry spell has parched all their cotton and corn . . .

Prolonged drought had driven blacks off the land; the fleeting reference to the killing floor describes those who were sent packing for Chicago, to work in its slaughterhouses. If rain did not come soon, House worried, more would flee the South and home. Other songs recounted the lives of the new migrants. They told of the conditions that led many, depressed by their inability to find work, to seek solace in the bottle. They spoke of adulterous dalliances that bolstered damaged egos. And with uncanny accuracy they recalled the pain of losing a lover and made promises to endure it no longer. Thus when Ma Rainey belted out "Don't Fish in My Sea" or Tampa Red, W.C. Handy, Bessie Smith, and many others sang their songs, the words struck a chord, because the stories they relayed were the stories of those in the audience. The blues enabled the roles of observer and participant to merge.[34]

Mass production of phonograph players and records enhanced the national popularity of the blues. The new technology bridged the perceived chasm separating the country and the city. Conceivably, many migrants who thronged to the Attucks and other music places in Norfolk knew the sound before they came to town; it was, as Levine and Baraka argue, instantly recognizable. But just to be sure, Okeh and Brunswick adorned their record covers with the words *Race Records*. The meaning was unmistakable. As ads in the *Norfolk Journal and Guide* suggest, blacks in the city went on to purchase works by Ethel Waters and other blues artists, as well as the down-home and urban tunes by Jim Towel, Tampa Red, and Georgia Tom on the labels of Brunswick, Vocalion, and Columbia.[35]

Blacks not only were connoisseurs of the blues; they also enjoyed a wide range of music. At home and in the workplace, they sang religious standards. They filled the concert halls and lined the parade routes to hear the Excelsior Band of Norfolk, the Norfolk and Western Male Chorus, and the Norfolk Jazz Quartette perform popular and gospel tunes.

Many were fans of the Philharmonic Glee Club, pictured in Figure 9 in the section of illustrations. Blacks sang work songs, race-conscious songs, and songs about recent events. A derisive melody entitled "Engineer Rigg," for example, followed a train accident that killed several black travelers bound for Norfolk. Apparently, the train's engineer forgot to inform a bridge operator of his schedule. As the speeding train approached, the drawbridge remained up, causing the train to land in the western branch of the Elizabeth River. As a few stanzas reveal, blacks left little doubt about whom they blamed:[36]

> Engineer Rigg was a good engineer,
> He told his fireman it was not to fear,
> But to pull off his overall and put on his pants,
> And get ready to dump them niggers in the Western Branch.
>
> . . . The drawbridge was open when they rounded the bend,
> And to have stopped that train, oh! an awful sin,
> So he let her go with still more steam,
> Till all but two cars went down in the stream.[36]

In this song, Afro-Americans struck back, and in the process they revealed aspects of the culture of expectations. In a Jim Crow society, blacks expected little justice. In a Jim Crow society, they expected life to be hard. The song allowed them to articulate this understanding and to school others in its broader meaning about differentials in power.

But culture is more than the summation of visible symbols such as music, movies, jokes, and other public displays. Culture also represents the transmittal of invisible elements such as ideas, values, and feelings. Studying the public displays is relatively simple because of the availability of artifacts from which one can deduce reasoned conclusions. To study the invisible elements, however, the historian is asked to delve into the area of psychology and to talk about the conjunction of attitudes and behavior. Needless to say, it is easier to demonstrate behavior than to explain the attitudes that underlie it. Luckily, one of the major instruments of attitudinal development was and remains the family. Historically, the black family has served from slavery through freedom as the agent that inculcated the values and developed the strategies to ensure survival.[37] This is not to imply that the family has not changed; it has. But so have the society and the culture (both that of the majority and that of the minority) in which it has operated.

## THE FAMILY, VISITING, AND CONGREGATION

The first generation of urban sociologists predicted a bleak future for those 1.5 million Afro-Americans who left the rural South between 1900 and 1920, including the breakup of the "traditional" family unit. But like many prognosticators, they erred. Blacks who moved to the cities married and had children. More important, as Borchert found in Washington and others noted elsewhere, black Americans adapted to their new surroundings with the same acumen that aided their adaptation to other conditions.[38] Furthermore, they developed a strategy for circumventing the deleterious effects of migration on both their culture and their ties to family and friends—they visited. Visiting proved to be an important extension of the congregative character of urban living.

Significantly, migration produced a change of venue but only seldom a shift in orientation. Marriage and maintaining relations with kith and kin remained important to Afro-Americans. Marriage, however, was structured by the undergirding economy, and, as a result, men and women had somewhat different experiences. Although the marriage rate for both males and females aged fifteen and older in 1910 approached 50 percent, males married later. A range of factors, including the desire for steady and remunerative employment, accounted for this difference. J. Williamson, for example, was forty-one when he married his twenty-five-year-old bride. Furthermore, in 1910 more than two fifths of all marriageable males opted out of matrimony altogether, as compared to three tenths of the females. Nor did these rates change much through 1930.[39]

Differences in mortality rates and in patterns of divorce also shaped the different experiences of men and women. From the beginning of sustained black migration to the cities, black males had a shorter life expectancy than black females.[40] Consequently, a black woman was four times as likely to be a widow as a black man was to be a widower and nearly three times as likely to have been divorced, statistics that time did little to change.[41]

Nevertheless, as Afro-Americans adapted to the vagaries of urban life, the family remained a strong and vital institution, with family members rendering vital assistance to one another. E. V. Johnson, for example, forty-eight and widowed, relied on her daughters, Lucy and S. B., to run the family-owned restaurant. When she first came to town, Susan J. moved in with relatives, who helped her adjust to the demands of city life. And later, after Susan married, she and her family moved in with an older brother, William, until they raised enough money to purchase a house. These examples and myriad others speak to the cultural adaptations of Afro-Americans.[42] So does visiting, which blacks used to reaffirm the bonds between relatives and friends.

The importance of visiting to black Norfolkians was captured weekly in a section of the *Norfolk Journal and Guide* that recorded the travels of both residents and nonresidents. A typical citation in this section listed the names of persons coming to or leaving Norfolk, the individuals they visited, the length of the trip, the size of the party traveling, and the type of familial unit, as in this fairly representative example: "Mr. Lonnie Jones, Norfolk, visited his parents, the Rev. and Mrs. Jones in Durham, North Carolina."[43]

From this brief example, we can determine several things about visiting, familial contact, and Afro-American culture. We know that a Lonnie Jones resided in Norfolk; there is no mention of a spouse or children. The description also indicates that Jones visited his parents in Durham. It is hard to say with certainty how long he stayed, but it seems reasonable to surmise that it was more than one day but less than a week (two to six days), simply because the *Journal and Guide* usually reported a day's trip or a week's trip as such. Further, it is clear that Jones traveled alone, as a son returning to his family of origin, albeit for a short time. The fact that the *Journal and Guide* printed this information suggests that its readers, many of whom lived in Norfolk, attached importance to visiting. This type of detailed micro-level information provides us with a new look at the Afro-American family and a composite portrait of visiting (which is actually a form of short-term migration, although demographers typically do not call it this), family patterns, and, ultimately, black culture.[44]

By surveying selected issues of the *Norfolk Journal and Guide* for the years 1916–1917, 1921, and 1925, we can begin to chart the cultural importance of visiting by looking at who visited and why they visited. In the 840 visits recorded, almost as many travelers entered the city as left. In two of every three cases, the primary visitor was female. Moreover, like Sarah Wills, slightly more than three quarters described their trips as social visits, indicating the possibility of contact with kin and kith. Borchert noted that many Washington alley dwellers returned home for crises, but Norfolk data show that few travelers were journeying to attend the funeral of a friend or a relative, and even fewer traveled to be at the bedside of an ill relative or friend.[45] Others traveled to a convention, for business reasons, or for an unspecified personal reason. In fewer than 1 percent of the cases, travel was necessary to make a permanent move or to attend a church revival.

Letters, interviews, and diaries underscore the importance attached to maintaining links with family and friends. The Reverend Ed Hunter, pastor of St. John AME Church, and his wife, Jennie, for example, often exchanged letters with their uncle in Raleigh, North Carolina. One letter in particular emphasized the significance of family ties, despite geographic separation and momentary lapses in corresponding. Dated 13 June 1914 and addressed to "My dear Uncle Charles," it began: "As you are not here and cannot see how greatly my time is drawn upon by the duties which press upon me for attention, I am sure you cannot under-

stand why I have delayed so long in replying to your splendid letter of
May 20th."[46] Such letters substituted for direct contact. Through them,
consanguineous links were maintained and celebrated. Nor was this peculiar to blacks in Norfolk; throughout black America, migrants sent
both letters and themselves to and fro. Clearly, they valued their affective ties with those from whom they were geographically separated.[47]

Efforts to maintain such contact required the establishment of a tacit,
if not explicit, visiting protocol. It cost a family of four twenty-five dollars
to travel by ship to New York from Norfolk, more than a fertilizer
worker or an oyster shucker earned in a week.[48] Thus it was not always
financially practical to send the entire household. Consequently, like
Little Floyd Godfrey, Jr., who visited his grandmother in Elizabeth City,
North Carolina, or Frances Ricks Price, who arrived from New York
City in 1925, six in ten travelers journeyed alone.[49]

Equally important, Afro-Americans selected certain relatives and
friends for visits more often than others. Nearly two fifths of those surveyed visited first-order relatives, that is, past or present members of
the family of procreation or orientation. The immediate family remained a salient reference, much as it had been for blacks who struggled
to reunite after slavery. Blacks traveled to reaffirm these ties throughout
the year, including holidays. Thanksgiving of 1925, for example,
brought Ruth Johnson Simpson to Norfolk to see her parents, Mr. and
Mrs. Robert Johnson.[50]

In contrast, only 16.1 percent visited second-order kin, such as grand-
parents and grandchildren, uncles, aunts, cousins, or in-laws. Even fewer
individuals called on persons of unspecified relation. Most of the others,
about 30.5 percent, traveled to see friends. This pattern suggests that although contact with all family members was important, the effort exerted to maintain it diminished as the blood ties became more distant.

The choice of whom to visit tells us something about the visits themselves. Most were designed to renew old ties and establish new connections. Virginia C.'s parents often returned to rural Norfolk County to see
friends and relatives. After moving to New York City, Mrs. J. W. Jones
and her husband returned to see her sister, Perlie Hall. T. Arrington of
Rocky Mount, North Carolina, chose late June to spend a weekend with
her friends Mr. and Mrs. Edward Andrews. During these visits, adults
gossiped, compared communities, and caught up on old times. For children, such visits often meant something more, for they sometimes introduced children to family they hardly knew. When Mildred and Gladys
Harris's father left them with relatives in Rocky Mount for the summer,
the boundary of their community grew considerably. Even more, the
trips facilitated the intergenerational perpetuation of culture. During
the summer months, Virginia C. and her two siblings regularly spent
time at their Aunt Mettie's farm. The three learned to pluck chickens,

feed livestock, and tend the fields; they heard different perspectives on family members and family traditions; and they experienced the rural life their parents had since abandoned.[51]

Although visits could be idyllic times, hidden in the shadows is the story of the struggle for power within the Afro-American household. Some have seen in these shadows evidence of sullied cultural patterns—crime, pathology, or abuse.[52] But Afro-Americans were neither all saints nor all sinners; most lived as balanced a life as possible. They struggled in a human sense to define their world, a struggle that sometimes put men and women in conflict. Clifton and Susan, for example, readily agreed on the need to purchase a house and set up an independent household. They agreed on the importance of educating their children. They even agreed that Susan should control the household finances. But they disagreed about work. In Clifton's eyes, he was the provider. Susan defied him and, he believed, assaulted his manhood when she got a job. Although the vast majority of working-class women were employed outside the home, Clifton clung to other notions. Susan, however, never recognized Clifton's presumption of power. After all, she was no martyr; she had not assumed two jobs, one at work and another at home, just to spite Clifton. She went to work because they needed the money and because she knew she could contribute. She did not defy Clifton; rather, she asserted herself.[53] The difference was critical to understanding where the two converged and diverged along gender lines.

Clifton and Susan were not unique. Her brother William married and divorced six times because he and his wives disagreed over the sharing of household decisions, over the issue of power. When the Depression cost James Ruffin his job, his marriage of twelve years ended. During the good times, the Ruffin family of seven had accumulated the symbols of progress and prosperity, even a piano. But after James lost his economic footing, he also lost his family, his sense of self-worth, and his direction. The major culprit, of course, was unemployment, but a contributing factor was James's demoted role in the family. He could not stay if he could not contribute. This dictum guided the actions of scores of black men.[54]

Sometimes the internal struggle exploded into the ugliness of parental violence. George Bennett spent his childhood in a series of North Carolina lumber camps. When he was only four, his mother died and his father remarried. The new wife bore a striking physical likeness to George's mother, but to George the similarities ended there. In an attempt to define her place and rights in her new household, his stepmother terrorized him and his sisters.

> She was the most unkind person to an innocent kid that I have ever known. I can say . . . I cannot recall her ever saying a kind word to me, nor did she do me one kind deed. . . . When she told me to do something, it was always a yell and a holler. She could not talk to me in a nice tone of

voice, and the many whippings she gave me were terrible. . . . But the scheme of my stepmother was that she wanted my father, but she did not want to raise his kids.[55]

George's own talents as a parent were little better. Later in life, he found himself in a situation he could not handle, and he simply left, as others did. George tried to explain away his actions: "The only thing about me was that I did not have a settled mind to drop anchor in one place too long. I had a restless nature, by which I liked to go from place to place." But he also admitted that he could never reconcile his tendency to gamble and cavort, on the one hand, with his wife's religious beliefs or his children's needs, on the other. Although he loved his family deeply and understood his responsibilities, he left anyway. Domestic struggles occasionally caused individuals like George to war with themselves, their loved ones, and their consciences.[56]

This internal battle for influence manifested itself in ways other than the splintering of families, as the pattern of male visiting suggests. Most of those who traveled in groups had only one other person with them; few nuclear families traveled all together. This is not to imply that families never traveled; rather, when they did, the group consisted of a parent, most often the mother, and children. In more than 80 percent of the cases in which husbands and fathers traveled, they had selected the person to be visited. This was true both when they traveled only with their wives and when they traveled as part of the nuclear family.[57]

This pattern has several possible explanations, all of which underscore the black woman's cultural role as kinkeeper, the one who maintained contact with family and friends.[58] In part, men's travels may have been determined by the outcome of intrafamilial gender politics. Restrained by work or constitution, men may have decided to travel only when they determined who would be visited. Or, given that fewer men than women traveled under any circumstance, perhaps couples decided that husbands should visit when their work schedules permitted. No doubt the pattern also highlights the little-addressed patriarchal and patrilineal structure of the historical black family, in which wives were viewed as part of the male line and were thus tied closely to both sides of the family, but husbands did not belong to the female line. The results also point to a possible artifact in the reporting procedure. Conceivably, husbands traveled at the suggestion of their wives. The newspaper in such instances might list the male as the primary visitor, when in actuality the female functioned as the real kinkeeper. More likely, the above pattern derived from a compilation of many factors, not any one.

The essential role of women as kinkeepers and conveyors of cultural continuity is underscored in another manner. Travel was occasionally necessitated by the death of a loved one or the serious illness of a relative or friend. On such occasions, men and women responded in equal fashion. Women, however, bore primary responsibility for making social trips and were the primary social visitors.

The length of visits worked to the advantage of a community strategy based on development in the home sphere. To sustain protest and reap the expected improvements, individuals had to be committed to the community. Although we know that some residents left during prolonged periods of economic retrenchment, visiting patterns suggest a strong attachment to black Norfolk. This is important to note, because some have questioned the commitment of blacks to urban-industrial America. Gottlieb, for example, argues that the frequent coming and going undermined community attachment and worked to the disadvantage of blacks in Pittsburgh. Instead of being a limiting factor, however, visits expanded the possibilities for Norfolk blacks, allowing them to identify with both place of origin and place of residency without one identification overriding the other. This attachment to dual communities manifested itself in numerous ways. Blacks in New York, for example, maintained an active chapter of the Sons of Norfolk; yet there is no reason to believe that membership in this social club lessened their commitment to improving conditions in New York. Likewise, Afro-Americans who left to visit old communities remained black Norfolkians; after all, the overwhelming majority returned home in two to three days.[59]

The length of their stays varied somewhat by gender, however. Men almost never went on extended visits. For example, H. R. Goodson returned to Clayton, North Carolina, after spending a few days with his daughter and son-in-law. Typically, a trip in which the male was the primary traveler lasted somewhere between one day and two to five days (63.2 percent of the known cases). Many women also took short trips (less than a week), but they were inclined, and were probably able, to stay longer.[60]

Unfortunately, the data lack a purely economic measure from which we could deduce something about attitudes. In lieu of such a standard, let us substitute seasonality of travel, assuming that when one traveled was part of a set of reasoned economic choices. And, indeed, the optimal time for travel coincided with a whole set of assumptions based on economic rationality. Summer, by far, was the most popular season for trips: 43.4 percent of the pool of travelers visited during that time. This choice of season probably had little to do with agricultural work rhythms, for, unlike the migrants described by Gottlieb and Grossman, relatively few blacks in Norfolk came from the Cotton South.[61] Most came from the timber and tobacco regions of North Carolina and the tobacco and grain-producing regions of Virginia. Moreover, few men traveled, and even fewer stayed long enough to help with a harvest. Black residents not only returned to the country; they also went North to see relatives, and in turn their northern relatives returned to see them. They chose summer months in many cases for convenience—children had school vacations, vacationing white families did not need their help, and the weather was more accommodating.

Fall was the second most popular time to travel, though it was a distant second. Approximately one quarter of the visits occurred during the autumn. Undoubtedly some traveled at this time to help with late harvests, but Thanksgiving and Christmas, two of the most popular holidays for visiting, also fell during this period. Winter was the least favorite season for travel, particularly during January, February, and March. Inclement weather and associated problems made winter travel dangerous and uncertain. Because of added safety precautions and possible delays, it was probably also more expensive.

In many respects, the length of stay, the timing of trips, and the inferred commitment to community emerged out of the points of origin and the destinations of travelers, that is, the travel fields. Although guests arrived from as far away as Illinois, Michigan, and Canada, and Norfolk residents visited kith and kin in Hawaii, California, and Arkansas, overall the social travel field had a much narrower range. Norfolk blacks most often visited or were visited by family and friends in Virginia, North Carolina, and the many cities and towns along the East Coast transportation corridor—Baltimore, Philadelphia, New York, and others.[62]

When George Gilmore rushed to Norfolk from Montclair, New Jersey, to be at the bedside of Joseph, his injured brother, he was one example of the many who flocked to Norfolk for all sorts of reasons.[63] Friends and relatives came from thirty-eight northern communities, thirty-two communities in North Carolina, twenty-one towns and cities in other parts of Virginia, and eleven other places in the South or elsewhere (excluding twenty-seven locales in the immediate Norfolk area). Conversely, Mrs. George Walker's three-week visit with cousins in New York City was an example of the counterflow.[64] Blacks visited a total of ninety different destinations outside the Norfolk area: twenty-nine communities in North Carolina, twenty-seven northern communities, twenty-three towns and cities in other parts of Virginia, ten communities elsewhere in the South, and Honolulu.

These points of destination and departure suggest more than a complex social travel field. Regardless of the motive for travel and how the decision to travel was made, it is clear that movement to the city did not result in the breakdown of lines of communication between those who stayed in rural areas and those who left. In noting the several reasons why people traveled, it is obvious that social trips helped to maintain contact over space and time. As others have noted in other settings, women served as the primary kinkeepers. They and their children traveled to see friends and relatives in communities as close as Norfolk County and as far away as New York and Chicago. Therefore, if the community was the cultural hub, the family functioned as the conduit through which values, feelings, expectations, and dreams flowed. Visitation sustained the continuity. Ostensibly, the social trip was the ideal situation in which to share new ideas and new experiences, to embrace old ideas and old experiences, and for those experiences to be passed on intergenerationally. The multiple directions of the trips enabled people to reaffirm their cultural past by reestablishing contact with relatives and friends who shared similar backgrounds.[65]

Visiting became an integral part of the congregative character of urban living and the attempt by Afro-Americans to define their world. In the context of a segregated urban environment, they chose to congregate, to interact with one another. Similarly, they chose to maintain contact with relatives and friends who lived elsewhere. Each decision illustrates their complex hold on elusive power. At first glance, it might seem that the forced nature of segregation robbed congregation of its obvious meaning. In Buxton, Iowa, no laws enforced segregation, and race relations generally were harmonious. When blacks there formed separate institutions, we can presume they wanted to. But this was equally true in Norfolk. There, congregation was even more important, because the organizations that evolved became part of the community's institutional advance guard, critical players in the battle for development in the home sphere.

Nevertheless, Afro-Americans saw the limits of their power. Congregation could never eliminate segregation. Therefore, the cultural variants of congregation produced something other than political, economic, or social power. In the varied faces of culture, blacks asserted self: they laughed, joked, cried, sang, danced, and argued. Deep in the creases of the social fabric, they found the means of affirming their humanity and rising above their second-class status, even if only for brief moments. This subtle display of power, this deconstruction of segregation, partially explains the value of visiting.[66] In addition to enabling Afro-Americans to affirm affective bonds, it allowed them to show the importance of those bonds and to validate the continued presence of self. Moreover, visiting underscored a refusal to be wrenched from community. This proved important, because community needs remained a central focus of the strategies developed during the next dozen years.

# FIVE

# Unemployment, Migration, and Material Decline: The Foundation for Change, 1929–1941

Little seemed to bolster Charlie Johnson's flagging spirits, but he never abandoned hope. Johnson was no Bigger Thomas, the enduring symbol of black suffering and rage in the Depression-era city, whose alienation from white society culminated in the death of his employer's daughter in Richard Wright's novel *Native Son*. Nevertheless, Johnson and the figure of Thomas were connected by race and by place in the social order. Johnson, a fifty-six-year-old fisherman, had known few good days; as he looked back in 1939, it seemed as if most of them had come before the Depression. Charlie and his wife had hit rock-bottom and bore the scars of unemployment and poverty. In Charlie's mind, his fate was simple: he had been dealt a bum hand, but one he had to play out. Charlie was no cynic, but this child of slaves and stepchild of a racially divided system had shouldered more than his share of pain—so much so that, in a melancholy mood, he once declared that he was grateful for the premature deaths of his five children, because death had spared them from suffering. Despite his many setbacks, however, Charlie remained always hopeful that circumstance and determination would combine to improve the conditions of his life.[1]

The Great Depression forever changed the lives and shaped the worldview of many who survived those tumultuous years. Few fell as low as the Johnsons, but hundreds in Norfolk lost jobs, businesses, families, and homes. In the end, a restructuring of social relations resulted in the complex rethinking of the work-home formula for empowerment. To understand why this happened, we must first understand the nature of the economic crisis that produced the foundation for change.

## THE NATURE OF THE ECONOMIC CRISIS

There were two Norfolks, one white and one black, a division accentuated by the Depression years. In white Norfolk, signs of a pending economic crisis appeared slowly; in black Norfolk, they appeared earlier.[2] Both the *Virginian-Pilot* and the *Norfolk Journal and Guide* gave scant coverage to the stock market crash in 1929, but their reasons were as different as the audiences to which they catered. For the majority of whites, the crash was a relative nonevent, for many still had jobs and a means of support. For blacks, a great many miles lay between Wall Street and Church Street; the social distance, even more than the geographic distance, placed Wall Street beyond their cognitive focus. The problem was more than distance, however. Blacks knew all to well that they were directly affected by the slightest change in the country's economic fortunes. What, then, accounted for the lack of press coverage? It was a matter of timing. To upper-middle-class whites who had prospered during the 1920s, the crash represented a sudden, jolting climax. For the majority of blacks, the crash was somewhat of an anticlimax.

Across the nation, black Americans sarcastically quipped that the Depression was a white man's creation, that blacks found it hard to discern the difference between 1929 and 1922. Historian William Harris remembered his father commenting "that black people were already so poor in the 1920s that in the 1930s they did not even know the Great Depression had come." Others echoed his sentiments. For residents of Stamps, Arkansas, remembers Maya Angelou, the Depression was in every respect a continuation of poverty: "The country had been in the throes of the Depression for two years before Negroes in Stamps knew it. I think that everyone thought that the Depression, like everything else, was for the white folks." Perhaps Clifford Burke best summarized popular thought when he told Studs Terkel that "the Negro was born in the depression. . . . It only became official when it hit the white man."[3]

Norfolk Afro-Americans did not have to wait for official news to realize that conditions were worsening. Early in the 1920s, many had lost jobs and businesses when the recession of 1921–1922 caused the local labor market to contract. Although the economy rebounded, unemployment among blacks had again reached critical levels by the spring of 1928. More than two hundred black residents representing benevolent associations, social welfare agencies, labor, business, the press, and the churches convened an unemployment conference at First Baptist Church to discuss conditions. Estimates showed that many black workers had been reduced to part-time hours, while many others could not find work at all. The job placement rate for women seeking work had dropped to 5 percent per month. These changes were precipitating the birth of a new class of unemployed:

> Those who are suffering are not the indolent and shiftless who would readily patronize a public soup kitchen or beg a public dole in order to buy life's necessities. The real sufferers are the self-respecting men and women of families who hitherto have been regular in their payments for rents, groceries, fuel, furniture and clothes, but who are being slowly but surely forced into insolvency and poverty.

Many also feared the impoverishment of working-class families meant the inevitable impoverishment of the "business, fraternal and professional people with whom they deal."[4] To thwart this downward slide, the conferees took the unprecedented step of asking the city to sponsor public works projects. Thus, by the time the stock market crashed in faraway New York, blacks had already spent the better part of a year dispensing casualty reports. It was no news to them that the country was—and had been—in serious economic trouble.

After the conference, conditions worsened, and blacks suffered serious reversals in occupations that traditionally had been major sources of employment. Summing up 1929, the *Norfolk Journal and Guide* moaned, "It may as well be frankly admitted that the Negro in this city suffered some unprecedented losses in menial jobs."[5] As employers made further cutbacks, losses mounted. Scores fell victim to the southern proclivity to replace black workers with jobless white workers, which altered established patterns of racial labor market segmentation. Norfolk's white Housewives League even threatened to replace black domestics with white women who had been formerly employed by one of the recently closed factories. Along the waterfront, the ILA proved powerless to stop the replacement of blacks with whites. Nor did the arrival of new business concerns counterbalance the general trend. In view of conditions, some new businesses openly acknowledged a reluctance to employ blacks.[6]

The result was a transformation of the local labor market. Black men—who had lost more than 3,000 jobs between 1920 and 1930—lost 2,024 jobs between 1930 and 1940. Even more so than in the past, the losses were scattered across the occupational spectrum.[7] Men who worked were either particularly resourceful or lucky—or both.

John Chase was such a person. Before the onset of the Depression, this longtime resident of Norfolk had moved to Baltimore to work as a longshoreman, earning better wages than those he had earned as an independent fisherman. The Depression drove him home, however, to the tenuous security of his old trade. Upon returning, he fished from the middle of April to the end of November to support himself and his wife, Laura. A typical day for Chase began at 11 P.M., when he caught a street car to Willoughby Beach. There he retired to a basement room in the home of a white fellow with whom he had arranged to stay. His day began anew at 4 A.M., when he launched his boat and set out for the fish-rich Chesapeake Bay. After catching the day's haul, he brought the boat in around 10 A.M., returned home, ate, and then hit the streets of his neighborhood to peddle his catch. Laura told a WPA interviewer that her husband worked an average of twelve to thirteen hours a day, six days a week, weather permitting. At the conclusion of the fishing season, Chase found work as an oyster shucker, or he sold clams to neighbors or to the proprietors of the Longshoremen's Hall.[8] For him, the decision to return to fishing grew out of a conflict between available options and the need to escape poverty.

Only black professionals registered a modest gain during this period. Principally, the gain reflected a growing number of ministers. The reasons for this growth are not clear, but across the country the number of black churches, and therefore clerics, increased during the 1930s. Perhaps many were like William J., who believed he had received the "calling" and used the mail-order route to obtain the appropriate credentials.[9]

Black women, who in the past had found employment when their menfolk could not, did not fare well either. They lost 1,812 positions, which exacerbated the problem of underemployment. Hardest hit were domestic and personal servants. Female factory operatives also received notices, especially when American Cigar closed in the mid-1930s.[10]

The 1930 census statistics on unemployment, meanwhile, substantiated the fears of those who worried about the development of a new class of unemployed. Citywide, a disproportionate number of the unemployed were black men and black women who attributed their joblessness to "economic conditions." Many were young workers between the ages of twenty and twenty-nine, although the ages of the unemployed ranged from fifteen to forty-nine. Nearly three quarters of the men and two thirds of the women headed households or contributed sizable portions to the household's budget. Most had only recently lost their jobs—that is, they had been without work two weeks or less.[11]

Thomas Hill's pension, which he supplemented by growing his own vegetables, enabled the retired navy yard worker to get by. Julia Jones, in contrast, relied on public assistance, particularly after a debilitating back injury.[12] As unemployment rose, the number who applied for help increased. By October 1933, 17.8 percent of the nation's urban blacks were receiving relief, compared to 9.5 percent of whites. In Norfolk, a smaller percentage of blacks (13.8 percent) depended on relief, but this figure was still considerably higher than the rate for whites (1.7 percent). Furthermore, when the government surveyed the extent of urban relief in seventy-nine cities in 1934, it found that blacks, who accounted for little more than a third of Norfolk's population, composed 79.6 percent of the households on relief in that city, the highest figure among the cities studied.[13]

We now know that the various censuses seriously undercounted, especially among blacks. But census statistics also veil another important reality: the actual victims of the Depression were most often families, rather than adults living alone. Fewer than one tenth of the households on relief had only one member.[14] Most relief recipients lived, at least for a period, in intact families. Moreover, as is the case during any period of protracted impoverishment, children were the hidden sufferers. Unemployment statistics measured the lack of jobs for parents or guardians but seldom the impact of joblessness on the young. By the fall of 1933, nearly half of the city's relief recipients were under seventeen. In fact, children between the ages of six and thirteen represented one quarter of all assisted, the largest single cohort.[15]

The Depression exacted a price that the numbers cannot begin to reveal. Economic deprivation forced many to enter a restricted labor market at the very time jobs for young workers disappeared. It also exaggerated differences, and youths from economically marginal families found themselves subjected to the critical review of peers, children who could be pointed social critics. Louis C. recalled that as a youngster he supplemented his family's budget and earned money for himself by selling the *Journal and Guide* and running errands for the merchants lining Church Street. Times were difficult for his family, but they paled in comparison to the hardships faced by others he knew. He described the story of a school-age chum whose family was particularly destitute. The family subsisted on collard greens and had little money to spend on school lunches. The youth insisted on continuing school, however, although he knew that his daily lunch, a sandwich of collard greens, would provoke gibes and taunts from his classmates. To avoid this, he ate his sandwich each day before he reached school.[16]

Time brought little improvement. Instead, the continuing difficulties put considerable strain on many families. Conditions were virtually unchanged in March 1935, when the government surveyed the number of workers on relief in the United States. Locally, almost five thousand Afro-Americans remained out of work, and, as in 1933 and 1934, blacks composed more than three quarters of those on relief. Females headed more than half of the families receiving relief, although 87.3 percent of all males on relief headed their households.[17]

For many, the experience of living in an impoverished, female-headed household was new. Mothers often became the primary economic providers for the first time because fathers, unable to secure employment and feeling emasculated, deserted. Lucille Johnson informed an interviewer for the Virginia Writers' Project that her husband had abandoned her and their five children when she reported him to the authorities for not providing adequate child support. According to Lucille, "he said I done showed him up a fore de white folks and shamed him," and he left. To make ends meet, Lucille worked as a laundress twice a week and received aid from the city's various charities and relief agencies.[18]

In restructuring some black households, the Depression also robbed them of the material amenities that had formerly provided the semblance of a middle-class life. When the Virginia Writers' Project interviewed James Ruffin's wife, Maria, she was caring for their five children, who ranged in age from six months to eleven years. She kept them healthy and fed, but austerity betrayed the impact of the Depression on their standard of living. A piano in need of repair symbolized the turn of events: its presence brought to mind better times; its current state of disrepair underscored how long ago those times were. Maria confessed that conditions had worsened after her husband left the family when it became clear he could no longer provide for them financially.[19]

Whereas more often the Depression tore families apart, it also forced others together. Across America, Afro-Americans turned to one another for aid and assistance as conditions deteriorated. Chicago tenement dwellers "shared facilities, hotplates, stoves and sinks." Others shared canned produce, livestock, and homegrown vegetables. Of course, some retreated into the narrow world of self-interest. Mrs. T. L., a resident of Jackson, Mississippi, complained, "You would have thought that the Depression would have pulled people together, but it sure didn't happen. Everybody went their separate ways. . . . I guess everybody was too busy trying to take care of themselves."[20] But this was not the dominant response. One Norfolk longshoreman managed a one-time contribution of ten dollars to support relatives, even though he had a young child, a wife who did not work outside the home, and family expenditures that equaled his earnings. Another Norfolk resident, who earned more than twelve hundred dollars as a cook in 1936, donated one hundred seventy-five dollars for the funeral of his brother.[21] For these families, the Depression was a time to come together.

In the aggregate, the negative effect of the Depression on the structure of the black family smoothed out by 1940. A comparison of 1930 and 1940 reveals a slight increase in the number of single adults and a very slight decrease in the number of those married. At both the beginning and the end of the Depression, roughly one third of all black men and one quarter of all black women over the age of fifteen lacked spouses. The most serious changes occurred during the middle years of the Depression, when conditions were worst.[22]

The undermining of the family unit also threatened the community at large. Through 1930, development in the home sphere had depended on a stable core population that identified with the community and its goals. The family helped direct this focus by functioning as an anchor. Individuals who lived in stable families put down roots and fought to improve conditions. When conditions deteriorated, the logic that informed earlier strategies faced new challenges. In part, this explains why some came to entertain different notions of how to win community empowerment.

Neither the family nor the community came completely undone, however. Black families often adapted to the changes wrought by the Depression in creative and stabilizing ways. Fewer marriages ended in divorce in 1940 than had been the case in 1930, but one quarter of all wives and one sixth of all husbands nevertheless lived in households with one spouse absent in 1940. Such conditions forced accommodations. Charlie Johnson and his wife, for example, moved in with her brother after the brother's wife deserted him and their children. In exchange for room and board, the Johnsons provided child care. Such an arrangement benefited both the underemployed couple and the splintered family.[23]

Young adults were required to make the greatest adaptations, for they proved to be the most frequent victims of unemployment. As the 1930s began, two fifths of jobless black men were under twenty-nine years of age. Nor did prospects improve as the group aged. Seven years later, nearly 60 percent of totally unemployed men were thirty-five or younger. Some had only recently entered the labor market, but three quarters of this group had been there for the seven-year duration. Gender brought little advantage, which many parents and relatives understood. Rather than see his recently divorced adult daughter endure the poverty of unemployment, for example, Thomas Hill took her in.[24]

Despite the disproportionate suffering of blacks, the problems that beset them were as much structural as racial. Like their black counterparts, young whites also found jobs hard to come by. Older, more experienced workers found full or partial employment more readily than those under thirty-five.[25] How many of either race understood this shared predicament is unknown, but such common ground would become the focus of organizers who attempted to modify the language of protest in the black community.

Whatever comfort blacks took in knowing that others also suffered failed to erase the pain they felt when the 1940 census showed how much they had lost. In 1920, 47.6 percent of working-age black women held jobs. Ten years later, this figure had risen to 49.3 percent; but by 1940 it had declined to 42.8 percent. Black men encountered even greater reversals. After World War I, their rate of participation in the labor force stood at 89.6 percent. A decade later, the figure had dropped to 80.3 percent. Because opportunities declined rapidly thereafter, fewer than 75 percent found employment in 1940.[26]

## RESTRUCTURING SOCIAL RELATIONS: SETTING THE STAGE

Norfolk blacks responded to the Depression and the conditions it created in several ways. For some, the deleterious conditions produced a change in philosophy: they took part in Communist-led marches, joined interracial unions, and supported radical political figures. For others, it occasioned only a change in setting.

Eliza Mason, a native of Norfolk, came of age on the eve of the Great Depression. Her father had died when she was quite young, and, like many widowed women with a family to support, her mother took a job as a domestic. This income could not support the household, however. When the three o'clock bell announced the end of the schoolday, Eliza headed for work. "The lady would send her butler for me and I would get in that car and go there and fix their supper, wash their dishes, put their kids to bed, and they would bring me all back home. I did that for years and years for that family," she remembered. When she finished high school, Eliza dreamed of going to a liberal arts college, but her family was too poor. She refused to let poverty dash her dreams; instead Eliza modified her aspirations and decided to become a nurse. She used the low tuition and her own earnings to enroll at Hampton Institute, where she completed the course of study. After graduation, she had little trouble finding a job, but she was also introduced to the two-tier wage structure. She noted bitterly, "I can't say that I had any problems getting jobs . . . but it was the money. They made a difference in the salaries between the colored nurses and the white nurses. . . . And you had to work beside the white nurse every day. That used to upset me terrible." Because of this discrimination and her desire to see another part of the country, Eliza left for New York in 1931. She never returned to Norfolk, except for brief visits.[27]

Hundreds of others left the city during the Depression decade, but the biggest exodus in fact occurred between 1920 and 1930. The city lost a net total of 2,297 men during that ten-year period. Although it gained a net total of 289 women, large numbers of young women, as well as men, fled. Most of those who left had entered the decade of the 1920s as young adults (between the ages of twenty and thirty-nine) and were likely to have had the most difficulty finding a job and later retaining that job (see Table 12).

TABLE 12  Net Migration Among Blacks by Cohort,
Norfolk, 1920–1930 and 1930–1940

| Age Group | 1920–30 | | 1930–40 | |
| --- | --- | --- | --- | --- |
| | Male | Female | Male | Female |
| 10–14 | 37 | 120 | 96 | 268 |
| 15–19 | 250 | 387 | 242 | 165 |
| 20–24 | 455 | 688 | 416 | 288 |
| 25–29 | 27 | 304 | 400 | 324 |
| 30–34 | −684 | −272 | 130 | 156 |
| 35–39 | −620 | −432 | 182 | 95 |
| 40–44 | −307 | −104 | 148 | −9 |
| 45–49 | −422 | −220 | −111 | −60 |
| 50–54 | −587 | −86 | −218 | −145 |
| 55–59 | −229 | −69 | −266 | −165 |
| 60–64 | −140 | −41 | −47 | −90 |
| 65–69 | −50 | −10 | −76 | −94 |
| 70–74 | −16 | 1 | −18 | −37 |
| 75+ | 7 | 17 | −7 | −21 |
| Total | −2,279 | 283 | 871 | 675 |

SOURCES: U.S. Bureau of the Census, *Fourteenth Census of the United States* (Washington, D.C.: Government Printing Office, 1921), vol. 2, *Population, 1920*, pp. 356–57; U.S. Bureau of the Census, *Fifteenth Census of the United States* (Washington, D.C.: Government Printing Office, 1932), vol. 3, pt. 2, *Population, 1930*, p. 1156; U.S. Bureau of the Census, *Sixteenth Census of the United States* (Washington, D.C.: Government Printing Office, 1943), vol. 2, pt. 7, *Population, 1940*, p. 194.

Surprisingly, the exodus during the 1930s was relatively small. In fact, the city added more black men and women than it lost. The largest gains in population were registered by younger workers, the same group that had left in great numbers the decade before.[28] Overall, there was a net surplus among Eliza Mason's peers in the twenty-five to twenty-nine age group. The somewhat older workers who had weathered the 1920s found the 1930s difficult. Particularly hard-pressed were black males and females aged thirty-five to forty-nine in 1930; they registered a net loss between 1930 and 1940. Nonetheless, we have a portrait of an essentially stable urban population, with a few notable exceptions. This stability was important, because it worked to the advantage of those who advocated staying the course, who argued that little had changed at work or at home, and who believed that time-honored efforts on behalf of development in the home sphere represented the best strategy for Afro-Americans.

If we consult the U.S. Census Bureau's study of internal migration, however, a slightly different picture emerges. Adopting 1935–1940 as its time frame, the Census Bureau discovered that the city lost an estimated 959 nonwhites during those years. This loss reflects an in-migration of 2,403 persons of color and an out-migration of 3,362. Moreover, in direct contrast to the patterns noted previously, the Census Bureau discovered that the biggest loss occurred among women: as a group, they lost an estimated 660 persons, whereas men lost only 299.[29] Perhaps the standardization of relief efforts during the second half of the decade made migration a less precarious venture. Or perhaps the differences reflect the insensitivity of measures of net migration. Whatever the reason, the patterns of movement we perceive vary, depending on the time frame chosen.

Inasmuch as it seems impossible to totally reconcile the differences, it is useful to pursue a corollary question: where were the migrants headed? Generally speaking, most nonwhite men (because Norfolk's nonwhite population was overwhelmingly black, we can assume a high correlation between the two groups) went to cities with populations of more than one hundred thousand. More than one quarter of the migrants who left Norfolk moved to rural, nonfarm areas. Indeed, as a group, black men returned to the countryside at a rate nearly equaling their movement to urban areas (46.8 percent versus 53.2 percent). This was particularly true of in-state migrants, 69.9 percent of whom returned to the country.[30]

The migration habits of women differed in one important respect. Whereas women who migrated primarily went to large cities or other urban places (62.5 percent of all cases), when they returned to the country—as they did in more than a third of the cases—they moved to small towns. The only departure from this pattern involved migration within Virginia, where black women, like black men, migrated to farm areas.[31]

What is important here is not the fact that people migrated, but that some actually opted to return to the countryside. Conventional wisdom holds that thousands of displaced rural folks jammed the cities of America looking for work during the Depression—which they did. Nonetheless, some also decided to return to the country, indicating that rural opportunities remained a salient choice during difficult times.

## NARROWING THE CLASS DIVIDE

The Depression not only robbed many of their livelihood and forced others to migrate; in essential ways it also narrowed the class divide in the black community. Real differences of course remained. During the day, for example, homeless men, women, and children, "nearly obscured by the smoke which cast a pall over the dump at nearly all times," rummaged through debris in search of anything salvageable, later molding their bounty into the makeshift living structures of a shantytown. But, as the 1928 unemployment conferees noted, what affected the working class eventually affected the middle class. As if to prove this true, the shantytown architects built their makeshift community next to the more affluent Lindenwood neighborhood, home for many members of the black middle class.[32]

Most Afro-Americans fared somewhat better than the shantytown dwellers, but even managing the family budget often proved troublesome. Toward the end of the Depression, the federal government surveyed 110 black families in the Norfolk-Portsmouth area, 66 of them in Norfolk. The family disbursement schedules provide a unique opportunity to examine a household's struggle to maintain its financial integrity. The survey respondents were relatively better off than many of their neighbors; participation in the survey required that at least one person in the household had been employed for the preceding twelve months as something other than a domestic.[33] But even these less impoverished working-class black families lived on the edge. Nearly a third of the nation's black households showed a deficit at year's end. Among black Norfolkians, fewer than half of the families came out ahead. Nor was their margin of security that large—no household saved more than fifty-two dollars, and most saved less than thirty-five dollars.[34]

This struggle to manage finances structured the urban housing market as well. Nearly four fifths of the families surveyed were renters. Areawide, the percentage of blacks who were homeowners dropped from 21.6 to 16.0 percent during the Depression. Despite an increase in the overall number of families, 490 fewer blacks owned homes at the end of the Depression than at the beginning.[35]

Many carried the pain of losing their home for years. Susan J. had used her initial stay in the city to save enough money to go to college. She had dreamed of becoming a nurse. Then her brother Luke died, and she took over his house payments. She married Clifton in 1926 with the hope that he would move into the Titustown residence, but he refused. Then the Depression hit. With only one hundred eighty dollars still owed on the mortgage, Susan began to fall behind on taxes. Eventually, she lost the house, the possession that had kept her from going to school. With the hurt still close to the surface, she later recalled, "The Depression came on . . . and the taxes . . . and I lost it. That got to me worse than I ever let anything get to me, leaving out death." For Susan, the loss was doubly painful because she had already paid the mortgage once. Her father had borrowed against the dwelling, leaving her to pay twice. The new debt wiped out her savings, while the Depression and taxes took part of her soul.[36]

At best, in cases in which a substantial erosion in the quality of life did not occur, we see stark evidence of only minimal improvement. This perception is reinforced by the information gleaned from the family disbursement schedules. Although the majority of survey respondents lived in detached family dwellings, 78.8 percent used coal and wood to fuel their stoves or heaters, and more than 57 percent lacked so basic an amenity as an indoor toilet.[37]

Still, the tenants sampled in the survey lived a better life than many. Citywide, only a third (32.8 percent) of the rental dwellings occupied by blacks at the end of the Depression had indoor toilets. The city did not lack the structural elements necessary for sewage hook-up; on the contrary, 81.9 percent of all white renters lived in units with indoor facilities. Rather, the disparity suggests a differential in standard of living created in part by different employment situations, lower earnings, and stingy landlords. Landlords undoubtedly played an important role in determining the quality of housing. The Census Bureau found that a third of all black renters lived in units needing major repairs, as compared to only one in every eight white renters. Some of the units in which blacks lived were so deplorable that a federal official described Norfolk's slums as the worst in the country.[38]

The worst housing in these slum areas was an average of forty years old and surrounded the black business district. The existence of these dwellings validated the ongoing need for improvement in the home sphere, because their placement reminded all of the link between the classes. Federal officials observed in 1939:

> Many of the frame shacks and other nondescript dwellings are in a dilapidated condition. Most of the large one family houses have been converted at minimum expense for two or more families. Most of the inhabitants are poor class Negroes and many are on relief. Collections are difficult and vacant property is subject to vandalism. Very few homes have central heating plants and practically none have bathrooms.

Nevertheless, the occupancy rate in these areas seldom fell below 90 percent. And when blacks encroached on previously all-white neighborhoods, either the contested neighborhood became the scene of interracial confrontations or a quick succession followed, transforming mostly white areas into mostly black areas.[39] This restricted range of alternatives left the black middle and working classes in competition for limited space. As a result, middle-class neighborhoods such as Haynes Tract frequently adjoined working-class neighborhoods or even slums.[40]

Interracial differences in access to urban amenities overshadowed many other differences among blacks themselves and illustrated anew the importance of the home sphere. For example, 85.8 percent of the city's white tenants used gas for cooking, whereas only 5.6 percent of black households had the equipment to do so. To the typical Afro-American resident, no fuel existed other than coal, as the residents of 2416 Courtney, 1012 Lancaster, and 705 Walker would tell an interviewer.[41] By 1940 half of the homes in Norfolk used mechanical refrigerators rather than iceboxes to store perishables; but whites in fact owned 95.1 percent of the refrigerators in the city. Whereas seven in ten white households owned a mechanical refrigerator, this appliance, like the gas stove, was virtually unknown to most blacks unless they had seen one in a display window, a catalog, or in the home of a white employer. The vast majority depended on ice to chill their food.[42] Thus, although the material gap set some blacks apart from other blacks, more generally it set all blacks apart from whites. Even the average white worker had a better standard of living than most middle-class blacks, let alone a black working-class counterpart.

During this period, black entrepreneurs acquired a deeper understanding of how the forces that impoverished black workers impoverished them. Nowhere was this more apparent than in the sequence of events that resulted in the collapse of the community's leading financial institution, the Metropolitan Bank and Trust. Throughout its history, the company had teetered on the edge of economic disaster. As William Rich had acknowledged in the 1920s, the bank could not survive by catering to small depositors. Officials tried to correct the problem by reinvesting in capital-intensive businesses during the 1920s. Then the Depression rocked the financial world. Many insolvent companies collapsed, sending a ripple effect throughout the financial community. Those who had invested in these companies were left with drastically undervalued stocks. Metropolitan, which had invested $25,000 in bonds in the Guarantee Title and Trust Company, sustained a major loss when Guarantee failed and its stocks depreciated by 40 percent. To exacerbate the situation, the recession led to a revaluation of the bank's capital stock. The net result was a loss of $55,000 in capital stock and another $32,000 in investments. Given the unavoidable drift toward insolvency, the state ordered the bank to suspend operations on 5 January 1931.[43]

Hope remained that the bank would eventually reopen. This prospect appeared likely when 99 percent of the depositors agreed to a reorganization plan calling for major sacrifices on their part. Under the terms of the plan, 50 percent of all deposits were earmarked for capital stocks and the other half for withdrawals. Furthermore, depositors agreed to delay all withdrawals for a year, after which they could remove no more than two fifths of their money.[44]

The much-heralded comeback actually amounted to a last gasp. Under the terms of the reorganization, the face value of the stock went from $50.00 per share to $5.00 per share. This allowed the bank to secure 4,500 stockholders and acquire $100,000 in liquid capital. But the government already had begun to make plans to close undervalued financial institutions.[45]

President Roosevelt temporarily suspended the operations of all banks in 1933. When approval came for banks to reopen, Metropolitan discovered that it lacked the needed resources. In large part, the depositors had little faith in the bank's leadership and questioned whether their money was safe. The situation was compounded by a fourth devaluation of the bank's capital stocks and a lukewarm response to a call for the depositors to buy the bank building. Metropolitan Bank and Trust went the way of a third of the nation's financial institutions when it closed its doors for good in June 1933. For the faithful, all that remained was collecting 15 percent of their initial deposit, all in cash.[46]

Metropolitan's closure reaffirmed the link between the working class and the middle-class business infrastructure. Commentators had foreseen in 1928 that as working-class fortunes went, so too went middle-class businesses. Another way of judging the impact on the lives of business owners and their constituency is to examine the rate of vacancies in the business district, especially Church Street, the main artery of black business (see Graph 1).

The fortunes of those who lived and worked along this commercial strip paralleled the downturn in the nation as a whole. At the beginning of the period, slightly more than one in every six units lacked an occupant; four years later, this figure had increased to one in every five. The percentage of those affected peaked in 1936, when 20.9 percent of all the units sat vacant. Thereafter, economic fortunes improved. So drastic was the turnaround that, by 1941, Church Street had a 92 percent occupancy rate.[47]

The Depression years were difficult for black residents, although people continued to visit friends and relatives, to laugh, to have babies, to go to the movies, and to attend church. For many, however, the quality of life declined as unemployment victimized a sizable portion of the black population. Structural changes in the labor force pushed blacks out of occupations they had traditionally dominated and pushed hundreds into a decade-long search for steady employment. Women and children were the hardest hit by the effects of unemployment and poverty.

Some Afro-Americans chose migration, moving to large cities or returning to the countryside. The extent of return rural migration, especially among those who stayed in the South, points to a new set of

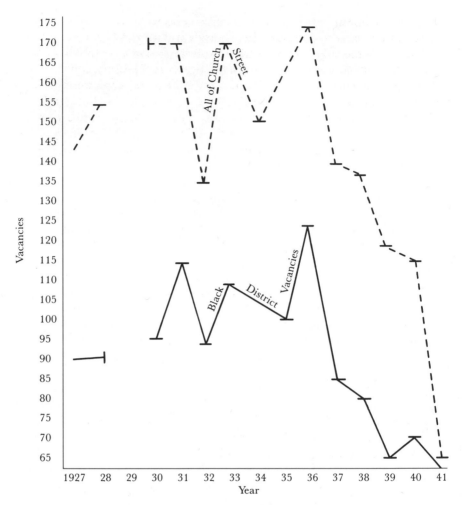

Graph 1. Business and Residential Vacancies Along Church Street, 1927–1941

SOURCE: *City Directory of Norfolk*, 1927 through 1941.
NOTE: No city directory exists for 1929.

assumptions. Before the Depression, blacks left rural areas in unprecedented numbers to go to the city in search of jobs. Undoubtedly, many saw a return to the countryside as a real alternative when the urban labor market constricted.

For the most part, however, Norfolk blacks stayed put. Those who remained struggled to maintain a modest standard of living, though most failed. More became renters and fewer owned their own homes. Although they lived in the city, their homes lacked the accoutrements of modern life. A third of the city's Afro-American renters lived in substandard housing; they used coal to heat their homes and ice to keep their perishables fresh. Generally speaking, they walked to work or took the bus.

In this social context, some residents began to question their world. They began to wonder if social conditions did not demand some radical changes. The shift in perspective and the corresponding behavioral shift suggest an alteration in the prevalent social philosophy. Ultimately, the 1930s were not one period, but several, bound by the dates 1929 and 1941. One story is the nature of the crisis; another is the response it engendered.

# SIX

# The Depression Years: Toward a Restructuring of Social Relations, 1929–1941

For Afro-Americans in the Depression years, the combination of unemployment, material decline, new actors, and new ideas led to a restructuring of social relations and a rethinking of how best to act in their own interests. The responses of Norfolk residents to the changing situation were complex and varied. Between 1929 and 1936, the depth of the economic crisis in conjunction with the arrival of radical organizers—first from the Communist party and then from the Congress of Industrial Organizations (CIO)—ushered in a change in the language and form of protest politics and a more concerted effort to link the workplace and the home sphere.[1] As a result, new examples of interracial working-class solidarity emerged.

Beginning in 1935, but more assertively after 1936, middle-class leaders, who had always been wary of the Communist party and its calls for interracial solidarity, reclaimed control. They continued to champion the strategy of developing the home sphere as the best course for blacks. In their view, little had changed, despite the leveling effects of unemployment. Racism still flourished, white workers maintained a privileged position in the local setting, and poverty and race limited access to city services. Their argument now lacked the full persuasiveness it had once carried, however. Instead, during the Depression years, Norfolk blacks entertained various alternatives. How residents reacted to those options altered the race and class dynamic and figured in the restructuring of social relations, especially in efforts to add blacks to the family of labor.

## THE INTRODUCTION OF A NEW PERSPECTIVE

As the 1930s began, very little in the past of either the city or the Afro-American community indicated a leaning toward radicalism. A few quasi-indigenous groups had indeed espoused philosophies that threatened the status quo. We need only recall the TWA, which began as a union for longshore workers during the 1910s and came to call for the organization of all black workers, regardless of job or gender. Yet, like the Garveyites, whom some also saw as "radical," the longshoremen constructed an agenda for social mobilization that was sensitive to racial calibrations.

Therefore, when radicals affiliated with the Communist party entered the area in 1929, their chances for success seemed slim. The Socialist party was the only other kindred group in the area, and the Socialists' efforts to mobilize locals had failed miserably throughout the 1920s. They experienced great difficulty in attracting either black or white recruits, let alone getting members to attend meetings and pay dues. Their greatest success actually came in attracting crowds to hear national spokespersons.[2] But, as the Communists quickly learned, the past did not mean as much during the 1930s.

Several reasons explained the measured success of the new radicals. At no time in American history had an economic crisis affected so many for so long. In Norfolk, as elsewhere, blacks composed a disproportionate number of those affected. Consequently, they began to look for solutions that would help them reclaim control over their own destinies. The Communists made an appeal to do just that. They were encouraged by the Soviet-dominated Communist International, which saw the plight of black Americans as a cause worth embracing.[3] From the start, Communist organizers actively sought out unemployed black workers. They also took up residence in the heart of the black community, in effect becoming part of the group they sought to mobilize. In addition, they organized community members around issues that affected them directly— work, hunger, housing, relief. Most important, they did what no other group had even contemplated: both in speech and in behavior, they tried to fuse the two worlds of work and home.

Lacking the industrial setting of Birmingham or a cause célèbre like the Angelo Herndon case in Atlanta, the history of Communists in Norfolk is one of agitation, confrontation, and harassment. It is a history of modest successes, as measured by early public support, which nevertheless diminished as the years passed. Although Harvey Klehr estimates the Communist party enrolled fewer than one hundred members statewide, the story of the radical mobilization of the black community goes beyond a quantification of adherents. Rather, that story deals mostly with the seizing of a historical moment. In the end, it was at the level of political mobilization and as a challenge to social conventions that the radicals were most successful.[4]

As in any attempt at mobilizing, it was necessary for certain mechanisms to be in place. Lawrence Goodwyn argues, in reference to the Populists, that building a democratic movement is the net result of the evolution of four sequential stages. He calls stage one "the movement forming." During this stage, the actors create their own independent institutions. Stage two he labels "the movement recruiting." This stage features the creation of organizational strategies for drawing people into the movement. During stage three, called "the movement educating," a new and perhaps more sophisticated analysis of the present situation is offered. The process of mobilization culminates in stage four, with "the movement politicized."[5]

Whether the Communist initiative constituted a democratic mass movement is debatable. That the Communists' vision of a raceless and classless society distinguished them and the coalition they sought to form from that of their predecessors is not. No other group overcame the dominant belief system that defined blacks as racial ethnics at work and at home. In the rural South and Midwest, the domain of the Populists, race framed their perspectives, as the later career of Populist leader Tom Watson vividly illustrated—after the collapse of populism, Watson became one of the South's more esteemed race-baiters. Likewise, the Knights of Labor, who held a vision of workers' cooperatives, resisted the call for black inclusion. In the urban North, where Garvey's movement was centered, his followers considered economic achievement inseparable from racial self-sufficiency. More important, the Garveyites cared little about the relationship of the masses to the means of production; for them, class-based issues ran second to their faith in the soundness of capitalism.[6]

Chiefly, therefore, the Communists had to create institutions that would free would-be participants from the guardianship of the status quo. Although acute unemployment and the rise of poverty called for a wholesale attack, the Communists first had to sell black Norfolkians on the soundness of their approach, which required a strategy. Because of the degree of material decline, the home sphere was targeted first; few would oppose a group that helped obtain shelter, food, and money. Norfolk residents, in this regard, joined with those in countless other cities in establishing an Unemployed Council to channel the needs and aspirations of the dispossessed.[7] Once the immediate crisis had been stabilized, the new radicals tried to organize the workplace. How they did this both challenged and left unchallenged fundamental views about the place of blacks in the industrial order.

Eventually, the hope for a complete radicalization of the population faded, plagued by the same problems encountered elsewhere: leftist factionalism and opposition from both national and local police as well as from an array of black and white individuals and groups.[8] As a result, historians have dubbed members of the Communist party the first champions of civil rights, rather than the architects of a new belief system.[9] Actually, they were both. The fact that historians ignore the latter role in favor of the former underscores the limits of the Communists' approach. To understand how they played this dual role, we must turn to those crucial years of the early 1930s.

Most Communists who came to Norfolk during that period resembled Stephen Graham—white and either foreign-born or the children of immigrant parents. They arrived with an idealized belief that communism was the panacea for all the world's problems. The 1930s offered them a laboratory in which to test that belief. Blacks and other similarly situated poor folks were the potential recruits for an army ripe for revolution. To Graham, the cause was noble: he wanted to "fight for race equality and unionization of the entire working class, white and black, for better conditions."[10]

From the start, such pronouncements marked the Communist organizers as outsiders—or, worse yet, as outside agitators. Communists exhorted workers of all races to join the left-leaning Trade Union Unity League (TUUL) and to help in the eventual overthrow of capitalism and the existing government. Neither black nor white citizens wanted to hear those words in 1930. Few objected when police in Norfolk and Portsmouth arrested and charged Graham with inciting a "race riot."[11] Most prayed that President Hoover was correct in his prediction that economic prosperity was just around the bend.

The next months did not bring renewed prosperity, however; they brought increased despair. For their part, the new radicals tempered their rhetoric to reflect the growing seriousness of the economic hard times. They continued their call for the replacement of the capitalist system, but they became even more vociferous in their demands that the immediate survival needs of the unemployed be met, regardless of race.

To accomplish their goals and dramatize the plight of the poor, the Communists employed a method of street theater. But instead of staging large amorphous marches and demonstrations whose only specific target was an abstract capitalism, Communists organized the local Unemployed Councils to demand free or reduced rents, major repairs to old buildings, and the right of tenants to negotiate directly with landlords. Focused demonstrations enabled organizers to channel the frustrations simmering among the ranks of the unemployed. Moreover, the nebulous oppressor acquired an identity: the real estate broker, the landlord, or the former employer. The council's strategy to defend the rights of the unemployed involved creating a program, establishing an agenda, and setting a timetable whereby people could evaluate results. For those Afro-Americans whose primary concerns were food, shelter, and then work, the Communists were doing something they could identify with.

To be fully successful, however, the new radicals had to get their message to those who were most likely to be receptive. This required a variety of strategies for concurrent recruitment and education. Frequently, organizers simply stood on street corners handing out leaflets describing their philosophy to passersby. This approach, however, discouraged the sustained personal contact between converter and potential convert so important to mobilization. Often, Communists organized mass rallies at strategic corners along Church Street, Olney Road, or Princess Anne Road. As many as five hundred people would gather to hear Fred Allen, Louis Seidman (both white), Rufus Beaverbrook, Rev. Haywood Parker, or Alexander Wright (the last three black) preach the Communist scripture. When the street corner proved inadvisable or unaccommodating, the group used recognized meeting places in the black community. Several rallies and demonstrations were held at Barraud Park, despite its geographic inconvenience and poor condition. (Through 1934, the city continued to lag in transforming the farmland into a park, and its undeveloped state discouraged use.) At other times, Communists persuaded the pastors of churches such as Garrett's Temple, Second Calvary Baptist, John M. Brown AME, or St. John AME to allow them to use their buildings. When these places were unavailable, they met at their own headquarters, located at first on Church Street and later on Princess Anne Road.[12] Finally, the Communists brought in black organizers who spoke in a language and tone that blacks understood.

Isaac Alexander Wright became such an organizer in Norfolk. He was a tall, angular, brown-complexioned man whose carriage recalled that of a country preacher. His face indicated that he had known hard work and hard times. Unlike the northern-born white organizers who preceded him, Wright was comfortable in an all-black southern environment. He was, recalled his progressive colleague and former friend Louise Thompson Patterson, a captivating, charismatic speaker. "He could," she remembered, "hold the workers, because he knew what he was talking about." Whereas others had come armed with the language of Marx, Wright related personal stories in his Texas voice, using them to draw the connection between Marxist analysis and individual experiences, as both FBI records and personal recollections indicate. Style in this instance was very important, because it was an effective vehicle for transmitting information. Patterson, who visited Norfolk often as an organizer for the International Workers' Order (IWO), noted: "He had all his stories linked up with the life of a black worker, farm worker particularly. . . . He would make parallels between doing something in the field and organizing in the union. . . . He seemed never to run out of the speeches."[13]

Even the existence of a structure for mobilization and the efforts of a spellbinding orator like Wright do not fully answer the question of what caused people to become engaged. Why did blacks and whites dare to defy the worldview that had shaped their behavior to that point? What did the Communists say and do that made their ideas palatable to black residents like Rufus Beaverbrook, head of the South Norfolk Unemployed Council, and the Reverend Haywood Parker? What caused 250 blacks and an equal number of whites to ignore a city ordinance and sit in an integrated fashion at public rallies in the city auditorium?[14]

Answers to these queries explain a great deal about the restructuring of social relations. For more than half a century, blacks had been locked out of the working class. This may seem a non sequitur, for blacks were disproportionately workers. But the working-class world often described by historians had few black faces. At one time, this omission reflected the paucity of black urbanites. But even after the number of blacks in Philadelphia, Boston, Detroit, Chicago, and Pittsburgh increased, barriers to inclusion remained. Blacks were often simply barred from industrial employment. Those who overcame the initial obstacles discovered another impediment: unlike other recent arrivals, blacks remained racial ethnics both at work and at home. The conditions that transformed the Irish, the Slavs, the Poles, the Italians, and others into workers at work and ethnics at home did not apply to blacks. As a consequence, few examples of interracial labor solidarity dot the historical record. Moreover, community concerns, which fragmented the working class, erased any hope for interracial common ground. Blacks in countless cities instead used their racial distinctiveness as the basis for community mobilization.[15]

Black southerners also faced the particular problems of living in an urban-industrial environment that consigned them to a separate world. With relatively few white ethnics in Southern cities, the distinctions between black and white were more pronounced, and examples of interracial solidarity even scarcer. Blacks and whites lived together but apart, with segregated unions, toilets, housing, cemeteries—segregated everything. Viewed as separate from the white working class, black Norfolkians cloaked their own class differences to fight like other "ethnics" on behalf of community concerns, on behalf of development in the home sphere.[16]

Then the new radicals stepped in. They argued that racism was a subterfuge (even though they themselves were not immune from it—Cyril Briggs reported in 1929 that most of the white members of the party in

Norfolk had been expelled for excluding blacks from party activities). The issue as the radicals saw it was class, not race. On numerous occasions, Fred Allen, Rufus Beaverbrook, and others demanded racial equality and a place for blacks in the world of the working class. As Harry Wicks, the Communist party's candidate for the U.S. Senate from Pennsylvania, told a gathering at the Norfolk city auditorium in October 1932, "Any party which does not raise its voice for the 12 million Negroes of this country is no workers' party, no organization of the masses." Two years later, James Ford, a black Communist and the party's candidate for the vice-presidency, assailed the old-line black leadership as "stool pidgeons [*sic*] of the bosses." More than seven hundred people attended the public rally for Ford; according to the reporter from the *Norfolk Journal and Guide,* they "were mostly of the working class." Those gathered listened attentively as Ford asserted that the old leaders, bound by the old worldview, were "not interested in the problems of the workers." His words drew encouraging exclamations of "You are right!" and "Tell the truth!" when he concluded that "the destiny of the Negro race lies in the working class."[17]

The speeches by Wicks and Ford were two of the more publicized gatherings. Words were enough to incite but perhaps not enough to engage many. Action persuaded James Olds more than rhetoric. Olds and his family were evicted from their home in the Berkley section of Norfolk. Soon after the landlord had the family's worldly possessions placed on the sidewalk, representatives from the Unemployed Council intervened, gathering the belongings and returning them to the family's home. E. C. Savage and Company, the real estate firm that owned the property, pressed charges against Olds, Fred Allen (local head of the Unemployed Council), and his wife, Sylvia Langdos Allen, for illegal entry and trespassing. Testimony revealed that neither Fred Allen nor James Olds had participated in the action. An unidentified black youth under the supervision and with the assistance of Mrs. Allen had returned the furniture. What was most significant, however, outside of the act itself, was the assembly of more than four hundred blacks and whites at the Berkley Liberty Hall to protest the arrests. To the continued consternation of public officials, who rewrote a city ordinance to minimize such gatherings, it seemed the Communists were acquiring more public support.[18]

The eviction of Julia Jones further inflamed public sentiment. Jones and her twelve-year-old daughter lived in a decaying, unheated, one-room tenement apartment on St. Paul Street, in a predominantly black section of town where 90 percent of the residents were renters. Most lived in structures built during the presidencies of Grover Cleveland and

Benjamin Harrison, dwellings described as "shacks" and "dilapidated" by government real estate investigators. Jones had sustained a back injury when the apartment's porch railing collapsed, sending her tumbling to the ground. Medical examiners prescribed bed rest, and she subsequently lost her job. Mother and daughter became dependent on friends and charity, neither of which covered basic needs. When their rent was late, landlord H. M. Hardee evicted the two.[19]

The Unemployed Council interceded in much the same way it had for the Olds family, which greatly angered Hardee. He decided to make living conditions so intolerable that the Joneses would voluntarily leave. Aided by two assistants, he removed the doors and windows of the apartment to allow the January cold to enter. Locking the doors and the window glass in a vacant apartment, the trio left. Their departure signaled the council's arrival. After deliberating over whether to break into the other apartment and take the doors and windows, the group decided to place heavy cardboard over the exposed openings instead. The cardboard, plus a little coal and wood, protected the mother and daughter from the elements.[20]

Soon thereafter Jones hired the council's lawyer, Ernest W. Merrill. Merrill, who remained active in radical causes through World War II, sued the landlord for faulty building maintenance that caused bodily injury and for subjecting his tenant to life-threatening weather conditions. For its part, the council claimed to have sent a telegram to "landlord Hardee," the owner of "2,000 miserable shacks," and demanded the reinstatement of Jones, full compensation for her injuries, the cessation of evictions, a reduction in rents, and repairs to all buildings. They threatened to organize a rent strike if Hardee ignored their demands.[21]

Generally, such threats proved to be more than braggadocio. Members of the Unemployed Council repeatedly led unemployed workers to city hall in search of an equitable distribution of relief funds. Black residents had engaged in protest politics before, but never to the point of marching on city hall. Clearly, the form of social protest had changed. Equally important, their efforts produced immediate results. After a deluge of demonstrators descended on his office, Mayor Mason pledged, as politicians are wont to do, a satisfactory adjudication of their demands. The council wanted the poor protected from evictions; a community chest fund of three hundred thousand dollars, to be administered by workers' committees; free hot meals; warm clothes and school supplies for children of the unemployed; and the unconditional release of all workers arrested and imprisoned for participation in rent strikes, as well as the promise of amnesty for those who took part in future demonstrations.[22] Little suggests that the city met all of these demands.

Nevertheless, such actions marked a significant break with the past. For the first time, a group committed to improving conditions for the working class included blacks.

Yet, however hard they tried to make it so, Communist party organizers discovered that racial distinctions would not disappear. And, in the end, the party used racial differences to attract Afro-Americans, a practice long feared by opponents of the Communists.[23] When responsibility for relief shifted from the city to state and federal agencies in 1933, demonstrators marched on the Virginia Emergency Relief Administration (VERA) office, demanding to know why some blacks were excluded from the relief rolls. They also demanded to know why it sometimes took several weeks to investigate a black family's case history to determine if the family qualified for relief. Joseph Kline, speaking for the Unemployed Council in 1934, informed the *Norfolk Journal and Guide* that his group planned future protests as long as city and federal officials discriminated.[24]

In another instance, the Unemployed Council and others complained bitterly when relief wages paid to black workers were reduced from $2.00 to $1.25 per day. Many whites believed that blacks could live more cheaply than they could, but most of those allied with the black community argued that even the initial sum had been inadequate and that the reduction was outrageous. This development, along with an attempt to remove seven hundred black women from the WPA rolls when white truck farmers complained that relief wages prevented them from attracting workers, brought further demonstrations.[25]

This willingness to fight for the rights of black workers, to draw them into the world of the working class by eliminating racial differences, registered with all blacks, including black leaders. P. B. Young warned Afro-Americans in 1930 to adopt a "safer and saner" way of rectifying their unenviable plight. But, two years later, writing in the NAACP's *Crisis*, he modified his position somewhat:

> The communists in America have commendably contended for and have practiced equality of all races, and in their many activities have accepted Negroes into their ranks both in high and lowly positions; more they have dramatized the disadvantages of the Negro by walking in a body out of a Jim-Crow Pittsburgh hospital, by aiding ejected tenement dwellers, and in industrial strikes directed by them fighting against the practice of excluding Negroes from labor unions. All these accomplishments go to the creditside for the communists.[26]

Nonetheless, he wondered whether the Communists' prescription promised the best remedy. Young's ambivalence was not shared by all. When scorned by his ministerial colleagues for allowing Ben Davis, Jr., a black Communist party official, to speak at his church, the Reverend C. P. Madison of Second Calvary Baptist retorted, "In my opinion there was nothing in the speech that would hurt anyone. He only told us what Negroes in this country should do to gain what is rightfully theirs."[27]

The black working class offered the Communists greater support. Afro-American workers attended the rallies and demonstrations; they went to mass meetings to dramatize the injustice of the Scottsboro Boys case, in which nine young black men were wrongly charged with the (fabricated) rape of two white women on an Alabama train. Because of this support, military investigators described Norfolk as the most "sensitive" spot in the entire Mid-Atlantic and South Atlantic regions. Similarly, in a tone of obvious regret, an editorial writer for the *Journal and Guide* observed that the Communists "have made some headway here" and "have a great many sympathizers among intelligent colored people." Norfolk was, he concluded, "fertile ground" for a larger Communist movement, because "every human factor that enters into the stifling of loyalty to the present social, political and economic system prevails in Norfolk." The writer found the present situation unfortunate, but, he lamented, the black community's identification with the radicals derived from the city's universal neglect of the needs of black residents.[28]

In spite of the concerns of government intelligence agencies and the assessments of black leaders, the threat was never as great as perceived. Any group who sought the allegiance of blacks competed with history. Afro-Americans realized that their community was stratified along lines of class, gender, and social orientation, but they feared that whites saw one undifferentiated mass connected by race. Race was a powerful connector, but it was never as adhesive as whites made out and as blacks allowed them to believe. Afro-Americans maintained the ruse because of their interpretation of white understanding: if whites saw them as one, they were one. Furthermore, they understood the nature of urban politics. Rewards went to blocs, seldom to individuals. Blacks knew that if they exposed themselves and their differences, they invited the kind of guerrilla warfare that threatened their collective power. Few would have consciously invited such disaster.

Those who believed this most strongly included many members of the black middle class. Some resembled P. B. Young. Young, the consummate "race man," advanced his position within the black community and the larger society by talking in terms of race. This nationalistic perspective was crucial to his survival both as a businessman and as a race leader. To entertain the centrality of anything other than race jeopardized this position. Of course, he found part of the Communist party's message cogent, which explains his 1932 comments in *Crisis*. But to Young and many others, race determined class, and race was the primary issue to consider in pursuing social and political concerns. Thus Young's ultimate view of the Communists was his first: blacks should shy away and find "safer and saner" means of achieving their goals.

A few made the leap of faith the Communist party encouraged. For a certain group of black workers, the symbolism in the Communists' language merged with their own perceptions and experiences. They knew their station in life differed immeasurably from that of the factory owner. The Marxists provided a common vocabulary for comparing experiences. These workers also knew that race, though important, did not always completely determine success or position in the marketplace; after all, the Depression had not spared whites because they were white. Some, therefore, saw the opportunity for common ground.

Across the urban South, a contingent of Afro-Americans made the hard connections. After surveying the miserable conditions in Birmingham, Hosea Hudson joined the party. Angelo Herndon, overwhelmed by Atlanta's blatant social inequities, joined the Communist party, was arrested, and became the focus of a celebrated international case. Meanwhile, in Norfolk, Alexander Wright became a liaison between the Communists and the black community, transmitting the radicals' ideology through a language his neighbors understood, even if they did not endorse the undergirding philosophy.[29]

Others took part in Communist activities not so much for what the radicals said as for what they did. Seldom had a group of whites made the fight for black civil rights a high priority, let alone attempted to include blacks in the broader world of the working class. While walking down the street one day in Norfolk, James Canaday happened on a demonstration. He stopped and asked someone what it was about and was told it was a hunger march. Because he had been unemployed for several months, requiring assistance from the Colored United Charities, he knew hunger, and he decided to join in. His participation landed him in jail. Yet it is hard to argue that Canaday's decision to join the march reflected the maturation of his political consciousness. By all indications, he never took part in another march. It is likely that he decided to participate simply because he was attracted by the energy of the social event and its stated purpose.[30]

We can only speculate about the reaction of the majority of the city's black citizens. Some of the hundreds who attended the rallies and took part in the demonstrations surely found the underlying message of the radicals appealing. Norfolk residents had long shown a tendency to accept new ideas. Others probably struggled to bring that message and the associated language in line with their own experiences. As Louise Patterson recalled, the majority of white organizers came from the North and felt out of place in Norfolk and somewhat uncomfortable among blacks.

It took Alexander Wright to break down the language of what Ralph Ellison, in *Invisible Man*, termed "scientific Marxism." Many harbored some doubt about the motives of the organizers and the legitimacy of their plan for a raceless and classless society, especially given the government's efforts to paint all progressives as un-American and undesirable.[31] And probably, as much as anything, the societal noise of those tumultuous years (race, class, reds, un-American, New Deal, FDR, Daddy Grace, and so on) blocked full receipt of the message. In the end, other groups and other perspectives competed successfully for the ear of Norfolk blacks.

The eventual drowning out of the Communists was related to the inability of Wright and others to fuse the struggles in the workplace and in the home sphere. When the Communist party failed to translate street-corner successes into workplace victories, and when the efforts of CIO organizers exposed the raw nerve of race in an urban-industrial context, many found comfort in the older social equation. Eventually, black citizens turned to more established alternatives. Nonetheless, the radicals and their followers had a significant impact on the restructuring of intergroup social relations by calling for the inclusion of blacks in the working class and by challenging the benefits of maintaining the status quo.

## PURSUING WORKPLACE ADVANCEMENT

When Congress passed the National Industrial Recovery Act (NIRA) in 1933, establishing legal sanction for union organization and collective bargaining in various industries, local radicals found their entry into the workplace. It proved to be a misguided step, however. Initially they stumbled, and then they completely faltered. In the end, a combination of poor tactical decisions, conflict within the ranks of labor, and the saliency of race undermined the attempt to successfully wed the workplace and the home sphere and balance the social equation. By 1938 the Communists had lost their position in the workplace and their base in the community.

Communist organizers began their foray into the work force with a pitch to longshoremen. Alexander Wright, long a local spokesperson for the Unemployed Council and the Communist party, organized a local of disgruntled dockworkers under the banner of the Marine Workers Industrial Union (MWIU). Its avowed purpose was simple: "The Marine Workers Industrial Union is organized to unite all workers in the Marine industry and lead them in their struggles against the employers for better working and living conditions and for the ultimate freedom from wage slavery."[32]

Local members and national leaders often heard Wright expound on a variation of this theme. At a National Recovery Administration (NRA) hearing in January 1934, Wright linked conditions in the home sphere to conditions in the workplace. The NRA regulated prices and wages in most basic industries. Wright feared that the agency was not prepared to go far enough to ameliorate conditions. Commenting on the situation in the area, he joked, "In Hampton Roads, Virginia, when the Blue Eagle stepped in the Bald Eagle flew out." His sarcastic reference to the symbol of the NRA, the Blue Eagle, drew both laughter and applause from the audience. But Wright wanted to be sure people understood that the MWIU's purpose was serious. He warned, "We are organized for only one thing—that is—struggle." Driving home the point, he continued, "We wrote the code in ink, and we wrote it with the intention of writing it in strikes. There is no use of being afraid to die, because we are not living anyhow." This last refrain brought even more applause from the audience.[33] It also put the MWIU in conflict with the ILA, which dominated the port.

Three months after Wright issued his proclamation, MWIU officials presented a list of demands to officials at six shipping lines. Union members demanded an eight-hour day and wages of sixty cents per hour, with time and a half for overtime. They also demanded that the companies, with assistance from the federal government, pay waterfront workers full relief and unemployment benefits. In addition, they wanted the wages of railroad gangs restored and speed-ups and abusive language eliminated. Perhaps most important, union officials wanted the companies to recognize the MWIU as the coastwide dockworkers' bargaining agent.

The union issued its demands on 30 April 1934, setting in motion its own demise. Three days later, nearly 90 percent of the 1,005 employees at Buxton, Merchant and Miners, Philadelphia and Norfolk, Chesapeake Bay, Seaboard and Portsmouth, and Southern Portsmouth shipping lines walked off their jobs. Company officials responded by calling in the police, who arrested nearly fifty striking workers for loitering and failing to heed the police directive to "move on." Working in concert, the companies hired four hundred scabs, most of them white, to replace the strikers. Afterward, Wright charged the companies with transforming what was essentially an employer-employee confrontation into a racial issue.[34] He knew all too well that this technique threatened any chance of real breakthroughs in interracial labor relations.

Neither the companies nor the police posed the greatest hindrance to the striking MWIU unionists, however. (Not all of the men who answered the call to strike actually joined the union.) More detrimental was the ILA's refusal to support the strike, despite Wright's claim that they "had the ships owners [sic] licked until the city decided to interfere and use the police force and the patrol wagons as strike-breaking machinery."

Since 1917, the majority of the Hampton Roads longshoremen had belonged to the ILA, generally considered the preeminent labor organization in the area. The success of any waterfront strike depended on ILA cooperation, which in this instance was denied. The ILA, backed by the Waterfront Council it dominated, actually offered to supply workers to the shipping lines being struck. It viewed the MWIU as "a dual organization to the ILA," one to which "no allegiance" was owed, because it was not "affiliated with the American Federation of Labor."[35]

Given these circumstances, the MWIU ended the strike a few days after it began. Wright described the decision as a "temporary retreat," but it was much more. The union disappeared from the local scene later that year. Wright's insistence that the strike had been merely a "dress rehearsal" proved to be nothing but hyperbole.[36]

On balance, the entire episode produced more minuses than pluses. Nearly a third of the workers who went on strike were not immediately recalled to work; some undoubtedly lost their jobs permanently. This somewhat misguided attempt both dampened the spirits of the dissident longshoremen and exposed the fragility of their power. The companies knew that the MWIU lacked critical resources and could not stop work on the docks. They realized too that the conflict between the MWIU and the ILA made the latter an ally of management; in fact, ILA officials seemed more than willing to thwart any future threat to labor peace.

Nonetheless, the strike marked the first time that a union had attempted to alter the meaning of race and class in the workplace, although the structure of the labor market meant that all the MWIU members were black. Previous labor groups such as the TWA had manifested a basic philosophy that subordinated class and elevated race; instead of being a worker, one was a *black* worker. But, as the radicals countered at a mass rally on Sunday, 6 May 1934, only days after the strike, the issues were not unique either to blacks or to whites—they were workers' issues.

Joseph Benson, a white speaker at the rally and a secretary of the local International Labor Defense (ILD), grandly suggested that the strikers might have achieved their demands if they had garnered the unwavering support of most laboring whites and Negroes. Despite the best efforts of earnest organizers, however, black and white workers generally did not make the connections between their racial interests and their collective interests; they were still too acutely aware of their places in the political economy. In this instance, many saw the MWIU strikers only as disgruntled longshoremen who had grown disenchanted with the ILA's conservatism. (Unwittingly, perhaps, the *Norfolk Journal and Guide* fed this view. Highly critical of a May Day speech by James Ford, which it believed had precipitated the ill-fated strike, the newspaper at the same time recognized the limits of current ILA policy and questioned the union's conservative posture, given the times.) Therefore, the strikers and their seven hundred supporters who gathered in Barraud Park as Wright, Benson, and others harangued the ILA, the "bosses," and the "capitalist press" were in many ways exceptional.[37]

With the passage of the Wagner Act in 1935, which guaranteed labor's right to bargain collectively, the newly founded Congress of Industrial Organizations (CIO) became the latest entrant in the workplace struggle. In Norfolk, several plants and industries experienced the organizing efforts of the CIO. Even ILA Local 978 became a CIO affiliate in 1938. Rank-and-file dissension had been brewing for some time before the members ousted international vice-president George Milner, local president David Alston, and two other union leaders in 1934. Thereafter, the local struggled to maintain its identity as an ILA affiliate, particularly after Milner and Alston succeeded in forming rival Local 1442. Thus, when it was approached by the CIO, Local 978 jumped at an opportunity to escape ILA control.[38]

CIO organizers successfully organized box makers at the Farmco Company, fertilizer workers, and peanut workers at the Planters Company in Suffolk. By the end of the Second World War, the CIO had even organized a local at the *Norfolk Journal and Guide.* Although blacks constituted a majority of the workers in these industries, the CIO made it clear that it was racially inclusive. In this respect, the organization tendered an organizing perspective closely resembling that of the Communists. Moreover, the ascendancy of the CIO put pressure on the more conservative AFL to actively recruit blacks, which culminated in the 1940s in new and lasting examples of labor solidarity.[39]

At the same time, many wondered if interracial labor solidarity might cost blacks the autonomy that allowed them to act in their own interests. Nowhere is this clearer than in the conflict between the Finkelstein Company and organizers for the Amalgamated Clothing Workers of America (ACWA), an AFL affiliate soon to become a charter CIO union. Finkelstein was a major employer of black labor. At the start of the Depression, nearly two hundred black women and men worked for the company, although they had a precarious position in its labor structure. Purposely restricted to the least skilled and lowest-paying jobs, they routinely became the first fired during periods of economic contraction.[40] In theory, union affiliation promised the job security they lacked, but their tenuous hold on these all-important industrial jobs made them cautious.

Afro-Americans worried that their white counterparts were not prepared to accept them in the world of the working class, and the union's early actions failed to erase their apprehensions. When Jacob Potofsky, vice-president of ACWA, came to Norfolk in 1934 to organize Finkelstein's, the workers had only a weak, largely meaningless company union with an open shop. On hearing of the ACWA's intentions, company officials threatened to bolt the area. Hailing from New York City, the plant's owners knew all too well that ACWA president Sidney Hillman had successfully orchestrated the organization of similar plants throughout the Northeast. They could only hope that conservative impulses would dampen the enthusiasm for a union in Norfolk. In the meantime, union officials made their intentions clear: they would not leave until all workers joined the union.[41]

Almost immediately, the union faced the problem of organizing a plant in a racially divided city. Allegations surfaced that certain whites refused to join a racially integrated body. Black women sensed an ominous scenario unfolding. Union officials intimated that they planned to support union members at all costs. Thus, if whites succeeded in excluding blacks from the union, and if the union succeeded in controlling the plant, some blacks feared, unionization could mean losing their jobs. As a result, they reacted coolly to the union's overtures. Most of the black women realized that jobs at Finkelstein's constituted their only real alternative to domestic service, especially since the closure of American Cigar. The union worked to overcome the women's doubts about the efficacy of unionization. On one occasion, Ruth Thornton, a black organizer from Philadelphia, came to town to address the women. She assured those gathered that the union sincerely desired to include them and their ideas.[42] Her appearance did little to assuage their fears, however.

In part, their reticence reflected a hesitation to join what to them was a dubious organization, one called Communist by plant manager Irving Lyons. The reluctance also reflected the campaign of coercion and intimidation undertaken by management, which increased when the U.S. Supreme Court ruled the NRA unconstitutional. For several months, while the NRA lay in abeyance and the Wagner Act awaited ratification, the company stepped up its efforts to drive the union out. Its primary objective became to "get rid of all bad eggs" who identified or associated with the ACWA. Workers were kept under constant surveillance at home and at work. Those seen talking to union officials, regardless of the locale, frequently lost their jobs; others received a strongly worded personal reprimand from the plant manager. These tactics, plus the presence of police in and around the plant, hampered recruitment efforts.[43]

Although the issue of race never disappeared, union organizers quickly turned to other concerns. From their perspective, the company's recalcitrance stemmed from a deep-seated antiunion sentiment. In response, the union went on the offensive, presenting the company with a new list of demands. Its leadership argued for guarantees that the NRA wage scale would be maintained, that thirty-six hours would constitute a full work week, that reemployment preference after a layoff would be given to union members, that work would be divided as practically as possible between all workers, and that the company would recognize ACWA Local 92 and the Norfolk Central Labor Union (CLU) as the employees' collective bargaining agent. This list represented a backing away from the initial request that the company reinstate all employees discharged for alleged union activity. In an attempt to show good faith, the union promised that "there shall be no strikes or lockouts during the life of the agreement, or any renewal thereof." In the event conflict arose, the union promised to allow a jointly approved third party to serve as arbiter.[44]

When he received the proposal, Finkelstein reiterated his threat to suspend his company's operations in Norfolk. He indicated it was not unions he opposed but the ACWA. He expressed a willingness to meet with William Green of the AFL, but those meetings proved unfruitful. Thus the ACWA, with CLU support, issued strike orders for the second week in August. Meanwhile, Ed Pickler, head of the local CLU, arranged for his body to have Finkelstein's name added to the national "unfair to labor" list.[45]

For black workers like Solomon Skinner and Edward Smith, the strike offered an opportunity to be part of the union's decision-making unit. Unlike black women, black men had allied with the union early on. In fact, they were conspicuous among Labor Day marchers who praised the advantages of belonging to the ACWA.[46] But neither they nor the black women who remained cool to unionization could control attempts to use them as pawns.

Hoping to divide the workers and break the union, company officials charged the union with encouraging race mingling on the picket lines and elsewhere. To the union's credit, it refused to back away from the position that equal pay and equal protection should be afforded every worker, regardless of race. The union contended that the company introduced race to deflect attention from the central issue, union representation. Black longshoremen who supported the strikers concurred, as did prominent residents, both blacks and whites.[47]

Company officials remained adamantly opposed to the unionization of their plant, but it became increasingly clear that they would have little choice. The passage of the Wagner Act and the constant presence of the Regional Labor Board and the U.S. Conciliation Service assured the ACWA of eventual success if the workers supported the union. Moreover, unlike the Communists, who vilified the government, ACWA leaders importuned the government to force the company to abide by the law. They also allied themselves with the local labor establishment, particularly the powerful Central Labor Union. And they played their

trump card—a strike—only at the last possible moment. Because they
had local labor support, cooperation from the government, and only a
weak in-house union as opposition, the strike worked to their benefit. To
ensure victory, union members picketed, held rallies, and bombarded
management with proposals. This highly visible campaign finally produced the desired result, union recognition.[48]

The victory also uncovered a split between the black leadership class
and those blacks who worked for an integrated union. George Streator,
a former assistant of W. E. B. Du Bois, worked for the ACWA in the
Finkelstein case. He maintained that Norfolk's leading black businessman—a thinly disguised reference to P. B. Young—opposed the unionization of the garment workers because he knew the precedent could affect management policies at his own company. Streator even went a step
further in his criticism, claiming that Young used race to prevent effective social change.[49]

Streator's assessment of Young was no doubt correct in the particu-
lars, but, as Du Bois informed him, he missed the larger issue.[50] Genu-
ine color-blind unionism meant that blacks became invisible. A reading
of the ACWA's involvement in Norfolk reveals that the union was not
anti-black. But neither was it pro-black. Its agenda called for the unionization of all workers in the garment industry. The organization of
blacks therefore depended on their presence in a particular plant. Nothing the union said or did, notwithstanding Streator's own philosophy, led
workers of either race to assume that workplace solidarity extended to
the home sphere. Moreover, the urban environment in which the plant
and the union operated could not accommodate such a belief system. A
color-blind workers' movement helped to actualize the Communists' earliest aspirations; but it also transformed the class and race dynamic in a
manner few black Norfolkians found comfortable.

## A TIME TO REFLECT AND REGROUP

During the second half of the 1930s, black residents struggled to reconcile the new changes with old philosophies and approaches. What unfolded contributed further to the restructuring of intraracial and interracial social relations. Before 1935, few had time to ponder the long-
term consequences of what the radicals and their black supporters
prescribed. This changed at mid-decade. The shift was neither swift nor
complete, however. Residual allegiance to the new orientation remained, as indicated by Rev. Harvey Johnson's address to delegates attending the seventy-third annual meeting of the Norfolk Baptist Union:

> Class hatred with its offspring of ostracism, segregation, Jim Crowism, etc.
> will be driven to the background, and people will move freely among

themselves, without class hate or rancor, and the equal rights of all men will be defended before the law and equal opportunities will be afforded all on the grounds of a common brotherhood.[51]

Yet some blacks began to murmur that few whites had changed their views that greatly. Depression conditions exacerbated rather than lessened interracial conflict in the home sphere, even as they increased workplace solidarity. With impunity, white toughs attacked black schoolchildren who journeyed through Brambleton on their way to school. In 1934 working-class whites, joined by members of the white middle class, attacked two black families who had moved into apartments on West Olney Road. These whites seemed intent on stopping changes in residential patterns that threatened to bring blacks to the border of one of the more comfortable white neighborhoods.[52]

Nor could blacks expect much assistance from the city government. Eight years after the purchase of Barraud Farm for parkland, the park remained relatively underdeveloped. And, to the consternation of most blacks, including Alexander Wright (who in 1936 garnered several hundred votes as the Communist party's congressional candidate), the city council passed a bus segregation ordinance. Wright denounced the law as "unconstitutional" and "uncivilized" and one bound to inconvenience blacks disproportionately. City officials responded that it was an extension of the state and local laws requiring racial separation on streetcars.[53]

Other events, meanwhile, unveiled the grand distance between the world some advocated and the one in which Norfolk residents operated. Since the codification of the first law delineating the role of blacks, Afro-Americans had occupied a particular but ever-evolving place in society. In time, they gained the rights and privileges of citizenship, which also gave them the power to challenge the existing order. Norfolk blacks had long understood this and agitated on behalf of improvements in the home sphere. But there was an irony: black residents adopted as allies members of the white elite. Although these upper-class whites accepted the right of blacks to ask for improvements, they firmly adhered to the doctrine of civility. This urban paternalism based on amicable race relations proved to be as limiting for blacks as the frontal attacks of the white working class, for it had as its foundation interracial coalitions that protected white interests.[54]

Because Norfolk was sandwiched between the Chesapeake Bay and the Atlantic Ocean, the last thing whites worried about was a beachfront. Blacks, however, imparted great significance to an article that appeared in the first edition of the 1930 *Journal and Guide*. The headline read: "Norfolk's Christmas Gift to Her Citizens." After searching for several years, members of the Interracial Commission and the city council had found a site for a Negro city beach: eleven miles of waterfront property owned by the Pennsylvania Railroad in the Little Creek section, several miles from the city's core.[55]

The brash optimism of one week faded the next, however, dulled by racial politics in a Jim Crow city. Opposition from segments of the white working-class population, particularly those who owned property near or adjacent to the proposed beach site, surfaced almost as soon as the council's decision became public. This opposition resurrected memories of other hotly debated civic issues, such as the selection of Barraud Park and the location of Booker T. Washington High School. White residents such as R. W. Turner charged that the beach would lower the property values of whites living nearby in Ocean View. Others screamed that the "beautiful shore drive [would] become a spectacle." Representatives of white business even opposed the beach as unfair public-sector competition. Some wondered aloud if blacks actually deserved a publicly financed beach, given that they paid "only negligible taxes." And others prefaced their comments with the patronizing refrain, "We have nothing against our darkies," and then told the fifteen hundred people who had gathered to debate the beach proposal that the city should "give them another spot, isolated, and segregated."[56]

To the dismay of the power brokers, both black and white, who had selected the site, opposition continued for nearly two years. On several occasions, the council reaffirmed its belief that this site was preferable to any other, and especially to none at all. Nonetheless, whites campaigned for public office on the strength of their opposition to the beach site. One trio—Burkard, Shultie, and Wilson—promised to use the fourteen thousand dollars earmarked for the project to improve the streets in the black community. (Civic improvements continued to lag behind the city's promises.) The typically unflappable P. B. Young responded that blacks were tired of whites who ignorantly spoke in the so-called best interests of blacks. He admonished the three to demonstrate their sincerity by offering to "sell the bathing beach and golf links at Ocean View . . . purchased at the city's expense for white people, and convert the proceeds to the paving of streets and the improvement of sanitary conditions for all people of Norfolk, whites and blacks."[57]

The three ignored Young's request. They lost the election, but the opposition intensified. In 1932 white opponents obtained an injunction prohibiting the city from taking control of the property from the railroad company. Foes of the beach accused the city of violating the terms of a 1930 ordinance when it agreed to renegotiate. Under the original terms, Norfolk paid the company fourteen thousand dollars, and, in return, the company deeded the city more than fourteen acres of land. Under a new proposed arrangement, the city would use ten acres, and the company would retain four acres for future dredging purposes. Enemies of the project argued that the new terms voided the original contract, and they sought an injunction to prevent the company from cashing the city's check. Circuit Court Judge O. L. Shackleford, substituting for Judge Allan R. Hanckel, granted the injunction. Upon his return, however, Hanckel overturned the decision, and the group indicated that it planned no further appeals.[58]

Frustrated by the delays and the public acrimony and fearful that the Depression would undercut the city's ability to pay for the project, the council had actually voted a month before this last-ditch attempt to withdraw its earlier appropriation. But, following the urging of many prominent citizens of both races, the council reversed itself. The fortuitous creation of the federal Civil Works Administration (CWA), which had monies for such civic ventures, made the decision easier. By June 1935, a modest city beach existed for Norfolk's forty-five thousand black residents.[59]

In dramatic fashion, the beach episode raised gnawing questions about the strategy for empowerment. Was it foolish for blacks to ally with whites in the workplace when those same whites opposed the creation of a beach? Was it any wiser to ally with upper-class whites who demanded acquiescence to paternalism in interracial dealings? Did acting in a manner dictated by others detour blacks from attaining the power they really sought? How could they use race, class, and power to their advantage? These questions commanded center stage as the community reflected on the changes and plotted future initiatives.

In addition to raising strategic questions, the beach episode once again placed blacks in the ironic position of abetting those who believed in the necessity of segregation. Many realized the irony in demanding equal rights by seeking a segregated beach. But, as one resident knowingly admitted at a gathering of blacks, in seeking power blacks sometimes had to do what seemingly contradicted their interests because in the long run it in fact served their interests:

> That little strip of sand is not very important—in fact, in principle I am opposed to it—but what is important is this—it is a symbol of the taking of justice from us. We should not have to submit to segregation for the sake of peace and then submit to the taking of this substitute for justice from us.[60]

In an urban setting where blacks lacked a bloc vote to barter with, such contradictions abounded.

Over the next few years, residents took further stock of their place in the political economy, and, as they did, they attempted to arrest their political impotence. Although robbed of surplus income by the Depression, many still managed to pay the poll tax and qualify to vote. The UNIA even encouraged its shrinking following to pay the tax. Of course, some who could pay refused, insisting "that they [wouldn't] pay $1.50 just for the privilege of voting for some white man." Others paid the tax but would not vote, for similar reasons. Overall, fewer paid in 1931 than had paid in 1927. Once the economy recovered, so did the number of registrants, which totaled more than fifteen hundred by 1936. Although the next downturn produced a drop in this figure, the 1940 total nevertheless approached the 1927 level of twelve hundred.[61] Perhaps equally interesting, many of those who paid the poll tax, both in the 1920s and the 1930s, came from the laboring classes—primarily laborers and domestics.

The powerful yet insidious expectations of civility created even greater problems. Although by this time white power brokers realized that it was in their vested interest to appoint blacks to parallel civic committees, and although blacks sought to serve on those committees, whites remained uncomfortable with blacks who presumed to influence civic affairs. When Rev. W. M. Harris, pastor of Grace Episcopal and an important member of the local black leadership, wrote to Lawrence Oxley, head of the Division of Negro Labor at the U.S. Labor Department, about appointing a black to the Virginia State Employment Service, he realized he had crossed the threshold of acceptable public behavior. The diffident Harris pleaded, "Please regard this letter as confidential as far as my name is concerned because I am not supposed to have certain political contacts and I mean this especially as far as any local people are concerned."[62] Such schooled caution diluted the potential political power the franchise might have produced.

By 1936 this caution had split the leadership elite into opposing political camps. After a long, troubled affiliation with the Republican party, black citizens in 1928 had begun a slow but eventually complete switch to the Democrats. In 1936 most of those in the black-dominated Twenty-First Precinct voted for Franklin Roosevelt. Established black leaders such as P. B. Young, Dr. Frank Coppage, and attorney J. Eugene Diggs in turn allied with the Citizens' Democratic League, which had close ties to the state Democratic political machine run by U.S. senators Harry Byrd and Carter Glass. Called the "Administration" forces in local parlance, this black group also included Helen Dancy, a social worker and head of the Negro Women's Democratic Club, which was the women's auxiliary of the Colored Citizens' Democratic Club.[63]

Opposed to this group were members of the Independent Democratic League, headed by Jerry O. Gilliam and I. Ione Diggs. Gilliam stood in direct contrast to the cautious, taciturn Young. Dark-complexioned, jovial, a railway mail clerk, past head of the National Alliance of Postal Employees union, Grand Exalted Leader of the Eureka Lodge of Elks, and president of the local NAACP branch, Gilliam was most comfortable with working-class blacks and saw himself as their advocate. He maintained that "college-bred boys are self-seeking and ambitious in a personal way." Likewise, Diggs, who abhorred the civility that governed both social and electoral politics in Norfolk, saw the Administration forces as too wedded to that approach. An administrator of a public assistance program, she was both secretary of the NAACP and president of the Negro Women's auxiliary to the Independent Democratic League. Her activities on behalf of the IWO and the CIO in Norfolk caused her to be branded a radical in certain quarters. Both Gilliam and Diggs encouraged blacks to strike an independent political course, to agitate if they wanted change, and to refrain from buying where they could not work.[64]

Despite the strong opposition, the Administration forces dominated local affairs. They preferred coalition politics, although for blacks such alliances bore a certain price. Ostensibly, for example, the beach proposal had grown out of the concern expressed by members of the Interracial Commission over conditions "inimical to the health and well-being of our Negro population, and militating against peaceable relations between the two races."[65] At the same time, Louis Jaffe, editor of the *Virginian-Pilot* and one of the South's leading white moderates, informed L. W. Windholz, chairman of the Public Works Committee, that Little Creek got the nod over other locations because it met certain requirements. He advised Windholz: "There is need for a permanent solution of the Negro Beach problem[:] a bay front tract reasonably accessible, separated from white developments, as far as possible, by natural barriers, and wholly immune from the mutations of real estate demand and caprice of speculators. The Little Creek tract . . . alone meets these requirements." Jaffe appeared impervious to the problems caused by the beach's geographic distance from the hub of the black community (see Map 3). His public denunciations of lynching, of the KKK, and of the media's penchant to cast all blacks as criminals make it hard to impugn all of his motives. Yet without question his proposal enabled the white leadership to maintain the social advantage that segregation brought without giving up the moral high ground.[66] Such was the price paid by blacks who relied on civility and coalition politics with the white elite.

## COMPETING NOISES

As the decade matured, the black community pulled further and further away from the world envisioned by the radicals. The New Deal, which redefined the relationship between the individual and the state, accounted for part of the retreat. In other instances, Afro-Americans

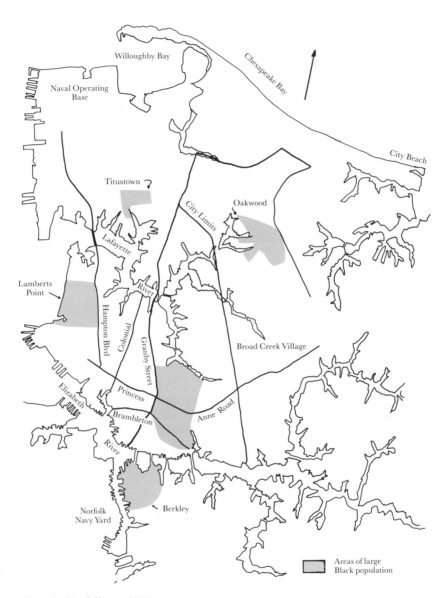

Map. 3. Norfolk, ca. 1935

turned to the sacred for protection from the secular or were lured by
worldly plans for salvation. Essentially, few crossed the racial divide. The
Communists were dangerous, some argued, for believing that interracial
relations were changing or could change. Increasingly, Norfolk Afro-
Americans countered that they did not live in a raceless and classless

society, but rather in an urban-industrial society in which they remained racial ethnics in every sphere.

The refocusing of efforts took on a class character within the black community. Black ministers led the retreat. When Marjorie Wyatt, the white assistant director of the Federal Emergency Relief Administration, asked ministers for their assistance in stopping the daily parade of Communist-led unemployed workers seeking relief, both the Baptist and the AME associations pledged to tell their congregations to turn away from the radicals. Rev. W. M. Harris of Grace Episcopal Church summarized the sentiment of most of the clergy when he counseled that what the Negro worker needed was more "efficiency" and "not Communism."[67]

Similarly, the executive committee of the local NAACP, whose national body was the nemesis of the International Labor Defense, voted ten to three to withhold support from a united campaign to free Robert Lee Johnson, a black man who faced life in prison for murdering a white police officer and whose case the ILD had taken on. Although the membership of the local NAACP branch questioned the authority of the executive committee to decide such a delicate matter, the decision stood. After being denied NAACP assistance, the ILD and its allies assailed their adversary. Alexander Wright blasted the NAACP as the "National Association for the Advancement of Certain People." With total antipathy, he charged that "the NAACP is merely a reformist organization, and it is willing to lick the boots of the bosses."[68] On the first count, he was correct; but the second was a shrill sign of desperation.

Sure of the continued integrity of their community base, opposition leaders grew more recalcitrant toward the Communists as the Depression continued. At the suggestion of David Alston, local ILA leader, organizers barred the radicals from taking part in the annual Emancipation Proclamation commemoration. The committee defended its position in a public statement:

> The Norfolk Emancipation Association is made up of delegates from various fraternal, civic, benevolent, social, and religious organizations and individuals who can join for the sum of 25 cents a year. It is not the object of the association to let any group use it in any way to espouse anything that will bring disrepute or mar the record that has been established over a period of 72 years.[69]

Such sentiment capsulized the growing objection to the Communists and their message. To many, the new radicals produced unwanted trepidation, and leaders responded by ostracizing them.

Some of the black residents who never fully identified with the Communist party and its philosophy found their own heroes, who offered them a salvation secular movements could not. In Harlem, Afro-

Americans hard-hit by the Depression flocked to Father Divine. In Norfolk and the Hampton Roads area, others embraced the theology of Bishop Charles Emmanuel "Sweet Daddy" Grace. Known throughout the Eastern seaboard simply as Daddy Grace, the bishop attracted an uncommon number of working-class folks to his United House of Prayer. Some estimate that during the 1930s his following soared to several hundred thousand nationwide.[70]

The Norfolk House of Prayer sat squarely in the heart of the black community. Located at the corner of Church Street and Seventeenth Street, it was easily accessible to the crowds who gathered when Daddy Grace came to town. Susan J. and her daughter attended some of those services. As Susan's daughter recalled, her mother liked the atmosphere, even though she was not "holy and sanctified." To the young girl, the pageantry—from the red, white, and blue building to the attendants fanning Daddy Grace to the vocal demonstrations of the congregants—satisfied her thirst for entertainment and contrasted with the humdrum days of the Depression.[71]

Numerous commentators argue that Daddy Grace's House of Prayer movement was simply a cult, one that drew its following from the ranks of the poor and dispossessed. Scholars similarly viewed Father Divine, the other Depression-era religious personality, before Robert Weisbrot rescued him from permanent historical caricature. Black Americans identified with Divine (who also had an interracial following) and Grace because of what they symbolized. It is true that Grace lacked a plan for solving vexing urban ills, but for thousands of blacks Daddy Grace offered hope that provided a two- to three-hour respite from the daily struggle. Moreover, Grace embodied all that capitalism promised: prosperity, wealth, conspicuous consumption, lavish consumerism. Against the sobering backdrop of unemployment, he interjected a vibrant image of America, all wrapped in red, white, and blue. The American colors became his colors because he firmly believed in the structure as it existed. For all his pomp, Grace represented a conservative alternative to the Communists, one rooted in the Afro-American religious tradition. He appealed to what Jerry Gilliam charged was a conservative tendency among the masses.[72]

Others ignored both the radicals and the not-so-radical. They entrusted a better life to fate or to the "poor man's stock market." Early in the Depression years, numbers playing began to increase. Local moralists castigated black residents for succumbing to this debilitating urban vice, and the police publicized crackdowns, but the *Norfolk Journal and Guide* constantly included ads enticing people to wager their spare change.[73]

A few others tapped a thriving underground economy, abandoning the idea that legitimate means would alleviate their despair. According to the testimony of a few longtime residents, bellhops and others at prominent white hotels subsidized their earnings by working as panderers. Earnings from prostitution and bootleg whiskey filled the pockets of quite a few.[74] Thus vice, games of chance, and religion—not the Communist party or the CIO—served as primary reference points for many. For these individuals, the most pressing issue was not home sphere development or workplace advancement, but survival.

Relief and reform programs implemented by the Roosevelt administration also lured some away from radical alternatives. Blacks were the primary beneficiaries of the Federal Emergency Relief Administration and its successor, the WPA. They found jobs at Civilian Conservation Corps camps and got a city beach through funding from the Civil Works Administration, a city hospital courtesy of Public Works Administration monies, and a sixty-thousand-dollar appropriation from the WPA to improve Booker T. Washington High School's physical plant. In addition, the 1935 passage of the Wagner Act encouraged the CIO to organize blacks in several previously unorganized industries.[75] In short, many gains realized during the 1930s came from federal sponsorship.

As a result, blacks hesitantly turned to Roosevelt. Initial reaction to the president and his new programs had ranged from lukewarm endorsement to outright hostility. At first, many blacks questioned his motives, arguing that he went out of his way to appease southern whites. Others charged that instead of promoting relief, recovery, and reform, New Deal programs promoted racism. Consequently, the national black community viewed many early programs as detrimental. The National Recovery Administration, created to set price controls for most industries, was derogatorily labeled the Negro Removal Act.[76]

Many black Norfolkians, struggling to stay employed and remain in business, agreed with the barb. When federal standards forced an increase in wages, white restaurateurs and hotel owners replaced formerly lower-paid porters, waiters, dishwashers, and other service personnel with whites. Other unskilled workers were similarly threatened. Black entrepreneurs, bound by the same standards, considered bankruptcy or willful violation of the law, because they lacked the capital to compete with whites. In the past, this fear of pending insolvency had fueled their pleas for blacks to "buy black."

Tension between black-owned and white-owned cleaning establishments, which had already reached a boiling point even before the NRA introduced a uniform pay scale, illustrated the mood in the black community. For some time, white cleaners had complained that black operators undermined the market by charging less for their services. The feud culminated in an ugly incident, repudiated afterward by many white operators. A group of whites approached C. P. Ricks and F. R. Scott, two black cleaners, and warned them that if they did not raise their prices, they would be assaulted. Other intimidation followed. Customers patronizing the black establishments often received parking tickets, and ads the businesses placed in white dailies were doctored to proclaim that specials were for "colored only."[77]

Given the intense nature of the competition, many blacks found the NRA's decision to standardize wages and rates for services without race-specific differentials both disheartening and potentially devastating. In a letter to Hugh S. Johnson, head of the NRA, black cleaner Henry Dolphin summarized the prevailing sentiment:

According to the reports as published in the daily press, it appears that complaints have been filed by a group of white dry cleaners in the city of Norfolk, Virginia, against colored people similarly enganged [sic] in the said city. . . .

The fact is, there is no correlativity between the two groups; each having resided in separate and distinct social, religious, industrial and economic worlds for ages past.

It is an undisputed fact that the Negro resides in a separate world; more especially is this so South of the Mason and Dixon Line. The colored dry cleaner, in this instance now in conflict, cannot occupy business premises in a neighborhood inhabited exclusively by white people—hence, we find him among his own people in his own locality, endeavoring to take advantage of his opportunity to improve his industrial status and contribute toward the solution of his economic problems. His charges for services rendered are less and of right ought to be so, since the wages received by his patrons—the colored neighbor—are likewise less in proportion to the wages paid the white neighbors.

Again, from the standpoint of competition, there is and cannot be any real competition between the white and colored dry cleaners in the city of Norfolk, Virginia. The white dry cleaners occupy premises in localities where colored people dare not loiter; while the colored cleaners are struggling to eke out a mere existence. . . .

If there is any just cause for complaint, then it seems to lie on the part and on behalf of the colored cleaners against the white cleaners cited, those prices are alleged to be the same as that charged by the colored cleaners.

It is to be wondered if there is not just one spot of sunshine for the colored American to enjoy. . . . They are forced to ride, eat, drink, walk, worship, and to do everything separate and apart from the white American; and this is constitutional. It therefore logically follows, (despite the fact that colored residential districts are overwhelmingly invaded and overrun by white and oriental business concerns which occupy the most advantageous points) that it would be unconstitutional to force the colored man into a fictitious equality of competition with a neighboring businessman whose district he is prohibited by law and custom to invade except as a servant.

> There can be no fairness in a competitive bargain where the opportunities are inequal [sic]; the result will ultimately be the rooting out of the struggling colored businessman, and the damning of his ambitious spirit as a true American, seeking to be self-supporting in working out his economic salvation and determining the future of his generations to come.

The letter was signed "Yours with much respect, Henry D. Dolphin."[78]

Dolphin's eloquence, his outrage, and his viewpoint explain why some found comfort in the old design for empowerment rather than the new. Before blacks could fully embrace a new perspective, they needed some sign that whites had reformed their belief systems. Nothing gave Dolphin reason to believe this had happened. As always, blacks and whites lived in two separate and unequal worlds. Under these conditions, class could not be elevated to a position alongside race. White cleaners and black cleaners, after all, shared a class similarity that disappeared because of race.

Other examples of discrimination, both real and perceived, reinforced long-held views that race defined Afro-Americans' place in the city. Barbers, for example, complained loudly and frequently throughout the 1930s about a new state law requiring licenses. They viewed certification as a thinly veiled attempt to eliminate them from the trade, a justified suspicion, for other means, legal and extralegal, had worked to reduce the number of black barbers elsewhere. In another instance, local WPA officials closed sewing rooms in the area, forcing the black women workers who sought to maintain their WPA benefits onto the streets as garbage collectors. Norfolk blacks reacted with horror at the prospect of "their" women digging ditches and hauling trash like men. Then word surfaced that white women had replaced the black women in the sewing rooms. This discovery erased any doubt that Norfolk was a Jim Crow city and that race, more than anything else, determined one's place in the social order.[79]

Other events both reinforced this conclusion and suggested alternatives. A major debate over the possible appointment of the first black police officer since Reconstruction dominated community discussions for a time. A crime wave, centered primarily in the black community, gripped the city in 1939. The situation became intolerable, and a delegation approached the city about hiring a black officer to patrol the worst areas. A group of citizens even promised to pay the officer's salary. Despite the support of several prominent white individuals and groups, including the Central Labor Union, the city refused.[80]

Later that year, Ernest Wright attempted to take the civil service exam to become a police officer. Although no city or state law gave it the authorization to do so, the Civil Service Commission barred black applicants. Feeling that his civil rights had been violated, Wright sued the city. During the trial, commissioners admitted a racial bar existed but defended their actions as being in the best interest of good race relations. The commissioners had an underlying doubt about the suitability of black police, even in black districts, they claimed. Discrimination, they quickly added, had little to do with their position. As proof, they pointed to black women who had been hired as clerks. Circuit Court Judge Luther B. Way thought otherwise. He ruled that the city's policy violated the Fourteenth Amendment's equal protection clause. Way ordered the city to administer a test to Wright forthwith, one that was "substantially the same" as that given recent white applicants.[81] The city abided by the order but found other means of barring black police officers.

Wright's efforts were not wasted, however. His initiative marked a turning point in the battle for empowerment. Slowly, more and more Afro-Americans made a connection between progress in the workplace and in the home sphere. But the way in which that understanding took public form marked a major departure. Throughout much of the industrial period, the working class played the central role in linking the two spheres. Now, in Norfolk, another scenario unfolded. First, the principals came from the upper end of the status-based class scale: police and teachers. Second, the goal was never to form a broad-based interracial or ethnic coalition, but rather to gain advantages for the black community; toward this end, the goal translated into a struggle for equal opportunity. Third, although the influence of the radicals was unmistakable, the new protests had an Afro-American resonance. Voice was extremely important, because in using their own symbols and vocabulary, blacks began the awkward but necessary step critical to a permanent restructuring of social relations. This step enabled them to take the next journey, one that more fully combined advancement in the workplace and the home sphere. The battle of the Norfolk Teachers Association for equal pay illustrates the subtlety—and the importance—of this change.

## TOWARD EMPOWERMENT: MODIFYING THE FORMULA

Norfolk, like most cities in the South, paid white teachers more than it paid black teachers. Throughout most of the 1930s, few people publicly questioned this arrangement. Many whites agreed with W. H. Venable, a prominent white attorney:

> It is not a new thing, or an accidental happening, that white teachers are paid higher salaries than Negro teachers in Virginia. . . . The white tax-payers of Virginia have cheerfully borne the heavy burden and appropri-

ated many millions of dollars from taxes paid by them for the education of Negro boys and girls since 1865. The white teachers have cheerfully carried part of the burden, although these large expenditures have kept down their pay.

To Venable, a recent demand to raise the salaries of black teachers to the level of the salaries paid whites was rash. "There is," he wrote, "no justice now in a demand, to . . . seek a reduction of the pay of white teachers, in order to add further to the pay of Negro teachers." Essentially, he rejected the basic assumption underlying the request. In his words:

> A generation and a half of advancement from the unlettered toward the learned is only a step and a half in the right direction for the Negro race. All right minded white people take pride in the educational progress made by the Virginia Negro race in a short period of 75 years; but don't fool yourself, Mr. or Miss Negro, with the idea that you have, in this short time, caught up with the white race of Virginia who started the climb of civilization's ladder hundreds of generations ahead of you. The white people have got alot more pulling to do, and you with their assistance, have a good deal more climbing to do before there can be any serious thought given by sensible people of either race, to your far-off dream—social equality in Virginia.[82]

Venable's reasoning captures the flavor of the argument typically used whenever blacks petitioned for redress. But, as he aptly noted, the stakes this time were higher. For the first time, a black segment of the labor force demanded the same salaries offered whites. The action was all the more surprising because the initiators were teachers, generally known for their conservatism.

Venable and those who agreed with him feared that the demand by black teachers for equal pay camouflaged their desire for social equality. In a sense, this was true, despite published denials that blacks wanted social equality. Of course, most blacks, including the teachers, did not define social equality as interracial social mingling, a prospect that many undoubtedly found totally foreign. Nevertheless, the teachers did want financial compensation to reflect the status of their jobs. P. B. Young put the issue to Venable this way: "I am sure Mr. Venable would not have the Negro teacher occupy a 'social strata' comparable to that of a common laborer, but the Negro teacher is put to the necessity of avoiding this on the wage of a common laborer." Norfolk in 1939 paid the white custodian at Booker T. Washington High School a higher annual salary than that received by any black teacher or principal.[83] This situation, teachers argued, demanded correction, as did all salary differentials. Thus, on a certain level, the call for equal pay was synonymous with a call for social equality, for a system in which persons would be compensated for skills, status, and class position without regard to race.

The Norfolk Teachers Association (NTA), the Virginia Teachers Association (VTA), and the NAACP combined forces and mounted a challenge to the discriminatory policy. For several years, the leadership of the black Virginia Teachers Association had ruminated over correcting the statewide pay inequities. But, as Thurgood Marshall, chief counsel for the NAACP, informed NAACP executive secretary Walter White, "many of the conservative teachers have always been able to influence the large majority of the teachers not to take the necessary steps to bring about such a case." The conservatism diminished somewhat after a massive education program on the merits of pursuing the case, sponsored by the NAACP. Finally, in 1937, the VTA and the NAACP received the authorization "to organize a Joint Committee for the equalization of teachers' salaries."[84]

The committee quickly agreed on several procedural matters. To minimize possible retribution against teachers, both parties agreed to have the head of the NAACP's committee function as the public head of the Joint Committee, despite a private agreement to share the leadership. In addition, the VTA agreed to establish a one-thousand-dollar defense fund to defray all legal costs, travel expenses incurred by the counsel, and injuries suffered by petitioning teachers. For its part, the NAACP donated legal assistance.[85]

After winning a minor victory in Maryland courts, the NAACP launched a major offensive in Virginia. Norfolk became the site for the first test case in the state. Aline E. Black, a young teacher at Booker T. Washington, volunteered to become the original plaintiff. The central legal question became whether pay differentials based solely on race violated the plaintiff's constitutional rights under the equal protection and due process clauses of the Fourteenth Amendment.[86]

Salary differentials based on race, sex, and educational level existed in the Norfolk school system. Whites, as a rule, earned more than blacks; men earned more than women; and those with college degrees earned more than those with teaching certificates. These general trends cloaked other important relationships, particularly racial differentials in proportional earnings. Blacks at both the elementary and secondary levels fared better at the minimum end of their salary ranges than those at the maximum end of the range. A black elementary school teacher with a teaching certificate received a minimum salary worth 70.3 percent of the salary of a comparably educated white teacher. This figure depreciated to 67.4 percent as the same teachers approached the upper limit of the range (see Table 13).

Ironically, those with a baccalaureate fared relatively worse than those with only a teaching certificate. A black elementary teacher who possessed a B.A. earned more than one with a certificate but less than a

TABLE 13    Salary Structure of the Norfolk School System,
ca. 1939–1941

| | Annual Salary (nine months) | |
| --- | --- | --- |
| | Minimum | Maximum |
| *Black teachers* | | |
| Elementary school teachers | | |
|   Normal certificate | $597.50 | $960.10 |
|   Degree | 611.00 | 960.00 |
| High school teachers | | |
|   Women | $699.00 | $1,105.00 |
|   Men | 784.50 | 1,235.00 |
| | | |
| *White teachers* | | |
| Elementary school teachers | | |
|   Normal certificate | $850.00 | $1,425.00 |
|   Degree | 937.00 | 1,425.00 |
| High school teachers | | |
|   Women | $970.00 | $1,900.00 |
|   Men | 1,200.00 | 2,185.00 |

| | Earning Power of Blacks as a Percentage of White Earning Power | |
| --- | --- | --- |
| | At Minimum Salary | At Maximum Salary |
| Elementary school teachers | | |
|   Normal certificate | 70.3 | 67.4 |
|   Degree | 65.2 | 67.4 |
| High school teachers | | |
|   Women | 72.1 | 58.2 |
|   Men | 65.4 | 56.6 |

SOURCE: Legal Files, Norfolk Branch, NAACP Papers, Library of Congress.

white counterpart. Beginning black elementary teachers with degrees took home paychecks worth 65.2 percent of what a similarly skilled white teacher earned. Thus a certificate-only teacher had greater proportional earning power (70.3 percent) than one with a B.A. As seniority increased, these differences disappeared; by the time both categories of teachers reached the upper pay limit, each earned 67.4 percent as much as comparable white teachers.

At the secondary level, the income disparities grew sharper. An entry-level black female teacher earned 72.1 percent of the salary earned by a similarly educated white female teacher. The same black teacher at the apex of her career earned only 58.2 percent of the salary of a tenured white teacher. Men as a rule earned more than their same-race female counterparts, and white men earned more than black men. A beginning black male teacher earned 65.4 percent of the salary earned by an entry-level white male. The differential increased in proportion to seniority. By the time a black male reached the maximum salary, he earned approximately fifty-seven cents for every dollar earned by a white.

The NAACP filed the original petition for adjudication in March 1939. Several months elapsed before the first public hearing on 1 July. At the hearing, counsel for the city asked Circuit Court Judge Allan R. Hanckel to dismiss the petition because it was insufficient in law. The city issued a demurrer in the case, indicating that it did not contest Black's presentation of the facts as they related to her case. Instead, the city reasoned that she had waived her rights to seek redress when she willingly signed her yearly contract. Teachers recognized this power, the city attorney argued, when they entered into contractual arrangements with the city. Because only the city had the right to determine personnel policy, the courts lacked the discretionary powers to change the city's practices, counsel concluded.[87]

NAACP lawyers accepted only part of the city's argument. They concurred that the city possessed the power to fix salaries and establish hiring guidelines. But they countered that this right did not bequeath the city "the discretion to violate the Constitution" and that paying similarly qualified teachers different salaries solely because of their race or color violated the equal protection and the due process clauses of the Fourteenth Amendment.

Privately, Marshall and his colleagues admitted that they never expected a decision in their favor. Hanckel proved them correct. He denied Black's request for a writ of mandamus to end discriminatory salary practices, and he maintained that the court had no right to substitute its discretion for that of the city school board. NAACP lawyers were pleased, however, that he sustained the demurrer, for now the city's admission that it intentionally paid teachers substantially different salaries based on race was part of the public record.[88]

Black's attorney filed an immediate appeal for a writ of error with the Virginia State Court of Appeals. But before a hearing date could be set, the principal of Black's school, Winston Douglas, notified her that the city had decided not to renew her contract. Her attorneys had admitted in private that her firing was a possibility, but they had not considered it likely. (Most never knew that the city had decided to fire Black two weeks before Judge Hanckel's ruling.)[89]

The school board's action stunned the entire city and solidified the black community. The *Virginian-Pilot* commented, "The School Board's failure to re-employ Aline Elizabeth Black, the Negro high school teacher who has been made the instrumentality of a salary-equalization test case, is an act of reprisal in which it can take no pride."[90] The Interracial Commission publicly denounced the action as injurious to amicable race relations. In the black community, where members of the Teachers Association and their allies kept local residents apprised of the case throughout the spring, there was an immediate outcry. Black schoolchildren led a demonstration from Dunbar School down Chapel Street to Rugby, down Rugby to Church Street, and up Church to St. John AME at the corner of Bute and Church. The youths carried placards comparing the school board's decision to fascist behavior worldwide: one sign read "Dictators—Hitler, Mussolini, and the School Board." Others characterized the board's action as an infringement of civil liberties. Students carried signs declaring "School Teachers Must Have the Right to Petition," "The Right of Petition Must Not Be Denied American Citizens," and "Our School Board Has Vetoed the Bill of Rights."[91] The language was Afro-American in its formulation: although it addressed issues of decency, fair play, and democracy, the statements allowed blacks to express their outrage over a grievous racial injustice. Others understood what was said, but black Norfolkians understood it better. As a result, twelve hundred students, parents, and other adults assembled at St. John to sign a petition demanding Black's reinstatement.

Support for Aline Black was great in part because her case had broad ramifications. Teachers had occupied a special place in the black community since well before the end of slavery. To pay them less than whites affronted all blacks and underscored the pervasiveness of social inequality. Hence, an adjustment of the disparities had considerable symbolic meaning in the black community: it suggested that whites respected the black community's best. More important, the elimination of the dual wage scale opened the door for an assault on other inequities of the segmented labor market. If salaries were equalized, local blacks and strategists throughout the South could point with new authority to both the violation of *Plessy* and the flaws in its doctrine. This congealing of work and home along racial lines was the all-important first step.

Despite the denunciations, appeals, and demonstrations, the decision held as long as Black remained a litigant. Moreover, her dismissal raised another question: could Black continue as a plaintiff in the case? Initially, her lawyers believed the firing had no bearing and told her so. But, after a prolonged review, Thurgood Marshall informed Black and Jerry Gilliam, president of the Norfolk NAACP, that the lawyers believed her termination invalidated her as a plaintiff because she no longer "had sufficient legal interest to maintain her suit." Further, he informed them that, as a result, the NAACP had decided to drop her case.

As previously agreed, the Joint Committee assumed her salary for the school year (approximately $1,105). Nevertheless, Black was understandably angered by the outcome.[92]

More dangerous, however, was the fear that infected the NTA's ranks after Black's termination. Many teachers wanted results without the risk of injury. They fully understood the gains to be reaped if they won, but no one else wanted to make the sacrifices. Conversely, the NAACP expected a few casualties along the way. It believed that the larger principle was more important than a personal sacrifice. The organization's attitude was not based on callousness. Thurgood Marshall, in fact, wrote letters to several black colleges on Black's behalf, describing her circumstances and asking them to hire her.[93] But the NAACP's national agenda sometimes pushed local blacks outside the accustomed comfort zones. When this happened, conflict resulted.

Tensions ran high on both sides between August and October of 1939. NAACP officials often found themselves mollifying the fears and reservations of the teachers. NTA president Melvin O. Alston, like Black, agreed to serve as a litigant if the need arose. When called on to do so, he requested certain protections—essentially, a *"written promise* signed by the *proper person,* to the effect that [he would] be compensated to the extent of one thousand dollars ($1,000) immediately upon *temporary* or *permanent* loss of present teaching position" (his emphasis).[94] On the surface, this request simply reflected a desire to protect his vital interests. But, in his capacity as president of the Norfolk Teachers Association, Alston surely knew that at least a thousand dollars had been set aside by the Joint Committee for such contingencies. In all probability, Alston harbored considerable apprehension about stepping forward. He even withdrew as a possible litigant in August, although he was eventually convinced that his participation was critical.

Alston was not alone in his doubts. On at least two occasions, the NTA also tried to distance itself from the case. Many members feared losing their jobs. They also openly questioned the legal wisdom of the team of lawyers designing the case. All parties realized this was unknown judicial territory, with many potential pitfalls. At a public meeting in November 1939, Marshall assured the apprehensive that in time they would win.[95]

After Alston agreed to serve as the second plaintiff and the NTA somewhat timidly agreed to function as co-plaintiff, the NAACP submitted a new petition challenging the legality of unequal salary schedules. The thrust of the petition dealt with the central charge of discrimination. Alston charged the city with paying equally qualified teachers and principals different salaries based "solely upon race and color":

> That the School Board of Norfolk in adopting and enforcing the said salary schedule, in administering it and in paying salaries to teachers thereunder in the manner herein before described, has discriminated, and con-

tinues to discriminate unjustly against the petitioner and other members of his race . . . solely because of their race and color, in violation of the Constitution and laws of the State of Virginia, and in denial of equal protection of the laws guaranteed by the Fourteenth Amendment of the Constitution of the United States.[96]

As in previous appeals registered by Norfolk Afro-Americans, the offended parties demanded that the wrongs incurred simply because of race be righted. Yet in one important aspect this appeal exceeded anything previously requested. In the past, racial appeals had called for the creation of an equal but separate park, beach, school, or playground. This time, blacks sought the elimination of distinctions altogether. Black teachers wanted the privileges guaranteed whites: a top salary without racial consideration.

Circuit Court Judge Luther B. Way heard arguments in the Alston case the following year. On 12 February 1940, he issued his opinion. Repeating often-heard judicial reasoning, he ruled that Alston had voluntarily entered into a contract with the city and that, because Alston freely performed part of his duty as a teacher under the terms of the said contract, he had "waived such Constitutional rights" enabling him to petition. Way sidestepped the entire issue of equal pay. He did, however, inexplicably void Alston's contention that his petition, filed jointly with the Norfolk Teachers Association, constituted a class-action suit.[97]

Alston and his attorneys appealed the decision to the U.S. Circuit Court of Appeals, with surprising results. On paper, the Fourth Circuit Court's three-judge tribunal seemed composed of unlikely friends. Judge John J. Parker presided; he had lost a bid to become a U.S. Supreme Court justice largely because of the NAACP. After reviewing Parker's early career, Walter White, head of the NAACP, judged him racist and told the Senate Judiciary subcommittee investigating Parker's nomination as much in 1930. Labor officials joined in the NAACP's denunciation when they learned of opinions Parker had written that undermined their cause. Although Parker defended his actions to the satisfaction of some labor critics, he never distanced himself from his earlier views on race, and it cost him in the hotly contested confirmation proceedings. Joining Parker on the bench was Armistead M. Dobie and Morris A. Soper. Soper seemed safe, but Dobie, who had joined the bench the previous year, did not. As a Norfolk native, he retained ties to the area; his father had, in fact, been the superintendent of the Norfolk school system at one time.[98]

As Richard Kluger describes it, neither Parker nor Dobie apparently harbored undue prejudices; Parker's warm embrace of the black lawyers following their presentation has become part of legal folklore. The Appeals Court proceeded to reverse the lower court's ruling. Parker, who wrote the decision, argued that fixing salaries was "action by the state which is subject to the limitations prescribed by the 14th Amendment." Appropriately, he ruled that the city's discriminatory policy violated the Constitution. He also disagreed with Judge Way and ruled that the petition constituted a class-action suit, meaning that all black teachers were party to the decision. Parker remanded the case to the lower courts with a directive to the Norfolk school board to end "discrimination on the grounds of race or color in fixing salaries to be paid school teachers."[99]

Following a protracted meeting between the city attorney, the mayor, the city council, school board officials, and the city manager, the city appealed the decision to the Supreme Court rather than abide by the decree. The U.S. Supreme Court in November 1940 refused to review the case on a writ of certiorari. The case was again remanded to the lower court for settlement.[100]

The teachers' battle with the school board and the city over a satisfactory adjudication of the case continued for the better part of the next year. In the end, the city agreed to correct the situation within three years. According to the final settlement, the city would increase the salary of black teachers by increments of one-third until parity was achieved.[101] But, in many ways, the final agreement stole from the building drama. At the very moment they had the city in a good bargaining position, the teachers abdicated power and reached a dubious compromise. The reasons for this outcome can be explained by the newness of this strategy and the continued importance given to development in the home sphere.

After the U.S. Supreme Court refused to review the case, the city wanted to compromise. City attorney Alfred Anderson called a meeting of the plaintiffs, black community leaders, representatives of the state teachers association, the mayor, the city manager, and members of the school board to discuss the possibility of reaching an equitable settlement. At this meeting, the city first proposed phasing in equal salaries over three years.

NAACP counsel, who refused to attend the meeting and had encouraged other blacks not to go, found the city's plan lacking. They doubted the good faith of the city, especially given that Anderson refused to submit the proposal in writing. They also wondered if the city merely sought to contravene the court's edict by delaying for three years.

Black power broker P. B. Young, who attended the meeting, reached a different conclusion: he saw an opportunity for development of the home sphere. Always the conservative militant and always pragmatic, Young viewed the teachers' good fortune as a bargaining chip. The black community needed a new elementary school, and the city wanted a gradual settlement of the teachers' case. Young deduced that blacks could trade one for the other and told Marshall as much privately.

Marshall, Leon Ransom, and Oliver Hill, after a conference with Young, addressed the teachers. They went over the city's proposal and discussed its ramifications. Then they explained their refusal to participate in the earlier meeting. Several teachers questioned the city's integrity: given that the city had posted a surplus of $117,000 at the end of the past fiscal year, three years seemed a long time to wait. L. F. Palmer, president of the Virginia Teachers Association, who had attended the meeting with city officials, addressed the mass meeting next. Looking beyond the Norfolk particulars, he asked the group to accept the proposal for the good of all teachers, because their acceptance would establish a pattern others could emulate. Other speakers followed with similar appeals.

Then Young was asked to speak. Although earlier in the day he had asked the attorneys not to interfere with the teachers' decision and had agreed not to interfere himself, Young accepted the invitation. He informed the teachers that the maintenance of good race relations hinged on their willingness to compromise. He mentioned the importance of the new school they stood to gain, and he assured them that he earnestly believed city manager Charles Borlund would call a statewide conference to address the equal pay issue. Though Young reneged, the attorneys kept their word and did not interfere. A vote was taken, and the teachers accepted the three-year plan with one stipulation: that if city funds were insufficient, they would accept a lump sum of thirty thousand dollars the first year, with the remainder to be paid in equal increments the next two years.[102]

In a memo apprising the top leaders of the NAACP, Walter White and Roy Wilkins, of the case's outcome, Marshall was livid. He indicated that he, William Hastie, Leon Ransom, and Oliver Hill felt "that this [was] the most disgraceful termination of any case involving Negroes in recent years, and further, that it was so worked that practically all members of the joint committee were placed in a position of being unable to suggest that the teachers not follow this disgraceful offer." A summary of the case, presumably written by Marshall, concludes:

> The case was filed for two purposes: (1) To get a court precedent and (2) to bolster the courage of Negro teachers. We obtained this but the "leaders" built up the courage of teachers to file the suit but destroyed it during the last month by encouraging them to accept whatever the City might see fit to offer. The effect of this on other teachers and Negroes in general will be to set us back 75 years.[103]

The teachers' compromise speaks to the currents and crosscurrents that permeated the search for empowerment. Clearly, the NAACP and local blacks had both similar and dissimilar objectives. Broadly stated, both wanted to eliminate salary disparities. But the NAACP wanted the teachers to settle for nothing less than what whites had. Leaders like Young and Palmer wanted immediate and tangible results; theirs was the world of civility and racial accord. The two unreconciled tendencies often accounted for different social and political strategies and brought into full view the various meanings of Afro-Americans' struggle in their own interests.

Within the years from 1929 until 1941, we can isolate two, possibly three, shorter periods that together make up the larger span of time. The first period, from 1929 to 1935, involved the near-convergence of the two worlds of work and home. The confluence of economic hard times, despair, and active mobilization efforts by Communists and others engineered the change. During this period, blacks—sometimes alone and sometimes in conjunction with radical whites—made a meaningful attempt to point out the interconnections between race and class.

The second period, 1935 to 1937, was a transitional phase, marked by backlash. Members of the black middle class began to question seriously the wisdom of convergence. Government agencies began to offer relief and other assistance and thereby usurped the radicals. As the New Deal became entrenched, reform eventually replaced revolution. Because the Communists willingly used the reform agencies, they became part of what they had challenged. Some came to question the party's intentions. Even such a black stalwart as Alexander Wright left the Communist party when he became a victim of inner-party politics and became convinced, according to Paul Crouch's testimony before the McCarran Committee, "that the communists were not interested in building his union but in using his union to build the Communist Party."[104]

It is difficult to determine whether the last four years of the phase, 1937 to 1941, constitute a separate period or, more likely, represent the culmination of patterns that emerged in the second period. During those last four years, a residual allegiance to the new orthodoxy remained. Communists still spoke in black churches; they continued to promulgate their message whenever and wherever possible. But as the crisis abated, so did their influence. Consequently, blacks were left on their own to sustain the early thrust for social change. And, to confound the picture further, integrated unions that emphasized worker solidarity without attempting to alter nonwork social relations developed. For many blacks, it became "safer and saner" to embrace some variation of the old orthodoxy in which race was central and to sprinkle that variation with a little of the message of social equality and class consciousness advanced by the Communists. Thus we have the story of the teachers' battle to equalize salaries, a racial battle fought to bring their earning power in line with their class status.

Collectively, the three phases led to a restructuring of social relations. Signaling a new vision of what was possible, working-class blacks and whites began to question their allegiance to perspectives that validated racial differences at work. Influenced by the Communist party, the CIO, and a long history of analyzing the conditions they faced, Norfolk workers began the process of forging a common ground. During the 1930s, they joined interracial unions, openly defied segregation ordinances, and criticized those who would use race to divide the working class. Although this new orientation did not take final form until World War II, in the interim blacks and whites struggled to reconcile the needs and interests of their respective communities.

# SEVEN

# World War II and the Crystallization of a New Perspective, 1941–1945

Near the end of the Depression, an interviewer for Gunnar Myrdal's historic study *An American Dilemma* asked Jerry O. Gilliam, head of the local NAACP, to assess black life in Norfolk. Gilliam had much to say about intraracial differences, conservatism, and racism. He criticized the black clergy for taking more from the working people than they gave. He criticized those in the black community who shied away from sustained involvement in social and political causes designed to improve conditions. Finally, he turned to the white majority and offered:

> The whites deprive the Negro of privileges here like the mythical rat bites. I once slept in a back room in Washington, D.C., and big rats would run over me every night. A friend . . . told me to get out of there or rats would eat me to death. . . . "The rat," he said, "will take a small bite off your toe, and then blow on it so you won't feel, then take another nibble and blow some more, until the blood starts flowing and you bleed to death in your sleep." That's the way the white people lull Negroes to sleep in Norfolk and then bite them till they're bled dry.[1]

Gilliam may have taken a certain metaphorical liberty, but he was correct in at least one respect: vigilance was needed if Afro-Americans were to protect their own interests. He, of course, had no way of predicting the profound changes that were to develop in the definition of those interests. During the war years, in fact, blacks came full circle. Like their predecessors at the conclusion of the Civil War, members of this later generation argued that it was in their own interests to link advancement in the workplace and progress in the home sphere. Changes in the industrial order, particularly the increased acceptance of black workers by their white contemporaries, enabled them to adopt new strategies. Although new examples of interracial labor solidarity did not eliminate all interracial tensions, Afro-Americans discovered that they could promote workplace improvements and pursue interracial alliances without abandoning their assault on Jim Crow. Understanding why this discovery came when it did, and not before, demands a closer examination of the war years.

## A COMMUNITY IN FLUX

Even before the bombing of Pearl Harbor, Norfolk had become a community in flux; the war accelerated the pace. Endowed with an array of military installations, shipbuilding facilities, harbors, and railroad terminals, the entire Hampton Roads area—consisting of Norfolk on the south side and Newport News on the north side—became one of the country's prime defense centers. As its centrality to the war effort expanded, so did its population. Between April 1940 and May 1942, the civilian population in Hampton Roads grew by a staggering 122,525 persons, or 37.9 percent. An additional 60,000 military personnel and dependents added to the pressures.[2]

In the early months, most new arrivals were white. Norfolk, the largest city in Hampton Roads, had a 1940 population of 144,332, approximately one third black. By November 1941, officials speculated that the population was approaching 194,000. According to WPA records, however, blacks accounted for an average of only 15 percent of the in-migration areawide; in Norfolk the rate was closer to 14 percent. Nor was the area unique. For various reasons, black Americans initially hesitated to answer the call for war workers, especially in comparison to their response in the early years of World War I.[3]

Several factors contributed to this hesistancy locally. The armed services informed blacks that quotas had been met, thus deterring many from joining the military and adding to that population. A slow housing market characterized by outdated structures, many of them in poor repair, also kept some away. Others feared they would move to Norfolk only to discover that employment opportunities were limited. Reports of racial discrimination in hiring did little to lessen such apprehensions. In addition, the structure of the local labor market was a deterrent. Unemployment among blacks, which dipped after 1942, still hovered around 10 percent in 1940. Local residents filled many of the available positions, decreasing the possibilities for migrants. These factors, individually and collectively, slowed in-migration during the first year or two.[4]

The number of new arrivals increased substantially after 1942. Unfortunately, no data exist that would enable us to plot migration patterns through 1945; instead, we must use data for 1950. If we assume that most of the increase correlated strongly with the war, then certain age groups, primarily young men and women, would have been more likely to migrate than others. Their position in the migrating pool is suggested by an earlier government survey. Although the data are incomplete, we can deduce that young men, particularly unattached men between the ages of eighteen and twenty-four, migrated in the greatest numbers. If the men were married, they left their families behind, at least in the beginning (through 1943). During the first wave, most migrants came from Virginia or North Carolina. This changed by mid-1942, according to Lyonel C. Florant, a black research associate on the staff of the Virginia State Planning Board; thereafter, the depletion of the local labor supply led to expanded recruiting efforts and the appearance of migrants from other states.[5]

By 1950 the city's black population had grown by 36.9 percent, or seventeen thousand new residents. Roughly two thirds of this number were actually migrants; the rest were children born to the migrants after their arrival. Most newcomers resembled Mrs. Sessoms, a native of Rocky Mount, North Carolina, who moved to the area with her husband after he landed a job at the Norfolk Navy Yard. A sizable proportion of new arrivals were young adults between the ages of twenty and thirty-five (see Table 14).[6]

A change in the composition of the migrating population must have occurred at some point after 1943. Whereas at the beginning of the war unattached young men streamed into the city, the large numbers of persons between the ages of ten and nineteen in 1950 indicate that migrants may have been more willing to bring or send for their families when living conditions improved.

The increased population, swollen by new defense workers and military personnel, had an immediate and profound impact on the social structures of both the city and the black community. Even before the war, it had become obvious that the housing situation, particularly for blacks, demanded immediate remedy. Many of the dwellings built at the end of the nineteenth century and the beginning of the twentieth had deteriorated into slums. And because the city failed to pursue slum clearance monies actively, the housing stock was both substandard and scarce.[7] Several thousand new arrivals simply exacerbated an already critical situation.

Between September 1939 and December 1941, the cost of living in Norfolk jumped by 17.9 percent. The comparable rate nationwide was 12.1 percent. This jump put Norfolk second only to Mobile, Alabama, the national leader.[8] Most of the increase in Norfolk resulted from large rises in the cost of housing. For the same period, rent for the average household increased 16.4 percent, whereas nationwide the increase in large cities averaged only 3.6 percent. Any rise in earning power lagged

TABLE 14   Net Migration
Among Blacks by Cohort,
Norfolk 1940–1950

| Age Group | Male | Female |
|---|---|---|
| 10–14 | 436 | 513 |
| 15–19 | 442 | 437 |
| 20–24 | 1,333 | 654 |
| 25–29 | 1,354 | 1,060 |
| 30–34 | 1,125 | 946 |
| 35–39 | 672 | 663 |
| 40–44 | 411 | 239 |
| 45–49 | 167 | 191 |
| 50–54 | 136 | 31 |
| 55–59 | 57 | −25 |
| 60–64 | 34 | 12 |
| 65–69 | −25 | −71 |
| 70–74 | −33 | −5 |
| 75+ | −24 | 0 |
| Total | 6,085 | 4,645 |

SOURCES: U.S. Bureau of the Census, *Six-teenth Census of the United States* (Washington, D.C.: Government Printing Office, 1943), vol. 2, pt. 7, *Population, 1940,* p. 265; U.S. Bureau of the Census, *Seventeenth Census of the United States* (Washington, D.C.: Government Printing Office, 1952), vol. 2, pt. 46, *Population, 1950,* p. 55.

NOTE: These figures are actually based on the entire nonwhite population and may thus be slightly inflated; blacks, however, represent 99 percent of that population.

hopelessly behind the huge increases in the cost of living. As one black tenant complained, her twenty-five-cent-a-week pay raise had "been more than offset by the increase in just a few foodstuffs," let alone what she now paid in rent.[9]

Across the nation, black migrants suffered tremendously. In Chicago, landlords gouged tenants mercilessly. At times, as many as ten families paid a premium to live in cardboard cubicles in windowless basements; others took up temporary residence in condemned buildings. Conditions in Detroit were little better. Blacks seeking to move into a federal public housing project to escape overcrowded conditions were attacked by whites and city police.[10]

Prices and living conditions may have been bad elsewhere, but it was little consolation to Norfolk blacks. J. E. Davis complained, "I am paying too much for rent. . . . The landowners take advantage of their tenants in that they know the people have to live somewhere. We either pay high rents or move into the streets." Residents in the 800 block of Henry Street watched their rents increase 65 percent between February 1940 and July 1941. A unit lacking even the basic comforts that had cost $10 per month now cost $16.50.[11]

The typical dwelling in the area averaged three rooms, with no indoor toilets or baths, no hot water, and a bathroom for every two families. In 1938 an upstairs apartment of this type cost $10 per month; in 1940 the same apartment cost $11. By the middle of 1941, the apartment went for $14 per month. In November of that year, the same tenant paid $15.50 for the same apartment. Therefore, between 1938 and November 1941, basic rent for the apartment jumped 55 percent. To the exasperation of many tenants, the rent kept outpacing any cost-of-living raises in their salaries. Odessa Jones spoke for many: "The rent in Norfolk is entirely too high in relation to salaries and wages."[12]

Eventually, price controls and the development of new housing helped to stabilize rents. But these controls came a full two years after the start of the population boom. Many in the first group of migrants had used porches as sleeping quarters. According to Florant, they slept "in shifts on the same bed without change of linen," a practice dubbed the "hot bed." Female migrants discovered that they were in disfavor with many landlords. Most rooming-house operators believed that women were "more of a nuisance to lodge than men" and simply refused to rent them rooms.[13]

The federal government realized that new housing had to be built if it planned to attract defense workers and accommodate military personnel. In establishing priorities, however, it minimized the problems faced by the black community. As always, the military's agenda took precedence. In October 1940, federal officials appropriated $1.98 million to build Merrimac Park for white enlisted personnel and their families on land adjoining the naval air station. Another $3.3 million was later allocated to build Ben Moreel, a 1,342-unit complex for white enlisted personnel stationed at the naval operating base.[14]

Navy administrators either forgot or chose to ignore the needs of black enlisted personnel and their families. Norfolk blacks jarred their consciences, however. Seven months after the groundbreaking ceremony at Merrimac, federal officials surrendered $47,771—a paltry sum in comparison to other housing appropriations—for the construction of twenty four-room frame houses with hot water and coal stoves and heaters. The structures, built in Titustown, the once-fashionable suburb that deteriorated into a slum after World War I, stood in stark contrast to the accommodations provided for residents of Merrimac and Ben Moreel.

Government investigators called the Titustown location "unfortunate in that it apparently perpetuates a slum." They did not emphasize the disparities in amenities: the Merrimac and Ben Moreel projects featured indoor and outdoor recreation facilities, full-time recreation workers, and a range of recreational activities.[15]

Nevertheless, the construction of the Titustown addition adumbrated a new chapter in the history of state-generated housing for blacks. During World War I, the federal government had created self-governing, race-exclusive workers' towns; this plan had been abandoned by World War II in favor of race-exclusive projects centered in established cities. But the main issue still remained the positioning of labor close to industries. Therefore, to the chagrin of longtime black residents, new construction brought little relief to those long in search of better housing. Instead, about $1.2 million went for the construction of Oak Leaf Park, a workers' project built near a major defense contractor in the Campostella section. Located some distance from Church Street, the three-hundred-unit structure solved neither the short-term nor the long-term needs of the community.[16]

Even the much-heralded completion of Roberts Park was not a solution; war workers again got first priority. The 230 units began accepting tenants in September 1942 exclusively from among those families of "essential war workers" who lacked local housing or a manageable commute. And although the rent at Roberts Park was expensive by local standards—$30 per month for a one-bedroom apartment, $32.50 for a two-bedroom, $35 for a three-bedroom, and $37.50 for a four-bedroom—this price included utilities (heat, water, gas, and electricity) and the use of a refrigerator, gas stove, and indoor toilet.[17] Ironically, when a developer finally built homes for blacks with all the modern conveniences, most of those homes went to newcomers.

A year later, the federal government constructed Liberty Park, temporary residences just east of Community Hospital, a black facility. The one-story demountable structures eased the tight housing market a bit. The frame dwellings, built on raised platforms with detached, front wooden steps, seemed less than adequate as replacements for long-term housing, even though they became just that. In any case, in comparison to older apartments in the center of town, the Liberty Park houses represented a vast improvement.[18]

The war created other problems for Norfolk as well. In addition to an undersupply of houses, the city had too little water, not enough schools, and a crippling amount of traffic congestion. These conditions made life in Norfolk miserable, as several national periodicals took pleasure in noting.[19]

The acute water shortage sprang from the frantic attempts by the city and the federal government to house the growing population. By the summer of 1942, two thousand housing units were being built each month. The new construction surpassed the city's ability to provide drinking or bathing water. Because Norfolk was such a vital defense center, federal officials underwrote the installation of several new pumping stations. They also promised to provide the resources (financial and otherwise) for laying several miles of new pipes to transfer the needed water.[20]

The government response to the school crisis was not as expeditious. Because of the rapid influx of school-age children, most schools operated on double shifts. Blacks got some relief after 1942 when, with federal monies, the city built an elementary school in Liberty Park and the R. A. Tucker Elementary School near Campostella. War conditions, however, dashed any hope of a new school in the heart of the black community.[21]

The problems of clogged traffic lanes and long lines of vehicles eased when the government improved the long-neglected traffic system. But because top priority went to high-volume thoroughfares linking various military installations, little improvement came to Uptown (the center of the older black community). Instead, military engineers busied themselves improving Sewells Point Road, Hampton Boulevard, and (Admiral) Taussig Boulevard near the naval base.[22]

To complicate matters further, in 1941 the city devised a complex formula for determining whether a street qualified for "curbing, guttering, grading, surfacing or paving." The formula took into account prevailing interest rates, the ability to secure a twenty-year bond, and whether a given street's property owners paid the appropriate city real estate tax. This formula limited the number of paved streets in the black community, and a 1945 amendment did not correct the situation. The amendment contained one noteworthy modification: residents living on streets that failed the basic test could as a unit "pay the difference in cost of the improvements and the amount the city would pay pursuant to the formula."[23] In most cases, black homeowners failed the basic test, and very few residents had the collective capital to pay for the work themselves. Rutted, dust-clouded streets remained an all-too-familiar sight.

## TOWARD A NEW CONSIDERATION OF EMPOWERMENT

War-produced changes not only dictated the city's ability to maintain itself; those changes also contributed to alterations in social calculations. World War II, and the role of Afro-Americans in it, unveiled a central paradox about American democracy. War mobilization both increased the integration of blacks into the larger community and heightened their isolation from it. Unable to ignore the contradictions, blacks in Norfolk joined the nationwide drive for full inclusion. In the process, a subtle difference in perspective crystallized.

Roosevelt and others argued that the war symbolized the struggle to protect individual liberties around the world. Yet, except for protests by blacks and some liberal-minded whites, little mention was made of anti-democratic practices at home. Black soldiers in uniform rode Jim Crow buses, and black civilians were trained for defense industry jobs in Jim Crow sections of town, endured racial invectives, and struggled against occupational ceilings based on race. Much was demanded of those asked to preserve democracy in a patently undemocratic society.[24]

Norfolk's position as a major defense center and a southern city heightened the sensitivity to the paradox. While blacks struggled to protect the nation's vital interests, they also had to wrestle with the realities of limited social and economic mobility caused by restrictive Jim Crow legislation. This confluence resulted in periodic expressions of outrage and public demonstrations. It also resulted in the visible blurring of the lines of demarcation between the work and the home spheres. This shading helped Afro-Americans to redefine their own interests. For the first time in a long while, blacks came to see and to express publicly that what affected them in the workplace had a direct bearing on conditions at home. This change in perspective meant that the community would take a more active role in fighting for workplace improvements, including better jobs, better wages, and the right to unionize.

The new strategy followed a series of events that took place in early 1941. A radio appeal went out for skilled crafts workers to fill fifteen hundred openings at the Fort Eustis construction project on the peninsula (the north side of Hampton Roads). The federal government had earmarked $5.1 million to renovate and construct new buildings at the fort. Working through the Virginia State Employment Service, it allowed local contractors to determine hiring procedures. Both the John T. Pettijohn Company of Lynchburg and the Hofheimer Construction Company of Norfolk opposed the hiring of black carpenters on the pretense of avoiding race mixing. Blacks saw through this flimsy rationale and called it what it was: "rank discrimination" intended to deny blacks the "right to work on defense projects in common with other Americans."[25]

Embarrassed federal officials sent word to delegates attending the Fifteenth Hampton Builders Conference, a black group, that they planned to correct all instances of discrimination at defense projects. George L. Zuidema, an executive officer and hiring agent for one of the contractors, addressed the same conference. He pleaded with those in attendance, "Don't bear down on me too hard. I am only trying to live up to a tradition." He sidestepped a question asked by one delegate, who demanded to know why black and white carpenters could work side by side without incident at the Fort Monroe construction site just a few miles from Fort Eustis, but not at Fort Eustis.[26]

Zuidema revealed his true feelings in a two-hour interview with a reporter. In a matter-of-fact manner, he commented, "We have always segregated our workers by trades in the past. It is a long established policy, and is still in effect because in my best judgment it is right. It has always been done by me." Zuidema still played the game by the old rules; in other words, he believed in the value of the segmented labor market. To illustrate his point, he claimed that the company did not object to employing blacks; in fact, 39.7 percent of its labor force was black (2,300 out of 5,800), and blacks frequently dominated entire job categories. Conveniently, he failed to emphasize that most worked in the lowest-paying, unskilled jobs.[27]

Afro-Americans viewed the war as a prime opportunity to enter the industrial labor force and had little use for Zuidema's traditions. But, as Robert Weaver, a black economist and government official discovered, opposition from white workers and employers blocked opportunities, even though the country desperately needed laborers.[28] That proved to be true until blacks mounted sufficient pressure to alter the behavior, if not the attitudes, of white employers.

Social psychologists find that there is usually a direct correlation between one's attitudes and one's subsequent behavior—that is, knowing someone's attitude about a particular subject increases the probability that you can predict that person's behavior. But such a generalization can be misleading. During the 1940s, for instance, most white Americans believed that democracy was worth preserving. They nevertheless separated this belief from their support of racially discriminatory laws and practices. On the surface, fighting to preserve democracy and then supporting undemocratic practices seem incongruous, but they were not to these actors. A different set of social norms and a different belief system shaped each attitude-behavior interaction. The first dealt with the question of whether democracy should be preserved, a question that most answered affirmatively. The second, however, asked whether blacks should have the same rights and protections as other citizens—to which most whites answered no. They did not view the second question as a necessary component of the first. But blacks did. To them, it seemed ludicrous for the U.S. government to expend considerable human and financial capital fighting to preserve democratic structures for allies, when that same government refused to protect the individual liberties and freedoms of many of its own citizens. The different interpretations caused considerable conflict and set the stage for the civil rights movement.[29]

Soon after the war started, blacks realized that most whites had not connected the fight to preserve democracy abroad to the struggle for democratic practices at home, and they began to mount pressure campaigns. The most successful, A. Philip Randolph's threatened march on Washington for jobs in the summer of 1941, caused Roosevelt to issue Executive Order 8802. Designed to placate black leaders, the order outlawed employment discrimination in defense industries. Following its issuance, FDR created the President's Committee on Fair Employment Practices (FEPC) to police the defense industry. In actuality, the FEPC lacked the personnel and the enforcement powers to punish violating employers or unions; but it did give the illusion of a supportive White House. Moreover, blacks saw it as a means of breaking the yoke of racist employment practices. When the FEPC expired in 1943, Norfolk blacks even raised two thousand dollars to help create a permanent agency.[30]

In Norfolk, the effectiveness of Executive Order 8802 was tested very early. To the dismay of many, the culprit was the body sworn to end discrimination in defense hiring—the federal government. Personnel officials at the Norfolk Navy Yard had notified the U.S. Employment Services (USES) of immediate openings. As a matter of practice, the navy never delineated jobs by race and in fact employed blacks in skilled, semi-skilled, and unskilled positions. Nevertheless, the USES inexplicably advertised the jobs with racial restrictions included. Thus, at the same moment one federal agency broadcast opportunities for advancement, another agency announced that the opportunities were for whites only.[31]

Black residents responded quickly and decisively, but the effect of their outcry is hard to gauge. Navy yard officials advised everyone to ignore the published advertisement and promised to give the jobs to the best qualified people. But it is doubtful that this happened. A review of FEPC cases for Norfolk and Portsmouth reveals that black workers filed discrimination charges against the navy yard more frequently than against any other local employer. In large measure, the federal government shared culpability for the continuation of racist hiring practices. As Lyonel Florant observed:

> It is in times of crises that the mores break down and new forms of adjustment arise. During World War I, the status of the Negro in American life was considerably enhanced by his economic, political and consequent social gains. Thus far there has not been much evidence of a change in status as far as Norfolk Negroes are concerned. . . .
>
> Despite the numerous requests and the great demand for training courses for Negroes in Norfolk, relatively little attention has been paid to the Negro labor market as a current and future reservoir of workers for skilled and semi-skilled tasks.[32]

Florant penned his gloomy assessment after observing defense training facilities in the area. Norfolk, one of the most strategic industrial centers along the South Atlantic coast, had a wide variety of training courses for white men and women; but, as late as 1942, there were only four shops for blacks, none of which trained black women. Lawrence Oxley, chief of the Negro Placement Service of the USES, called it an outrage that an area so vital to the nation's security and war effort lagged in fulfilling its responsibility to train skilled workers for defense industries.[33]

To make matters worse, the shops that trained Afro-Americans contained insufficient equipment and were staffed by improperly trained, overworked instructors. Classes often bisected the normal workday, meeting from 1 to 7 P.M. Contemporaries speculated that those hours were chosen to discourage black men from applying, because they typically held other full-time jobs and could not afford to forego twelve weeks' wages while receiving the necessary training. City officials openly disagreed with this charge, however.[34]

Furthermore, Florant's report told only part of the story. Aside from the glaring inequities, more insidious racism was often encountered. For example, when black residents approached T. B. Rydingsvaard, director of the school board's trade section, about correcting the imbalance in the number and quality of training shops, he brushed them aside by reciting the overused claim that the city could not find qualified black instructors. The protesters agreed that qualified black instructors were hard to find. But, they countered, a fair wage would certainly increase the probability of locating qualified candidates.[35]

Regardless of whether Rydingsvaard and the city were motivated by ignorance or by racism, blacks were determined to use the call for labor to gain well-paid, permanent industrial jobs. Dissatisfied with Rydingsvaard's response, a committee of fifteen prominent Afro-Americans went directly to Charles Borlund, Norfolk's city manager. Borlund, a champion of amicable race relations during the war years, obtained Rydingsvaard's assurance that the city would do all in its power to procure necessary training equipment. That very afternoon, Rydingsvaard obtained the authorization to purchase the required machinery.[36]

But blacks must have felt as if they were aiming at targets in a shooting gallery, for as quickly as they eliminated one challenge, another appeared. This time, VEPCO, the local utility and bus company, informed all parties that government restrictions on the use of scarce commodities prevented it from wiring the training site. Robert Weaver promised to use his influence to help the city. The authorization came, but an old problem resurfaced: the city still lacked the equipment to transform Booker T. Washington High School into a fully operational training center. A total of six months elapsed between the first conversation with Rydingsvaard and the center's opening. Even then, no one had successfully addressed the question of training for black women.[37]

The employment needs of black women would not go unattended for long, however, because World War II marked a profound turning point in black Norfolk. As a group, black women had the highest female labor force participation levels in the country, although most were mired in low-paying, domestic service jobs. When men left for the war, black women stepped in to fill the void. Their presence was not always wanted or accepted, but they were not deterred. Equally important, Norfolk's black community threw its full support behind the women. After all, better-paid black women benefited the entire community, especially when so many black women worked for wages.

Like their sisters across the country, black women in Norfolk were determined to land industrial jobs. In March 1942, for example, an urgent call went out for two thousand women to learn the bench and lathe trade. Alice Knight inquired at the USES office about the training course. Office personnel innocently directed her to a training site at Twenty-Fifth Street and Hampton Boulevard. The instructor informed Knight that their facilities were for the exclusive use of white women and steered her to the Booker T. Washington night school. She went there, only to learn from Rydingsvaard that the city had made no provisions for black women. Despite a desperate need for war workers, it seemed that a reservoir of labor would go untapped. Across the nation, black women were equally victimized by racism and sexism.[38]

This time, however, individual workers did not fight alone. With scenes of unemployment lines permanently etched in their minds—and supported by an observable change in white labor—many Afro-Americans encouraged black workers to organize; they tied workplace advancement to improving the general welfare of both individual households and the community. In a letter to the editor, local resident Eugene Jones counseled other blacks to "cast [their] lot with labor generally, and be encouraged in doing so." Members of the Baptist and AME clergy proposed a labor educational drive with a twofold goal: an increased number of unionized workers and better employment opportunities. Even the UNIA Progressive Club supported the new approach. Club president L. L. Booth urged Afro-Americans to maintain any employment gains for the betterment of all.[39] When Alice Knight's problem became public knowledge, blacks pressured the city for some type of accommodation. In April, city officials outlined tentative plans for a training course in the machine shop and hand-and-tool trades.[40] Needless to say, more time elapsed before the plans were implemented.

Training, of course, never ensured that women would receive fair employment opportunities. Several key industries had heretofore barred women in general, and black women in particular. A. E. Jakeman, personnel director for the Norfolk Shipbuilding and Drydock Company, joked: "Standards for hiring were at first reasonably high, but gradually subsided to the popular ironic specifications, if it's warm, I'll work it."[41] Jakeman's sarcasm was intended to highlight management's perception of the quality of female labor.

Even those who successfully overcame the barriers of race and gender found new obstacles after they were hired. Industrial employers, who preferred to hire white women rather than black women regardless of training, hired blacks only as manual laborers. But by September 1942, many area installations desperately needed labor because scores of qualified men had joined the armed services. Nineteen-year-old Cerona Browner, a recent graduate of a welders' training course from a National Youth Administration center in Washington, D.C., applied for work at the Norfolk Navy Yard. Officials first denied her request by claiming that the only restrooms and drinking fountains in the work area were reserved for white women. Fearing resistance from white women, personnel officials instead offered Browner a job as a custodian, which she promptly refused. She took her case directly to the installation's ranking officer and demanded a job in keeping with her training.[42]

During the interim, the rancor over her placement went well beyond the boundaries of the yard. Senator Harry Byrd of Virginia, Senator Burnet R. Maybank of South Carolina, Secretary of the Navy Frank Knox, several of FDR's advisors, and the Metal Trades Council of the Norfolk Navy Yard convened a conference. They all agreed that the presence of black women in skilled positions threatened to increase racial antipathy and thereby undermine the war effort. White women, they offered, bound by segregation and guided by a belief in white supremacy, refused to share their work space with black women. That black men worked side by side with whites without major conflict, and had done so for many years, was not mentioned.[43]

Navy yard officials rejected this rationale, however, and assigned Browner to a job as a welder trainee. They even informed her she could use the water fountain reserved for white women. But after she had been on the job for nine days, administrators decided that the training she had received fell below the yard's standards, and she was terminated. Browner admitted that the procedure she had learned differed from the one used in the yard, but she argued that she could learn the new technique.

Rear Admiral Felix Gygax disagreed. He concluded that she lacked the necessary aptitude and that her discharge emanated from her inability to keep pace. The FEPC investigator concurred, thereby exonerating the yard of racial discrimination. Meanwhile, Gygax asserted that those who insisted that the yard practiced racial discrimination were themselves blinded by racial prejudice. In the end, the pretext for terminating

Browner was "upholding standards," rather than capitulation to segregationist influences. Whatever the explanation, this was not the last time the yard would complain that a black woman lacked suitable training.[44]

Unquestionably, employers experienced great difficulty accepting a black "Rosie the Riveter." The country had entered a different phase in the industrial age, and the shortage of males made women's labor indispensable. Despite this situation, where their white counterparts found the door to advancement partly ajar, black women workers found the door nearly shut. Perennial candidates for the last openings and the first firings, they nevertheless demonstrated a new resolve to secure industrial jobs. Conditioned by the 1930s, when Afro-Americans encountered a federal government poised to challenge the conventional, female workers turned to that government for assistance in the 1940s. Most knew that the stakes were high, that economic advancement brought with it financial security and an enhancement of the material base of the wider black community. Thus they used the FEPC to push for change.

For complex reasons, as a variety of examples indicate, the FEPC frustrated as many women as it helped. Jocelyn Tucker turned to the agency for help after she lost her job. She accused officials at the Norfolk Naval Supply Department of firing her solely because of her race. Department officials countered that she was "slow and inept in her work, loitered on the job, and absented herself from the post without permission for unreasonable periods of time."[45] Other sources claimed that many women lacked the skill or temperament for industrial work. Hence, where many black women saw discrimination, many companies saw incompetence. Either may have been correct in individual cases; it was sometimes hard to know when termination followed worker ineptitude or company bias. This made it all the more important for blacks to protest and petition when advisable.

Individual proclivities could also prevent conclusive determinations of employee or employer guilt. FEPC procedures required a follow-up investigation whenever a complaint was filed. In Tucker's case, she had disappeared by the time of the investigation. Heartened by increased job opportunities elsewhere, many complainants saw no purpose in following their FEPC cases to closure. Moreover, black women understood that the FEPC could not provide remuneration. Realizing that industrial jobs were nice but that any job was better than no job, many acted conservatively and practically. And when faced with a missing complainant, the FEPC simply closed the case.

In other instances, black women and company officials disagreed about what a job entailed. After completing a defense training course at Booker T. Washington High, Rachel V. Fleakes, Hallie Britt, and Ellamae Reid obtained jobs as helper trainees. Navy yard administrators directed them to sweep floors; the women refused. Instead, they informed their supervisors that sweeping floors contradicted the purpose of their training and fell outside their job classification. The navy yard summarily fired the three on the grounds of insubordination. The women charged discrimination, but FEPC investigators decided in favor of the navy yard, upholding the firings because the positions were all temporary.[46]

Industrial-sector jobs did not offer the only advancement opportunities for black women. A few applied for white-collar positions. In such instances, the discrimination could be even more blatant. The naval hospital in Portsmouth, for example, advertised for registered nurses, and Rebecca Watson applied. She presented her application to the head nurse, who, in a state of obvious shock, indicated that she had not been instructed to hire colored nurses. Only after conferring with the head of personnel did the nurse correct herself and inform Watson that all vacancies were filled. Watson subsequently charged the U.S. Navy with racial discrimination. She bolstered her case by showing that the same hospital had proceeded to hire a white nurse, who remained on the job only eighteen days. Clearly, the navy had violated the letter of the law and the spirit of the constitution, but it managed to circumvent both the FEPC ruling and the civil service hiring guidelines by assigning only navy nurses to openings at the hospital thereafter.[47]

Such discrimination was frequent. When Mary B. Cook called the civil service office about a job as an employee relations assistant, they told her to come in the next morning for an interview. The civil service worker apparently did not detect the caller's race over the phone. When Cook arrived, the receptionist tried to cover her mistake by suddenly announcing that the opening had disappeared. Cook approached the FEPC for assistance, believing that her credentials warranted consideration: a B.S. from Hampton Institute, an M.S. from Columbia University, and nineteen years of experience teaching at I. C. Norcom High School in Portsmouth and one year at Virginia State College, a black institution. The FEPC decided that her qualifications did not meet the exact specifications for the job and ruled that the employment decision was not capricious.[48]

This sample of cases typifies both the quality and the types of charges brought to the attention of David Longley, the local investigator, and Thomas Houston, the area representative in Washington. Longley in particular believed that discrimination accounted for many personnel decisions.[49] But discrimination based on gender and race was often difficult to prove, especially if an employee's work habits became an issue. The larger employment record indicates that by 1943 nearly thirty thousand Afro-Americans worked at various defense centers in the area. A survey of seventeen thousand of these black workers reveals that 11.8

percent of them labored in skilled occupations and 41.2 percent held semi-skilled positions. These two categories combined equal the 47.0 percent who worked in unskilled jobs, suggesting that some vertical occupational mobility did occur.[50] Moreover, the fluidity of the job market led the FEPC to close a number of cases without a full adjudication of the merits of the original charges.

Black men also viewed the war years as a time for advancement. Gender, however, created different emphases. Men worried about the possibility of retrogression, so any loss of skilled or semi-skilled positions caused alarm. A report by Longley confirmed their worst suspicions. He wrote, "We have every reason to believe that there exists in this area a well organized effort to replace Negroes in skilled work with whites." Individual cases gave credence to Longley's charges. Skilled black men did lose jobs for what sometimes seemed to be petty offenses. Lonnie Myers worked at the naval operating base as a fireman first class for better than a year. He had previously worked eight years for Seaboard Railroad. Base officials let him go after four whites and one black employee accused him of ignoring directions and cursing his supervisors. Myers labeled the charges fabrications. But he could not find witnesses to corroborate his story, and the decision stood.[51]

Others did not feel comfortable approaching the FEPC. They were skittish about being identified and reprimanded by their bosses. This conservatism bore the imprint of the scarcity of the 1930s: a high-paying job in the 1940s was to be cherished. Behavior by employees in Shop #51 at the navy yard reflected this caution. A group of them repeatedly wrote to FEPC area representative Thomas Houston in Washington, D.C., charging that rampant racial discrimination took place in the yard in general and in their shop in particular. Each time, the letter arrived without a return address or any means of identifying the petitioners. Finally, an explanation clarified the mysterious conduct: the letter writers feared reprisals. And clearly they had doubts about the FEPC's power to intercede effectively.[52]

Other workers realized that the time had come to correct the pattern of underemployment that had plagued black workers for so long, and they responded less circumspectly. To protect themselves, they informed the wider community of their problems and enlisted its assistance. These workers realized that most residents now understood the importance of workplace advances in the overall struggle for progress, including development in the home sphere. Such cases underscore the depth of the change in perspective.

One of the more public of these cases came to the attention of the FEPC in May 1944. Employees in the all-black shop at the metal works division of the naval air station protested because the installation refused to promote the men in their unit. At the time they filed the complaint, only one of the fifty-seven had a rating higher than helper, and this man was a machinist first class. The men maintained that the government installation created a bottleneck to fair advancement.

News of conditions at the shop circulated through the black community for two months before the first letter reached George Johnson, deputy chairman of the FEPC. The workers embroiled in the controversy held a community meeting to present their side of the story. Two sets of interrelated issues surfaced: one involved the men in the all-black shop, and the other involved black employees in other units at the air station. But the major concern was the contention that the navy kept the workers trapped in low paying jobs and ignored their request for a fair settlement. Rather than fighting the navy in the press or the community, the men proposed a compromise. In exchange for the eventual addition of blacks to the thirteen-member shop committee that mediated internal complaints, they would temporarily support the formation of an all-black shop committee. But they argued that this should not militate against the addition of a black to the "real" shop committee. Nor, they added, should anyone interpret it as an abrogation of their desire for fair remuneration and promotion.[53]

The air station's intransigence prompted the black employees to form a quasi-labor unit. This unit in turn wrote to George Johnson in Washington, D.C., soliciting FEPC help. John L. Perry, electrician second class, and John F. Burrell II, machinist second class, wrote that although their group had filed twenty-one separate complaints with the air station's internal committee, the committee had never responded. Instead, the captain of the base told two representatives that the cases were groundless. The workers found the committee's negligence and the captain's behavior inexcusable. They told Johnson basically what they had told the black community two months earlier: "Skilled Negroes are placed in positions far below their training and ability," and "the upgrading of Negroes is seriously retarded and . . . they are discharged promiscuously."

They also added a point they chose not to share with the general public. In addition to their concern about management procedures, they questioned whether the shop superintendent displayed the proper sensitivity to the black workers in his employ. In their view, the lieutenant who headed the shop was a racist. There was no other way to interpret his comments that "the average Negro is by far below the average white" or that "it will take fifty generations for the Negro to become as efficient as any White." The black men found his attitude and behavior offensive and clearly disadvantageous to them; as they wrote, "quite a few colored employees . . . graduated from outstanding Negro colleges . . . and the average education of the Negro in trades here is way above that of the white."[54]

Against this backdrop, the FEPC began its investigation. When the investigation was completed, it referred the twenty-one individual charges of discrimination back to the internal grievance committee, which found very little evidence to substantiate the allegations. Progress occurred only when laborer Vanders Williams became the first black member of the naval air station shop committee.[55]

The actions of black workers caused middle-class black leaders to abandon at least part of their earlier cautiousness. In this respect, Norfolk was but a microcosm of events elsewhere in the South and throughout the nation.[56] Blacks demonstrated a new resolve to make the "system" work for them. P. B. Young, for example, joined fifty-nine other conferees in Durham, North Carolina, in October 1942. Sometimes called a militant Booker T. Washington, Young, like others, had historically displayed a willingness to work within the framework of the South's biracial system. Now, however, many middle-class blacks, reacting to pressures exerted by the laboring classes, had tired of the go-slow tactics of southern whites. They understood, and black workers reminded them, that amicable race relations would follow a change in Jim Crow policies.

It was a result of both pressure from black workers and a disgust with the slowness of change that the Durham conferees enthusiastically drafted the Durham Manifesto, or the Southern Black Declaration of Independence. The manifesto contained several planks, among them a call for the end of segregation in all its forms, an endorsement of the FEPC, the open encouragement of blacks to join the labor movement, and a demand for an end to inequities in housing, medicine, and education.[57] The Durham Manifesto represented the first time that southern blacks had merged the separate elements of their existence into one coherent appeal for redress.

The changing views of white labor officials also aided blacks in their quest for increased union participation and in their adoption of a new orientation. The AFL, which dominated the powerful Central Labor Union (CLU), and the CIO competed for control of organized labor. The CIO's willingness to organize black labor pressured the AFL to modify its policies. In response, the state AFL body appointed David Alston, longtime black laborite and longshore official, to the hitherto unheard-of position of labor recruiter among Afro-Americans. Alston, in turn, called on whites in the state body to root out discrimination in labor circles.[58]

Locally, the CLU answered this challenge with more than a little ambivalence. In cases where the contacts were old and the jobs predominantly black, the CLU courted black workers—the ILA and the oyster shuckers' union being good examples. Even certain progressive social issues led white labor to ally with blacks. When the city had an opportunity in 1939 to adopt the food-stamp program and aid needy families, many of whom were black, the CLU led the charge, with the *Norfolk Labor Journal* declaring: "It is to be hoped that the Council which was not liberal enough to give us slum clearance because the slum owners did not seem to like the idea, will at least give themselves and the needy families of the city a break by speedily approving the stamp system."[59]

The CLU took a similarly tough, if ironic, stance in favor of eliminating the poll tax. (Half a century earlier, white workers had applauded its imposition.) All too often, however, the tax disfranchised both black and white workers and consigned them to second-class status. Therefore, the CLU declared the "abolition of the poll taxes an imperative war necessity. It will reassert America's abiding faith in the principles of democracy. . . . It will release ten million second-class citizens from political peonage." The CLU further muted the cynics by encouraging union members to root out the cancer of prejudice in the workplace. Its new prominence in race-related matters enlivened the words embossed on the banner of the *Labor Journal,* the CLU newspaper, which read: "The Strongest Bond of Human Sympathy, Outside of the Family Relations Should Be One Uniting All Working People."[60]

Nonetheless, the steps that had brought the CLU to its current position were unsteady ones. One issue of the *Labor Journal* that included an article chastising the city for its failure to support slum clearance also included this joke:

> *Rastus:* "Sambo, does yo' all know why dere ain such an affinity 'tween a colored man an' a chicken?"
>
> *Sambo:* "Must be 'cause one am descended from Ham and de odder from eggs?"[61]

Such "humor" derived from the historical setting of the 1930s and 1940s, when the only contact many whites had with black America came through a culturally filtered medium like the radio and shows like "Amos and Andy." The old orthodoxy, which depicted blacks as inferiors, clearly lingered.

Meanwhile, some white labor organizations questioned the appropriateness of color-blind unionization. In such cases, the issue became whether to establish a parallel all-black local or to accept blacks in already established and recognized white locals. In late 1944, members of Painters' Local 1100 (Norfolk) and Local 474 (Portsmouth) agonized over this issue. Harry Bratt, vice-president of Local 1100, paraphrasing the international president of the union and its constitution, concluded that no provision expressly authorized the creation of a separate union for blacks. Wrestling with the conflict between past practices and common sense, he recognized that other unions in the area admitted blacks because it made sense. To exclude Afro-Americans from the world of the working class helped no one, he admitted. Furthermore, Bratt understood that others had changed in the face of new realities, and "they do not do it for love. They are very far from it. They do it for the sole reason that they see the unorganized colored craftsmen as a competitor of their's and they finally came to the conclusion that for their own benefit it is better to have the Negroes organized."[62]

For all the Harry Bratts who considered change a possibility, equal numbers of white workers viewed blacks as competitors and sought their elimination from the labor market. But blacks demonstrated a new determination to hold their own, and they managed to challenge those whites who opposed them without attacking white labor generally. This strategy enabled them to find common ground without abandoning an assault on Jim Crow. In the case of the Association of Colored Railway Trainmen and Locomotive Firemen (ACRT) and the Brotherhood of Locomotive Firemen and Enginemen, a white union, the U.S. Supreme Court became the final arbiter. The legal case grew out of a collective bargaining agreement between the white union and the railroads. Under the terms of the agreement, the white union represented all workers. But blacks maintained that this white union had entered into a contract with the Norfolk and Southern Railway that discriminated "against negro members of the craft." The case that grew out of the original complaint bore the name of Tom Tunstall, a Norfolk County resident. Tunstall lost his job when the union refused to take precautions to protect the jobs of black firemen. Under the terms of the union contract, nonpromotable workers were not to be given priority on the better routes, and black firemen fell into this category. Tunstall filed suit on behalf of himself and all members of the ACRT.

The NAACP, with support from the American Civil Liberties Union, won an impressive victory on behalf of the ACRT. Motions had been filed in both the District Court and the U.S. Court of Appeals for the Fourth Circuit contending that the Railway Labor Act did not give the courts the jurisdiction to intervene in what was essentially an administrative matter. The U.S. Supreme Court disagreed. A mere four days after hearing the case on 18 November 1944, the Court decided five to two in favor of the black plaintiffs. Justice Stone wrote in his opinion: "For reasons stated in our opinion in the Steele case the Railway Labor Act itself does not exclude the petitioner's cause of action from the consideration of the Federal Courts." The Court further concluded that when a plaintiff is without "available administrative remedies," the plaintiff may petition the court for "equitable relief." The justices reversed the lower courts and remanded the case for proper review.[63] On 9 April 1945, the Fourth Circuit revised its earlier decision. In doing so, it noted that this was indeed a class-action suit. The case wound its way back to the District Court, which reversed its decision, finding in favor of Tunstall and the ACRT.[64]

The Tunstall case, one of the period's most publicized race-related labor initiatives, also had full community backing. The *Norfolk Journal and Guide* carried eight feature stories on either the ACRT or Tom Tunstall. One of its final stories featured the headline: "Firemen Score Another Victory in Tunstall Case." In the body of the story, the paper proudly quoted from Supreme Court Justice Murphy's concurring opinion: "The Constitution voices its disapproval whenever economic discrimination is applied under authority of law against any race, creed or color. A sound democracy cannot allow such discrimination to go unchallenged."[65] These words captured the essence of everything blacks had been saying since the war's beginning. They also underscored the effectiveness of wedding class-based economic issues to racial concerns. Clearly, what benefited the worker paid dividends to the community.

Thus even opposition by white laborites did not stymie the groundswell of support building in the black community for protecting the gains achieved in labor circles. For the first time, black labor officials— frequently without, but sometimes with, the support of whites—emphasized the common world shared by blacks at work and at home. Gone were the principals who in the 1930s had attempted to organize black workers. Gone too was much of the rhetorical excess about revolutionizing America. In its place, labor officials tied unions to bread-and-butter issues such as better pay, job security, and structured hours. Local constituents listened as black and white representatives of the International Hod Carriers Union and the Building and Common Laborers Union of America Local 307 encouraged blacks to don union buttons and pay the poll tax.[66] Many whites helped by welcoming blacks into their ranks, enthusiastically in some cases, coolly in others.

## THE CONTINUED IMPORTANCE OF
## HOME SPHERE DEVELOPMENT

Although shifts in the economy enticed blacks to seek workplace improvements, few abandoned the older strategies concerned with developing the home sphere. The route to community empowerment continued to be focused on obtaining better roads, schools, and city services, as well as a greater say in city affairs. This time, however, some of the obstacles to interracial labor solidarity had been cleared. For the first time, certain blacks were considered workers at work. This change ironically placed them more squarely in the center of the working class. And, like working-class folks elsewhere, they discovered that the battle for the city remained an ethnic one. In this milieu, Afro-Americans reaffirmed an older orientation instead of embracing a newer one. As before, they would fight a racial battle for community empowerment.[67]

A war-produced subplot complicates the storyline, however. We might explain what happened between 1941 and 1945 as a reaction to the country's failure to breathe life into the words of the constitution or the Declaration of Independence; but it was more. Like most blacks across the nation, blacks in Norfolk believed in the principles that led the country to engage in the war. They wanted to contribute; they sincerely wanted to achieve—or overachieve—in every aspect. As a consequence, a collision took place between the conflicting tendencies to protest angrily and point the finger when city officials, neighbors, or the federal government violated the basic precepts of democracy, on the one hand, and a tendency to mute opposition lest it be construed as somehow unpatriotic, on the other. It was this collision that helped to shape strategic rethinking.

The world of Norfolk blacks changed tremendously when the city became involved in the war. The federal government, in conjunction with the city, established several governing boards and councils to coordinate civilian-military affairs. Blacks, of course, wanted proportional representation, and the assurances came. City manager Borlund appointed P. B. Young and David Alston, both respected members of the black leadership, to the Civilian Defense Council in 1942. In other instances, the city established separate but parallel units on which blacks served, such as the all-black Rationing Board No. 2, the all-black Draft Board, and the all-black USO.[68] These creations mollified public concern but did little to rechannel the undercurrent of fear and uneasiness that troubled the city.

Representation on these boards reflected the effectiveness and forcefulness with which Afro-Americans challenged city officials, a challenge that frightened whites. Blacks made it clear that certain affronts would no longer be peacefully endured. Whites interpreted all signs of black assertiveness as impudence. Marvin Schlegel wrote in the official municipal history of Norfolk during the Second World War: "Some Negroes asserted their rights with insolence, and some whites arrogantly tried to put them in their place."[69] Schlegel's assessment referred to a series of incidents beginning in 1942, some of them public, others private.

Privately, the little transgressions in civility that blacks had once obediently ignored now became intolerable. B. T. Holmes, director of an organization called the Negro Council for National Defense, wrote to

R. M. Marshall, coordinator of the Civilian Defense Office, to complain about such breaches. He was particularly offended by the Civilian Defense Office's practice of issuing identification cards bearing the phrases "woolly hair and maroon eyes." To Holmes, this was a throwback to a traditional practice that had little to do with proper identification. He was emphatic that "such descriptions are . . . positively resented." He also raised a much more sensitive concern that went to the heart of interracial protocol: "Also many colored volunteers detest equally as much to be referred to as Sam, George, Susie or boy. Such practices and the philosophy which makes for them are no help to [national] unity during times of peace nor war." Reportedly representing some thirty civic, political, labor, social, and benevolent groups, Holmes sternly demanded that Marshall's office "issue specific instructions to all personnel to terminate the discourteous practices mentioned above."[70]

Marshall recognized the legitimacy of Holmes's first complaint and confessed to P. B. Young in a separate letter that he honestly hoped the directive he sent to his employees would end the practice. He professed great displeasure, however, with Holmes's second charge. He refused to believe that anyone in his office had made such disparaging comments. More telling, he wondered whether Holmes had a right to raise the issue.[71] It is likely, therefore, that Marshall did little to correct a problem he did not believe existed.

Publicly, blacks fumed over the obtrusiveness of the various segregation ordinances, many codified three decades earlier. None of the laws proved as troublesome or tiresome as the one authorizing the separation of blacks and whites on buses and streetcars. The wartime restrictions imposed on gasoline, tires, and driving, coupled with the increase in population, meant that more people rode buses, seriously taxing the public transportation system. Indeed, blacks in the new developments of Roberts Park and Liberty Park were at first excluded from the VEPCO bus lines.[72] Given the dimension of the crisis, blacks argued that any attempt to observe segregation was ludicrous.

A few whites agreed. Virginius Dabney, editor of the *Richmond Times-Dispatch,* penned an editorial calling for the repeal of the state ordinance. The Norfolk Interracial Commission voiced its approval of the editorial and the philosophy it embraced. But the officials of the bus and streetcar companies and city officials, including the police and the local courts, refused to bend.[73]

Perhaps the most honest critique was offered by Louis Jaffe, editor of Norfolk's *Virginian-Pilot.* He wrote Dabney to ask how he could endorse the abolition of segregated accommodations in transportation without realizing the implications for dismantling the entire system of racial segregation. Dabney retorted that he foresaw no such threat. Yet neither the city nor the state approved Dabney's plan, leaving blacks and whites to battle over the merits of segregation.[74]

At first, white bus drivers and streetcar conductors simply enforced the segregation order one-sidedly. They turned their heads when whites ignored the imaginary dividing line separating the races and sat in the black section. Instead of arresting the offending white, the driver would force black passengers to move. But when blacks violated the seating arrangements, white drivers were quite vigilant. In one case, bus driver Clyde Horner noticed Sara Morris Davis, a black schoolteacher, seated between two white passengers at the front of the bus. Horner told her to vacate her seat immediately. Reportedly in a firm but even voice, Davis explained to the driver that the bus was full and that the seat in front was the only one available. Where else, she asked, was she to sit? The driver answered gruffly that he did not care, as long as she vacated that particular seat. She refused, the police were summoned, and she was arrested.

Upset by the entire episode, Davis initiated one of the first legal challenges to a state's segregation laws, a decade before the now-famous Montgomery bus boycott, which sparked the direct action phase of the civil rights movement. Davis's attorney contended that the bus driver willfully ignored a white passenger sitting in the black section and enforced the law in only one direction. The Virginia Supreme Court of Appeals agreed with Davis, in a June 1944 split decision. It ruled that the law was to be enforced in a nondiscriminatory manner. Thus, in this narrowly focused case, the court decided that the actions of the bus drivers—and not the law—discriminated.[75]

The decision brought only mixed blessings to the black community, because it failed to address the real issue: segregation on public conveyances. Neither did it direct bus drivers to employ common courtesy in dealing with black passengers. Streetcar drivers could continue to tease black passengers by accepting their money and then pulling away when they went to the back door to board. And it did not protect blacks when a bus driver, often a newcomer, chose to impose the most rigid interpretation of the law. In one such instance, a driver noticed that three blacks were the only remaining passengers at the end of his route and that they were sitting in seats in front of the dividing line. Rather than ignoring the violation, he zealously instructed the three to move to the back of the bus. One man refused. The police were summoned, but, after they arrested the wrong man, all charges had to be dropped.[76]

Competitive race relations clearly had not disappeared as a central component of day-to-day life. In fact, race-related disagreements caused great dissension. White Americans, claimed a *Negro Digest* poll, believed that blacks did not deserve the same guarantees and privileges that whites enjoyed. Blacks began to ask why "at this time when all of us should be united and working for one common cause, prejudice is raising its ugly head, snapping and biting at a group of people in whose veins flow the blood of patriotism just as strong as in any white person that ever trod American soil." Blacks were concerned with "minor" issues like segregated buses because they believed the war was being fought for a nobler cause—the extension of democratic liberties worldwide. This was why the Young Men's Civic Organization (YMCO) in nearby Portsmouth asked in a newspaper article what they were to tell black soldiers fighting abroad to preserve democracy about democracy at home.[77]

Of course, the white community was not a monolith. On occasion, public officials spoke of interracial civility, if not civil rights. Early in 1942, city manager Borlund pleaded. "Do not let anyone draw you into an argument because a man's skin is black, or his religion is something or other. This is not the time . . . and no time is the right time . . . for racial or religious intolerance, especially not in Virginia."[78] But for Davis, members of the YMCO, and countless others who no longer agreed to accept segregation, there was more at stake then civility.

The new determination of blacks frightened whites. Rumors even spread through the white community that blacks planned to massacre the white citizens of Norfolk during one of the periodic war-related blackouts. Each time the lights dimmed between June and August of 1942, whites braced themselves for an attack by blacks armed with ice picks. This ludicrous charge was actually investigated by the police department, who found sales of "the obsolescent kitchen utensil" normal. Most of the rumormongers were whites. Officials tried to assuage fears by blaming the rumors on "enemies of our domestic peace." But the problem went deeper. During the same period, allegations surfaced that one of those ubiquitous "Eleanor Clubs"—supposedly, formally organized groups of black women who took direction from Eleanor Roosevelt's tendency to challenge conventions on racial matters—operated in the city. According to many white housewives, the "Eleanorites would insist on the right to enter the kitchen by way of the front door"; they might become surly and refuse to don servants' uniforms or work limitless hours, or they might commit an even more grievous error like refusing to answer when addressed by their first names.[79]

Astonished by the allegations, blacks tried to limit the damage by dismissing both claims as unfounded. They neither had any intentions of starting a race war nor had they heard of an "Eleanor Club." Many declared that it was preposterous to think blacks would plan to attack whites, particularly with ice picks. When asked about the rumors, Clifton T. Epps answered, somewhat indignantly, "Like most other people of Norfolk, I heard the rumors but I didn't think much about it because I felt Negroes were generally too sensible to launch an attack against whites armed with meager ice picks." Overwhelmed by the incredible nature of the charges and offended by the underlying assumptions, Tom McClain chimed in, "It hardly seems reasonable that they would attempt riots and disorder, using only ice picks while thousands of soldiers, sailors, marines and police officers are virtually ringed around the city."[80] Even in attempting to placate whites, however, no one denied wanting a change in the basic social arrangements. It became apparent that along with democracy they expected dignity.

The black community was not a monolith, either. The same internal tensions and conflicts that had existed between 1910 and 1941 still existed during the war. Some older leaders criticized younger leaders when the latter championed too fast a pace. When B. T. Holmes wrote to R. M. Marshall about the terms of address used in referring to blacks, P. B. Young criticized the young man for being brash and hotheaded. And even when the debate over segregation on buses reached its high point, some quarters of the community objected more to the indiscriminate manner in which whites addressed blacks than to the existence of Jim Crow. The courts, the *Norfolk Journal and Guide* charged, seemed more willing to believe "half illiterate bus or streetcar operators" than responsible and educated black citizens. As a result, "the better class of Norfolk's colored citizens, particularly those of well defined cultural sensibilities, have become victims of the state segregation law in effect on streetcars and buses."[81]

Meanwhile, indigenous black institutions performed an invaluable role in inculcating values and beliefs central to winning the war, even as they also served the interests of the black community. Long the conduit through which important messages traveled, the black church assumed a more visible role, especially in the early years of the war, serving as host to city officials and providing them with a direct pipeline to blacks. When Mayor Woods spoke at the Men's Day Celebration at St. Paul CME Church in February 1942, he delivered a plain and straightforward message: while the war lasted, citizens must work toward racial cooperation and avoid racial discord. On another occasion, when the level of volunteer support lagged behind expectations, black leaders went to ministers, who in turn used their pulpits as a rallying place. Similarly, when the longshoremen threatened a strike, the ministers directed the workers to place the needs of the whole community ahead of the priorities of a few. From the church came socially transmitted guidelines for acceptable behavior.[82]

And regardless of how many times they challenged social customs, most blacks did aim to fulfill their patriotic duties. Some were token representatives on various bureaucratic boards concerned with matters such as rationing, the draft, and civilian defense. Many spent a great deal of time and energy involved in other programs. The entire collection of indigenous social welfare institutions—from the YMCA and YWCA to the Boy Scouts to the Colored United Charities—donated volunteers to the Civilian Mobilization and Civilian Defense programs. These women and men became office helpers and program consultants; they served as hostesses, dance partners, and chaperons for the USO; and they worked in hospitals and for the Red Cross.[83] Such participation enabled Norfolk Afro-Americans to help the country and to help themselves by demonstrating their competence.

Competence and patriotism were not the only reasons for their participation. Service on the various boards and councils increased the role of blacks in local affairs—even on a segregated basis. In large part, this explains why the placement of an office of the Rationing Board in the Uptown district was deemed so important. Located on Church Street, "Board #48–65–5 was administered entirely by Negro citizens," and blacks composed nearly the entire clientele, although they could patronize the white board if necessary. The board regulated prices and buying procedures for consumers as well as merchants. Encouraged to abide by the guidelines established for food prices by the Office of Price Administration, many simply did not understand how to do this and probably chose not to learn. Some citizens ignored the directives or misinterpreted them. Consequently, price maintenance surfaced as a major problem. In addition, many owners of small businesses experienced difficulty getting merchandise delivered. Burdened with an unpredictable inventory, they increased prices to stay afloat. To alleviate these and other problems, the board organized an "institute and conducted regular classes in how to mark up the goods for sale."[84]

Norfolk Afro-Americans viewed representation rather than education as the most important aspect of the board. In their quest to realize improvements in the home sphere, black Norfolkians were broadening the range of what was possible. Many entertained new ideas about their place in the city and their role in its governance. Some even considered black representation on previously off-limits bodies like the school board. Norfolk resident Loscie Ridley commented, "Any group that is without personal representation is bound to suffer and we as a group have suffered long enough. It is high time we were represented by someone who has our interest at heart, not only on the school board but on all other civic boards where the advancement of the Negro is at stake." George Jones understood, too, that representation alone was not sufficient, that those who represented Afro-Americans had to have their interests at heart. He observed, "The advantages of such an appointment are too numerous to mention, provided the City Council selects a man who has the interest of his race at heart and not a 'Judas.' " Most recognized that such representatives shouldered the dual responsibility of changing white attitudes and protecting the interests of the black community. If inroads could be made in both areas, most believed that progress in the home sphere would follow.[85]

One of the primary reasons blacks demanded representation on various boards and remained racially vigilant was that certain elements of the community's infrastructure remained hopelessly underdeveloped, particularly its recreational facilities. Federal officials recognized this as a problem. P. N. Binford, field recreation representative, wrote to Mark A. McClosky, director of recreation at the Office of Defense Health and Welfare Services in June 1942 that, as a result of the rapid influx of workers and the consequent overexpansion, "facilities of all kinds are sadly lacking."[86]

Another federal report issued in early 1941 painted a similarly bleak picture. The city operated five so-called community centers for blacks. Each center ran its own program, and each was open only during the school year. Black residents had access to only one gym in the city, at Booker T. Washington High. Moreover, most recreation centers were small wooden-frame buildings. Given both the undeveloped physical plant and the size of the structures, juveniles rather than adults became the primary patrons.[87] As a result, black enlisted men who came to Norfolk in 1941 discovered few diversions other than hanging out at bars and tippling houses, visiting prostitutes, or playing basketball twice a week at the local high school. More frustrating, families with children quickly found that only two of the seven playgrounds had any equipment and that none remained open during the school year.

The black community therefore continued its long struggle to improve the poor recreational facilities, especially for black military personnel. When the mobilization first began, all sources admitted that "Negro Naval Personnel were the most neglected young men in this community." Groups soon organized to correct that wrong. Following meetings with the navy and the Central YMCA, the Hunton Branch of the Y opened part of its facility as a dormitory, and its director became a part-time social coordinator. With assistance from the navy, the Hunton Y obtained about seventy beds for navy, army, and other military and civilian personnel. And, before the construction of the Smith Street USO, the Y also sponsored weekly dances at Booker T. Washington High School.[88]

The story of the Smith Street USO underscores why some believed that there was an ongoing need for vigilance in racial matters. Given the rules of segregation, Afro-Americans in Norfolk welcomed the addition of a USO for black men. They were especially proud that William Houston, dean of Howard University and civilian aide to Secretary of War Henry L. Stimson, agreed to dedicate the building on 9 February 1942. But the USO eventually became a cruel reminder of their second-class status in a Jim Crow town. Locals had argued that the USO should be located in one of the better sections of town, but most would have settled for any place besides Smith Street, which bisected one of the city's worst slums. Many complaints came from members of the black middle class, whose class position did not blind them to the obvious: Smith Street was like a checkerboard of cobblestones and mud. During the rainy season, passage became inconvenient if not impossible. Mud from the street splattered the building, giving it a drab, greyish appearance. The street and the slum location became so bad that many parents forbade their daughters to serve as hostesses, refusing to allow them to walk the dark, threatening streets and alleys leading to the building.[89]

Nevertheless, black military personnel and the civilians who befriended them were denied access to other USOs and had nowhere else to go. And the digest of services rendered by the Smith Street USO was impressive. During the war years, 1,924,075 persons attended activities at the building. More than 230,000 utilized the recreational, educational, and personal service equipment. More than 47,000 used the USO's sleeping quarters, and 11,725, victimized by the harshness of wartime life, sought counseling. Thus, despite its poor location and the associated problems, the USO provided an invaluable service.[90]

Norfolk residents also increased their efforts to influence electoral politics during these years, although they obviously did not abandon protest politics. Politics, the franchise, and voting assumed a new importance to many who were influenced by the rhetoric of the period. An unidentified citizen, distraught over enforcement of the segregation laws, wrote a letter to the newspaper encouraging all blacks to use the ballot to elect those who had their best interests in mind. He had some harsh words for blacks in Portsmouth who helped reelect the very people who in the past had supported the segregation ordinances, the police, and the courts. If blacks were determined to change the system, he counseled, they had to stop voting for such people. And the leadership had to stop "sell[ing] their people down the river" for a few privileges. The advancement of the race and the improvement of the home sphere were perceived to be directly related to the acquisition of greater political power.[91]

Dr. Luther P. Jackson, a graduate of the University of Chicago and a professor of history at Virginia State College in Petersburg, heard the plea and spearheaded a statewide voter registration drive, which began in April 1941. Jackson surveyed voting habits in Norfolk, where he found to his dismay that between 4.1 and 4.6 percent of the 27,920 eligible black voters paid the poll tax—and only a fraction of that number actually voted. Jackson and a group he headed to increase black voter participation formed an alliance with labor and other organizations to increase the number of taxpayers and voters.[92]

Black labor leaders played an important role in the campaign. Members of the Labor-Citizen League formed a Colored Poll Tax Committee, which was led by Rev. W. H. Bowe, local head of the Pile Drivers Union. Joining Bowe on the committee were P. J. Chessom, Samuel Hill, Charlie Williams, Southall Bass III, John W. Ruffin, Ernest Fazzaro, and Fred Trotman. This committee set an immediate and attainable goal of reaching those individuals who, for whatever reason, could not go downtown to pay the treasurer. This effort was aided when the courts, at the behest of labor, agreed that a person could send a proxy to pay his or her poll tax.[93]

Within the first year of the campaign, an additional 250 Norfolk blacks paid the poll tax. This number might seem small, but it should be compared to figures for 1940–1941, when the ranks grew by only 40 people. To measure the effectiveness of the campaign fully, we need only look at statistics for 1944. In that year, 5,297 black residents paid the poll tax in full, resulting in the addition of 4,113 registrants between 1940 and 1944. More important, most of this growth—4,098 of the new registrants, or an increase of 347 percent—occurred after Jackson's initial survey. This vividly testifies to both the effectiveness of the campaign and the newfound importance blacks assigned to paying the tax and voting. Residents knew that political power ultimately followed political clout and that clout would be developed only when blacks availed themselves of all opportunities.[94]

This political upsurge was reflected in the personal philosophies of residents, too. Percy Walton grew up in Norfolk, but he had never voted. After the registration drives, he commented, "I have lived here all my life and only last year did it occur to me how important it was to pay the poll tax and vote. . . . I am going to vote too because I think it's the only way of saying just whom you want to run the city." John Wood added, "Once we have a strong voting population we will be heard on such matters as housing, streets, sanitation." Dolly Jones also wanted to make the system work for Afro-Americans. She summed up the prevailing sentiment: "Five thousand qualified voters would make a lot of difference in the attitude of other people toward us, and many of our desires for a better Norfolk."[95]

Certainly blacks in the pre–World War II era had expressed political consciousness. And they continued to possess the political acumen to determine when a political candidate did or did not have their interests at heart. In 1942, for example, many residents in the heavily black Twenty-

First Precinct voted for the Communist party or the Socialist party candidate after they found the Democratic candidate lacking.[96] But a qualitative and quantitative change occurred, beginning in 1943 and intensifying in 1944. Primarily, the tenor and the frequency of political activity increased dramatically. Individually, more and more residents took part in the public debate over the importance of the franchise. Collectively, blacks joined organizations such as the Adams Ward Voters League, which held regular meetings in 1944 with the purpose of attracting a broad cross-section of the population. Afro-Americans even succeeded in getting one of their own to attend the Norfolk City Democratic Committee, reportedly as a full member. We need only note some of the league's speakers—David Alston, black labor recruiter for the Virginia State Federation of Labor, and Mrs. J. P. Giddings, national field worker for the UNIA—to get a sense of its actual population base, even though the black middle class, from all accounts, dominated the leadership positions.[97]

Ironically, however, greater political integration would eventually mean the death of many of the race-exclusive organizations that had served black Norfolkians so well over the years. The changes would also bring an end to the careers of race leaders such as P. B. Young, who in 1943 was the chair of the Southern Conference on Race Relations, the presiding officer of the board of trustees of Howard University, and a member of the second FEPC; in their drive to improve race relations, these leaders inadvertently set the stage for their own obsolescence.[98] In any case, we can only speculate that they would not have opposed the changes even if they could have stopped them. The battle for empowerment produced some notable successes. One of the most striking and most specific was that, after constant public pressure, two blacks received regular appointments to the Norfolk police force in late November 1945, for the first time in seventy years.[99]

The addition of Afro-Americans to the regular police force marked the culmination of three generations of social agitation. Since the end of the Civil War, Norfolk blacks had waged a determined battle to empower themselves. They had accepted as their motto a personal philosophy once expressed by Norfolk resident Annie Dryer: "We, like all the rest of the people on this earth, can't get anything unless we fight for it. Nobody is giving more than they think they are compelled to."[100] This willingness to fight for their rights cut through the various strategies adopted over the years. What materialized during the war years was but the latest variation.

Although there was considerable continuity in this latest strategy, there were also notable breaks with the past. For the first time, the industrial world was configured in such a way as to allow blacks to become workers at work. Once this was accomplished, black residents supported workplace advancement as a key to developing the home sphere. They did not abandon efforts in other areas, for little had changed in the battle for city services. Rather, a more complex view of the world evolved. Henceforth, Afro-Americans could be workers at work and blacks at home. How they viewed themselves determined the strategies they adopted as they struggled to act in their own interests.

# Conclusion:
# Everything Has Changed, but
# Everything Remains the Same

The southern urban landscape has changed impressively since Norfolk resident Ada Forest advised in 1943, "Voting is the only way we can do our part to be sure that our boys have a better home when they come back from the war."[1] Forest knew that voting was no cure-all, but she viewed increased political participation as part of a process that would ultimately lead to the dismantling of Jim Crow. Many who came of age during the Depression and World War II believed this, too, and they acted on those beliefs. More than four decades after the end of World War II, and a generation beyond the 1963 March on Washington, Afro-Americans occupy positions of responsibility and authority in ever-increasing numbers—more than six thousand by 1985, mostly in the South. In Norfolk, too, conditions have changed. Today, the vice-mayor is black, as are the superintendent of schools and several other top-ranking city administrators and public officials.[2]

In the light of these dramatic changes, both the benefits and the limits of earlier strategies become even more obvious. Ada Forest and her contemporaries inherited and refined a formula for group advancement based on life in a particular stage of America's industrial history. Racial barriers to advancement, they believed, prevented blacks from securing a social, political, or economic safe haven. The elimination of Jim Crow therefore became their highest priority.

Only now is it clear that segregation was but one head of the hydra blocking the path to empowerment. Few possessed such clarity of analysis in 1955 or 1965; most were blinded by the success of their own powerful actions and were often unable to see that America was changing in profound ways. As more and more blacks moved into the urban core, for example, more and more manufacturing jobs moved to the urban fringe or out of America altogether.[3] The simultaneous transformation of America's racial and economic profiles meant that the path others had followed to material success no longer existed; ironically, just as strategies for improvement began to pay dividends, the nation entered a new historical epoch. As a result, even in Atlanta, with its politically powerful black leadership and expanding economic base, the benefits and limits of earlier formulas so taunt present-day strategists that on the twenty-fifth anniversary of the Washington march, Rev. Joseph Lowery, president of the Southern Christian Leadership Conference, made the seemingly contradictory claim, "Everything has changed and nothing has changed."[4] His charge underscores both the importance of the Norfolk story as a window on a certain period and the need for more detailed examinations of black communities in the urban South.

### QUASHING JIM CROW

"Most historians would agree that the modern civil rights movement did not begin with the Supreme Court's decision in *Brown* v. *Board of Education*," Robert Korstad and Nelson Lichtenstein argue.[5] Historians may be the only believers, however. If Americans were asked to identify a signal event in the nation's race relations, most would surely mention the Supreme Court's landmark ruling. From 17 May 1954 forward, popular perception goes, America changed forever. Nor is this interpretation without merit. Amazingly, a system of dominance that had taken four generations to assemble was in many respects disassembled in fourteen trying years. During that span, black Americans and their allies put their lives on the line to win benchmark victories in Montgomery, Little Rock, Greensboro, Birmingham, and Selma. Even the 1968 murder of Martin Luther King, Jr., and the election of Richard Nixon as president could not completely undo what had been accomplished. Of course, there were defeats along the way, but in the end the postwar generation had achieved what Ada Forest could only dream of in 1943. It is not surprising, therefore, that to a nation addicted to instant analysis the "modern" civil rights movement began with the *Brown* decision.[6]

To their credit, Korstad and Lichtenstein correctly, but incompletely, challenge this perception. "The civil rights era began, dramatically and decisively, in the early 1940s when the social structure of black America took on an increasingly urban, proletarian character," they maintain. "A predominantly southern rural and small town population was soon transformed into one of the most urban of all major ethnic groups." In many respects, this analysis is correct, for the actions of Afro-Americans during the 1940s certainly played a central role in shaping the modern social movement. From Norfolk to Baton Rouge, Afro-Americans fought to improve their position in the region's political economy.[7]

Nevertheless, as the Norfolk story suggests, there is something lacking even in Korstad and Lichtenstein's important corrective. Norfolk blacks began the battles that culminated in the civil rights movement in the 1860s, not the 1940s. From the start, they sought more than a transformation of race relations. Black Norfolkians—and they were hardly alone—sought full participation in the range of daily life; they sought to share power. For this reason the authors of the *Equal Suffrage Address* warned all Afro-Americans to secure the franchise, promote labor associations, and do everything necessary to protect their collective interests. To argue that the civil rights movement began in the 1940s disregards the enabling actions of Norfolk blacks and their long search for group advancement. The 1940s were not important because they "generated a rights consciousness that gave working-class black militancy a moral justification in some ways as powerful as that evoked by the Baptist spirituality of Martin Luther King, Jr., a generation later." Rather, the 1940s were important because of the way blacks in Norfolk, Birmingham, Winston-Salem, and Detroit redefined their own interests: as dependent on both advancement in the workplace and improvement in the home sphere.[8]

Ironically, however, the long-overdue opportunity to quash Jim Crow reoriented strategies and narrowed choices. The tone of the early years of the civil rights movement was established against a backdrop of increasing white resistance to any breach in the status quo. Virginia's Senator Harry Byrd spoke for many when he openly declared, "If we can organize the Southern States for massive resistance . . . I think in time the rest of the country will realize that racial integration is not going to be accepted in the South."[9] Byrd and his peers initially failed to appreciate the determination of Afro-Americans to change the social order. Eloquently, Martin Luther King, Jr., captured the spirit of that resolve in a speech at the inaugural gathering of the Montgomery bus boycott movement. As his words rose above swelling choruses of "Amen," King insisted, "There comes a time when people get tired. We are here this evening to say to those who have mistreated us so long that we are tired—tired of being segregated and humiliated, tired of being kicked about by the brutal feet of oppression."[10]

By 1955 hundreds of Afro-American indeed felt tired. Some had been residents of the urban South for many years; others had arrived in the past ten years. Together, newcomers and old-timers changed the racial profile of many southern cities. Between 1940 and 1960, the black populations of Montgomery and Birmingham, for example, jumped 84 and 40 percent, respectively; by 1950 blacks were nearly 40 percent of the population in both cities.[11] A similar wave of black migration had accompanied World War I without appreciably altering the social order, but the 1950s were different. Primarily, though the rate of suburbanization was lower in the South than in the North, it was large enough to have an effect. Consequently, more and more downtown merchants found themselves dependent for economic survival on the blacks who remained in the urban centers. This in turn increased the real and symbolic buying power of Afro-Americans.[12]

But too few blacks had any real economic security, a point that is increasingly discussed today. Recently, Harold Cruse criticized the leadership of the NAACP for endorsing a plan of noneconomic liberalism; by inference, he indicted the entire civil rights establishment.[13] The degree to which the NAACP and other organizations simply reflected entrenched attitudes in the black community is not clear, however. In addition, statistics supported those who believed blacks were making measured economic progress: though parity was not attained, the income gap between blacks and whites narrowed between 1940 and 1960.[14]

We now know that blacks made the greatest financial and occupational gains in areas that had long been open to them. Few new opportunities materialized during the period. As a result, Afro-Americans, the most urbanized of all citizens by 1960, remained disproportionately working-class (more than 70 percent, according to Landry), especially in the South.[15] Far too many blacks stood on the economic margins; it was imperative but not always obvious that they needed to pursue economic rights as vigorously as civil rights. But this did not happen.

For reasons that are clear given the times yet in hindsight intellectually frustrating, blacks in communities across the South accepted the primacy of removing Jim Crow. It was not that blacks of the civil rights era totally ignored economic issues. In Baton Rouge, Montgomery, and Tallahassee, they organized successful economic boycotts, and in Montgomery they made the hiring of black bus drivers a chief demand. Nevertheless, through 1966, almost all major civil rights groups and local communities failed to balance the empowerment equation. When the Reverend Andrew White of Nashville stressed the importance of economic as well as legal improvement, one of his contemporaries countered, "We did not disagree with the fact that [the economic issue] was most important, but our view was that sit-ins would lend themselves to kind of a public presentation of the issue." When asked why he favored a frontal attack on Jim Crow over any other plan, White's friend confessed that it "would be better than any procedures of which we were aware when dealing with economics."[16]

Even in Norfolk, priorities and strategies shifted after 1955. Although in general the city adjusted to the end of segregation better than most, desegregation came because blacks pushed. Feelings ran deep on both sides of the color line when several black students agreed to challenge the constitutionality of a state law requiring the closing of any public school that desegregated. Although nearly two years had passed since the 1957 turmoil in Little Rock when black students attempted to attend Central High School, school desegregation remained an explosive issue. In accordance with state law, Norfolk closed its schools for a time to avoid the inevitable—six schools were actually closed for five months, affecting nearly ten thousand students. When schools reopened in early 1959, the nation watched.[17]

The explosion many feared never materialized, but for several months the city teetered on the edge. Members of Norfolk's white community opposed desegregation with as much passion as any resident of Little Rock. Blacks who moved into the Green Hill Farms and Coronado sections in 1954, near all-white Norview High School, experienced that passion firsthand—they were welcomed by bombs and blazing crosses. The most diehard segregationists belonged to the Defenders of State Sovereignty, a small, ultraconservative, pro-segregationist body that exerted influence disproportionate to its size in the early days of the school struggle. The group used threats, a well-orchestrated direct-mail campaign, and the establishment of alternative private schools to influence public opinion. In the end, most whites capitulated, believing that closing the public schools was too great a price to pay to preserve segregation. One white housewife spoke for the majority when she told Samuel Lubell, "I was more satisfied with segregated schools but this is better than closed schools."[18]

Upon deeper reflection some whites even admitted that blacks deserved equal treatment. Some, however, had a keen understanding of the subtleties of Jim Crow and were well aware that a shift in policy did not always produce a change in behavior or social practices or a sharing of power. "When the buses were desegregated only a few of the younger Negroes sat up front with the whites. Most of them didn't change at all. Isn't that what would happen if everything was free? Things wouldn't be too different. But the Negroes wouldn't have an issue to fight about," one white resident shrewdly and proudly proclaimed.[19]

This speculation proved to be prophetic. Modifications of the racial and social order produced tremendous change; yet, paradoxically, much remained the same. We should not forget that the death of Jim Crow was a tremendous feat, occasioned by a thoughtful, well-executed plan. The black schoolchildren who entered the formerly segregated schools of Norfolk, for example, trained for sixteen weeks for their roles as agents of social change. Because nothing could be left to chance, they received instruction in deportment, in handling racial conflict, and in meeting the academic challenges. And although they entered the schools alone, none acted individually. Civil rights activist Vivian Mason spoke for most in the community when she said: "The children understood completely that the whole community was behind them."[20] Other black communities made similar commitments. But the power of their successes also revealed the limits of the civil rights approach.

## AN OUT-OF-DATE CULTURE OF EXPECTATIONS

James Farmer, former head of the Congress of Racial Equality, poignantly analyzed the shortcomings of this approach in a 1967 address. A sinister mood gripped the country that year. A few years earlier, Harlem and Watts had exploded, and that year Newark and Detroit had done the same. Many feared that inner-city residents had adopted the chant "Burn, baby, burn!" as a personal anthem. Farmer, hoping to explain the dramatic turn of events, revisited Little Rock, site of the Central High School crisis ten years earlier. He ran into an old acquaintance there who offered: "Brother Farmer, everything has changed, but everything remains the same. Yes, I can now buy a hot dog at the lunch counter. Big deal." He went on to complain:

> Yes, I can go downtown and check into a hotel, if I had the money, which I don't. I have been out of work for six months. And furthermore, if I go three miles outside the city, I won't know that there ever was a Civil Rights Act of 1964. And yes, we can sit on the front seat of a bus. We can go to the theater and sit in the audience; we can buy a hot dog and a hamburger. Everything has changed but everything remains the same.[21]

Without realizing it at the time, perhaps, the Little Rock resident anticipated the next twenty years of Afro-American history. Clearly, his comments captured the degree of dissonance between expectations and conditions.

Afro-Americans entered the 1950s with a culture of expectations that quickly fell out of step with the march of time. By *culture of expectations*, I mean a socially and culturally generated sense of what is attainable. Dan (a pseudonym), for example, was born in the late 1950s to parents who migrated from rural North Carolina to Norfolk. His parents stressed hard work and responsibility, but not education. Dan dropped out of school after the eighth grade; this was not unusual in his family, for only two of his five siblings finished high school. His lack of formal education did not trouble him at the outset, because he harbored a certain set of expectations. Dan had a brother seven years his senior, who had also left school after the eighth grade and had landed a well-paid job as a longshoreman. The muscular Dan expected to duplicate this success, given his family ties—his father was a longshore crew leader. But Dan's world had changed in profound ways, without his knowledge. Mechanization, a worldwide recession, and stiffer eligibility requirements conspired against him; even his family contacts were not enough. Dan came of age, out of step.[22]

There are thousands of Dans. Some will live out their lives as members of the respectable but economically disadvantaged Afro-American working class. Others will slide into the amorphous grouping labeled the underclass or the truly disadvantaged. And, of course, a few will become members of the new black middle class.[23] Regardless of their class position, Dan's peers inhabit a desegregated world in the throes of a radical structural realignment. In Philadelphia, for example, just as Afro-Americans moved into the urban core, the jobs they expected to fill moved in the opposite direction—to surrounding suburbs, to other states, or to other countries. As Hershberg and his colleagues discovered, the economic opportunity structure for Afro-Americans in central cities changed even as racial barriers to occupational mobility became illegal.[24] In a number of ways, the dismantling of Jim Crow proved to have been an easier task than realigning the economic opportunity structure and the culture of expectations.

With only a few exceptions, however, strategies after 1965 often seemed frozen in time. Much of the civil rights effort was designed to tackle the most egregious aspects of southern segregation. The thousands of Afro-Americans who lived outside the region in the nation's decaying inner cities felt abandoned. Few could answer the question raised by Claude Brown in *Manchild in the Promised Land*: "For where does one run to when he is already in the promised land?"[25] For instance, although Martin Luther King's venture into Chicago forcefully reoriented the civil rights warrior, he and his associates discovered that tackling the concomitant problems of urban unemployment, underemployment, and poor housing required a different approach. That such an approach escaped them underscored how much conditions had changed and were changing. Increasingly, black Americans began to understand that attacks on segregation and discrimination addressed only part of the problem.

Unfortunately, years of fighting to change the ugly side of American life left strategists spent. Even the 1968 Poor People's March on Washington lacked a certain freshness. King's untimely death and the state of disarray in which it left the Poor People's Campaign, combined with the state's hostile response to locally produced black initiatives and a conflict of visions over guarantees of opportunity and assurances of outcome, rendered many solutions ineffective.[26] We are still positioned today at a historical crossroads, searching for new strategies. What remains constant is a desire to share power in a plural society and the need for Afro-Americans to balance their interests at work and at home. Unless this is done, and unless economic achievements follow the notable political advancements, we jeopardize the longevity of hard-won gains.

## CONCLUSION

Untangling the mysteries of the past requires one to explain the inexplicable, the complex, and the contradictory. In the process, one also comes to understand the importance of the stumbles, missteps, and wrong-headed actions. Such is the case with the history of blacks in Norfolk, Virginia, between 1862 and the 1960s. The men, women, and children who called this city home for those many years struggled to secure a place in the local setting. Their efforts tell us a great deal about a city, a region, and a time in American history.

Norfolk blacks entered the Reconstruction years with a universal desire to share the fruits of American life. More forcefully than some, they articulated a strategy: group advancement hinged on development in both the workplace and the home sphere, they informed the nation. As the century drew to a close and access to political and economic power declined, black residents astutely modified this strategy. They did not change their goal, but they did alter the path they would take. Thus, by the beginning of the twentieth century, black residents were focusing on improvements in the home sphere rather than on advancement in the workplace.

It is clear that the black community was never monolithic. Intraracial class differences shaped perspectives almost as much as life in a Jim Crow city did. Black business people and their working-class patrons had different views about whether "buying black" buttressed the community's economic foundation. Garveyites and middle-class leaders openly debated the best means of securing their rightful place in the city. Black labor leaders and their working-class constituents often ignored middle-class sages who advised them to eschew labor activism. Nevertheless, the wide range of persons and personalities who called Norfolk home shared a point of agreement: throughout the years, they were determined to act in their own interests.

This ability to agree on fundamental matters had a lot to do with the importance of the home sphere. Today, the word *home* has an important meaning in black America. But home is not a new concept. Afro-Americans have always searched out "homeboys" and "homegirls." And, as I have tried to suggest, home was always more than the house in which one lived. It was the community, the streets, the neighborhood; it was one's church, friends and relatives; it was a shared culture and shared expectations; it was what one sought to improve, because it was a place worthy of improvement. The multifaceted character of home also made it possible to enlist the aid of so many when it was threatened. For this reason, black residents found it easy to agitate to develop the home sphere further.

Perspectives began to shift in the 1930s. The Depression narrowed the gulf between the well-to-do and the disadvantaged. Locally, blacks were the first to feel the impending economic crisis. Although their experiences were eventually shared by whites, their special place in the political economy meant that they suffered first and longer than others. As a result, they proved more willing to listen to those who promised an alternative to despair and privation. In the beginning, they listened to Communist activists who called for a shift in social discourse. Even the most conservative race leaders applauded the Communists for their willingness to challenge the government and working-class whites on behalf of blacks. Still, the inexorable power of race could not be denied. Black residents understood that they lacked full membership in the working class. In an attempt to come to terms with their particular status, they embraced, rejected, and then reembraced a modified formula for advancement resembling the one advocated by the authors of the *Equal Suffrage Address,* as the attempt to equalize the salaries of black schoolteachers clearly illustrates.

In a way, the salary case prefigured a brief closing of the historical circle; for a moment during the Second World War, perspectives and strategies changed. The war set in motion certain events critical to the realignment. Primarily, it elevated the discussion of what democracy meant. The inconsistency between public rhetoric and social conditions was not lost on blacks; more so than at any time in recent memory, they were determined to obtain a safe place in American life. Equally important, the state introduced laws that aided such efforts; working-class whites sought alliances with blacks on certain issues; and the infrastructure of the black community more successfully supported agitation. Agitation, moreover, took place at work and at home. Black residents demanded better jobs and more security; they sought a greater say in the city's social and political affairs.

The swirl of events that became the civil rights movement promised to produce such a world. Caught in the vortex of a period of intense social change, Norfolk blacks joined in the regionwide campaign to destroy Jim Crow. This decision produced remarkable dividends even as it also exposed the flaws of pursuing development in the home sphere more than in the workplace. Today, we are still evaluating the full effect of this decision. And we are left with the impression that everything has changed and nothing has changed.

Yet to conclude on that point misses the larger story. Possessed by one overriding concern, blacks in Norfolk struggled to take their place as full citizens. Over the course of four generations, they tilled the soil of social change, and in the 1960s they were there to collect the harvest. Now a new season has arrived, and a new crop needs planting. Frederick Douglass said it best: "Those who profess to favor freedom and yet deprecate agitation are men who want the crops without plowing up the ground; they want the rain without the awful roar of its many waters. . . . Power concedes nothing without a demand. It never did and it never will."[27] From the end of the Civil War to the modern civil rights movement, Norfolk residents like Ada Forest understood this point very well. Theirs was an enduring struggle, which reflected their faith in the promise of democracy and their commitment to act in their own interests.

# NOTES

## INTRODUCTION

1. Frederick Douglass is quoted in William H. Chafe, *Civilities and Civil Rights: Greensboro, North Carolina, and the Black Struggle for Freedom* (New York: Oxford University Press, 1980), p. 2. Francis Grimké and A. Philip Randolph are quoted in Philip S. Foner, ed., *The Voice of Black America* (New York: Capricorn Books, 1975), vol. 2, pp. 54–55, 208, respectively.

2. Thomas Hill, interview by Edith Skinner, 2 February 1939, Virginia Writers' Project (VWP 58–71), Virginia State Library, Richmond. The Virginia Writers' Project was an initiative sponsored by the Work Projects Administration (WPA), which culminated in publication of *The Negro in Virginia* (New York: Hasting House, 1940).

3. George C. Wright, *Life Behind a Veil: Blacks in Louisville, Kentucky, 1865–1930* (Baton Rouge: Louisiana State University Press, 1985), pp. 1–10.

4. It was Kenneth Kusmer ("The Black Urban Experience in American History," in *The State of Afro-American History*, ed. Darlene Clark Hine [Baton Rouge: Louisiana State University Press, 1986], pp. 105–6) who first suggested that urban historians examine the interaction among internal, external, and structural factors. Internal factors refer to the world blacks created—their institutions, cultural perspectives, and evolving worldview. External factors refer to the role played by whites in the shaping of black life expectations. Structural factors are nonracial elements, such as the economic organization of the city.

5. The literature concerning urban blacks that focuses on either race relations or ghetto formation is voluminous. Representative studies include W. E. B. Du Bois, *The Philadelphia Negro* (Philadelphia: University of Pennsylvania, 1899); Mary White Ovington, *Half a Man: The Status of the Negro in New York* (New York: Longmans, Green, 1911); St. Clair Drake and Horace Cayton, *Black Metropolis: A Study of Negro Life in a Northern City*, rev. ed. (New York: Harper and Row, 1962); Gilbert Osofsky, *Harlem: The Making of a Ghetto, Negro New York, 1890–1930* (New York: Harper and Row, 1963); Allan H. Spear, *Black Chicago: The*

*Making of a Negro Ghetto, 1890–1920* (Chicago: University of Chicago Press, 1967); and Kenneth L. Kusmer, *A Ghetto Takes Shape: Black Cleveland, 1870–1930* (Urbana: University of Illinois Press, 1976).

6. Joe William Trotter, Jr., *Black Milwaukee: The Making of an Industrial Proletariat* (Urbana: University of Illinois Press, 1985), p. 277.

7. Ibid. The broader theoretical implications of how racial and class views promoted or hampered labor solidarity are broached in Ira Katznelson, *City Trenches: Urban Politics and the Patterning of Class in the United States* (Chicago: University of Chicago Press, 1981), introduction.

8. The implication of the home-work bifurcation for blacks has been most directly addressed by Olivier Zunz, *The Changing Face of Inequality* (Chicago: University of Chicago Press, 1982), pp. 6, 372–98; and Katznelson, *City Trenches*, pp. 17–20 and chaps. 5–8. *Ethnic* is an imprecise word when applied to blacks, primarily because it disregards the ethnic variations among people of African descent. Nevertheless, in certain settings blacks were indeed viewed and treated as an undifferentiated aggregate, much as European immigrant groups were treated. In recognition of this, I substitute the phrase *racial ethnics* to denote a common, yet different, industrial experience.

9. See Herbert Gutman, *Power and Culture,* ed. Ira Berlin (New York: Pantheon Books, 1987), esp. introduction and chap. 8.

10. Since the appearance of Stanley Elkins's provocative treatise on slavery (*Slavery: A Problem in American Institutional and Intellectual Life* [Chicago: University of Chicago Press, 1959]), a generation of historians has implicitly or explicitly debated the degree to which blacks carved out measurable physical and psychic space. The fine points of the debate are most noticeable in the slave historiography. But, as James Borchert's important book suggests, it has also been a concern of urbanists (*Alley Life in Washington* [Urbana: University of Illinois Press, 1980]).

CHAPTER 1

1. Toni Morrison, *Beloved* (New York: Alfred A. Knopf, 1987), pp. 148–53.

2. David L. Goldfield, *Urban Growth in the Age of Sectionalism: Virginia, 1847–1861* (Baton Rouge: Louisiana State University Press, 1977), pp. 195, 197, 205–8; Thomas J. Wertenbaker and Marvin W. Schlegel, *Norfolk: Historic Southern Port* (Durham, N.C.: Duke University Press, 1962), chaps. 5, 8, 9 and p. 299. For further elaboration, see Carville Earle and Ronald Hoffman, "Urban Development in the Eighteenth-Century South," *Perspectives in American History* 10 (1976): 39–48; and David Goldfield, "Pursuing the American Dream: Cities in the Old South," in *The City in Southern History,* ed. Blaine Brownell and David Goldfield (Port Washington, N.Y.: Kennikat Press, 1977), pp. 55–90.

3. Charles L. Perdue, Jr., Thomas E. Barden, and Robert K. Phillips, eds., *Weevils in the Wheat: Interviews with Virginia Ex-Slaves* (Bloomington: Indiana University Press, 1980), p. 115.

4. Ibid., pp. 111–19. See also Leon Litwack, *Been in the Storm So Long* (New York: Alfred A. Knopf, 1979), chaps. 1–5; Ira Berlin et al., eds., *Freedom: A Documentary History of Emancipation, 1861–1867,* Series I (Cambridge: Cambridge University Press, 1985), vol. 1, *The Destruction of Slavery,* esp. chap. 1.

5. Perdue, Barden, and Phillips, *Weevils in the Wheat,* p. 118.

6. Manuscript Census, Norfolk City, 1870, microfilm reel M593–1666, U.S. Bureau of the Census, Record Group 29, National Archives; Perdue, Barden, and Phillips, *Weevils in the Wheat*, pp. 99–103, 268.

7. Ira Berlin, *Slaves Without Masters* (New York: Oxford University Press, 1974), pp. 208–11, 306, 317–18. For an understanding of slavery and its various forms, see Stanley Elkins, *Slavery: A Problem in American Institutional and Intellectual Life* (Chicago: University of Chicago Press, 1959); Robert William Fogel and Stanley L. Engerman, *Time on the Cross: The Economics of American Negro Slavery* (New York: Little, Brown, 1974); and Herbert G. Gutman, *The Black Family in Slavery and Freedom, 1750–1925* (New York: Pantheon Books, 1976). Few studies highlight both the inconsistencies and the rationality of the system as well as Eugene D. Genovese's *Roll, Jordan, Roll: The World the Slave Made* (New York: Vintage Books, 1976).

8. Wertenbaker and Schlegel, *Norfolk*, pp. 233–35. The overall response to emancipation was very complex, with some blacks favoring certain actions over others. But nothing suggests that those blacks who fled to Norfolk or lived there before the war maintained a view of freedom in conflict with the authors of the *Equal Suffrage Address.*

9. *Equal Suffrage: Address from the Colored Citizens of Norfolk, Virginia, to the People of the United States, 1865* (reprint, Philadelphia: Rhistoric Publications, 1969), p. 5. For descriptions of the three authors of the *Address* mentioned in the text, see Luther P. Jackson, *Negro Office-Holders in Virginia, 1865–1895* (Norfolk: Guide Quality Press, 1945), p. 3; Peter Rachleff, *Black Labor in the South: Richmond, Virginia, 1865–1890* (Philadelphia: Temple University Press, 1984), pp. 46, 48, 78; Henry Lewis Suggs, ed., *The Black Press in the South, 1865–1979* (Westport, Conn.: Greenwood Press, 1983), p. 379; and the booklet *St. John A.M.E. Church: 119th Anniversary, 1863–1982* (Norfolk: St. John A.M.E. Church, 1982). See also David Howard-Pitney, "The Jeremiads of Frederick Douglass, Booker T. Washington, and W. E. B. Du Bois and Changing Patterns of Black Messianic Rhetoric, 1841–1920," *Journal of American Ethnic History* 6 (Fall 1986): 47–62.

10. *Equal Suffrage Address*, pp. 7–8.

11. Roger Ransom and Richard Sutch, *One Kind of Freedom* (Cambridge: Cambridge University Press, 1977), chaps. 4–7; John Blassingame, *Black New Orleans* (Chicago: University of Chicago Press, 1974), pp. 64–65; Gerald Jaynes, *Branches Without Roots* (New York: Oxford University Press, 1986), chap. 13; Tommy Lee Bogger, "The Slave and Free Black Community in Norfolk, 1775–1865" (Ph.D. diss., University of Virginia, 1976), pp. 177–79; Kenneth M. Stampp, *The Era of Reconstruction* (New York: Vintage Books, 1965), pp. 79–81.

12. Howard N. Rabinowitz, "Continuity and Change: Southern Urban Development, 1860–1900," in Brownell and Goldfield, *The City in Southern History*, pp. 105–11.

13. Allen W. Moger, "Industrial and Urban Progress in Virginia from 1880 to 1900," *Virginia Magazine of History and Biography* 66, no. 3 (July 1958): 327; Wertenbaker and Schlegel, *Norfolk*, pp. 272–87.

14. Moger, "Industrial and Urban Progress in Virginia," p. 327.

15. *Annual Reports of Officers, Boards, and Institutions of the Commonwealth of Virginia*, Year Ending September 30, 1899, vol. 2, *Report of the Labor Commission,* p. 140, located in the Virginia State Library, Richmond. See also U.S. Bureau of

the Census, *Report of the Social Statistics of Cities* (Washington, D.C.: Government Printing Office, 1887), pt. 2, *Southern and Western States*, p. 70.

16. Manuscript Census, Norfolk City, 1870, reel M593–1666, U.S. Bureau of the Census, Record Group 29. For a discussion of occupational patterns among blacks during the early national and antebellum periods, consult Bogger, "The Slave and Free Black Community in Norfolk," pp. 161–91; and Luther P. Jackson, *Free Negro Labor and Property Holding in Virginia, 1830–1860* (1942; reprint, New York: Antheneum, 1968), pp. 57–58, 93, 98, 139. For comparative examples, see Howard Rabinowitz, *Race Relations in the Urban South* (New York: Oxford University Press, 1978), pp. 77–96.

17. Manuscript Census, Norfolk City, 1870, reel M593–1666, U.S. Bureau of the Census, Record Group 29. Elizabeth Pleck notes similar patterns in Boston. (*Black Migration and Poverty: Boston, 1865–1900* [New York: Academic Press, 1979], pp. 137–60).

18. Jackson, *Negro Office-Holders in Virginia,* p. 79; *City Directory of Norfolk,* annual volumes for 1872–1880, located in the Norfolk Public Library. The class composition of the black community has never mirrored that found among whites, as numerous commentators have noted. Consequently, care must be exercised in using occupational status as a proxy for social class. The black doorman at the best white hotel or the butler for a prestigious white family often had high status in the black community, status that could exceed his material state. Classic statements on this theme include Hylan G. Lewis, "The Negro Business, Professional, and White-Collar Worker," *Journal of Negro Education* 8 ( July 1939): 430–45; E. Franklin Frazier, *Black Bourgeoisie* (New York: Free Press, 1957); and August Meier and David L. Lewis, "History of the Negro Upper Class in Atlanta, Georgia, 1890–1958," *Journal of Negro Education* 58 (Spring 1959): 128–39. For a more recent discussion, see William Julius Wilson, *The Declining Significance of Race: Blacks and Changing American Institutions,* 2d ed. (Chicago: University of Chicago Press, 1980), chap. 8.

19. Manuscript Census, Norfolk City, 1870, reel M593–1666, U.S. Bureau of the Census, Record Group 29; Jackson, *Free Negro Labor and Property Holding in Virginia,* pp. 97, 154; Bogger, "The Slave and Free Black Community in Norfolk," pp. 171–74.

20. *City Directory of Norfolk,* 1881.

21. Manuscript Census, Norfolk City, 1870, reels M593–1666, 1667; 1880, reels T9–1380, 1381, 1382; 1900, reels T623–1735, 1736; 1910, reels T624–1637, 1638; U.S. Bureau of the Census, Record Group 29.

22. Myers is quoted in Philip S. Foner, *Organized Labor and the Black Worker, 1619–1973* (New York: International Publishers, 1974), p. 35; more generally, see chap. 2. See also Charles H. Wesley, *Negro Labor in the United States, 1850–1925* (New York: Vanguard Press, 1927), p. 181; and Sterling D. Spero and Abram L. Harris, *The Black Worker* (New York: Columbia University Press, 1931), pp. 16–35.

23. Olivier Zunz argues that blacks lived history in reverse (*The Changing Face of Inequality* [Chicago: University of Chicago Press, 1982], p. 6). For an understanding of black involvement in the Knights of Labor, see Melton A. McLaurin, *The Knights of Labor in the South* (Westport, Conn.: Greenwood Press, 1978), p.

135; U.S. Congress, Senate, *Report on Conditions of Women and Child Wage Earners in the U.S.*, 61st Cong., 2d sess., 1910, S. Doc. 645, vol. 10, *History of Women in Trade Unions*, p. 130; and Sidney H. Kessler, "The Organization of Negroes in the Knights of Labor," *Journal of Negro History* 37 (July 1952): 251–52, 258–59. Also see Foner, *Organized Labor and the Black Worker*, pp. 50, 62, for examples of solidarity and opposition.

24. *Richmond Planet*, 2 September 1899, 21 October 1899; Rachleff, *Black Labor in the South*, p. 200.

25. Spero and Harris, *The Black Worker*, p. 477.

26. Ibid., pp. 53–73. The move toward all-black locals was national.

27. William F. Ainsley, Jr., "Changing Land Use in Downtown Norfolk, Virginia: 1680–1930" (Ph.D. diss., University of North Carolina, Chapel Hill, 1977), pp. 148, 160.

28. Berlin, *Slaves Without Masters*, pp. 253–57; Leonard P. Curry, *The Free Black in Urban America, 1800–1850* (Chicago: University of Chicago Press, 1981), pp. 78–79.

29. Manuscript Census, Norfolk City, 1870, reel M593–1666, U.S. Bureau of the Census, Record Group 29.

30. Ibid., 1900, reel T623–1735, U.S. Bureau of the Census, Record Group 29.

31. Ira Katznelson, *City Trenches: Urban Politics and the Patterning of Class in the United States* (Chicago: University of Chicago Press, 1981), pp. 17–20; *Norfolk Labor Journal*, 14 December 1939.

32. Wertenbaker and Schlegel, *Norfolk*, pp. 235–37.

33. The *Norfolk Journal* is quoted in ibid., p. 245; more generally, see pp. 236–45. See also Alrutheus Ambush Taylor, *The Negro in the Reconstruction of Virginia* (1926; reprint, New York: Russell and Russell, 1969), pp. 219–20, 233; and Jackson, *Negro Office-Holders in Virginia*, pp. ix, 2–3, 21, 32–33, 51, 53, 59, 65, 71–72, 79.

34. Charles E. Wynes, *Race Relations in Virginia, 1870–1902* (1961; reprint, Totowa, N.J.: Rowan and Littlefield, 1971), chaps. 1–3; Richard L. Morton, *The Negro in Virginia Politics, 1865–1902* (Charlottesville: University Press of Virginia, 1919); Andrew Buni, *The Negro in Virginia Politics, 1902–1965* (Charlottesville: University Press of Virginia, 1967), chap. 1.

35. *Richmond Planet*, 22 February 1896, 4 July 1896.

36. *Report of the Proceedings and Debates of the Constitutional Convention, State of Virginia, 1901–1902* (Richmond, 1906), p. 2974. Read pp. 2958–93 for a full rendering of Thom's attitude.

37. Ibid., p. 3076.

38. Glass is quoted in *The Negro in Virginia* (New York: Hasting House, 1940), p. 239.

39. Buni, *The Negro in Virginia Politics*, p. 24. Also see the Capitation Tax Rolls for 1910, located in the Norfolk Public Library.

40. James Sidney Kitterman, Jr., "Reformers and Bosses in the Progressive Era: The Changing Face of Norfolk Politics, 1890–1920" (M.A. thesis, Old Dominion University, 1971), pp. 29–56, 96–110, 152–56.

41. Ibid., pp. 96–110. See also Michael B. Chesson, "Richmond's Black Councilmen, 1871–96," in *Southern Black Leaders of the Reconstruction Era*, ed. Howard

Rabinowitz (Urbana: University of Illinois Press, 1982), pp. 191–222. Norfolk blacks suffered political losses but not the degree of verbal and physical thuggery used to intimidate blacks in Richmond (Rabinowitz, *Race Relations in the Urban South,* pp. 319–20).

42. Ainsley, "Changing Land Use in Downtown Norfolk," pp. 155–56.

43. August Meier and Elliott Rudwick, "Negro Boycott of Segregated Streetcars in Virginia, 1904–1907," *Virginia Magazine of History and Biography* 83, no. 4 (October 1973): 479–87.

44. Students of slavery have dominated this debate over autonomy. Since Stanley Elkins's *Slavery,* most scholars have attempted to ascertain the degree to which slavery was a totally controlling institution. As the debate has matured, a spectrum of perspectives has emerged. At one end is Elkins's "damage school," which characterizes slavery as a total institution that produced a childlike, culturally adrift black population. At the other is a group I call the near-total autonomists, scholars such as Herbert Gutman, Lawrence Levine, John Blassingame, and George Rawick, who keenly understand the limits placed on the individual by slavery but who ably document and celebrate the degrees to which slaves were able to carve out psychic and social space, that is, degrees of autonomy. Between these extremes are works by Robert Fogel and Stanley Engerman that describe the plantation as a firm and slaves as workers with roughly the autonomy bestowed on their nineteenth-century "free" counterparts. Between the view of the plantation as firm and the views of the near-total autonomists is Eugene Genovese's paternalism model, in which he argues that masters viewed their slaves as children and treated them as such. Interestingly, the only urbanist to actively join the debate has been James Borchert (*Alley Life in Washington* [Urbana: University of Illinois Press, 1980]).

45. *City Directory of Norfolk, 1865–1870; St. John A.M.E. Church: 119th Anniversary;* Robert Engs, *Freedom's First Generation: Black Hampton, Virginia, 1861–1890* (Philadelphia: University of Pennsylvania Press, 1979), p. 209; *The Negro in Virginia,* pp. 247, 254.

46. Engs, *Freedom's First Generation,* pp. 52, 87; Henry Rorer, "History of Norfolk's Public Schools, 1681–1968" (typescript, ca. 1968, Norfolk Public Library), pp. 2, 82; Wertenbaker and Schlegel, *Norfolk,* p. 255.

47. *Norfolk Journal and Guide,* 12 August 1922; *Annual Reports of Officers, Boards, and Institutions of the Commonwealth of Virginia,* Year Ending September 30, 1887, *Report of the Superintendent of Public Instruction; The Negro in Virginia,* p. 270.

48. Rorer, "History of Norfolk's Public Schools," p. 82; *Norfolk Journal and Guide,* 12 August 1922.

49. Rorer, "History of Norfolk's Public Schools," pp. 82–83.

50. Many black benevolent and social organizations were mentioned in the *City Directory of Norfolk* (various years) and in black newspapers such as the *Richmond Planet;* the list in the text was compiled from those sources.

51. *Richmond Planet,* 31 July 1897.

52. See Walter B. Weare, *Black Business in the New South: A Social History of the North Carolina Mutual Life Insurance Company* (Urbana: University of Illinois Press, 1973).

53. Jesse Edward Moorland, "The Young Men's Christian Association Among Negroes," *Journal of Negro History* 9 (April 1924): 134–35; "Progress of

the Y in Norfolk Through Thirty-Five Years of Existence," *Norfolk Journal and Guide,* 13 October 1923. Soon after this article appeared in the *Journal and Guide,* the YMCA ceased to exist. In 1918 the colored and the white associations had sponsored a joint fund-raising drive, during which the black YMCA was shortchanged by $4,600. This shortfall contributed to the economic woes of the black branch and culminated with the building at the corner of Queen Street being sold to the Elks Lodge (*Norfolk Journal and Guide,* 6 October 1923). Without a building, the entire association soon fell apart. The national body sent Channing Tobias to Norfolk in 1927 to try to revive the movement; by this time the Boys Club had filled the void and Tobias's effort failed (*Norfolk Journal and Guide,* 19 March 1927).

54. "YMCA, Norfolk, Virginia, 1911–1962" (folder, Norfolk Public Library); *Norfolk Journal and Guide,* 19 September 1925.

55. Rayford Logan, *The Betrayal of the Negro* (New York: Collier-Macmillan, 1965); Louis R. Harlan, *Booker T. Washington: The Making of a Black Leader, 1865–1901* (New York: Oxford University Press, 1972); Louis R. Harlan, *Booker T. Washington: The Wizard of Tuskegee,* 1901–1915 (New York: Oxford University Press, 1983); August Meier, *Negro Thought in America, 1880–1915* (Ann Arbor: University of Michigan Press, 1966), pp. 171–255.

56. Henry Lewis Suggs, "P. B. Young of the Norfolk *Journal and Guide:* A Booker T. Washington Militant, 1904–1928," *Journal of Negro History* 64 (Fall 1979): 365–76.

57. Randy Roberts's *Papa Jack: Jack Johnson and the Era of White Hopes* (New York: Free Press, 1983), pp. 85–113, offers the best description of the Johnson-Jeffries bout and its implications and consequences.

58. Stephen Graham, *The Soul of John Brown* (New York: Macmillan, 1920), p. 50; Roberts, *Papa Jack,* pp. 108–10.

59. B. Charney Vladeck, a Jewish socialist newly arrived from Russia and on a tour of the South, happened to be in Norfolk during the riot. He begged members of the Jewish community to intercede on behalf of blacks, but they branded him a "greenhorn," claiming that "blacks were nothing but animals." Vladeck in turn castigated his critics, calling them "all-rightnik Jews," meaning those who were newly middle-class (Franklin L. Jones, "The Early Life and Career of B. Charney Vladeck, 1880–1921: The Emergence of an Immigrant Spokesman" [Ph.D. diss., New York University, 1972], pp. 86–87).

60. *Virginian-Pilot and Norfolk Landmark,* 5 July 1910.

61. Roberts, *Papa Jack,* pp. 169–84. Also see Al-Tony Gilmore, Jr., *Bad Nigger! The National Impact of Jack Johnson* (Port Washington, N.Y.: Kennikat Press, 1975).

62. *Virginian-Pilot and Norfolk Landmark,* 5 July 1910; *New York Times,* 5 July 1910.

## CHAPTER 2

1. See Gilbert Osofsky, *Harlem: The Making of a Ghetto, Negro New York, 1890–1930* (New York: Harper and Row, 1963); Allan H. Spear, *Black Chicago: The Making of a Negro Ghetto, 1890–1920* (Chicago: University of Chicago Press,

1967); and Kenneth L. Kusmer, *A Ghetto Takes Shape: Black Cleveland, 1870–1930* (Urbana: University of Illinois Press, 1976). Compare Joe William Trotter, Jr., *Black Milwaukee: The Making of an Industrial Proletariat* (Urbana: University of Illinois Press, 1985).

2. George W. Bennett, *Life Behind the Walls of My Self-Made Fate* (self-published, 1964), pp. 28–29, 48–49; Stephen Graham, *The Soul of John Brown* (New York: Macmillan, 1920), pp. 32–33.

3. *Black Workers in the Era of the Great Migration, 1916–1925,* microfilm collection (Bethseda, Md.: University Publications of America, 1985), reel 24, frame 26; U.S. Department of Labor, *Report of the United States Housing Corporation* (Washington, D.C.: Government Printing Office, 1919), vol. 2, p. 270. Thousands of blacks nationwide answered the call for workers; see Osofsky, *Harlem,* chaps. 2, 9; Spear, *Black Chicago,* chap. 1; Florette Henri, *Black Migration: Movement North, 1900–1920* (Garden City, N.Y.: Anchor Books, 1976), esp. chap. 2; Elliott Rudwick, *Race Riot at East St. Louis, July 2, 1917* (New York: Meridian Books, 1965); and Trotter, *Black Milwaukee,* pp. 40–47. Numerous contemporaries debated the consequences of the out-flight, particularly the movement North; see, for example, George Edmund Haynes, "Negroes Move North," *Survey* 40 (4 May, 1918): 115–22; and Emmett J. Scott, *Negro Migration During the War* (New York: Oxford University Press, 1920).

4. Concerning the second population surge in northern cities, see Trotter, *Black Milwaukee,* p. 45.

5. U.S. Department of Commerce, *Negroes in the United States, 1920–1932* (Washington, D.C.: Government Printing Office, 1935), pp. 53–55. When put in context, the overall increase in Norfolk's black population during the war decade was quite significant. If we consider the twenty-five largest southern cities during the war decade, Norfolk's 73.3 percent growth rate ranked second. If we restrict our discussion to the region's ten largest cities, excluding the nation's capital, Norfolk had the most rapid war-associated population increase. Furthermore, between 1910 and 1930 Norfolk's median growth rate (3.8 percent) exceeded the median for the ten cities (3.5 percent); and only three cities—Houston, Memphis, and Birmingham—had an annual average population increase larger than that of Norfolk. Norfolk differed from the other cities primarily in its inability to sustain growth during the postwar decade.

6. Henri, *Black Migration,* chap. 2; Peter Gottlieb, *Making Their Own Way: Southern Blacks' Migration to Pittsburgh, 1916–30* (Urbana: University of Illinois Press, 1987), pp. 22–24; James Richard Grossman, "A Dream Deferred: Black Migration to Chicago, 1916–1921" (Ph.D. diss. University of California, Berkeley, 1982).

7. Earl Lewis, "At Work and at Home: Blacks in Norfolk, Virginia, 1910–1945" (Ph.D. diss., University of Minnesota, 1984), pp. 68–69; U.S. Bureau of the Census, *Thirteenth Census of the United States* (Washington, D.C.: Government Printing Office, 1911), vol. 3, *Population, 1910,* p. 951; U.S. Bureau of the Census, *Fourteenth Census of the United States* (Washington, D.C.: Government Printing Office, 1921), vol. 3, *Population, 1920,* p. 1069; U.S. Bureau of the Census, *Fifteenth Census of the United States* (Washington, D.C.: Government Printing Office, 1932), vol. 3, pt. 2, *Population, 1930,* p. 157.

8. Lloyd D., conversation with the author, 9 March 1983, Norfolk. Chain migration is defined in John S. MacDonald and Leatrice D. MacDonald, "Chain Migration, Ethnic Neighborhood Formation, and Social Networks," *Milbank Memorial Fund* 42 (1964): 82. See also John Bodnar, Roger Simon, and Michael P. Weber, *Lives of Their Own* (Urbana: University of Illinois Press, 1982), pp. 35–36, 58–59.

9. U.S. Bureau of the Census, *Fourteenth Census*, vol. 3, *Population, 1920*, p. 665; U.S. Bureau of the Census, *Fifteenth Census*, vol. 2, *Population, 1930*, p. 203.

10. Maria Ruffin, interview by Edith Skinner, 23 December 1938, Virginia Writers' Project (VWP 58–71), Virginia State Library, Richmond.

11. Bennett, *Life Behind the Walls*, pp. 48–49; Gottlieb, *Making Their Own Way*, pp. 4–7, 16–32.

12. See Theodore Hershberg et al., "A Tale of Three Crities: Blacks, Immigrants, and Opportunity in Philadelphia, 1850–1880, 1930, 1970," in *Philadelphia: Work, Space, Family, and Group Experience in the Nineteenth Century*, ed. Theodore Hershberg (New York: Oxford University Press, 1981), pp. 461–91, for the historical application of the concept of opportunity structure.

13. Lewis, "At Work and at Home," pp. 72–74. Annual reports by the Department of Labor and Industry of Virginia published in Richmond between 1922 and 1930 further attest to this point concerning the occupations of black youths (*Twenty-Fifth and Twenty-Sixth Annual Reports of the Department of Labor and Industry of the State of Virginia* [1922–1923], pp. 216–17; *Twenty-Seventh Annual Report* [1924], p. 102; *Twenty-Eighth Annual Report* [1925], p. 109; *Twenty-Ninth Annual Report* [1926], p. 106; *Thirtieth Annual Report* [1927], p. 102; *Thirty-First Annual Report* [1928], p. 81; *Thirty-Second Annual Report* [1929], p. 88; *Thirty-Third Annual Report* [1930], p. 37). The jobs of errand boy and bootblack were open to blacks and whites alike, but the number of black youths engaged in this type of street trade exceeded their proportion of the population. The number of blacks listed as errand boys declined over the period, however, to a point roughly equaling their proportion of the population (27.8 percent). Conversely, by 1930 nearly all bootblacks were Afro-Americans. Whites retained supremacy as newsboys and caddies, much as they did in New York City (David Nasaw, *Children of the City* [New York: Oxford University Press, 1985], p. 68). Other scholars have found similar patterns; see, for example, James Borchert, *Alley Life in Washington* (Urbana: University of Illinois Press, 1980), pp. 145–47.

14. Charlie Johnson, interview, 24 February 1939, Virginia Writers' Project. The dual, or segmented, labor market is discussed, with a somewhat different emphasis, in Gavin Wright, *Old South, New South* (New York: Basic Books, 1986), esp. chap. 6.

15. Records of the Federal Mediation and Conciliation Service (File 33/661, Record Group 280, National Archives) identify Skinner not only as a longshoreman but also as president of one of the local all-black unions.

16. U.S. Bureau of the Census, *Fourteenth Census of the United States* (Washington, D.C.: Government Printing Office, 1923), vol. 4, *Occupations, 1920*, pp. 1184–85; Edward Weller, interview, 24 February 1939, Virginia Writers' Project.

17. The figures are derived from a tabulation of occupations noted in an October 1919 house census of Truxton residents (U.S. Housing Corporation, Record Group 3, National Archives).

18. *Black Workers in the Era of the Great Migration,* reel 24, frames 16–19.

19. Charles N. Hunter to Hon. W. H. Hays, 23 March 1921, box 6, folder 1921, Charles N. Hunter Papers, Perkins Library, Duke University, Durham, N.C. See also other correspondence in this collection.

20. Lewis, "At Work and at Home," pp. 78–80 and chap. 4; Gottlieb, *Making Their Own Way,* pp. 56–57; Trotter, *Black Milwaukee,* p. 45.

21. U.S. Bureau of the Census, *Fifteenth Census of the United States* (Washington, D.C.: Government Printing Office, 1933), vol. 4, *Occupations, 1930,* pp. 1673–74. Jacqueline Jones (*Labor of Love, Labor of Sorrow: Black Women, Work, and the Family from Slavery to the Present* [New York: Basic Books, 1985], chaps. 4, 5) outlines a similiar pattern of dependence on female labor nationwide.

22. Helen Bryan, field representative, to Mary Anderson, director, U.S. Women's Bureau, 5 December 1919; Women's Bureau Bulletin no. 10 (December 1919), surveys; both in Record Group 86, National Archives. See also Jones, *Labor of Love, Labor of Sorrow,* pp. 134–42; Delores Janiewski, *Sisterhood Denied* (Philadelphia: Temple University Press, 1985), chap. 6.

23. Bryan to Anderson, 5 December 1919; Women's Bureau Bulletin no. 10, surveys; both in Record Group 86.

24. Bryan to Anderson, 11 December 1919; Women's Bureau Bulletin no. 10, Hosiery and Knit Goods folder; both in Record Group 86. Surveys for other companies reveal that all the other black women workers were unskilled laborers.

25. U.S. Bureau of the Census, *Fourteenth Census,* vol. 4, *Occupations, 1920,* pp. 1184–85. The story of Ruth V. was reported to the author by Rudolph C. Lewis following his conversation with Ruth V., 29 May 1984, Norfolk.

26. *Norfolk Journal and Guide,* 25 December 1926.

27. *Norfolk Journal and Guide,* 24 March 1928. Washington's contact with blacks in the region dated from his days at Hampton. Afro-Americans in the area often called on him to endorse local enterprises; see, for example, J. E. Mills to Booker T. Washington, 20 July 1908, box 791, file 1908, Booker T. Washington Papers, Library of Congress.

28. *Norfolk Journal and Guide,* 20 January 1923.

29. *Norfolk Journal and Guide,* 30 September 1916. Comparable accounts are offered by Spear, *Black Chicago,* pp. 111–18; and Bertha Hampton Miller, "Blacks in Winston-Salem, North Carolina, 1895–1920: Community Development in an Era of Benevolent Paternalism" (Ph.D. diss. Duke University, 1981), p. 108.

30. *Norfolk Journal and Guide,* 15 October 1921, 9 April 1921, 16 April 1921. For other examples of cooperative ventures, see Janet Sharp Herman, *The Pursuit of a Dream* (New York: Oxford University Press, 1981), esp. sec. 3; and Spear, *Black Chicago,* pp. 116–18.

A review of the business section of the *Journal and Guide* for the 1910s and 1920s indicates that a score of black merchants came to own shops in a wide array of areas. R. F. Riddick bought out Dr. McCurdy's drugstore on the corner of Calvert and Church streets; John D. Riddick owned his own construction company; Blanche Chambliss was the owner and operator of a small dressmaking business, with four sewing machines; and Alonzo Dozier came to own and run A. Dozier Grocery on Church Street. See also the *City Directory of Norfolk* (various years; located in the Norfolk Public Library) for listings of the racial ownership of business enterprises.

31. *Norfolk Journal and Guide*, 20 March 1926.

32. Louis R. Harlan, *Booker T. Washington: The Making of A Black Leader, 1865–1901* (New York: Oxford University Press, 1972), p. 218.

33. *City Directory of Norfolk*, 1910–1930. Although the ethnicity of all these merchants cannot be confirmed, most blacks viewed them as Jewish and continue to do so to this day. The depth of the antagonism is described in Chapter 3.

34. General treatments of Asians in the South include James W. Loewen, *The Mississippi Chinese* (Cambridge: Cambridge University Press, 1971); and Lucy M. Cohen, *Chinese in the Post–Civil War South* (Baton Rouge: Louisiana State University Press, 1984). Also see Ivan Light, *Ethnic Enterprise in America: Business and Welfare Among Chinese, Japanese, and Blacks* (Berkeley and Los Angeles: University of California Press, 1972); and John Modell, *The Economics of Racial Accommodation* (Urbana: University of Illinois Press, 1977). The courts decided in the *Gong Lum* case (*Gong Lum v. Rice*, 275 U.S. 78 [1927]) that an Asian girl should be considered colored and therefore could not attend school with whites in Mississippi.

35. Once substantial numbers of Asian merchants began to encroach on black businesses in the 1930s, however, sentiment changed. See *Norfolk Journal and Guide*, 28 December 1929.

36. *Norfolk Journal and Guide*, 14 January 1922 (editorial). Trotter made a similar observation (*Black Milwaukee*, pp. 124–34). See also *Norfolk Journal and Guide*, 20 March 1926. Interestingly, a study commissioned by the Phelps-Stokes Fund found that real estate brokers in Richmond at the time believed that working-class blacks were better credit risks than comparably employed whites; see Charles Louis Knight, *Negro Housing in Certain Virginia Cities* (Richmond: William Byrd Press, 1927), p. 119.

37. See stories and ads chronicling the achievements of these three men in the *Norfolk Journal and Guide*, esp. 28 April 1923, 29 December 1923, 17 July 1926. The experience of black artisans in Norfolk was not unlike that in Cleveland, Chicago, and Milwaukee.

38. *Norfolk Journal and Guide*, 22 January 1921, 29 December 1923. Also see *Richmond Planet*, 4 September 1897.

39. See the *Norfolk Journal and Guide*, 14 May 1927, for a history of Brown and the bank. Loan sharks plagued working-class blacks despite the efforts of various financial institutions, including the Norfolk Credit Union, which was created expressly to eliminate these social parasites (*Norfolk Journal and Guide*, 13 March 1928).

40. *Norfolk Journal and Guide*, 14 May 1927, 4 March 1922. At the end of the 1921 calendar year, Tidewater Bank and Trust publicly disclosed resources and liabilities equaling $412,492. Thus, when it merged with Metropolitan, Tidewater was totally extended financially (*Norfolk Journal and Guide*, 14 January 1922). See also Abram L. Harris, *The Negro as Capitalist* (New York: Haskell, 1936), pp. 84–89; and *Annual Reports of Officers, Boards, and Institutions of the Commonwealth of Virginia*, table 3 in each vol. for the years 1917–1926, located in the Virginia State Library, Richmond; *Negro in Virginia* (New York: Hasting House, 1940), pp. 298–99.

41. *Norfolk Journal and Guide,* 4 February 1922, 4 March 1922. Strangely, at the same time Tidewater and Metropolitan merged, the Union Commercial Bank opened its doors, headed by a different group of black men. These men too were all prominent members of the community: Rev. C. P. Madison, pastor of Second Calvary Baptist Church, chairman of the board; S. B. Noble, president; Dr. J. T. Given, vice-president; J. T. P. Cross, cashier; and labor leader George W. Milner, vice-president (*Norfolk Journal and Guide,* 14 January 1922). By all accounts, the bank did not survive the 1920s.

42. Rich is quoted in the *Norfolk Journal and Guide,* 14 May 1927. See also *Norfolk Journal and Guide,* 7 April 1923, 7 June 1924, 3 April 1926; Harris, *The Negro as Capitalist,* pp. 89–92.

43. Henry Lewis Suggs, "P. B. Young and the Norfolk *Journal and Guide,* 1910–1954" (Ph.D. diss., University of Virginia, 1976), pp. 1–33; Henry Lewis Suggs, ed., *The Black Press in the South, 1865–1979* (Westport, Conn.: Greenwood Press, 1983), pp. 397–403. This account also draws on Dr. Cecil Lewis's conversation with the author, 12 August 1983, Minneapolis. Lewis graduated from Hampton Institute in the 1920s and taught school in rural North Carolina before he went to work for the *Baltimore Afro-American.* He contended that the *Journal and Guide's* physical plant was inferior to most of those owned by the other leading black papers of the time.

44. Charles S. Johnson, *Patterns of Negro Segregation* (New York: Harper and Brothers, 1943).

45. Virginia C., conversation with the author, 23 September 1984, Norfolk; Clifton J., numerous conversations with the author, 1965–1976, Norfolk.

46. Trotter *(Black Milwaukee),* for example, discusses the rise of a class-conscious urban proletariat primarily in terms of industrial workers. In Norfolk, both nonindustrial and industrial workers organized. Tuttle and Zunz argue that blacks eschewed unionization (William M. Tuttle, Jr., *Race Riot: Chicago in the Red Summer of 1919* [New York: Atheneum, 1975], chap. 4; Olivier Zunz, *The Changing Face of Inequality* [Chicago: University of Chicago Press, 1982], introduction and chap. 14). Black Norfolkians, however, favored unions when blacks remained in control.

47. See Norfolk Industrial Commission, *Norfolk, Virginia: The Sunrise City by the Sea* (Norfolk: Burke and Gregory, 1914), pp. 7–19; Arthur Kyle Davis, "Norfolk City in War Time: A Community History," in *Virginia Communities in War Time* (Richmond: Virginia War History Commission, 1925), p. 295; "Report on Housing Conditions at Norfolk and Portsmouth, December 19, 1917," in *Black Workers in the Era of the Great Migration,* reel 23, frame 930.

48. Davis, "Norfolk City in War Time," pp. 322–27; Paul Nasca, "Norfolk in the First World War" (M.A. thesis, Old Dominion University, 1979), pp. 29, 51, 60.

49. *Norfolk Journal and Guide,* 17 April 1917.

50. Davis, "Norfolk City in War Time," p. 332. An examination of the U.S. Housing Corporation files, however, indicates that blacks who came to live in Truxton, a housing development for black war workers near the U.S. navy yard in Portsmouth, also landed semi-skilled and skilled positions (U.S. Housing Corporation, Record Group 3).

51. Davis, "Norfolk City in War Time," p. 332; *The Negro in Virginia,* p. 313. Norfolk blacks belonged to a smattering of all-black unions representing carpenters, railroad workers, postal employees, and domestic servants (*Norfolk Journal and Guide,* 19 May 1917, and 26 May 1917). This assessment of black labor activity is based on a close review of issues of the *Norfolk Journal and Guide* published between 1916 and 1929 as well as on Sterling D. Spero and Abram L. Harris, *The Black Worker* (New York: Columbia University Press, 1931), pp. 59, 103, 104, 118, 123–27, 149–81; and Herbert R. Northrup, *Organized Labor and the Negro* (New York: Harper and Brothers, 1944), pp. 37, 41, 73.

52. Spero and Harris, *The Black Worker,* pp. 195–96; Northrup, *Organized Labor and the Negro,* p. 146. Milner's name is also given as "Millner" in some records.

53. Very few records of the Transportation Workers Association remain, other than a few extant newspaper articles and reports filed with the Federal Mediation and Conciliation Service. For a description of the TWA and its early history, see Esther Levinson, "A History of the Hampton Roads Longshoremen's Association" (M.A. thesis, Old Dominion University, 1968); *Norfolk Journal and Guide,* 12 October 1917, 29 July 1922; and File 33/661, Federal Mediation and Conciliation Service, Record Group 280. Also see a longshoreman's ad in the *Norfolk Journal and Guide,* 16 January 1945, describing the union's early history; Theodore Kornweibel, ed., *Federal Surveillance of Afro-Americans (1917–1925): The First World War, the Red Scare, and the Garvey Movement,* microfilm collection (Bethseda, Md.: University Publications of America, 1986), reel 9, frames 199–207; and Files for Philadelphia, Military Intelligence Department, Record Group 165, National Archives.

54. See, for example, Tuttle, *Race Riot,* chap. 4; Bodnar, Simon, and Weber, *Lives of Their Own,* p. 214; Kusmer, *A Ghetto Takes Shape,* chap. 4; Stanley B. Greenberg, *Race and State in Capitalist Development* (New Haven, Conn.: Yale University Press, 1980), pp. 328–34; and William Julius Wilson, *The Declining Significance of Race: Blacks and Changing American Institutions,* 2d ed. (Chicago: University of Chicago Press, 1980), pp. 70–76.

55. Kornweibel, *Federal Surveillance of Afro-Americans,* reel 8, frames 506–7.

56. *Norfolk Journal and Guide,'* 5 September 1917.

57. For a more extensive discussion of the question of underemployment, see Wright, *Old South, New South,* pp. 177–97.

58. *Sixth Annual Report: Norfolk Chamber of Commerce—Board of Trade 1919* (Norfolk: Norfolk Chamber of Commerce, ca. 1920), p. 8, located in the Norfolk Public Library.

59. Spero and Harris, *The Black Worker,* pp. 59, 103, 104, 118, 123–27, 149–81.

60. File 33/661, Federal Mediation and Conciliation Service, Record Group 280; Levinson, "History of the Hampton Roads Longshoremen's Association," p. 21.

61. File 33/661, Federal Mediation and Conciliation Service, Record Group 280.

62. Ibid.

63. Ibid. Paul Faler comments that workers sometimes believed that the daily ingestion of spirits enhanced their work performance; management, however,

routinely argued that anything that distracted the worker was unacceptable (*Mechanics and Manufacturers in the Early Industrial Revolution* [Albany: State University of New York Press, 1981], pp. 131–33). On a similar point, see Bruce Laurie, *Working People of Philadelphia, 1800–1850* (Philadelphia: Temple University Press, 1980), pp. 54–56.

64. Jones, *Labor of Love, Labor of Sorrow*, pp. 137–41; *Norfolk Journal and Guide*, 22 September 1917, 29 September 1917. Stemming, in this craft-oriented trade, was considered the worst job in all aspects and one reserved for black women (Patricia Cooper, *Once a Cigar Maker* [Urbana: University of Illinois Press, 1987], pp. 15, 164; Janiewski, *Sisterhood Denied*, pp. 100–102).

65. Philip S. Foner, *Women and the American Labor Movement: From World War I to the Present* (New York: Free Press, 1980), p. 65. Cooper (*Once a Cigar Maker*, pp. 247–66) documents the efforts of white women who led strikes in the industry.

66. "Report on Wages and Rents in the Norfolk District," in *Black Workers in the Era of the Great Migration*, reel 23, frames 948, 971–72; *Norfolk Journal and Guide*, 22 September 1917, 29 September 1917.

67. *Norfolk Journal and Guide*, 29 September 1917.

68. *Virginian-Pilot and Norfolk Landmark*, 25, 26, 28, 29 September 1917, 2, 3, 5 October 1917.

69. *Virginian-Pilot and Norfolk Landmark*, 25 September 1917.

70. *Norfolk Journal and Guide*, 22 September 1917, 29 September 1917; *Virginian-Pilot and Norfolk Landmark*, 2, 3, 5 October 1917. Without question, stemmers earned the least of all industry workers (Cooper, *Once a Cigar Maker*, pp. 174, 176–77).

71. *Virginian-Pilot and Norfolk Landmark*, 25, 26, 28, 29 Septembeer 1917, 2, 3, 5 October 1917.

72. Bryan to Anderson, 13 December 1919; U.S. Women's Bureau Bulletin no. 10, folder title obscured; both in Record Group 86. Also see Beverly W. Jones, "Race, Sex, and Class: Black Female Tobacco Workers in Durham, North Carolina, 1920–1940, and the Development of Female Consciousness," *Feminist Studies* 10 (Fall 1984): 441–51.

73. *Norfolk Journal and Guide*, 12 May 1917.

74. *Virginian-Pilot and Norfolk Landmark*, 2 October 1917; *Norfolk Journal and Guide*, 6 October 1917.

75. *Virginian-Pilot and Norfolk Landmark*, 2 October 1917; *Norfolk Journal and Guide*, 6 October 1917. Also see William Taylor Thom, *The Negroes of Litwalton, Virginia: A Social Study of the 'Oyster Negro,'* U.S. Department of Labor Bulletin no. 37, November 1901.

76. *Virginian-Pilot and Norfolk Landmark*, 5 October 1917.

77. *Virginian-Pilot and Norfolk Landmark*, 5 October 1917. The police played a central role in regulating the action of workers in the industrial age; see Roger Lane, *Roots of Violence in Black Philadelphia, 1860–1900* (Cambridge: Harvard University Press, 1986), pp. 10–13.

78. David Katzman, *Seven Days a Week: Women and Domestic Service in Industrializing America* (New York: Oxford University Press, 1978), pp. 72–94, 290 and chap. 3; Edward Weller, interview, 24 February 1939, Virginia Writers' Project.

79. *Norfolk Journal and Guide*, 19 May 1917, 26 May 1917.

80. *Norfolk Journal and Guide,* 6 October 1917; *Virginian-Pilot and Norfolk Landmark,* 4 October 1917.

81. *Virginian-Pilot and Norfolk Landmark,* 16 September 1917; Kornweibel, *Federal Surveillance of Afro-Americans,* reel 8, frame 433.

82. *Norfolk Journal and Guide,* 6 October 1917; *Virginian-Pilot and Norfolk Landmark,* 4 October 1917.

83. *Norfolk Journal and Guide,* 6 October 1917.

84. Norfolk was an especially sensitive site during the war; see the Bureau of Investigation reports in Kornweibel, *Federal Surveillance of Afro-Americans,* reel 8, frames 538–39. Also see Military Intelligence Department Files in Record Group 165, National Archives.

85. Northrup, *Organized Labor and the Negro,* pp. 146–47; Spero and Harris, *The Black Worker,* pp. 196–97.

86. Northrup, *Organized Labor and the Negro,* pp. 146–47; Spero and Harris, *The Black Worker,* pp. 196–205; Levinson, "History of the Hampton Roads Longshoremen's Association," p. 37.

87. Article by Claude Barnett, director, Associated Negro Press, 24 March 1920, Legal Files, box D-1, NAACP Papers, Library of Congress.

88. *Norfolk Journal and Guide,* 13–20 October 1923; "Longshoremen, Norfolk," File 170/2271, Federal Mediation and Conciliation Service, Record Group 280; George E. Haynes to Negro Economic Committee, 20 May 1919, Re: Large Strike Among Seafront Workers, Folder 81102C, Federal Mediation and Conciliation Service, Record Group 174; "Labor Union Survey, Virginia, 1926–28," Series 6, box 89, National Urban League Papers, Library of Congress.

89. *Norfolk Journal and Guide,* 11 August 1923.

90. Bryan to Anderson, 13 December 1919; U.S. Women's Bureau Bulletin no. 10, folder title obscured; both in Record Group 86; Jones, *Labor of Love, Labor of Sorrow,* pp. 137–42.

91. Bryan to Anderson, 13 December 1919; U.S. Women's Bureau Bulletin no. 10; both in Record Group 86.

92. Bryan to Anderson, 9 December 1919; U.S. Women's Bureau Bulletin no. 10, Bakeries and Other Food Products folder; both in Record Group 86.

93. "Local Tobacco Industry Gives Steady Employment to Hundreds of Race Women and Girls of This Vicinity," *Norfolk Journal and Guide,* date unknown; the reporter estimated that five hundred to eight hundred black women worked at the plant. Blacks also sang in the Winston-Salem tobacco plants; see Julian Ralph, "The Very Old and Very New at Winston-Salem," *Harper's Weekly,* 20 July 1895, p. 681. Concerning the antebellum period, see Robert Starobin, *Industrial Slavery in the Old South* (New York: Oxford University Press, 1975), p. 18.

94. The literature on Afro-American work practices during slavery is growing. See, for example, Philip D. Morgan, "Work and Culture: The Task System and the World of Low Country Blacks, 1700–1880," *William and Mary Quarterly* 39 (1982): 563–99; John Scott Strickland, "Traditional Culture and Moral Economy," in *The Countryside in the Age of Capitalist Transformation,* ed. Steven Hahn and Jonathan Prude (Chapel Hill: University of North Carolina Press, 1985), pp. 141–78; Janiewski, *Sisterhood Denied,* pp. 108–9; and E. P. Thompson's pioneering "Time, Work-Discipline, and Industrial Capitalism," *Past and Present* 38

(1967): 56–97. In some cases, music played a central role in labor organization as well.

95. *Norfolk Journal and Guide*, 3 October 1925. A letter from Dr. Bowen, written on the letterhead of the American Chain Company, is contained in the NAACP Branch Files for Norfolk, box G-208, NAACP Papers.

96. Throughout America, company paternalism was viewed as a time-tested way of ensuring employee loyalty and thwarting union activity; see, for example, Daniel J. Walkowitz, *Worker City, Company Town* (Urbana: University of Illinois Press, 1981); and Tamara K. Hareven, *Family Time and Industrial Time* (Cambridge: Cambridge University Press, 1982).

97. *Norfolk Journal and Guide*, 28 July 1923. The following year, black employees formed the Social and Beneficial Association of Colored Employees of Miller, Rhoads and Swartz; nothing suggests this was a bona fide labor organization (*Norfolk Journal and Guide*, 21 June 1924). D. P. Penders sponsored a picnic for three hundred poor black children in July 1926 (*Norfolk Journal and Guide*, 31 July 1926). In September of that year, the VEPCO company sponsored a trip to Little Bay Beach on the peninsula for its black employees. (*Norfolk Journal and Guide*, 25 September 1926).

98. *Child Labor and the Work of Mothers on Norfolk Truck Farms*, U.S. Children's Bureau Publication no. 130, 1935, p. 203.

99. Susan J., interview, 2 January 1981, and numerous conversations between 1965 and 1983 with the author, Norfolk; Virginia C., follow-up conversation with the author, 23 September 1984, Norfolk.

100. *Child Labor and the Work of Mothers on Norfolk Truck Farms*, pp. 3–27.

101. *Norfolk Journal and Guide*, 10 February 1923, 17 February 1923.

102. *Norfolk Journal and Guide*, 12 May 1917, 30 June 1917, 29 September 1917, 21 May 1921, 13 May 1922, 11 August 1923, 6 September 1924, 5 May 1928.

103. *Norfolk Journal and Guide*, 12 May 1917, 12 August 1922.

## CHAPTER 3

1. Baker's words are taken from the film *"Fundi": The Story of Ella Baker*, produced by Joanne Grant, Fundi Productions, 1981, distributed by New Day Films, New York.

2. *Norfolk Journal and Guide*, 30 June 1917.

3. Nancy Bergmann Cuthbert, "A Social Movement: The Norfolk Klan in the Twenties," *Virginia Social Science Journal* 2 (1967): 101–18; David Chalmers, *Hooded Americanism* (New York: Franklin Watts, 1981), pp. 230–35; *Norfolk Journal and Guide*, 8 October 1921, 1 September 1923; "Ku Klux Klan," box 1, folder 1920–1924, Louis Jaffe Papers, University of Virginia, Charlottesville.

4. *Virginian-Pilot,*, 22 July 1923.

5. Charles S. Johnson, *Patterns of Negro Segregation* (New York: Harper and Brothers, 1943), p. 195.

6. The belief system of southern whites was long in forming and complex in its manifestations. See, for example, George Frederickson, *The Black Image in the White Mind: The Debate on Afro-American Character and Destiny, 1817–1914*

(New York: Harper and Row, 1971), chaps. 7–10; Gunnar Myrdal, *An American Dilemma: The Negro Problem and Modern Democracy* (1944; reissued, New York: Pantheon Books, 1972); and Johnson, *Patterns of Negro Segregation.*

7. The literature on ghetto formation is extensive. For a fair representation of the range, see Gilbert Osofsky, *Harlem: The Making of a Ghetto, Negro New York, 1890–1930* (New York: Harper and Row, 1963); Allan H. Spear, *Black Chicago: The Making of a Negro Ghetto, 1890–1920* (Chicago: University of Chicago Press, 1967); David Katzman, *Before the Ghetto: Black Detroit in the Nineteenth Century* (Urbana: University of Illinois Press, 1973); and Kenneth L. Kusmer, *A Ghetto Takes Shape: Black Cleveland, 1870–1930* (Urbana: University of Illinois Press, 1976). For the southern counterexample, see Thomas J. Woofter, *Negro Problems in Cities* (New York: Doubleday/Doran, 1928), chap. 3.

8. U.S. Bureau of the Census, *Fourteenth Census of the United States* (Washington, D.C.: Government Printing Office, 1921), vol. 3, *Population, 1920,* p. 1078; James Sidney Kitterman, Jr., "Reformers and Bosses in the Progressive Era: The Changing Face of Norfolk Politics, 1890–1920" (M.A. thesis, Old Dominion University, 1971), p. 12.

9. Arnold R. Hirsch, *Making The Second Ghetto: Race and Housing in Chicago, 1940–1960* (Cambridge: Cambridge University Press, 1983), p. 15. Many new residential pockets emerged concurrent with the appearance of new housing developments. Many were in or near the central city, or Uptown, area. There was even an "Own Your Own Home" movement (see "Movement to Stimulate Home Ownership Launched in City," *Norfolk Journal and Guide,* 16 April 1921). New developments appeared in Villa Heights, Lindenwood, and Barboursville in the early 1920s. Other new sections were far from the central city. In 1921 Lincoln Park was built some fifteen minutes (by streetcar) outside the city near Oakwood. Homes in what was advertised as the "Queen of Norfolk Colored Suburbs" routinely sold for three to four thousand dollars (*Norfolk Journal and Guide,* 19 March 1921). Promoters of such developments often mentioned their countryside attributes. For instance, the Titustown development, built in 1901, was billed as a place divorced from the "crowded, filthy, deadly rookeries" that characterized urban life in most cities. By 1915 the area had its own church, school, lodge, and other institutions and amenities. See William Anthony Avery, "Titustown: A Community of Negro Homes," *Southern Workman* 45 (August 1915): 432–41; *Black Workers in the Era of the Great Migration, 1916–1925,* microfilm collection (Bethseda, Md.: University Publications of America, 1985), reel 23, frame 979.

10. C. Vann Woodward, *The Strange Career of Jim Crow,* 3d ed. (New York: Oxford University Press, 1974), p. 100.

11. "Segregation of White and Colored Residents," *Norfolk City Code, 1920,* pp. 107–8 (Sargeant Memorial Room, Norfolk Public Library). Also see "Calvary Cemetery Set Apart for Colored Persons," *Norfolk City Code, 1920,* pp. 301–2, and other segregation codes.

12. *Norfolk Journal and Guide,* 21 November 1925. See also *Black Workers in the Era of the Great Migration,* reel 23, frame 970; U.S. Department of Labor, *Report of the United States Housing Corporation* (Washington, D.C.: Government Printing Office, 1919), vol. 2, p. 270.

13. U.S. Bureau of the Census, *Census of Religious Bodies, 1916* (Washington, D.C.: Government Printing Office, 1920), vol. 1, pp. 458–59; U.S. Bureau of the Census, *Census of Religious Bodies, 1926* (Washington, D.C.: Government Printing Office, 1930), vol. 1, pp. 494–96. A more detailed breakdown of churches by denomination is provided by examining the *Norfolk Journal and Guide* and the *City Directory of Norfolk* for various years (located in the Norfolk Public Library). Such a perusal reveals a list including these religious bodies, among others: Queen Street Baptist, First Baptist, Jerusalem Baptist, Bethel Baptist, Shiloh Baptist, Second Calvary Baptist, Monticello Baptist, St. John AME, John M. Brown AME, Metropolitan AME Zion, St. Luke CME, Grace Protestant Episcopal, First United Presbyterian, and St. Joseph's Catholic Church. The number of storefront churches—often Holiness churches—may never be known, but some, such as Holy Temple, are referenced in one source or another.

14. U.S. Bureau of the Census, *Census of Religious Bodies, 1916*, vol. 1, pp. 458–59. The booklet *St. John A.M.E. Church: 119th Anniversary, 1863–1982* (Norfolk: St. John A.M.E. Church, 1982) includes pictures of several church committees; many were dominated by women. See also Stephen Graham, *The Soul of John Brown* (New York: Macmillan, 1920), pp. 45–48; and Joe William Trotter, Jr., *Black Milwaukee: The Making of an Industrial Proletariat* (Urbana: University of Illinois Press, 1985), pp. 130–31.

15. *St. John A.M.E. Church: 119th Anniversary;* U.S. Bureau of the Census, *Census of Religious Bodies, 1916,* vol. 1, pp. 458–59.

16. U.S. Bureau of the Census, *Census of Religious Bodies, 1916,* vol. 1, pp. 458–59. Graham (*Soul of John Brown,* pp. 35–48) describes Bowling as well as his church (p. 37). Brief biographies of Bowling appear in a *Richmond Planet* article (21 December 1895) and in Henry S. Rorer, "History of Norfolk's Public Schools, 1681–1968" (typescript, ca. 1968, Norfolk Public Library), p. 55. For another description of the churches, see Claude Barnett, director, Associated Negro Press, Legal Files, box D-1, NAACP Papers, Library of Congress.

17. U.S. Bureau of the Census, *Census of Religious Bodies, 1926,* vol. 1, pp. 494–96; Graham, *Soul of John Brown,* pp. 45–46.

18. *Norfolk Journal and Guide,* 29 January 1921. James Borchert found that the working-class residents of Washington's alley dwellings were especially attracted to the storefront churches. (*Alley Life in Washington* [Urbana: University of Illinois Press, 1980], pp. 199–201). See also Trotter, *Black Milwaukee,* pp. 130–32.

19. C. Eric Lincoln, "Foreword," in *Black Religion and Black Radicalism,* by Gayraud S. Wilmore (New York: Anchor/Doubleday, 1973); *Norfolk Journal and Guide,* 20 March 1926, 29 January 1921.

20. Benevolent associations, social clubs, and secret societies played a prominent role in the day-to-day lives of black Norfolkians. Many of the organizations are listed in various issues of the *City Directory of Norfolk* for the period. The social activities of these groups are vividly depicted in the pages of the city's black newspaper, the *Norfolk Journal and Guide.* Some were strictly social clubs. Others, such as the Knights of Gideon, also functioned as burial societies; see the ad in the *Norfolk Journal and Guide,* 12 August 1922, describing the history of the

Knights of Gideon. Also see *Norfolk Journal and Guide*, 7 January 1922, 15 April 1922; W. E. B. Du Bois's classic study *The Philadelphia Negro* (Philadelphia: University of Pennsylvania, 1899), pp. 221–30; Abram L. Harris, *The Negro as Capitalist* (New York: Haskell, 1936), p. 192; Edward N. Palmer, "Negro Secret Societies," *Social Forces* 23 (December 1944): 207–12; *The Negro in Virginia* (New York: Hasting House, 1940), pp. 292–94; and William Muraskin, *Middle Class Blacks in a White Society: Prince Hall Freemasonry in America* (Berkeley and Los Angeles: University of California Press, 1975), introduction and chaps. 7, 9, 12. At no time did black residents resemble the alienated urban migrants described by Peter Gottlieb (*Making Their Own Way: Southern Blacks' Migration to Pittsburgh, 1916–30* [Urbana: University of Illinois, 1987], chap. 7).

21. *Norfolk Journal and Guide*, 15 April 1922.

22. See Charles Flint Kellogg, *NAACP* (Baltimore: Johns Hopkins University Press, 1967); and Robert Zangrando, *The NAACP Campaign Against Lynching, 1909–1950* (Philadelphia: Temple University Press, 1980); as well as biographies of various NAACP officials such as James Weldon Johnson, W. E. B. Du Bois, Moorfield Storey, and J. E. Spingarn.

23. See E. David Cronon, *Black Moses: The Story of Marcus Garvey and the Universal Negro Improvement Association* (Madison: University of Wisconsin Press, 1955); Tony Martin, *Race First: The Ideological and Organizational Struggles of Marcus Garvey and the Universal Negro Improvement Association* (Westport, Conn.: Greenwood Press, 1976); Robert A. Hill, ed., *The Marcus Garvey and Universal Negro Improvement Association Papers*, 6 vols. to date (Berkeley and Los Angeles: University of California Press, 1983–); Robert A. Hill, ed., *Marcus Garvey: Life and Lessons* (Berkeley and Los Angeles: University of California Press, 1987); and Judith Stein, *The World of Marcus Garvey* (Baton Rouge: Louisiana State University Press, 1986).

24. The earliest mention of a Norfolk branch of the NAACP dates from 2 April 1913, although the first application for charter was not received and accepted until 1917; see letter from E. H. Hunter, 1 August 1913, and "Application for Charter, January 22, 1917," Norfolk Branch, box G-208, NAACP Papers; and *Norfolk Journal and Guide*, 27 January 1917. Later in 1917, a local branch of the Urban League also formed, but it was unable to sustain public support in Norfolk. Thus, for almost the entire period of this study, Norfolk was in effect without an Urban League (*Norfolk Journal and Guide*, 15 September 1917; Hollis Lynch, *The Black Urban Condition: A Documentary History* [New York: Thomas Y. Crowell, 1973], p. 50). A perusal of the Urban League Papers in the Social Welfare History Collection of the University of Minnesota failed to produce additional information, nor is a branch listed in the Library of Congress collection. See also Kelly Miller, *Radicals and Conservatives, and Other Essays on the Negro in America* (New York: Schocken Books, 1968).

25. The membership files of the local branches are part of the NAACP Papers at the Library of Congress. The Tucker case is discussed in a series of letters dated August 1921 found in the Legal Files, box D-2.

26. Martin (*Race First*, pp. 367–68) and the *Norfolk Journal and Guide* (5 February 1921, 2 April 1921, 7 May 1921, 14 May 1921, 18 June 1921) list the vari-

ous Liberty Halls in the Norfolk area. The UNIA's journal, the *Negro World,* provided the database for determining the occupational makeup of the membership of the local Liberty Halls during the 1920s. Only ninety of the several hundred listed could be both positively identified and traced through the city directory. Eighty-one of 214 UNIA members identified were women (37.8 percent). See also Stein, *The World of Marcus Garvey,* pp. 227–47; and Emory J. Tolbert, *The UNIA and Black Los Angeles* (Los Angeles: Center for Afro-American Studies, University of California, Los Angeles, 1980), pp. 92–98.

27. Lawrence Levine, "Marcus Garvey and the Politics of Revitalization," in *Black Leaders in the Twentieth Century,* ed. John Hope Franklin and August Meier (Urbana: University of Illinois Press, 1982), pp. 118–19; Stein, *The World of Marcus Garvey,* introduction and conclusion. The level of Garvey support in Norfolk was impressive; see the *Norfolk Journal and Guide* (5 February 1921, 1 July 1922) and read the UNIA's *Negro World* to get a sense of local activity. Also see Hill, *Marcus Garvey and Universal Negro Improvement Association Papers,* vol. 2, pp. 176, 203, 214, 366, 368, 393, 493, 523, 534–35, 537, 548, 582–83. Norfolk was also the site of departure for the Black Star Line (Cronon, *Black Moses,* pp. 87, 96).

28. The Baptist Pastors' Union published its denunciation in full in the *Norfolk Journal and Guide,* 26 January 1924. Also see *Norfolk Journal and Guide,* 6 August 1921; Hill, *Marcus Garvey and Universal Negro Improvement Association Papers,* vol. 2, pp. 518–19.

29. Young's opinion appeared in the *Norfolk Journal and Guide,* 6 August 1921; Brown's letter appeared in the *Negro World,* 13 November 1926.

30. See correspondence between W. L. Martin, special assistant to the attorney general, and N. S. Small, secretary of the UNIA (Berkley-Norfolk, Va.), 15 July 1923 and 19 July 1923, in Theodore Kornweibel, ed., *Federal Surveillance of Afro-Americans (1917–1925): The First World War, the Red Scare, and the Garvey Movement,* microfilm collection (Bethseda, Md.: University Publications of America, 1986), reel 16, frame 3. See also the *Negro World,* 1 September 1923. Easton's letter appeared in the *Negro World,* 31 March 1928.

31. Levine, "Marcus Garvey and the Politics of Revitalization," pp. 118–20.

32. See August Meier, *Negro Thought in America, 1880–1915* (Ann Arbor: University of Michigan Press, 1963), chap. 3; Emma Lou Thornbrough, "T. Thomas Fortune: Militant Editor in the Age of Accommodation," in Franklin and Meier, *Black Leaders in the Twentieth Century,* pp. 19–38; Louis R. Harlan, *Booker T. Washington: The Making of a Black Leader, 1865–1901* (New York: Oxford University Press, 1972); and Louis R. Harlan, *Booker T. Washington: The Wizard of Tuskegee, 1901–1915* (New York: Oxford University Press, 1983).

33. Thomas J. Wertenbaker and Marvin W. Schlegel, *Norfolk: Historic Southern Port* (Durham, N.C.: Duke University Press, 1962), pp. 319–24; *Buchanan v. Warley,* 245 U.S. 60 (1917).

34. Norfolk City Council minutes, *Record Book* 28, p. 397, located in the office of the Norfolk City Clerk; *Norfolk Journal and Guide,* 14 July 1923.

35. *Norfolk Journal and Guide,* 17 February 1923, 24 February 1923. So testy were Brambleton whites that they attacked any black unfortunate enough to be found on the wrong turf, including black teachers and schoolchildren (see *Virginian-Pilot,* 10 July 1923).

36. *Norfolk Journal and Guide,* 21 March 1925.

37. See Kusmer, *A Ghetto Takes Shape,* pp. 167–70; Spear, *Black Chicago,* pp. 208–13; Hirsch, *Making the Second Ghetto,* esp. chap. 3.

38. Robert Bagnall to P. B. Young, 18 September 1925; Young to Bagnall, 23 September 1925; both in Norfolk Branch, box G-208, NAACP Papers.

39. Press release by the NAACP National Office, 26 February 1926, outlining victory in the Falls case and in a companion case involving Samuel Coston, who had moved into Brambleton, Norfolk Branch, box G-208, NAACP Papers; *Norfolk Journal and Guide,* 26 February 1926, 27 March 1926, 3 July 1926, 17 July 1926. See also George C. Wright, *Life Behind a Veil: Blacks in Louisville, Kentucky, 1865–1930* (Baton Rouge: Louisiana State University Press, 1985), pp. 119–22, 232–34.

40. Norfolk File, Home Owners Loan Corporation (HOLC) City Survey Files, 1935–1940, Record Group 195, National Archives; Louis C. and Virginia C., conversation with the author, 12 June 1985, Norfolk.

41. David H. Edwards to James Weldon Johnson, 13 January 1926; flyer announcing mass meeting to discuss the murder of Leroy Strother; Edwards to National Office, 13 January 1926; Edwards to Johnson, 3 April 1926; all in Norfolk Branch, box G-208, NAACP Papers. See also Robert G. Weisbord, *Bittersweet Encounter* (New York: Negro Universities Press, 1970), p. 321; *Norfolk Journal and Guide,* 17 April 1926.

42. The issue of road improvement in the black sections of Norfolk was perennial; see *Virginian-Pilot,* 2 July 1910, 9 July 1910. The black physician's comments were reported in Graham, *Soul of John Brown,* p. 41. The editorial appeared in the *Norfolk Journal and Guide,* 21 July 1917.

43. *Norfolk Journal and Guide,* 7 July 1923.

44. *Black Workers in the Era of the Great Migration,* reel 23, frame 987; "Housing in Southern Cities," *Southern Workman* 45 (July 1915): 371; *Norfolk Journal and Guide,* 5 February 1921. Health reports submitted to state officials support Schneck's findings. See *Annual Reports of Officers, Boards, and Institutions of the Commonwealth of Virginia,* table 2 in each vol. for the years 1922–1931, located in the Virginia State Library, Richmond; Bertha Hampton Miller, "Blacks in Winston-Salem, North Carolina, 1895–1920: Community Development in an Age of Benevolent Paternalism" (Ph.D. diss., Duke University, 1981); Earl Lewis, "At Work and at Home: Blacks in Norfolk, Virginia, 1910–1945" (Ph.D. diss., University of Minnesota, 1984), pp. 129–30; U.S. Bureau of the Census, *Fifteenth Census of the United States* (Washington, D.C.: Government Printing Office, 1932), vol. 6, *Population, 1930,* p. 1376.

45. *Norfolk Journal and Guide,* 22 January 1921, 7 July 1923. See also Blaine A. Brownell, *The Urban Ethos in the South* (Baton Rouge: Louisiana State University Press, 1975), p. 151.

46. George Haynes to Secretary of Labor, 1 July 1919, File 81102C, U.S. Department of Labor, Record Group 174, National Archives; *Norfolk Journal and Guide,* 29 January 1921; Wertenbaker and Schlegel, *Norfolk,* p. 319. Blacks admitted that a shift to the city manager type of city government resulted in an increase in the allotment of monies spent to improve their communities.

47. *Norfolk Journal and Guide,* 11 August 1923, 18 August 1923.

48. I. Walke Truxton to the Honorable City Council of Norfolk, Virginia, 23 July 1926, box 2, folder 1926, Louis Jaffe Papers.

49. *Norfolk Journal and Guide,* 5 November 1927.

50. Miller, "Blacks in Winston-Salem," esp. introduction and chaps. 1, 4, 7; Trotter, *Black Milwaukee,* chap. 4; Faye Welborn Robbins, "A World-Within-a-World: Black Nashville, 1880–1915" (Ph.D. diss., University of Arkansas, 1980), chaps. 4–5; Kusmer, *A Ghetto Takes Shape,* esp. chaps. 6, 11.

51. The description of the park appeared in the *Norfolk Journal and Guide,* 4 August 1923. Problems of this nature were not new to the city; see David Goldfield, "Continuity and Change: Southern Urban Development, 1860–1900," in *The City in Southern History,* ed. Blaine Brownell and David Goldfield (Port Washington, N.Y.: Kennikat Press, 1977), pp. 77–78. In 1915 a research group from New York studying urban problems recommended that the city of Norfolk expand the recreational opportunities for blacks, pointing out that "the two playgrounds and a section of Lafayette Park" were not enough ("Report on a Survey of the City Government," Bureau of Municipal Research, New York, 1915, pp. 516–17). Additional complaints about the lack of recreational options for blacks appeared in petitions to the city council to hold block parties. See, for example, Rev. Vincent Warren to City Council, 25 June 1923, *Record Book* 22, p. 271; James E. Smith, President of Sons of Norfolk, to City Council, 25 May 1930, *Record Book* 29, p. 464.

52. *Norfolk Journal and Guide,* 9 April 1921, 23 July 1921.

53. *Norfolk Journal and Guide,* 4 August 1923, 10 May 1924.

54. *Norfolk Journal and Guide,* 30 June 1923.

55. *Norfolk Journal and Guide,* 4 August 1923, 30 January 1926, 15 May 1926.

56. *Norfolk Journal and Guide,* 29 May 1926, 5 June 1926; I. Walke Truxton to City Council, 18 May 1926, Norfolk City Council minutes, *Record Book* 18, p. 219.

57. *Norfolk Journal and Guide,* 3 March 1928.

58. Wertenbaker and Schlegel, *Norfolk,* pp. 318–19; Capitation Tax Rolls, located in the Norfolk Public Library.

59. To ensure that the sample, although small, was random, a random number table was utilized for selecting the starting point. Also, a random internal was selected to ensure that we went through the entire list of entries for the years selected. These individuals were then traced through the *City Directory of Norfolk* for 1915.

60. The person reporting the story referred to the club's membership as "representative." According to the newspaper account, most of the individuals were young people, just starting out (*Norfolk Journal and Guide,* 3 November 1923).

61. Very little additional information accompanied the newspaper article (*Norfolk Journal and Guide,* 25 April 1925), and I have been unable to trace the club's origins further.

62. See note 59 above. The same procedure was followed, using the *City Directory of Norfolk* for 1927.

63. Andrew Buni, *The Negro in Virginia Politics, 1902–1965* (Charlottesville: University Press of Virginia, 1967), pp. 84–88; *Norfolk Journal and Guide,* 8 October 1921, 22 October 1921, 21 November 1925. Newsome was an attorney who lived in Newport News.

## CHAPTER 4

1. Ralph Ellison, *Invisible Man* (New York: Vintage Books, 1972), pp. 247–61; Robert Park, "Human Migration and the Marginal Man," *American Journal of Sociology* 33 (May 1928): 881–93.

2. Melville Herskovits (*The Myth of the Negro Past* [New York: Harper and Brothers, 1941], pp. x, 1–32, 292–99) was one of the first dissenters.

3. Lawrence Levine, *Black Culture and Black Consciousness: Afro-American Folk Thought from Slavery to Freedom* (New York: Oxford University Press, 1977), p. xi.

4. The Emancipation Day celebration received prominent coverage in the *Norfolk Journal and Guide* and dominated the community's social calendar; see that newspaper's December and January issues for the period. Also see the 1925 program for the Emancipation Day celebration, filed in the Norfolk Public Library. A review of the sports section of the *Journal and Guide* reveals the prominence and, we assume, the importance of sports in black life (*Norfolk Journal and Guide*, 26 May 1917). Luther D., for example, maintained that he was recruited by St. Joseph's Catholic High School to play football (Luther D., conversation with the author, 9 March 1983, Norfolk; see also "Dedicated to the Franciscan Sisters for Seventy-Two Years of Dedicated Service in St. Joseph's Parish, Norfolk, Va., 1889–1961" [typescript, n.d., Norfolk Public Library]).

5. As one who grew up in Norfolk, I can remember many weekends beginning with my grandfather purchasing a bottle of "good" scotch and retiring to his back porch to philosophize. He assured me—as a grandfather assures a grandson—that he had spent hours on that stoop over the years. From my experiences in post-1945 Norfolk, I know my grandfather was not alone.

6. The importance of food to the cultural world of Afro-Americans is well documented; see, for example, Charles Joyner, *Down by the Riverside: A South Carolina Slave Community* (Urbana: University of Illinois Press, 1984), chap. 3. Also note the food ads in the *Norfolk Journal and Guide*, and see "Family Disbursements of Wage Earners and Salaried Workers," Negroes, Norfolk Schedules, 1936, boxes 286–88, U.S. Bureau of Labor Statistics, Record Group 257, National Archives.

7. I ascertained the spatial layout by combining examinations of assorted maps in the Norfolk Public Library and old photographs with personal observations of the city.

8. See *The Negro in Virginia* (New York: Hasting House, 1940), p. 351; Richard W. Hull, *African Cities and Towns Before the European Conquest* (New York: W. W. Norton, 1976). One of the rarely discussed and, I might add, greatly misunderstood dimensions of urban life has been congregation. Some have assumed that segregation produced the congregative character of Afro-American urban life, but later observations challenge this assumption. Even in integrated settings, blacks congregated, despite Chicago-style de facto segregation or Norfolk-style de jure segregation. Illustrations can be found in St. Clair Drake and Horace Cayton, *Black Metropolis: A Study of Negro Life in a Northern City*, rev. ed. (New York: Harper and Row, 1962); Allan H. Spear, *Black Chicago: The Making of a Negro Ghetto, 1890–1920* (Chicago: University of Chicago Press, 1967), pp. 167–80; and Dorothy Schwieder, Joseph Hraba, and Elmer Schwieder, *Bux-*

ton: *Work and Racial Equality in a Coal Mining Community* (Ames: Iowa State University Press, 1987), pp. 20–38.

9. Joyner, *Down by the Riverside*, chap. 3; Eugene Genovese, *Roll, Jordan, Roll: The World the Slave Made* (New York: Vintage Books, 1976), pp. 540–50; *Norfolk Journal and Guide* advertisements; "Family Disbursements of Wage Earners and Salaried Workers," Negroes, Norfolk Schedules, 1936, boxes 286–88, U.S. Bureau of Labor Statistics, Record Group 257.

10. Louise Thompson Patterson, interview with the author, 2 September 1986, Oakland.

11. *City Directory of Norfolk*, 1910, 1918, located in the Norfolk Public Library; ad in the *Norfolk Journal and Guide*, 14 August 1926.

12. Helen Bryan, field representative, to Mary Anderson, director, U.S. Women's Bureau, 13 December 1919; Women's Bureau Bulletin no. 10 (December 1919); both in Record Group 86, National Archives; Stephen Graham, *The Soul of John Brown* (New York: Macmillan, 1920), p. 51.

13. *City Directory of Norfolk*, 1923; *Norfolk Journal and Guide*, 19 March 1921, 16 April 1921.

14. Virginia C., conversation with the author, 21 July 1984, Norfolk.

15. Joseph B. Earnest, *The Religious Development of the Negro* (Charlottesville, Va.: Michie Company, 1914), pp. 166–67.

16. Levine, *Black Culture and Black Consciousness*, pp. 68–78. Numerous ads fill the *Norfolk Journal and Guide*; see, for example, the ones by Anita and John Jones, 20 April 1929.

17. *Norfolk Journal and Guide*, 22 January 1921, 22 February 1930, 1 March 1930.

18. *Norfolk Journal and Guide*, 22 January 1921.

19. Gerald L. Davis, *I Got the Word in Me and I Can Sing It, You Know* (Philadelphia: University of Pennsylvania Press, 1985).

20. See, for example, *Negro World*, 1 November 1924, for a description of the Men's Day celebration; and Randall K. Burkett, *Garveyism as a Religious Movement* (Metuchen, N.J.: Scarecrow Press, 1978), introduction.

21. The quotation is taken from *The Negro in Virginia*, p. 351. These gatherings were a common experience throughout urban black America—indeed, throughout all urban America. See James Borchert, *Alley Life in Washington* (Urbana: University of Illinois Press, 1980), pp. 60–61, 75, 109, 148.

22. The continuity between the past and present was recounted by Louis C. in a conversation with me, 15 June 1986, Norfolk. I also observed similar gatherings while growing up in Norfolk.

23. For a description of baseball's democratic underpinnings, see Gunther Barth, *City People: The Rise of Modern City Culture in Nineteenth-Century America* (New York: Oxford University Press, 1980), pp. 159–91. The term *democratic* is not to be confused with *egalitarian* in this context. Rob Ruck offers a compelling portrait of the importance of sports to urban blacks in his *Sandlot Seasons: Sport in Black Pittsburgh* (Urbana: University of Illinois Press, 1987), esp. p. 37.

24. See Lawrence W. Levine, "William Shakespeare and the American People: A Study in Cultural Transformation," *American Historical Review* 89 (February 1984): 37–46. Gunther Barth offers an insightful rendering of the importance

of vaudeville to city people (*City People*, chap. 6). Also see Nathan Huggins, *Harlem Renaissance* (New York: Oxford University Press, 1973), pp. 280–86. The changes at the Palace Theater are described in the *Norfolk Journal and Guide*, 5 May 1917. Roy Rozenzweig (*Eight Hours for What We Will* [New York: Cambridge University Press, 1983], pp. 215–21) discusses the ability of working-class people to influence dispensers of culture.

25. See movie advertisements featured in the *Norfolk Journal and Guide*, 1 January 1921, 15 January 1921, 21 December 1929. See David Nasaw's fine study *Children of the City* (New York: Oxford University Press, 1985), pp. 120–29; and Rozenzweig, *Eight Hours for What We Will*, p. 215.

26. All of the theaters were located in the Church Street business district.

27. *Birth of a Nation* was in one sense an important film for a country trying to heal the wounds of sectional differences. Those who were predisposed to accept such a view—and there were many—had cinematic proof of the evils of Reconstruction. Concerning Stepin Fetchit, some argue that this character was so exaggerated that the actor may in fact have been engaging in a subtle form of protest. See Thomas Cripps, *Slow Fade to Black: The Negro in American Film, 1900–1942* (New York: Oxford University Press, 1977), pp. 45–55, 238–42.

28. Ibid., pp. 188–90.

29. *Norfolk Journal and Guide*, 7 September 1927. See Herbert Gutman's classic treatise on the power of the working class to bring form to its culture: *Work, Culture, and Society in Industrializing America* (New York: Vintage Books, 1977), pp. 3–78.

30. Robert C. Toll, *Blacking Up: The Minstrel Show in Nineteenth-Century America* (New York: Oxford University Press, 1974), pp. 270–74; Huggins, *Harlem Renaissance*, pp. 244–301.

31. Jervis Anderson, *This Was Harlem: A Cultural Portrait, 1900–1950* (New York: Farrar, Straus and Giroux, 1982), pp. 37–41; *Ethnic Notions*, video, directed and produced by Marlon Riggs, distributed by California Newsreel, San Francisco; Huggins, *Harlem Renaissance*, pp. 280–86. The high school minstrel show was reported in the *Norfolk Journal and Guide*, 24 March 1921.

32. Jeff Todd Titon, *Early Downhome Blues* (Urbana: University of Illinois Press, 1977); Levine, *Black Culture and Black Consciousness*, pp. 226–34; LeRoi Jones (Amiri Baraka), *Blues People* (New York: Morrow Quill, 1963).

33. *Norfolk Journal and Guide*, 21 January 1921. Smith returned on several occasions.

34. Lyrics from Titon, *Early Downhome Blues*, pp. 120–21; see also Eric Sackheim, ed., *The Blues Line* (New York: Schirmer Books, 1975), esp. p. 47. See also Houston A. Baker, Jr., *Blues, Ideology, and Afro-American Literature: A Vernacular Theory* (Chicago: University of Chicago Press, 1984), pp. 1–14 and chap. 3, for suggestions on what a decoding of the lyrics might tell.

35. Levine, *Black Culture and Black Consciousness*, pp. 217–39; Jones, *Blues People*, chap. 8. Through 1930, the *Journal and Guide* regularly ran ads bearing the names of these labels. See, for example, *Norfolk Journal and Guide*, 21 January 1921, 27 April 1929, 4 May 1929. Also see *The Negro in Virginia*, pp. 290–91.

36. Newman I. White, *American Negro Folk-Songs* (Cambridge: Harvard University Press, 1928), pp. 220–21.

37. Herbert Gutman makes this point well in his *The Black Family in Slavery and Freedom, 1750–1925* (New York: Pantheon Books, 1976).

38. Borchert, *Alley Life in Washington*, esp. chap. 2. For other examples, consult John Bodnar, Roger Simon, and Michael P. Weber, *Lives of Their Own* (Urbana: University of Illinois Press, 1982); and Elizabeth Rauh Bethel, *Promiseland* (Philadelphia: Temple University Press, 1981).

39. U.S. Bureau of the Census, *Thirteenth Census of the United States* (Washington, D.C.: Government Printing Office, 1911), vol. 3, *Population, 1910*, p. 935; U.S. Bureau of the Census, *Fourteenth Census of the United States* (Washington, D.C.: Government Printing Office, 1921), vol. 2, *Population, 1920*, p. 508; U.S. Bureau of the Census, *Fifteenth Census of the United States* (Washington, D.C.: Government Printing Office, 1932), vol. 4, *Population, 1930*, p. 996; Manuscript Census, Norfolk City, 1910, microfilm reel T624–1637, U.S. Bureau of the Census, Record Group 29, National Archives.

40. Frank Furstenberg, Theodore Hershberg, and John Modell, "The Origins of the Female-Headed Black Family: The Impact of the Urban Experience," *Journal of Interdisciplinary History* 6 (1975): 211–33; *Annual Report of the [Virginia] State Board of Health*, table 2 in each vol. for the years 1921–1930, located in the Virginia State Library, Richmond.

41. U.S Bureau of the Census, *Thirteenth Census*, vol. 3, *Population, 1910*, p. 935; U.S. Bureau of the Census, *Fourteenth Census*, vol. 2, *Population, 1920*, p. 508; U.S. Bureau of the Census, *Fifteenth Census*, vol. 4, *Population, 1930*, p. 996; divorce columns in the *Norfolk Journal and Guide*, 1921–1930; *Annual Report of the [Virginia] State Board of Health*, table 9 in each vol. for the years 1921–1930.

42. Gutman, *The Black Family*, pp. 477–544; Manuscript Census, Norfolk City, 1910, T624–1637, U.S. Bureau of the Census, Record Group 29; Susan J., interview with the author, 2 January 1981, Norfolk.

43. *Norfolk Journal and Guide*, 26 March 1921. Virtually no work has been done using newspapers to plot visiting patterns, with the exception of a study by Jane M. Pederson: "The Country Visitor: Patterns of Hospitality in Rural Wisconsin, 1880–1925," *Agricultural History* 58 (July 1984): 347–64. For a complete discussion of this section of the text, see Earl Lewis, "Afro-American Adaptive Strategies: The Visiting Habits of Kith and Kin Among Black Norfolkians," *Journal of Family History* 12, no. 4 (1987): 407–20.

44. To test the usefulness of this approach, I sampled every fourth issue of the *Norfolk Journal and Guide* for the years September 1916–October 1917, 1921, and 1925, for a total of thirty-seven issues and 840 recorded visits. The study was not extended beyond 1925 for two reasons. First, I sought both a time frame that paralleled the peak of the Great Migration and a period that encompassed the less intense post-migration years, when visiting might have become institutionalized. Second, because of the increasing socioeconomic stratification of the black community, one's appearance in the newspaper columns after 1925 derived from one's status in the community. This was not true in 1916–1917 or in 1921 but had become increasingly the case by the end of 1925. Even with this bias, the results are not likely to be severely skewed, because all economic groups visited. There is no way to capture the entire population, of course, because the

information was self-reported; therefore only those individuals who chose or were able to report this type of information are included.

45. *Norfolk Journal and Guide*, 13 August 1921; Borchert, *Alley Life in Washington*, p. 84; Gilbert Osofsky, *Harlem: The Making of a Ghetto, Negro New York, 1890–1930* (New York: Harper and Row, 1963), p. 30.

46. J. M. Hunter to Charles Hunter, 13 June 1914, box 4, folder 1913–1914, Charles N. Hunter Papers, Perkins Library, Duke University, Durham, N.C.

47. James Richard Grossman, "A Dream Deferred: Black Migration to Chicago, 1916–1921" (Ph.D. diss., University of California, Berkeley, 1982), pp. 57–61; Peter Gottlieb, *Making Their Own Way: Southern Blacks' Migration to Pittsburgh, 1916–30* (Urbana: University of Illinois Press, 1987), chap. 2 and pp. 205–10; Martin Fishbein and Icek Ajzen, "Attitudes Towards Objects as Predictors of Single and Multiple Behavior Criteria," *Psychological Review* 81 (1974): 59–74.

48. Florette Henri, *Black Migration: Movement North, 1900–1920* (Garden City, N.Y.: Anchor Books, 1976), pp. 66, 68; *Annual Reports of Officers, Boards, and Institutions of the Commonwealth of Virginia*, 1920, *Report of the Labor Commission*, pp. 32, 37, located in the Virginia State Library, Richmond.

49. *Norfolk Journal and Guide*, 5 September 1925.

50. *Norfolk Journal and Guide*, 7 November 1925.

51. Virginia C., conversation with the author, 7 June 1985, Norfolk; *Norfolk Journal and Guide*, 22 January 1921, 25 June 1921, 1 August 1925.

52. Roger Lane, *Roots of Violence in Black Philadelphia, 1860–1900* (Cambridge: Harvard University Press, 1986), pp. 156–58.

53. Susan J., conversation with the author, July 1977, Norfolk.

54. Papers of William J. in the author's possession, including one divorce decree; Susan J., interview with the author, 2 January 1981, Norfolk; Maria Ruffin, interview by Edith Skinner, 23 December 1938, Virginia Writers' Project (VWP 58–71), Virginia State Library, Richmond. See also the divorce decrees published weekly in the *Norfolk Journal and Guide*. Elizabeth Pleck (*Black Migration and Poverty: Boston, 1865–1900* [New York: Academic Press, 1979], pp. 186–87) describes a similar process for an earlier period.

55. George W. Bennett, *Life Behind the Walls of My Self-Made Fate* (self-published, 1964), p. 9.

56. Ibid., pp. 48–49. The desertion rate for black families increased substantially between 1910 and 1930, according to state records.

57. Lewis, "Afro-American Adaptive Strategies," pp. 412–13. Three quarters of the groups consisted of two travelers, and 4.8 percent were nuclear families.

58. *Kinkeeper* is a neologism that aptly conveys the importance of black women's social function. Tamara Hareven used it as a phrase conveying a similar meaning (*Family Time and Industrial Time* [Cambridge: Cambridge University Press, 1982], pp. 105–6).

59. Gottlieb, *Making Their Own Way*, chap. 7. Of those who came from or went to faraway places, few stayed more than a week. See Lewis, "Afro-American Adaptive Strategies," pp. 413–14.

60. *Norfolk Journal and Guide*, 14 March 1925. The difference in length of visit by gender had a strong statistical association ($\chi^2 = 22.68393$, 6df, significance = .0009) (Lewis, "Afro-American Adaptive Strategies," pp. 413–14).

61. Grossman, "A Dream Deferred," pp. 57–62; Gottlieb, *Making Their Own Way*, chaps. 1–2.

62. Frederick Stutz, "Distance and Network Effects on Urban Social Travel Fields," *Economic Geographer* 49 (1973): 135; John S. MacDonald and Leatrice D. MacDonald, "Chain Migration, Ethnic Neighborhood Formation, and Social Networks," *Milbank Memorial Fund* 42 (1964): 82.

63. *Norfolk Journal and Guide*, 14 February 1925.

64. *Norfolk Journal and Guide*, 13 August 1921.

65. The geography of the movement is more fully explicated in Lewis, "Afro-American Adaptive Strategies"; and Earl Lewis, "At Work and at Home: Blacks in Norfolk, Virginia, 1910–1945" (Ph.D. diss., University of Minnesota, 1984), pp. 223–34.

66. Schwieder, Hraba, and Schwieder, *Buxton*, pp. 20–38. In many respects, I am arguing that much as contemporary scholars decode text, blacks in Norfolk decoded the world in which they lived. Thus, where historians have seen power-lessness, black residents experienced something altogether different.

## CHAPTER 5

1. Charlie Johnson, interview, 24 February 1939, Virginia Writers' Project (VWP 58–71), Virginia State Library, Richmond. Bigger Thomas is the central character of Richard Wright's *Native Son* (1940; reprint, New York: Harper and Row, 1966).

2. Ronald L. Heinemann, *Depression and New Deal in Virginia: The Enduring Dominion* (Charlottesville: University Press of Virginia, 1983), pp. 8–14.

3. William H. Harris, *The Harder We Run: Black Workers Since the Civil War* (New York: Oxford University Press, 1982), p. vii; Maya Angelou, *I Know Why the Caged Bird Sings* (New York: Bantam Books, 1969), p. 41; Studs Terkel, *Hard Times: An Oral History of the Great Depression* (New York: Pantheon Books, 1970), p. 82.

4. *Norfolk Journal and Guide*, 10 March 1928. Norfolk's Afro-Americans were not alone; see Robert S. McElvaine, *The Great Depression* (New York: New York Times Books, 1984), p. 187.

5. *Norfolk Journal and Guide*, 4 January 1930.

6. See "Domestic Servants Here May Lose Places to White Competitors," *Norfolk Journal and Guide*, 21 February 1931; and "White Waitresses Replace Colored in W. G. Swartz Company's Cafe," *Norfolk Journal and Guide*, 17 October 1931. Business manager Samuel Lyons admitted that the Finkelstein Company, a garment concern, harbored real reservations about employing black women; see "Negroes Proving Efficiency in Finkelstein," *Norfolk Journal and Guide*, 13 October 1928. Harvard Sitkoff (*A New Deal for Blacks* [New York: Oxford University Press, 1978], p. 36) describes other efforts to deny jobs to blacks.

7. U.S. Bureau of the Census, *Fourteenth Census of the United States* (Washington, D.C.: Government Printing Office, 1923), vol. 4, *Occupations, 1920*, pp. 1183–84; U.S. Bureau of the Census, *Fifteenth Census of the United States* (Washington, D.C.: Government Printing Office, 1933), vol. 4, *Occupations, 1930*, pp.

1673–74; U.S. Bureau of the Census, *Sixteenth Census of the United States* (Washington, D.C.: Government Printing Office, 1943), vol. 3, *The Labor Force, 1940*, pp. 772–73.

8. Laura Chase, interview by E. C. Skinner, 17 February 1939 ("The Fisherman's Wife, Laura Chase"), Virginia Writers' Project.

9. Private papers, including correspondence from a mail-order divinity school in Chicago, in the possession of the author. William J. did successfully change careers, and for several years he was the pastor of a large Baptist church in Norfolk. For increased numbers of professionals, etc., see n. 7.

10. U.S. Bureau of the Census, *Fourteenth Census*, vol. 4, *Occupations, 1920*, pp. 1184–85; U.S. Bureau of the Census, *Fifteenth Census*, vol. 4, *Occupations, 1930*, p. 1675; U.S. Bureau of the Census, *Sixteenth Census*, vol. 3, *The Labor Force, 1940*, p. 776. Black women did not weather the downturn as successfully as some white women did. Excluded from clerical positions, most were not as fortunate as the white women Lois Helmbold describes in her research ("Making Choices, Making Do: Black and White Working-Class Women's Lives and Work During the Depression, 1929–1941" [Ph.D. diss., Stanford University, 1983])—or even as fortunate as some of the black women described by Jacqueline Jones (*Labor of Love, Labor of Sorrow: Black Women, Work, and the Family from Slavery to the Present* [New York: Basic Books, 1985], pp. 208–13).

11. U.S. Bureau of the Census, *Fifteenth Census of the United States* (Washington, D.C.: Government Printing Office, 1932), vol. 1, *Unemployment, 1930*, p. 1031.

12. Thomas Hill, interview by Edith Skinner, 2 February 1939, Virginia Writers' Project; *Norfolk Journal and Guide*, 21 January 1933.

13. Gladys L. Palmer and Katherine D. Wood, *Urban Workers on Relief, Part 2* (Washington, D.C.: Works Progress Administration, 1936), pp. 4–6; *Unemployment Relief Census, October 1933* (Washington, D.C.: Federal Emergency Relief Administration, 1934), pp. 8, 112.

14. Palmer and Wood, *Urban Workers on Relief*, pp. 7–11; *Unemployment Relief Census, October 1933*, pp. 86–87.

15. *Unemployment Relief Census, October 1933*, pp. 112–13.

16. Louis C., Sr., conversation with the author, 11 March 1983, Norfolk.

17. Philip M. Hauser, *Workers on Relief in the United States in March 1935* (Washington, D.C.: Works Progress Administration, Division of Social Research, 1938), vol. 1, *A Census of Usual Occupations*, pp. 1002, 1011.

18. Lucille Johnson, interview by Edith Skinner, 20 January 1939, Virginia Writers' Project.

19. Maria Ruffin, interview by Edith Skinner, 23 December 1938, Virginia Writers' Project.

20. Jones, *Labor of Love, Labor of Sorrow*, p. 279; Lawrence Gordon, "A Brief Look at Blacks in Depression Mississippi, 1929–1934: Eyewitness Accounts," *Journal of Negro History* 64 (1979): 382, 385; U.S. Department of Labor, "Consumers' Cooperative Among Negroes in Gary, Indiana," *Monthly Labor Review* 42 (February 1936): 370.

21. "Family Disbursements of Wage Earners and Salaried Workers," Negroes, Norfolk Schedules, #37 and #79, 1936, boxes 286–88, U.S. Bureau of Labor Statistics, Record Group 257, National Archives.

22. U.S. Bureau of the Census, *Fifteenth Census of the United States* (Washington, D.C.: Government Printing Office, 1932), vol. 2, *Population, 1930,* p. 996; U.S. Bureau of the Census, *Sixteenth Census of the United States* (Washington, D.C.: Government Printing Office, 1943), vol. 4, pt. 4, *Population, 1940,* pp. 685, 690.

23. U.S. Bureau of the Census, *Fifteenth Census,* vol. 2, *Population, 1930,* p. 996; U.S. Bureau of the Census, *Sixteenth Census,* vol. 4, pt. 4, *Population, 1940,* pp. 685, 690; Charlie Johnson, interview, 24 February 1939, Virginia Writers' Project.

24. U.S. Bureau of the Census, *Census of Partial Employment, Unemployment, and Occupations: 1937* (Washington, D.C.: Government Printing Office, 1938), vol. 3, pp. 538, 563 (this census was plagued by significant undercounting, as officials later admitted); Thomas Hill, interview by Edith Skinner, 2 February 1939, Virginia Writers' Project.

25. U.S. Bureau of the Census, *Census of Partial Employment, Unemployment, and Occupations: 1937,* vol. 3, p. 538.

26. U.S. Bureau of the Census, *Sixteenth Census,* vol. 3, pt. 5, *Population, 1940,* p. 748.

27. Dean W. Morse, *Pride Against Prejudice* (Montclair, N.J.: Allanheld, Osmun, 1980), pp. 77–78.

28. To approximate out-migration levels, one starts by taking the population at the beginning census date (p), multiplying that figure by the known survival rate for the population during the time period (r), and subtracting the product from the population at the terminal census date ($p^1$). From this, we can estimate net out-migration by age and sex among Norfolk's black residents. See Everett S. Lee et al., *Population Redistribution and Economic Growth, United States, 1870–1950* (Philadelphia: American Philosophical Society, 1957), vol. 1, pp. 15–16, 22.

29. U.S. Bureau of the Census, *Sixteenth Census of the United States: Population, 1940—Internal Migration, 1935 to 1940, Color and Sex of Migrants* (Washington, D.C.: Government Printing Office, 1943), p. 26.

30. Ibid., pp. 315, 338, 361, 384, 453.

31. Ibid., pp. 407, 430, 453, 476.

32. See the picture essay entitled "These Pictures and Facts Should Arouse Somebody's Civic Pride," *Norfolk Journal and Guide,* 12 May 1934.

33. "Family Disbursements of Wage Earners and Salaried Workers," Negroes, Norfolk Schedules, 1936, boxes 286–88, U.S. Bureau of Labor Statistics, Record Group 257. Also see Faith M. Williams and Alice C. Hanson, "Expenditure Habits of Wage Earners and Clerical Workers," *Monthly Labor Review* 39 (December 1939): 1311–34.

34. Williams and Hanson, "Expenditure Habits," p. 1326. Copies of the original schedules were recoded and analyzed using the Statistical Package for the Social Sciences (SPSS).

35. U.S. Bureau of the Census, *Sixteenth Census of the United States* (Washington, D.C.: Government Printing Office, 1945), vol. 2, pt. 5, *Housing, 1940,* p. 619.

36. Susan J., interview with the author, 2 January 1981, Norfolk.

37. "Family Disbursements of Wage Earners and Salaried Workers," Negroes, Norfolk Schedules, 1936, boxes 286–88, U.S. Bureau of Labor Statistics, Record Group 257.

38. U.S. Bureau of the Census, *Sixteenth Census*, vol. 2, pt. 5, *Housing, 1940*, p. 623.

39. Norfolk File, p. 41, Home Owners Loan Corporation (HOLC) City Survey Files, 1935–1940, Record Group 195, National Archives.

40. Ibid., p. 43; "Application of Broad Creek Plaza Corporation for Loan Under NIRA," Rejected Applications File, U.S. Public Housing Administration, Record Group 196, National Archives.

41. U.S. Bureau of the Census, *Sixteenth Census*, vol. 2, pt. 5, *Housing, 1940*, p. 628; "Family Disbursements of Wage Earners and Salaried Workers," Negroes, Norfolk Schedules #6, #8, #27, 1936, boxes 286–88, U.S. Bureau of Labor Statistics, Record Group 257.

42. U.S. Bureau of the Census, *Sixteenth Census*, vol. 2, pt. 5, *Housing, 1940*, p. 627.

43. *Norfolk Journal and Guide*, 10 January 1931; Abram L. Harris, *The Negro as Capitalist* (New York: Haskell, 1936), pp. 89–91.

44. *Norfolk Journal and Guide*, 24 January 1931, 7 February 1931, 27 June 1931, 11 July 1931.

45. Harris, *The Negro as Capitalist*, pp. 95–101.

46. *Norfolk Journal and Guide*, 18 July 1931, 24 June 1933. Closure also led to transferrals of ownership for the seven drugstores operated by blacks in 1927; only one was controlled by blacks by 1939 (*The Negro in Virginia* [New York: Hasting House, 1940], p. 305).

47. Vacancy rates were obtained by tracing the overall number of vacancies and businesses in operation as noted in the *City Directory of Norfolk* (located in the Norfolk Public Library) between 1927 and 1941.

## CHAPTER 6

1. Trotter saw a somewhat similar convergence among blacks in Milwaukee as early as 1925 (Joe William Trotter, Jr., *Black Milwaukee: The Making of an Industrial Proletariat* [Urbana: University of Illinois Press, 1985], pp. 64–65).

2. The Socialist party met with great difficulty in Norfolk in the later 1920s and early 1930s. Early in 1929, only thirteen members remained in good standing. By March 1931, the Norfolk chapter had accrued a debt of $263.37. By February 1931, the leadership had begun to issue urgent pleas for members to attend meetings regularly. See Virginia, 1919–1937, State and Local Files, microfilm reels 111, 132, Socialist Party Papers, Perkins Library, Duke University, Durham, N.C.; File 10110–2663–3, p. 3, Military Intelligence Department (MID) Files, Record Group 165, National Archives. Some argue that the Wobblies (the IWW) were the first to infiltrate the black community, but a reading of the MID files on IWW activity fails to corroborate this assertion.

3. Mark Naison, *Communists in Harlem During the Depression* (Urbana: University of Illinois Press, 1983), pp. 11–25.

4. Harvey Klehr, *The Heyday of American Communism: The Depression Decade* (New York: Basic Books, 1984), p. 273. Angelo Herndon, a black member of the Communist party in Atlanta during the Depression, was arrested for distribut-

ing Communist leaflets and charged with violating an old slave law that forbade inciting insurrection. Herndon's legal case became a central concern of activists in the South. See Charles S. Martin, *The Angelo Herndon Case and Southern Justice* (Baton Rouge: Louisiana State University Press, 1976).

5. Lawrence Goodwyn, *The Populist Moment* (New York: Oxford University Press, 1978), p. xviii.

6. See C. Vann Woodward, *Tom Watson: Agrarian Rebel* (New York: Oxford University Press, 1977); Richard Jules Oestreicher, *Solidarity and Fragmentation: Working-Class Consciousness in Detroit, 1875–1900* (Urbana: University of Illinois Press, 1986), pp. 35–36, 242–44; and Peter Rachleff, *Black Labor in the South: Richmond, Virginia, 1865–1890* (Philadelphia: Temple University Press, 1984), esp. chaps. 10–12. On communism, see Bert Cochran, *Labor and Communism* (Princeton, N.J.: Princeton University Press, 1977), esp. chap. 2; and Harvard Sitkoff, *A New Deal for Blacks* (New York: Oxford University Press, 1978), p. 142. On Garveyism, see Robert A. Hill, ed., *The Marcus Garvey and Universal Negro Improvement Association Papers* (Berkeley and Los Angeles: University of California Press, 1983), vol. 1, pp. xli–l.

7. Naison, *Communists in Harlem*, pp. 34–38; Daniel J. Leab, "United We Eat: The Creation and Organization of the Unemployed Councils in 1930," *Labor History* 8 (Fall 1967): 700–15; Martin, *The Angelo Herndon Case*, pp. 52–53, 405; Paul Dennis Brunn, "Black Workers and Social Movements in the 1930s in St. Louis" (Ph.D. diss., Washington University, 1975), pp. 182–96.

8. See Naison, *Communists in Harlem*, chap. 6, on the united front phase.

9. Sitkoff, *New Deal for Blacks*, p. 154; St. Clair Drake and Horace Cayton, *Black Metropolis: A Study of Negro Life in a Northern City*, rev. ed. (New York: Harper and Row, 1962), pp. 87, 734–37.

10. Oddly, Graham (whose real name was Grahovac) aired his position in the Garveyite paper, the *Negro World*; see "Negro and White Workers Will Not Let Them Kill Me!" *Negro World*, 1 February 1930; and *Norfolk Journal and Guide*, 2 November 1929. His philosophy and that of other organizers did not go unnoticed. Earlier details of organizational activity are mentioned in U.S. Congress, House, Special Committee, *Hearings Before a Special Committee to Investigate Communist Activities in the United States*, 71st Cong. 2d sess., 1930, pt. 6, vol. 1, esp. pp. 9, 11, 55, 225–29 (hereafter called Fish Committee Report).

11. *Norfolk Journal and Guide*, 2 November 1929; *Negro World*, 1 February 1930; Fish Committee Report, pt. 6, vol. 1, pp. 225–29.

12. *Norfolk Journal and Guide*, 12 November 1932; File 10110–2663–7, MID Files, Record Group 165; "Communist Hauled In by Local Police," *Norfolk Journal and Guide*, 15 October 1932; "Gathering to Be Addressed by Richard B. Moore," *Norfolk Journal and Guide*, 22 April 1933; "I.L.D. to Sponsor Meeting Thursday Night," *Norfolk Journal and Guide*, 10 March 1934. Military intelligence operatives described Norfolk as the most sensitive spot in the Mid-Atlantic and South Atlantic regions during this period. Local police attempted to break up the radical activity and were successful in a few instances. See Files 10110–2663–7, 10110–26635, Third Corps Area Reports for 1 February 1932, p. 6, and 1 May 1932, p. 4, MID Files, Record Group 165.

Concerning the speakers mentioned in the text, biographical information is available for Allen and Wright only. (See note 13, below, for information on Wright.) Allen's real name was Paul Crouch. Government officials indicated that he was born in North Wilkesboro, North Carolina. His radical activity began in the army in 1924 and brought him a dishonorable discharge in 1925. Between 1929 and 1932, he worked in several southeastern states as a Communist organizer, eventually ending up in Norfolk. Later, Crouch became a notorious government informer of dubious truthfulness. See Klehr, *Heyday of American Communism*, pp. 273–74.

13. Little is known about Wright's origins. On separate job applications obtained by the FBI, (Isaac) Alexander Wright listed his country of birth as Canada and his birth year variously as 1880 and 1887. Louise Patterson, however, a frequent associate in the early 1930s, recalled that he had a distinctive southern drawl. Later newspaper clippings released by the FBI reveal that Wright was a native of Texas. According to the same FBI records, he was nearly six feet tall and weighed between 174 and 190 pounds. Because other evidence contained in the FBI files seems in error, caution is advised in interpreting the information found there. It does appear that Wright may have worked at several shipyards before coming to Norfolk. See File 10110–2663–3, appendix, MID Files, Record Group 165; Isaac Alexander Wright, Internal Security File 65–1594–1 through 35, FBI; and Louise Thompson Patterson, interview with the author, 2 September 1986, Oakland.

14. *Norfolk Journal and Guide*, 22 October 1932. Initially the white press gave scant coverage to Communist party activities among blacks.

15. Gary B. Nash, *Forging Freedom* (Cambridge: Harvard University Press, 1988), pp. 224–27, 272–79; Bruce Laurie, *Working People of Philadelphia, 1800–1850* (Philadelphia: Temple University Press, 1980), pp. 62–66, 94–95, 155–58; Roger Lane, *Roots of Violence in Black Philadelphia, 1860–1900* (Cambridge: Harvard University Press, 1986), pp. 38–44; Elizabeth Pleck, *Black Migration and Poverty: Boston, 1865–1900* (New York: Academic Press, 1979), chap. 5; Oestreicher, *Solidarity and Fragmentation,* chap. 2; Olivier Zunz, *The Changing Face of Inequality* (Chicago: University of Chicago Press, 1982), chap. 14; David Katzman, *Before the Ghetto: Black Detroit in the Nineteenth Century* (Urbana: University of Illinois Press, 1973), pp. 62–63, 107–17; William M. Tuttle, Jr., *Race Riot: Chicago in the Red Summer of 1919* (New York, Atheneum, 1975).

16. Clearly, Afro-Americans were more than "ethnics." Unlike others, they could never blend into the social and cultural fabric by merely changing names, speech patterns, or religious affiliations. Nonetheless, the same factors that made the Irish a distinct social and cultural group made blacks one. Thus, for comparison's sake, the word *ethnic* is used, although guardedly.

17. Cyril Briggs, "Our Negro Work," *Communist* 8 (September 1929): 497; Myra Page, "Inter-Racial Relations Among Southern Workers," *Communist* 9 (February 1930): 154–65. Wicks and Ford are quoted in the *Norfolk Journal and Guide*, 22 October 1932, 5 May 1934, respectively.

18. *Norfolk Journal and Guide*, 22 October 1932. The city passed Ordinance 6574, which prohibited parades, speeches, demonstrations, or other assemblies

in public places without a written permit from the city manager, subject to a fine of between five and five hundred dollars and/or up to six months in jail. See "Judge to Report on Motions for New Trials," *Norfolk Journal and Guide*, 11 February 1933; and *Norfolk City Ordinances*, vol. 30, Ordinance 6574, p. 303, located in the Norfolk Public Library.

19. Norfolk File, Home Owners Loan Corporation (HOLC) City Survey Files, 1935–1940, Record Group 195, National Archives; *Norfolk Journal and Guide*, 21 January 1933; *Daily Worker*, 28 January 1933.

20. *Norfolk Journal and Guide*, 21 January 1933; *Daily Worker*, 28 January 1933.

21. *Norfolk Journal and Guide*, 21 January 1933; telegram quoted in the *Daily Worker*, 28 January 1933. After the formation of the CIO, Merrill, who spoke with a German accent but on at least one occasion claimed black ancestry, spent several years representing CIO-affiliated black dockworkers. At one point, he accused the local NAACP branch of being concerned exclusively about white-collar blacks (E. Frederic Morrow to Executives in National Office, 11 October 1939, Norfolk Branch, box G-208, NAACP Papers, Library of Congress).

22. "Political Status of the Negro," W. Jackson Field Notes, Norfolk, memoranda, box 85, folder 29, Ralph Bunche Papers, University of California, Los Angeles; File 10110–2663–7, MID Files, Record Group 165; *Norfolk Journal and Guide*, 3 December 1932, 10 December 1932. This strategy impressed blacks in Harlem as well (Naison, *Communists in Harlem*, chaps. 4–5).

23. The level of government concern for Communist activity can be seen in the MID files for the Third Corps Area (Record Group 165). Also see Richard Powers, *Secrecy and Power: The Life of J. Edgar Hoover* (New York: Free Press, 1987).

24. *Norfolk Journal and Guide*, 15 December 1934.

25. File 10110–2663–117, MID Files, Record Group 165; *Norfolk Journal and Guide*, 18 May 1935.

26. *Norfolk Journal and Guide*, 8 March 1930; "Negro Editors on Communism," *Crisis* 39 (April 1932): 117.

27. *Norfolk Journal and Guide*, 26 March 1938.

28. "Summary of the Subversive Situation," Third Corps Area Report, 1 May 1932, p. 4, MID Files, Record Group 165; "The 'Red' Menace In Norfolk," *Norfolk Journal and Guide*, 21 July 1934. In 1929 the *Journal and Guide* pleaded with blacks to join the more sanctioned AFL rather than ally with "labor agitators whose chief objective is to intensify class hatred" (2 November 1929).

29. Nell Painter, *The Narrative of Hosea Hudson: His Life as a Negro Communist in the South* (Cambridge: Harvard University Press, 1979); Martin, *The Angelo Herndon Case*, pp. 52–53.

30. *Norfolk Journal and Guide*, 11 March 1933, 18 March 1933; File 10110–2663–49, MID Files, Record Group 165.

31. Louise Thompson Patterson, interview with the author, 2 September 1986, Oakland; Ralph Ellison, *Invisible Man* (New York: Vintage Books, 1972). The story of Nate Shaw (i.e., Ned Cobb) addresses the efforts of the Communists in the rural South (Theodore Rosengarten, *All God's Dangers* [New York: Vintage Books, 1974], pp. 296–305, 326, appendix). No doubt many wondered if the party fully understood what it hoped to accomplish, for its blueprint

changed with successive Cominterns; see Naison, *Communists in Harlem*, chaps. 1, 6, 11.

32. *Marine Workers' Voice*, November 1933.

33. Alexander Wright, representative of Coastwide Longshoremen for the Eastern Coast, Shipping Code Hearings, January 1934, box 6507, National Recovery Administration, Record Group 9, National Archives.

34. *Norfolk Journal and Guide*, 12 May 1934; editorial by Alexander Wright, *Marine Workers' Voice*, June 1934; "ILA Head Helps Bosses Break MWIU Strike," *Marine Workers' Voice*, June 1934.

35. *Norfolk Journal and Guide*, 12 May 1934. Also see *Norfolk Journal and Guide*, 27 October 1934; *Marine Workers' Voice*, July 1934.

36. *Norfolk Journal and Guide*, 12 May 1934.

37. *Norfolk Journal and Guide*, 12 May 1934. Klehr (*Heyday of American Communism*, pp. 125–28) describes similar strike efforts on the docks in San Francisco. Other problems with the ILA involved practices that limited the numbers who worked. Because gang leaders did the hiring, personal predilections resulted in some 30 percent of the workers going without work. Those who did work supposedly returned portions of their earnings as kickbacks (Herbert R. Northrup, *Organized Labor and the Negro* [New York: Harper and Brothers, 1944], pp. 144–47; *Norfolk Journal and Guide*, 3 December 1932).

38. *Norfolk Journal and Guide*, 27 October 1934, 19 January 1935, 4 January 1936, 8 May 1937; Files 20912680, 4741570, Federal Mediation and Conciliation Service, Record Group 280, National Archives.

39. Paul A. Askew, president of the Norfolk Central Labor Union, interview with the author, 18 September 1983, Norfolk.

40. *Norfolk Journal and Guide*, 13 October 1928.

41. *Norfolk Journal and Guide*, 24 August 1935; Clemmie I. Shuck to Bennett F. Schauffler, director, National Labor Relations Board, Baltimore Region, 20 June 1935, Administrative File, Baltimore Region, box 207, National Labor Relations Board, Record Group 25, National Archives; *Virginian-Pilot*, 19 June 1935; Steve Fraser, "Dress Rehearsal for the New Deal," in *Working-Class America*, ed. Michael H. Frisch and Daniel Walkowitz (Urbana: University of Illinois Press, 1983), pp. 212–55.

42. *Norfolk Journal and Guide*, 3 November 1934, 10 November 1934.

43. Edith Christianson to Bennett Schauffler, 29 July 1935; written statement by Florence Thornton, 29 July 1935, about intimidation by management; transcript, telephone conversation between Schauffler and Nathan Finkelstein, son of the company's owner, 21 June 1935; news clipping, "Finkelstein Employees Seek an End of Intimidation," dated 9 August 1935; all in box 207, National Labor Relations Board, Record Group 25.

44. Jacob S. Potofsky to Bennett F. Schauffler, 7 July 1935, box 207, National Labor Relations Board, Record Group 25. Included with the letter was a copy of the labor agreement submitted by the Norfolk Central Labor Union to Irving Lyons, manager of the Norfolk plant. Potofsky stated that the agreement had been shown to Charles Borlund, who was chief of police at the time, and to local arbitrators and other prominent citizens; supposedly, they all agreed that the terms seemed fair.

45. Memo: summary of conferences between Bennett Schauffler and Sam and Nathan Finkelstein, 3 July 1935, 10 July 1935; summary of conference between Schauffler and William F. Green, Sidney Hillman (president, ACWA), Ed Pickler (president, Norfolk CLU), Jacob Potofsky, and Mike Smith, 10 July 1935; summary of telephone conservation between Schauffler and Potofsky, 10 July 1935; all in box 207, National Labor Relations Board, Record Group 25; *Norfolk Labor Journal,* 25 July 1935.

46. See the picture of the Labor Day parade in the *Norfolk Journal and Guide,* 21 September 1935. Moreover, black labor organizer George Streator arrived from New York to lend support (*Norfolk Journal and Guide,* 31 August 1935).

47. *Norfolk Journal and Guide,* 24 August 1935. Black longshoremen reportedly aided the strikers' efforts by joining in picketing and demonstrations.

48. See copy of the labor agreement reached by Sam Finkelstein and the ACWA to end the strike. The company promised Commissioner of Conciliation Anna Weinstock on 20 November 1935 that they would reinstate fired employees, whereas the union agreed not to strike for one year. See Local 92, ACWA, to Anna Weinstock, 20 November 1935, and Hyman Blumberg to Anna Weinstock, 20 November 1935, box 207, National Labor Relations Board, Record Group 25. The terms were met, but in 1937, amid rumors that the company was about to leave the area, labor problems resurfaced.

49. George Streator to W. E. B. Du Bois, 18 April 1935, 7 July 1935, W. E. B. Du Bois Papers, University of Massachusetts Library.

50. W. E. B. Du Bois to George Streator, 24 April 1935, 9 July 1935, reel 44, W. E. B. Du Bois Papers.

51. *Norfolk Journal and Guide,* 22 August 1936.

52. *Norfolk Journal and Guide,* 17 March 1934; Norfolk File, HOLC City Survey Files, 1935–1940, Record Group 195.

53. *Norfolk Journal and Guide,* 6 March 1937, 13 March 1937, 23 January 1937. A coalition of police agencies and patriotic groups informally planned measures to drive the Communist party out of town, particularly after it began distributing leaflets at a white junior high school; see *Norfolk Ledger-Dispatch,* 2 March 1936, 3 March 1936; File 10110–2663–117, MID Files, Record Group 165; James W. Ford, "Uniting the Negro People in the People's Front," *Communist* 16 (August 1937): 732.

54. William Chafe discusses civility in race relations in his *Civilities and Civil Rights: Greensboro, North Carolina, and the Black Struggle for Freedom* (New York: Oxford University Press, 1980), esp. introduction.

55. *Norfolk Journal and Guide,* 4 January 1930.

56. *Norfolk Journal and Guide,* 11 January 1930, 18 January 1930; Norfolk City Council minutes, *Record Book* 28, 14 January 1930, pp. 390–98, located in the office of the Norfolk City Clerk.

57. *Norfolk Journal and Guide,* 7 June 1930, 28 June 1930, 12 July 1930.

58. *Norfolk Journal and Guide,* 20 February 1932.

59. *Norfolk Journal and Guide,* 30 January 1932, 6 February 1932, 9 December 1932, 23 February 1935, 16 April 1938; S. I. Slover, mayor, to T. P. Thompson, city manager, 5 December 1933, box 2, Louis Jaffe Papers, University of Virginia, Charlottesville.

60. *Norfolk Journal and Guide,* 20 February 1932.

61. Capitation Tax Rolls, located in the Norfolk Public Library; quotation from a report found in box 85, folder 29, Ralph Bunche Papers. The Bunche Papers also include information on voting and the UNIA.

62. Rev. W. M. Harris to Lawrence Oxley, 8 December 1937, also 3 December 1937, 7 December 1937, 14 December 1937, 17 December 1937, box 1389, Lawrence Oxley Papers, Negro Division of the Virginia State Employment Service, Record Group 183, National Archives; Thomas J. Wertenbaker and Marvin W. Schlegel, *Norfolk: Historic Southern Port* (Durham, N.C.: Duke University Press, 1962), p. 336.

63. Material found in box 85, folder 29, Ralph Bunche Papers, includes a vivid discussion of the various political groups. See also Andrew Buni, *The Negro in Virginia Politics, 1902–1965* (Charlottesville: University Press of Virginia, 1967), p. 116.

64. Box 85, folder 29, Ralph Bunche Papers.

65. Louis I. Jaffe, editor, *Virginian-Pilot,* and Douglass Gordon, editor, *Norfolk Ledger-Dispatch,* to the State Corporation Commission, 25 September 1930, box 2, Louis Jaffe Papers.

66. Louis I. Jaffe to L. H. Windholz, chairman, Norfolk Public Works Committee, 21 June 1933, box 2, Louis Jaffe Papers; Morton Sosna, *In Search of the Silent South: Southern Liberals and the Race Issue* (New York: Columbia University Press, 1977), p. 136; George Brown Tindall, *The Emergence of the New South, 1913–1945* (Baton Rouge: Louisiana State University Press, 1967), p. 215.

67. *Norfolk Journal and Guide,* 19 May 1934; 8 December 1934.

68. *Norfolk Journal and Guide,* 16 February 1935, 23 February 1935. The NAACP chose not to ally with any radical group for fear of ruining its reputation. See W. P. Milner, secretary, Norfolk branch of NAACP, to Walter White, 25 March 1935, about the executive committee's decision not to join with the ILD in the Johnson campaign. In 1939 the local branch refused to ally with the CIO against the Atlantic Coast Lines, a major employer of longshoremen, because NAACP officials viewed the CIO as "unpopular here" (E. Frederick Morrow to National Executives, 11 October 1939). However, the local branch did adopt a more forceful posture in selected areas. For example, it pushed the Woolworth's on Church Street to hire blacks (David E. Longley to Walter White, 13 July 1935). These three letters are found in box G-208, NAACP Papers. The Communists interpreted any reneging on a promise of cooperation as a personal affront; see, for example, *Norfolk Journal and Guide,* 22 July 1933.

69. *Norfolk Journal and Guide,* 30 November 1935.

70. John W. Robinson, "A Song, a Shout, and a Prayer," in *The Black Experience in Religion,* ed. C. Eric Lincoln (Garden City, N.Y.: Anchor Books, 1974), pp. 212–35; Joseph R. Washington, Jr., *Black Sects and Cults* (Garden City, N.Y.: Doubleday, 1972), pp. 158–59.

71. *Norfolk Journal and Guide,* 7 April 1934; Virginia C., conversation with the author, 9 September 1984, Norfolk.

72. Washington, *Black Sects and Cults,* pp. 15–16, 77, 127; Albert N. Whiting, "The United House of Prayer for All People: A Case Study of a Charismatic Sect" (Ph.D. diss., American University, 1952), esp. chaps. 1–2; Robert Weisbrot,

*Father Divine and the Struggle for Racial Equality* (Urbana: University of Illinois Press, 1983). Although Weisbrot rescues Divine, he dismisses Grace as only a cult figure (pp. 41–42). Gilliam's charge is disclosed in Ralph J. Bunche to Gunnar Myrdal, 7 March 1940, Memorandum II: "Extended Memorandum on the Problems, Ideologies, Tactics and Achievements of Negro Betterment and Inter-racial Organizations," microfilm reel 1, pp. 181–82, Carnegie-Myrdal Collection, Schomburg Library, New York Public Library.

73. *Norfolk Journal and Guide*, 23 April 1932. See issues of the *Journal and Guide* during the 1930s for ads soliciting games of chance. See also J. Saunders Redding, "Playing the Numbers," *North American Review* 238 (December 1934): 533–42.

74. Five longtime male residents of black Norfolk, taped interview session with the author, 18 September 1983, Norfolk; Howard S., conversation with the author, 7 March 1983, Norfolk.

75. John B. Kirby, *Black Americans in the Roosevelt Era: Liberalism and Race* (Knoxville: University of Tennessee Press, 1980), pp. 17–32 and chap. 6; Ronald L. Heinemann, *Depression and New Deal in Virginia: The Enduring Dominion* (Charlottesville: University Press of Virginia, 1983), p. 87.

76. Sitkoff, *New Deal For Blacks*, p. 55.

77. Wertenbaker and Schlegel, *Norfolk*, pp. 336–37; *Norfolk Journal and Guide*, 23 April 1932, 19 August 1933, 9 December 1933, 16 December 1933.

78. Henry D. Dolphin to General Hugh S. Johnson, NRA administrator, 6 December 1933; O. J. Libert, assistant deputy administrator, to Henry D. Dolphin, 12 December 1933; both in Code Files, Complaints—Cleaning and Dyeing Industry, box 1407, National Recovery Administration, Record Group 9.

79. On the barbers, see *Norfolk Journal and Guide*, 15 February 1930, 5 August 1933, 18 November 1933, 7 January 1939. On the women, see Local NAACP Committee to Thomas P. Thompson, city manager, 20 December 1935, box G-208, NAACP Papers; *Journal and Guide*, 12 March 1938. Jacqueline Jones (*Labor of Love, Labor of Sorrow: Women, Work, and the Family from Slavery to the Present* [New York: Basic Books, 1985], p. 24) discusses earlier examples of the intersection of gender construction and "women's " work.

80. *Norfolk Journal and Guide*, 2 February 1939, 4 March 1939; *Norfolk Labor Journal*, 2 March 1944. See also Dennis C. Rousey, "Yellow Fever and Black Policemen in Memphis: A Post-Reconstruction Anomaly," *Journal of Southern History* 51 (August 1985): 359.

81. Ted Poston, "Law and Order in Norfolk," *New Republic*, 7 October 1940, pp. 472–73; reel 1, p. 112, Carnegie-Myrdal Collection.

82. *Norfolk Ledger-Dispatch*, 3 July 1939; *Norfolk Journal and Guide*, 22 July 1939.

83. *Norfolk Ledger-Dispatch*, 3 July 1939; Young's comment quoted from the *Norfolk Journal and Guide*, 22 July 1939. Also see *Norfolk Journal and Guide*, 19 January 1935, 22 January 1938, 29 October 1938; P. B. Young to Walter White, 12 July 1939, Legal Files, box I-D-91, NAACP Papers. The Carnegie-Myrdal Collection, reel 1, p. 112, includes a discussion of the teachers' case and its local importance.

84. Thurgood Marshall to Walter White, 29 November 1937, Legal Files, box I-D-91, NAACP Papers. Mark V. Tushnet (*The NAACP's Legal Strategy Against*

*Segregated Education, 1925–1950* [Chapel Hill: University of North Carolina Press, 1987], pp. 77–81) offers a synopsis of the case and its importance to the NAACP's strategy but does not discuss the case's significance to the Norfolk community.

85. Draft of minutes of the meeting of the committee from the Virginia State Teachers Association and the Virginia State Conference of the NAACP, 26 November 1937, Legal Files, box I-D-91, NAACP Papers.

86. *Norfolk Journal and Guide*, 29 October 1938, 5 November 1938.

87. "Demurrer Granted by Judge in Virginia Teachers' Salary Case," Legal Files, box I-D-91, NAACP Papers; *Richmond Times-Dispatch*, 1 June 1939.

88. Thurgood Marshall to the Joint Committee on Teachers' Salaries in Maryland, 5 June 1939, Legal Files, box I-D-91, NAACP Papers.

89. Telegram, Aline Black to Thurgood Marshall, 14 June 1939; Marshall to White, 14 September 1939; both in Legal Files, box I-D-91, NAACP Papers.

90. *Virginian-Pilot*, 16 June 1939.

91. *Norfolk Journal and Guide*, 10 July 1939, 15 July 1939.

92. Black to Marshall, 21 February 1940, Legal Files, box I-D-91, NAACP Papers.

93. Aline Black to Dr. J. M. Tinsley, 28 September 1939; Jerry O. Gilliam to Charles H. Houston, general counsel, NAACP, 29 August 1939; Thurgood Marshall to Jerry O. Gilliam, president, Norfolk branch, NAACP, 31 August 1939; Tinsley to Black, 26 September 1939; all in "Equalization Cases," Legal Files, boxes IIB—133, 153, 187, 188, NAACP Papers.

94. Thurgood Marshall to Melvin O. Alston, 27 July 1939; Alston to Marshall, 28 July 1939; both in "Equalization Cases," Legal Files, boxes 133, 153, 187, 188, NAACP Papers.

95. Alston to Marshall, 21 August 1939; Marshall to Alston, 29 August 1939; Alston to Marshall (no date, ca. 21 September 1939); Alston to Marshall, 8 October 1939; all in "Equalization Cases," Legal Files, boxes 133, 153, 187, 199, NAACP Papers.

96. Petition to the School Board of the City of Norfolk, Virginia, September 1939, "Equalization Cases," Legal Files, boxes 133, 153, 187, 188, NAACP Papers.

97. Opinion by Justice Luther B. Way, *Alston v. School Board of City of Norfolk*, 12 February 1940, Legal Files, box I-D-91, NAACP Papers.

98. Richard Kluger, *Simple Justice* (New York: Vintage Books, 1975), pp. 141–44, 215–16, 485.

99. Ibid., pp. 141–44, 215–16; *Alston et al. v. School Board of City of Norfolk et al.*, 112 F.2d (1940); *School Board of City of Norfolk et al. v. Alston et al.*, 311 U.S. 693 (1940).

100. Alfred Anderson, city attorney, to Oliver Hill, 12 July 1940, 24 July 1940; Oliver Hill to Thurgood Marshall et al., 27 June 1940; all in Legal Files, box 188, NAACP Papers.

101. *Melvin O. Alston and the Norfolk Teachers Association v. School Board of the City of Norfolk*, Civil Action File no. 50, Legal Files, boxes 133, 153, 187, 188, NAACP Papers.

102. Memo from Thurgood Marshall to Walter White and Roy Wilkins, 8 November 1940, "Equalization Cases," Legal Files, boxes 133, 153, 187, 188, NAACP Papers.

103. Ibid. Melvin Alston denies that he, the others, and the city struck a deal (Melvin Alston to Earl Lewis, 9 January 1984, personal correspondence in the possession of the author). See also reel 1, p. 186, Carnegie-Myrdal Collection. The case reportedly led to a reorganization of the local branch of the NAACP.

104. U.S. Congress, Senate, Committee on the Judiciary, *Communist Activities Among Aliens and National Groups, Hearings Before the Subcommittee on the Judiciary,* 81st Cong., 1st sess., 1949, p. 154. The testimony about Wright was given by Paul Crouch, who used the alias Fred Allen while working in Norfolk during the 1930s (see note 12, Chapter 6, above).

Jerry O. Gilliam, head of the Norfolk branch of the NAACP in 1939 and delegate to the National Negro Congress, commented on another occasion that although he did not believe there was much hope that blacks would ever realize democracy in Norfolk, neither did he believe the Communist party was an alternative; see reel 1, pp. 173, 192–93, 195–96, Carnegie-Myrdal Collection.

Recently released FBI and State Department documents reveal that Wright led a double life after his expulsion from the Virginia Communist party (ca. 1939). After being unemployed for two years, he was approached by the FBI and began a career as both a party "stalwart" in Pennsylvania and an FBI informer. He maintained both roles well into the mid-1950s, when government testimony against party colleagues forced him to make a public confession (FBI files 65–1594).

CHAPTER 7

1. Microfilm reel 1, frames 113, 181, 198, Carnegie-Myrdal Collection, Schomburg Library, New York Public Library.

2. *Population in Flux in the Hampton Roads Area: A Study of Population Trends in the Hampton Roads Area, 1890–1942,* Population Study Report no. 2 (Richmond: Virginia State Planning Board, 1942), p. 7.

3. "Study of Community Recreation Facilities in Relation to Defense Housing Projects in Norfolk, Virginia," p. 3, War Housing Program Geographic Dockets, U.S. Department of Housing and Urban Development, Record Group 207, National Archives; Lyonel C. Florant, "The Impact of the War on the Norfolk Negro Community," 26 May 1942, p. 1, box 6, Recreation Division, Office of Community War Services, Record Group 215, National Archives; Gunnar Myrdal, *An American Dilemma: The Negro Problem and Modern Democracy* (1944; reissued, New York: Pantheon Books, 1972), vol. 1, p. 1301.

4. *Norfolk Journal and Guide,* 30 March 1940, 13 July 1940, 23 November 1940; *Population in Flux in the Hampton Roads Area,* pp. 39–46.

5. Florant, "Impact of the War," 26 May 1942, pp. 1–2, box 6, Recreation Division, Office of Community War Services, Record Group 215.

6. *Norfolk Journal and Guide,* 10 July 1942. U.S. Bureau of the Census, *Seventeenth Census of the United States* (Washington, D.C.: Government Printing Office, 1952), vol. 2, pt. 46, *Population,* 1950, p. 55.

7. Florant, "Impact of the War," 26 May 1942, p. 4, box 6, Recreation Division, Office of Community War Services, Record Group 215; *Population in Flux in the Hampton Roads Area,* pp. 55–57; "Most of Norfolk Slighted by One-Sided

City Council," *Norfolk Labor Journal,* 2 March 1944; *Norfolk Ledger-Dispatch,* 7 April 1941; Norfolk File, Home Owners Loan Corporation (HOLC) City Survey Files, 1935–1940, Record Group 195, National Archives.

8. "Analysis of Increases in Living Costs, August 1939 to December 1941," *Monthly Labor Review* 54 (April 1942): 834.

9. Ibid.; "Inquiring Reporter," *Norfolk Journal and Guide,* 5 September 1942. See also *Norfolk Journal and Guide,* 18 October 1941.

10. Arnold R. Hirsch, *Making the Second Ghetto: Race and Housing in Chicago, 1940–1960* (Cambridge: Cambridge University Press, 1983), pp. 16–27; August Meier and Elliott Rudwick, *Black Detroit and the Rise of the UAW* (Urbana: University of Illinois Press, 1979), pp. 176–87; Dominic J. Capeci, *Race Relations in Wartime Detroit: The Sojourner Truth Housing Controversy of 1942* (Philadelphia: Temple University Press, 1984).

11. *Norfolk Journal and Guide,* 26 July 1941, article accompanied by picture with caption: "Rents Almost Doubled Inside a Year."

12. *Norfolk Journal and Guide,* 18 October 1941. Through August 1942, blacks filed three quarters of the complaints that landlords were inflating prices; see *Norfolk Journal and Guide,* 2 August 1941, 5 September 1942.

13. Florant, "Impact of the War," 26 May 1942, p. 5, box 6, Recreation Division, Office of Community War Services, Record Group 215.

14. "Study of Community Recreation Facilities," pp. 5–10, War Housing Program Geographic Dockets, Record Group 207.

15. The government investigators are quoted in ibid.; *Norfolk Journal and Guide,* 10 May 1941. In a blistering editorial, the *Journal and Guide* (12 April 1940) criticized federal and city officials for not providing housing for black personnel moving to the area for defense work.

16. An alternative example is discussed in Earl Lewis and David Organ, "Housing, Race, and Class: The Government's Creation of Truxton, Virginia, a Model Black War Workers' Town," in *Race, Class, and Urban Social Change,* ed. Jerry Lembcke (Greenwich, Conn.: JAI Press, 1989), pp. 53–78. Also see the booklet *This Is It* (Norfolk: Norfolk Housing and Redevelopment Authority, 1946), p. 11. The war also transformed the public debate over housing. Unlike blacks in Milwaukee (Joe William Trotter, Jr., *Black Milwaukee: The Making of an Industrial Proletariat* [Urbana: University of Illinois Press, 1985], pp. 185–87), blacks in Norfolk believed that slum clearance was a greater priority than the elimination of restrictive barriers. As it did for black Chicagoans, shelter remained a primary concern through the earlier years of the war; see Hirsch, *Making the Second Ghetto,* pp. 16–23.

17. *Norfolk Journal and Guide,* 19 September 1942.

18. Florant, "Impact of the War," 26 May 1942, p. 5, box 6, Recreation Division, Office of Community War Services, Record Group 215; *Norfolk Journal and Guide,* 11 August 1945; "Locality Analysis—Justification for Exception to the Termination . . . of . . . Federally Owned Housing Projects," Virginia Samples of Locality Files, U.S. Department of Housing and Urban Development, Record Group 207. Both Roberts Park and Liberty Park eventually came under the jurisdiction of the Public Housing Authority. Although Liberty Park was first envisioned as temporary housing, it was not razed until June 1986.

19. Thomas J. Wertenbaker and Marvin W. Schlegel, *Norfolk: Historic Southern Port* (Durham, N.C.: Duke University Press, 1962), pp. 348–61.

20. Marvin W. Schlegel, *Conscripted City: Norfolk in World War II* (Norfolk: Norfolk War History Commission, 1951), p. 257; Wertenbaker and Schlegel, *Norfolk*, p. 349; Committee for Congested Production Areas, Hampton Roads Area, Virginia, 16 March 1944, U.S. Department of Housing and Urban Development, Record Group 207.

21. Schlegel, *Conscripted City*, p. 176; survey of black public schools in Norfolk War History (NWH) Collection, located in the Norfolk Public Library.

22. Wertenbaker and Schlegel, *Norfolk*, p. 350.

23. *Norfolk Journal and Guide*, 17 November 1945.

24. See John Temple Graves, "The Southern Negro and the War Crisis," *Virginian Quarterly Review* 18 (Autumn 1942): 510–17; "Color, Unfinished Business of Democracy," special issue, *Survey Graphic* 31 (November 1942): 453–505; and Charles Johnson et al., *To Stem This Tide* (1942; reprint, New York: AMS, 1969), chaps. 7–8.

25. *Norfolk Journal and Guide*, 4 January 1941.

26. *Norfolk Journal and Guide*, 15 February 1941.

27. *Norfolk Journal and Guide*, 15 February 1941.

28. Robert C. Weaver, "Racial Employment Trends in National Defense," *Phylon* 2 (1941): esp. 354–58.

29. Stuart Oskamp, *Attitudes and Behavior* (Englewood Cliffs, N.J.: Prentice-Hall, 1977), pp. 165–245. See also Martin Fishbein and Icek Ajzen, "Attitudes Towards Objects as Predictors of Single and Multiple Behavior Criteria," *Psychological Review* 81 (1974): 59–74.

30. Robert C. Weaver, *Negro Labor: A National Problem* (New York: Harcourt, Brace, 1946), pp. 238–39. P. B. Young was appointed to the second FEPC; he later resigned, however. See also Louis C. Kesselman, *The Social Politics of FEPC: A Study in Reform Pressure Movements* (Chapel Hill: University of North Carolina Press, 1948), p. 79; Louis Ruchames, *Race, Jobs, and Politics: The Story of FEPC* (New York: Columbia University Press, 1953), pp. 57–58, for mention of Young; and Herbert Garfinkel, *When Negroes March* (1959; reprint, New York: Atheneum, 1969), for the best description of the movement to organize the march on Washington.

31. "Want Only Whites in Defense Skills," *Norfolk Journal and Guide*, 28 February 1942. All thirty-five skilled and semi-skilled positions went to white males; white females received preference for clerical positions. The listing locked black men and black women into service and laborer jobs.

32. Florant, "Impact of the War," 26 May 1942, pp. 8–9, box 6, Recreation Division, Office of Community War Services, Record Group 215.

33. *Norfolk Journal and Guide*, 21 February 1942.

34. Florant, "Impact of the War," 26 May 1942, p. 10, box 6, Recreation Division, Office of Community War Services, Record Group 215; Philip S. Van Wyck, acting director, War Production Training, to Robert Weaver, 9 July 1942, General Files, Record Group 215.

35. *Norfolk Journal and Guide*, 21 February 1942.

36. *Norfolk Journal and Guide*, 28 February 1942.

37. *Norfolk Journal and Guide,* 14 March 1942. Jerry Gilliam, head of the local NAACP, summarized black sentiment in a newspaper column ("The Negro and . . . the National Emergency," *Norfolk Journal and Guide,* 14 March 1942). His criticism centered on the irony of fighting for democracy abroad and being denied it at home. See also *Norfolk Journal and Guide,* 18 April 1942, 9 May 1942, 22 August 1942.

38. Jacqueline Jones, *Labor of Love, Labor of Sorrow: Black Women, Work, and the Family from Slavery to the Present* (New York: Basic Books, 1985), pp. 235–60; *Norfolk Journal and Guide,* 7 March 1942.

39. Numerous groups and individuals took part in this effort; see *Norfolk Journal and Guide,* 9 October 1943, 15 January 1944, 27 October 1945, 9 January 1945. The Committee on Negro Affairs held a meeting in September 1943 to promote the "Hold Your Job" campaign (*Norfolk Journal and Guide,* 11 September 1943).

40. *Norfolk Journal and Guide,* 18 April 1942.

41. A. E. Jakeman, "History and Commentary of Norfolk Shipbuilding and Drydock Corporation in World War II," p. 13, files of Norfolk Shipbuilding and Drydock Corporation, NWH Collection.

42. *Norfolk Journal and Guide,* 12 September 1942, 19 September 1942, 3 October 1942.

43. *Norfolk Journal and Guide,* 12 September 1942, 3 October 1942; Karen Tucker Anderson, "Last Hired, First Fired: Black Women Workers During World War II," *Journal of American History* 69 (June 1982): 88–89. Private contractors such as Ford also barred black women when the call for workers went out in the early years of the war (Meier and Rudwick, *Black Detroit,* pp. 136–56).

44. *Norfolk Journal and Guide,* 19 September 1942, 3 October 1942, 10 October 1942. Administrators at the naval ammunition depot at St. Julian Creek also refused to hire black women as helper trainees, maintaining, as had the navy yard, that they lacked adequate restroom accommodations (*Norfolk Journal and Guide,* 7 November 1942). See also the case of Mrs. Thelma McIntyre vs. Norfolk Navy Yard, 8 June 1944, Records of the Committee on Fair Employment Practices, boxes 630–40, Record Group 228, Philadelphia branch of the National Archives (hereafter called FEPC Papers).

45. Case of Mrs. Jocelyn P. Tucker vs. Norfolk Naval Supply Department, 8 November 1943, FEPC Papers.

46. Case of Mrs. Rachel V. Fleakes, Mrs. Hallie Britt, and Mrs. Ellamae Reid vs. Norfolk Navy Yard, 31 May 1944, FEPC Papers.

47. Case of Rebecca Watson vs. Portsmouth Naval Hospital, 7 April 1944, FEPC Papers.

48. Case of Mary B. Cook vs. Army Base, 4–GR–398, 13 November 1944, FEPC Papers.

49. David Longley to Joseph H. B. Evans, 8 March 1945, FEPC Papers.

50. "30,000 Race Workers Being Used in War Industries Here," *Norfolk Journal and Guide,* 9 January 1943.

51. Longley to Evans, 8 March 1945; case of Lonnie Myers vs. Norfolk Naval Operating Base, 6 February 1945; both in FEPC Papers. Also illustrative are the cases of Jesse C. Hawkins vs. Norfolk Navy Yard, 22 February 1945, and Aaron

Budd vs. Norfolk Navy Yard, 5 May 1945, 4–GR–526, both found in the FEPC Papers.

52. Case of Orville Hines and the Electrical Alliance vs. Norfolk Navy Yard, 7 October 1943, FEPC Papers. Blacks working in West Coast shipyards harbored similar apprehensions; see William H. Harris, "Federal Intervention in Union Discrimination: FEPC and West Coast Shipyards During World War II," *Labor History* 22 (Summer 1981): 342–43.

53. *Norfolk Journal and Guide*, 18 March 1944. For a general history of the naval air station, see Ira R. Hanna, "The Growth of Norfolk Naval Air Station and the Norfolk-Portsmouth Metropolitan Area Economy in the Twentieth Century" (M.A. thesis, Old Dominion University, 1967), esp. pp. 38–48.

54. John L. Perry and John F. Burrell II to George M. Johnson, deputy chairman, FEPC, 3 May 1944, FEPC Papers.

55. Case of John L. Perry et al. vs. Naval Air Station, 3 May 1944, FEPC Papers.

56. Raymond Gavins, *The Perils and Prospects of Southern Black Leadership: Gordon Blaine Hancock, 1884–1970* (Durham, N.C.: Duke University Press, 1977), pp. 122–37.

57. Ibid.

58. Paul A. Askew, president of Norfolk Central Labor Union, interview with the author, 18 September 1983, Norfolk; *Norfolk Labor Journal*, 6 September 1945; *Norfolk Journal and Guide*, 27 May 1944. Also see Shipbuilding Committee Dispute Case Files, case 111–12781–D, box 7805, Norfolk Shipbuilding and Drydock Company, National War Labor Board (WWII) Record Group 202, National Archives; and Barbara S. Griffith, *The Crisis of American Labor* (Philadelphia: Temple University Press, 1988), esp. chap. 5.

59. *Norfolk Labor Journal*, 14 December 1939.

60. *Norfolk Labor Journal*, 2 November 1939, 18 February 1943, 25 March 1943, 2 March 1944.

61. *Norfolk Labor Journal*, 21 December 1939.

62. *Norfolk Labor Journal*, 28 June 1945.

63. *Tunstall v. Brotherhood of Locomotive Firemen and Enginemen et al.*, 140 F.2d 35 (1944); *Tunstall v. Brotherhood of Locomotive Firemen and Enginemen, Ocean Lodge No. 76, et al.*, 65 S. Ct. 235 (1944). See also *Norfolk Journal and Guide*, 17 October 1942, 13 March 1943, 24 April 1943, 15 January 1944, 17 February 1945; and Ruchames, *Race, Jobs, and Politics*, pp. 70–72.

64. *Tunstall v. Brotherhood of Locomotive Firemen and Enginemen, Ocean Lodge No. 76, et al.*, 148 F.2d 403 (1944).

65. *Norfolk Journal and Guide*, 6 October 1945.

66. Black laundry workers, chemical plant workers, bottle and distillery workers, and lumber yard workers, among others, joined unions; see *Norfolk Journal and Guide*, 22 May 1943, 25 September 1943; and *Norfolk Labor Journal*, 1 May 1941. There was also a jurisdictional dispute that pitted the ILA Local 1221 against the CIO's ILWU 978; see File 20912680, Federal Mediation and Conciliation Service, Record Group 280, National Archives.

67. Few new studies have compared black and white workers during World War II. Notable exceptions are Meier and Rudwick, *Black Detroit*, esp. chap. 4; Herbert Hill, *Black Labor and the American Legal System* (Madison: University of

Wisconsin Press, 1985), esp. chaps. 4–11; Trotter, *Black Milwaukee*, pp. 162–75; and Griffith, *Crisis of American Labor*, pp. 62–87. The critical questions of when Afro-Americans became workers at work and how this shaped their struggle for community empowerment remain to be addressed.

68. Charles B. Borlund to J. H. Wyse, coordinator of the state Office of Civilian Defense, 11 June 1942, NWH Collection. See the NWH Collection for a description of the various all-black boards.

69. *Norfolk Journal and Guide*, 20 March 1943; Schlegel, *Conscripted City*, p. 194.

70. B. T. Holmes to R. M. Marshall, 29 June 1942, NWH Collection.

71. R. M. Marshall to P. B. Young, 6 July 1942, NWH Collection.

72. *Norfolk Journal and Guide*, 13 March 1943.

73. *Richmond Times-Dispatch*, 21 November 1943, 27 November 1943. The *Norfolk Journal and Guide* asked four white and two black citizens to state their position on the editorial; all six agreed the law was outdated. One of those commenting was a bus driver (*Journal and Guide*, 4 December 1943). Johnson et al., *To Stem This Tide*, chap. 3, recounts similar problems across the South.

74. Morton Sosna, *In Search of the Silent South: Southern Liberals and the Race Issue* (New York: Columbia University Press, 1977), p. 136.

75. *Norfolk Journal and Guide*, 31 July 1943, 1 July 1944. Leaders of both blacks and whites met to discuss the situation (Johnson, *To Stem This Tide*, p. 36).

76. *Norfolk Journal and Guide*, 18 July 1942, 5 September 1943; Schlegel, *Conscripted City*, p. 195.

77. *Norfolk Journal and Guide*, 18 July 1942, 3 February 1945.

78. *Norfolk Journal and Guide*, 28 March 1942.

79. *Virginian-Pilot*, 20 August 1942.

80. "Inquiring Reporter," *Norfolk Journal and Guide*, 29 August 1942.

81. P. B. Young to Richard M. Marshall, 7 July 1942, NWH Collection; *Norfolk Journal and Guide*, 11 December 1943.

82. *Norfolk Journal and Guide*, 29 January 1944, 11 March 1944; R. S. Hummel to Corrington Gill, 17 January 1944, Central File—Virginia, Recreation Division, Office of Community War Services, Record Group 215.

83. See the NWH Collection or the *Norfolk Journal and Guide* for 1941–1945 for descriptions of the efforts of each unit.

84. *Norfolk Ledger-Dispatch*, 18 December 1942; "Norfolk Prices and Rationing Among Negroes in War Time," NWH Collection. See also listings for "Colored Volunteers For Colored Rationing Office," NWH Collection.

85. "Inquiring Reporter," *Norfolk Journal and Guide*, 26 February 1944.

86. P. N. Binford, field recreation representative, to Mark A. McClosky, director of recreation, 25 June 1942, Virginia, box 6, Recreation Division, Office of Community War Services, Record Group 215.

87. Report, "Recreation in Norfolk," 3 March 1941, Virginia, box 6, Recreation Division, Office of Community War Services, Record Group 215.

88. "Three Years Report, 1940–1943, Hunton Branch YMCA," NWH Collection. The federal government was aware of this complaint; see Charles T. Guild to John I. Neasmith, 23 November 1941, Recreation Numbered Projects, Virginia, box 6, Recreation Division, Office of Community War Services, Record Group 215.

89. *Norfolk Journal and Guide,* 7 March 1942, 23 October 1943.

90. "Smith Street USO Wartime Services," NWH Collection; *Norfolk Journal and Guide,* 7 March 1942, 23 October 1943. When a fire destroyed much of the edifice and all of the building's furniture, prominent black leaders launched a letter-writing campaign. When the community was threatened with no USO at all, the Smith Street building became worth saving; see letters by Winston Douglass and the Norfolk Committee on Negro Affairs, in Recreation Numbered Projects, Virginia, box 6, Recreation Division, Office of Community War Services, Record Group 215. In addition, the navy placed the entire black district off-limits to white military personnel; see Schlegel, *Conscripted City,* pp. 322–23.

91. *Norfolk Journal and Guide,* 27 May 1944.

92. *Norfolk Journal and Guide,* 5 April 1941, 29 November 1941, 6 May 1944.

93. *Norfolk Journal and Guide,* 27 November 1945.

94. Luther P. Jackson, "Race and Suffrage in the South Since 1940," *New South* (June-July 1948): 1–26; Capitation Tax Rolls for 1940–1944, housed in the Norfolk Public Library.

95. "Inquiring Reporter," *Norfolk Journal and Guide,* 11 December 1943.

96. *Norfolk Journal and Guide,* 7 November 1942.

97. *Norfolk Journal and Guide,* 10 June 1944, 17 June 1944, 1 July 1944, 15 July 1944, 29 July 1944; Charles S. Johnson, *Into the Main Stream* (Chapel Hill: University of North Carolina Press, 1947), p. 42.

98. Ruchames, *Race, Jobs, and Politics,* pp. 57–58; Laurel K. Gutterman, "The Political Thought of a Southern Negro Editor, 1921–1940: P. B. Young of the *Norfolk Journal and Guide*" (M.A. thesis, Old Dominion University, 1966).

99. *Norfolk Journal and Guide,* 23 May 1944; Dennis C. Rousey, "Yellow Fever and Black Policemen in Memphis: A Post-Reconstruction Anomaly," *Journal of Southern History* 51 (August 1985): 358–60. For further information on blacks and the police, see Federal Security Agency, Social Protection Division, Record Group 215, National Archives.

100. "Inquiring Reporter," *Norfolk Journal and Guide,* 26 February 1944.

## CONCLUSION

1. "Inquiring Reporter," *Norfolk Journal and Guide,* 11 December 1943.

2. Eddie N. Williams, "Black Political Progress in the 1970s: The Electoral Arena," in *The New Black Politics,* ed. Michael B. Preston, Lenneal J. Henderson, and Paul Puryear (White Plains, N.Y.: Longman, 1982), pp. 73–108; *Virginian-Pilot,* 30 June 1988.

3. Theodore Hershberg et al., "A Tale of Three Cities: Blacks, Immigrants, and Opportunity in Philadelphia, 1850–1880, 1930, 1970," in *Philadelphia: Work, Space, Family, and Group Experience in the Nineteenth Century,* ed. Theodore Hershberg (New York: Oxford University Press, 1981), pp. 461–91; William Julius Wilson, *The Declining Significance of Race: Blacks and Changing American Institutions,* 2d ed. (University of Chicago Press, 1980), pp. 92–96; *The Truly Disadvantaged: The Inner City, the Underclass, and Public Policy* (Chicago: University of Chicago Press, 1987), pp. 20–62.

4. *New York Times,* 26 August 1988. Others have made similar observations, as recent articles in the *New York Times* indicate: "Poverty of Blacks Spreads in Cities" (26 January 1987); "Twenty Years After Kerner Report: Three Societies, All Separate" (29 February 1989).

5. Robert Korstad and Nelson Lichtenstein, "Opportunities Found and Lost: Labor, Radicals, and the Early Civil Rights Movement," *Journal of American History* 75 (December 1988): 786.

6. Jack M. Bloom, *Class, Race, and the Civil Rights Movement* (Bloomington: University of Indiana Press, 1987), pp. 131–32.

7. Korstad and Lichtenstein, "Opportunities Found and Lost," p. 786; Aldon Morris, *The Origins of the Civil Rights Movement* (New York: Free Press, 1984), pp. 40–81.

8. A comparison of this study of Norfolk, Korstad and Lichtenstein's article, and Morris's discussion of activities in the several movement centers (cited in note 7, above) clearly suggests this convergence. Also see Robert J. Norrell, "Caste in Steel: Jim Crow Careers in Birmingham, Alabama," *Journal of American History* 73 (December 1986): 669–94. The comment on the importance of the 1940s is quoted from Korstad and Lichtenstein, "Opportunities Found and Lost," p. 787.

9. Byrd is quoted in Benjamin Muse, *Virginia's Massive Resistance* (Bloomington: University of Indiana Press, 1961), p. 22.

10. King is quoted in Stephen B. Oates, *Let the Trumpet Sound* (New York: Plume Books, 1982), p. 70.

11. Morris, *Origins of the Civil Rights Movement,* pp. 6, 41.

12. Bloom, *Class, Race, and the Civil Rights Movement,* pp. 103–4; Morris, *Origins of the Civil Rights Movement,* pp. 48–50; Bart Landry, *The New Black Middle Class* (Berkeley and Los Angeles: University of California Press, 1987), pp. 73–75. The best and most direct discussion of the buying power of blacks is presented in the NBC White Paper, *Sit-In* (16mm film, 1961).

13. Harold Cruse, *Plural But Equal: A Critical Study of Blacks and Minorities and America's Plural Society* (New York: Quill Books, 1987), pp. 75–98.

14. Reynolds Farley and Walter Allen, *The Color Line and the Quality of Life in America* (New York: Oxford University Press, 1987), pp. 293–307.

15. Landry, *New Black Middle Class,* pp. 21, 67–70.

16. Morris, *Origins of the Civil Rights Movement,* p. 177.

17. Luther J. Carter, "Desegregation in Norfolk," *South Atlantic Quarterly* 58 (Autumn 1959): 507–20; Ernest Q. Campbell, *When a City Closes Its Schools* (Chapel Hill, N.C.: Institute for Research in Social Sciences, 1960); Muse, *Virginia's Massive Resistance,* pp. 92–94, 111–18.

18. Carter, "Desegregation in Norfolk," p. 517; Samuel Lubell, *White and Black: Test of a Nation* (New York: Harper and Row, 1964), p. 98.

19. Lubell, *White and Black,* p. 178.

20. Carter, "Desegregation in Norfolk," p. 514. Norfolk, like many southern cities, waited until the early 1970s to fully comply with the law. Today, it has the dubious distinction of winning federal support for a neighborhood school format, with some black support; see *Wall Street Journal,* 22 October 1985.

21. The Little Rock resident is quoted in an address given by James Farmer to the American Studies Conference at Lincoln University, reprinted in Philip S. Foner, ed., *The Voice of Black America* (New York: Capricorn Books, 1975), vol.2, p. 428.

22. "Dan" has been a personal friend of the author for more than twenty years.

23. The implications of an out-of-step culture of expectations are dramatically narrated in Sylvester Monroe, *Brothers, Black and Poor* (New York: William Morrow, 1988).

24. Hershberg et al., *Philadelphia*, pp. 461–91.

25. Claude Brown, *Manchild in the Promised Land* (New York: New American Library, 1965), p. viii.

26. The literature on this period is voluminous. See David J. Garrow, *Bearing the Cross: Martin Luther King, Jr., and the Southern Christian Leadership Conference* (New York: Vintage Books, 1988), pp. 421–624; Kenneth O'Reilly, *Racial Matters: The FBI's Secret File on Black America, 1960–1972* (New York: Free Press, 1989); Joel Dreyfuss and Charles Lawrence III, *The Bakke Case: The Politics of Inequality* (New York: Harcourt Brace Jovanovich, 1979); and Cruse, *Plural But Equal*, pp. 62–64, 364–70.

27. Philip S. Foner, ed., *The Life and Writings of Frederick Douglass* (New York: International Publishers, 1950), vol. 2, p. 437.

# BIBLIOGRAPHIC ESSAY

Research for this study included a close examination of many pertinent primary and secondary sources. A detailed listing of sources can be found in the endnotes; this essay provides an annotated review of the most valuable.

## 1862 TO 1910

Norfolk's role in the economy of the Chesapeake region dates from the eighteenth century. For an understanding of this background, see Carville Earle and Ronald Hoffman, "Urban Development in the Eighteenth-Century South," *Perspectives in American History* 10 (1976): 7–78.

An understanding of the city's role in the state and regional economy during the antebellum period is also imperative. See David L. Goldfield, *Urban Growth in the Age of Sectionalism: Virginia, 1847–1861* (Baton Rouge: Louisiana State University Press, 1977); and Thomas J. Wertenbaker and Marvin W. Schlegel, *Norfolk: Historic Southern Port* (Durham, N.C.: Duke University Press, 1962). This latter work is the only true general history of the city of Norfolk.

Very little has been written about Norfolk blacks during the antebellum period. The exceptions are useful studies by Tommy Lee Bogger and Luther P. Jackson. See Bogger's "The Slave and Free Black Community in Norfolk, 1775–1865" (Ph.D. diss., University of Virginia, 1976), which should be read in conjunction with the manuscript censuses for Norfolk between 1860 and 1910 (U.S. Bureau of the Census, Record Group 29, National Archives) and Jackson's *Free Negro Labor and Property Holding in Virginia, 1830–1860* (1942; reprint, New York: Atheneum, 1968).

Perhaps the most important primary document providing some insight into the nineteenth-century black community is *Equal Suffrage: Address from the Colored Citizens of Norfolk, Virginia, to the People of the United States, 1865* (reprint, Philadelphia: Rhistoric Publications, 1969). This address should be read in conjunction with two secondary works on blacks in the early labor movement: Charles H. Wesley, *Negro Labor in the United States, 1850–1925* (New York: Vanguard Press, 1927); and Sterling D. Spero and Abram L. Harris, *The Black Worker* (New York: Columbia University Press, 1931).

Several books and theses are useful in understanding the shift in race relations in the late nineteenth century and the early twentieth century. Those interested in black Norfolk should definitely read William F. Ainsley, Jr., "Changing Land Use in Downtown Norfolk, Virginia: 1680–1930" (Ph.D. diss., University of North Carolina, Chapel Hill, 1977). A limited but interesting master's thesis on progressivism and reform in the city is James Sidney Kitterman, Jr., "Reformers and Bosses in the Progressive Era: The Changing Face of Norfolk Politics, 1890–1920" (M.A. thesis, Old Dominion University, 1971). See also Andrew Buni, *The Negro in Virginia Politics, 1902–1965* (Charlottesville: University Press of Virginia, 1967); Alrutheus Ambush Taylor, *The Negro in the Reconstruction of Virginia* (1926; reprint, New York: Russell and Russell, 1969); Luther P. Jackson, *Negro Office-Holders in Virginia, 1865–1895* (Norfolk: Guide Quality Press, 1945); Charles E. Wynes, *Race Relations in Virginia, 1870–1902* (1961; reprint, Totowa, N.J.: Rowan and Littlefield, 1971); and Henry Lewis Suggs, "P. B. Young of the Norfolk *Journal and Guide*: A Booker T. Washington Militant, 1904–1928," *Journal of Negro History* 64 (Fall 1979): 365–76.

### 1910 TO 1930

The most valuable primary source on black Norfolk is the well-edited *Norfolk Journal and Guide.* Microfilm copies of this black newspaper are available at several depositories for the years 1916–1917, 1921–1945, and beyond; most scholars will find the liberal lending policy of the Center for Research Libraries in Chicago to their liking. The *Journal and Guide* should be read in conjunction with the city's two white dailies, the *Virginian-Pilot* and the *Norfolk Ledger-Dispatch.* Also see the Garvey newspaper, the *Negro World,* and the Hampton Institute publication the *Southern Workman.*

Those particularly interested in labor should also consult the U.S. Women's Bureau Bulletin no. 10, with its survey reports, in Record Group 86 in the National Archives. Esther Levinson's master's thesis, "A

History of the Hampton Roads Longshoremen's Association" (Old Dominion University, 1968) is valuable as a brief history of black longshoremen in the Hampton Roads area. Also consult the Federal Mediation
and Conciliation Service Papers, Record Group 280 in the National Archives; these papers contain important information on strike activity for
the entire period covered by this study. Two additional sources are Herbert R. Northrup, *Organized Labor and the Negro* (New York: Harper and
Brothers, 1944); and Philip S. Foner, *Organized Labor and the Black
Worker, 1619–1973* (New York: International Publishers, 1974).

In studying both the workplace and the home sphere, useful statistical information can be drawn from many published census compilations.
Included in this list are the U.S. Department of Commerce, *Negroes in the
United States, 1920–1932* (Washington, D.C.: Government Printing Office, 1935); and the census volumes themselves, for 1910, 1920, 1930,
and 1940 (the Thirteenth, Fourteenth, Fifteenth, and Sixteenth censuses). The *Twenty-Fifth* through the *Thirty-Third Annual Reports of the Department of Labor and Industry of the State of Virginia,* published in Richmond from 1922 to 1930, are also useful.

Invaluable material is provided by the files of the Norfolk branch of
the NAACP, located in the NAACP Papers in the Library of Congress.
Unfortunately, Norfolk did not have a functioning Urban League at this
time. Very useful materials were located in the Charles N. Hunter Papers in the Perkins Library at Duke University and the Louis Jaffe Papers in the Alderman Library at the University of Virginia (Jaffe was the
editor of the *Virginian-Pilot* for several years). The papers of P. B. Young
have been collected by Professor Henry Lewis Suggs, but to my knowledge they remain his personal collection and have not been reviewed.
Suggs has recently finished a biography of Young (*P. B. Young, Newspa-
perman: Race, Politics, and Journalism in the New South, 1910–1962* [Char-
lottesville: University Press of Virginia, 1989]), but I was unable to obtain it before completing this book.

One can learn a great deal by consulting the Capitation Tax Rolls, as
well as the annual *City Directory of Norfolk,* both located in the Norfolk
Public Library. Arthur Kyle Davis's work on Norfolk during World War
I ("Norfolk City in War Time: A Community History," in *Virginia Communities in War Time* [Richmond: Virginia War History Commission,
1925], pp. 291–357) is also helpful. Personal reminiscences round out
the list of useful sources: see especially Stephen Graham, *The Soul of John
Brown* (New York: Macmillan, 1920), a paternalistic, often racist, travel
account; and the autobiography of George W. Bennett, a black former
resident of Norfolk, *Life Behind the Walls of My Self-Made Fate* (self-
published, 1964).

## 1929 TO 1941

Aside from the census data noted previously and U.S. Bureau of the Census, *Fifteenth Census of the United States* (Washington, D.C.: Government Printing Office, 1932), vol. 1, *Unemployment, 1930,* a number of special studies were commissioned during the 1930s to study the impact of the Depression. Among them are Gladys L. Palmer and Katherine D. Wood, *Urban Workers on Relief, Part 2* (Washington, D.C.: Works Progress Administration, 1936); *Unemployment Relief Census, October 1933* (Washington, D.C.: Federal Emergency Relief Administration, 1934); Philip M. Hauser, *Workers on Relief in the United States in March 1935* (Washington, D.C.: Works Progress Administration, Division of Social Research, 1938), vol. 1, *A Census of Usual Occupations*; and U.S. Bureau of the Census, *Sixteenth Census of the United States: Population, 1940—Internal Migration, 1935 to 1940, Color and Sex of Migrants* (Washington, D.C.: Government Printing Office, 1943), esp. p. 26.

Manuscript documents at the National Archives and the Virginia State Library are also very useful. At the National Archives, see in particular "Family Disbursements of Wage Earners and Salaried Workers," Negroes, Norfolk (Virginia) Schedules, 1936, boxes 286–88, U.S. Bureau of Labor Statistics, Record Group 257; Shipping Code Hearings, 1934, box 6507, National Recovery Administration, Record Group 9; Home Owners Loan Corporation (HOLC) City Survey Files, 1935–1940, Record Group 195; Administrative Files, Baltimore Region, box 207, National Labor Relations Board, Record Group 25; the Lawrence Oxley Papers, Negro Division of the Virginia State Employment Service, box 1389, Record Group 183; and Code Files, Complaints—Cleaning and Dyeing Industry, box 1407, National Recovery Administration, Record Group 9. At the Virginia State Library, consult the Virginia Writers' Project list of interviews of black residents of Norfolk (VWP 58–71). Exchanges between George Streator and W. E. B. Du Bois in the Du Bois Papers microfilm collection (from the originals at the University of Massachusetts) provide an interesting subtext to the Finkelstein case. Likewise, the Carnegie-Myrdal Collection (from the originals in the Schomburg Library, New York Public Library) contains snippets from a valuable survey of the local NAACP and its leadership. Researchers would also find it useful to review fieldnotes of investigators for the Myrdal study in the Ralph Bunche Papers at the University of California, Los Angeles.

Invaluable information on the equalization case is located in the legal files of the NAACP Papers in the Library of Congress. Brief reference is made to Socialists in Norfolk in the microfilm collection of the Socialist Party Papers at Duke University; see Virginia 1919–1932, State and Local Files, reels 111, 132. Extant copies of the radical *Marine Workers' Voice*, coupled with selections from the *Daily Worker* and the *Communist*, are informative. See also the testimony of Paul Crouch, who used the alias Fred Allen while active in Norfolk Communist circles during the 1930s, in U.S. Congress, Senate, Committee on the Judiciary, *Communist Activities Among Aliens and National Groups, Hearings Before the Subcommittee on the Judiciary*, 81st Cong., 1st sess., 1949; additional testimony is found in U.S. Congress, House, Special Committee, *Hearings Before a Special Committee to Investigate Communist Activities in the United States*, 71st Cong., 2d sess., 1930 (the Fish Committee Report). Other information on Communist activities is noted, although with some bias, in the *Norfolk Journal and Guide*; in the Military Intelligence Department Files, Record Group 165 in the National Archives; and in Alexander Wright's Internal Security File (FBI), 65–1594–1 through 35, and 65–1594 more generally.

## 1941 TO 1945

Several specially commissioned reports and bodies of papers are crucial for anyone studying the Hampton Roads area, and Norfolk in particular, during World War II. See, for instance, *Population in Flux in the Hampton Roads Area: A Study of Population Trends in the Hampton Roads Area, 1890–1942*, Population Study Report no. 2 (Richmond: Virginia State Planning Board, 1942). Similarly, the Norfolk War History Collection, housed in the Norfolk Public Library, is very useful; within the larger collection, there is in fact a special collection on wartime activities among black Norfolkians. At the National Archives, one should review the records of the Committee on Fair Employment Practices (FEPC Papers) for the Norfolk area, boxes 630–40, Record Group 228 (actually located at the Philadelphia regional branch office of the National Archives). These sources are very valuable in documenting the redefinition of priorities that occurred during the war years. Also see Lyonel C. Florant, "The Impact of the War on the Norfolk Negro Community," 26 May 1942, box 6, Recreation Division, Office of Community War Services, Record Group 215; as well as several other pertinent files in this record group.

Several other sources have some bearing on labor activities in the area during the war years. The *Labor Journal*, newspaper of the Norfolk Central Labor Union, is available on microfilm (from Stanford University) for the years 1939 to 1945. Also see the Circuit Court and Supreme Court decisions in the Tunstall case (*Tunstall v. Brotherhood of Locomotive Firemen and Enginemen et al.*, 140 F.2d 35 [1940]; *Tunstall v. Brotherhood of Locomotive Firemen and Enginemen, Ocean Lodge No. 76, et al.*, 65 S. Ct. 235 [1944]. Finally, Marvin W. Schlegel's *Conscripted City: Norfolk in*

*World War II* (Norfolk: Norfolk War History Commission, 1951) is very useful in outlining the broad changes that occurred within the city and within the black community.

## PERSONAL INTERVIEWS AND CONVERSATIONS

Among the individuals who submitted to interviews or engaged me in conversations about events relating to black Norfolk between 1910 and 1945, I would like to thank Louise Thompson Patterson; Virginia C.; Louis C., Sr.; Paul Askew; Lloyd D.; Luther D.; Cecil L.; the late Susan J.; Ruth V.; and four longtime residents whose identities are not to be made public.

# INDEX

Compositor: BookMasters
Text: 10/12 Baskerville
Display: Baskerville